P9-AGS-407

The **Rough Guide** to

Barcelona

written and researched by

Jules Brown

ROUGH
GUIDES

roughguides.com

Contents

OPPOSITE CASTELLERS AT THE FESTES DE LA MERCÈ **PREVIOUS PAGE** STAINED-GLASS ROOF, PALAU DE LA MÚSICA CATALANA

Introduction to
Barcelona

Barcelona – Spain's second city, and the Mediterranean's most exciting destination – sets the template for urban style, hip design and sheer nonstop energy. Where others tinker at the edges, time and again Barcelona has reinvented itself, from medieval maritime power to Olympic city, from neglected Franco-era backwater to dominant national force, while its celebrated – often outrageous – architecture speaks volumes about the city's tireless self-confidence. This is a place whose most famous monument, Antoni Gaudí's Sagrada Família, is an unfinished church of indescribable invention; whose most celebrated street, the Ramblas, is a dawn-to-dark maelstrom of human activity; and whose vibrant restaurants, bars, shops and galleries are in the vanguard of European style and fashion. Visit for the first time, expecting a traditional city break, or the fiftieth, thinking you know it inside out, and Barcelona never fails to surprise.

Much of the impetus for Barcelona's almost overpowering self-promotion stems from its political and cultural identity. You're left in no doubt – by way of language, tradition, cuisine, even sport – that, whatever the map might show, you're no longer in Spain but in the autonomous province of **Catalunya** (Catalonia in English), which can trace its distinct history back as far as the ninth century. This makes Barcelona the capital of what many regard as a nation, and adds another level to the pride the locals naturally feel for their city. Galleries and museums, for example, hold "national" collections of Catalan art and history, while the 1992 Olympics – which kick-started the dynamic rebuilding process – were indisputably Barcelona's Games, and not Spain's. The city fosters an independent spirit, setting itself apart from the wider country and single-mindedly pursuing its own social, economic and cultural agenda.

Nowhere is this separate face of Barcelona seen more perfectly than in the otherworldly *modernista* (Art Nouveau) buildings that stud the city's streets and avenues, dating from

ABOVE FRANK GEHRY'S FISH

an earlier period of renewal in the nineteenth century. Antoni Gaudí is the most famous of those who have left their mark on Barcelona in this way: his Sagrada Família church is rightly revered, but just as fascinating are the (literally) fantastic houses, apartment buildings and parks that he and his contemporaries designed.

Barcelona also boasts an extensive medieval old town – full of pivotal buildings from an even earlier age of expansion – and a stupendous artistic legacy, including major galleries containing the life's work of the famous Catalan artists Joan Miró and Antoni Tàpies (not to mention a celebrated showcase of the work of Pablo Picasso). The city is equally proud of its cutting-edge restaurants – featuring some of the best chefs in Europe – its late-night bars and clubs, and most of all its football team, the mercurial, incomparable FC Barcelona. Add a spruced-up waterfront, 5km of sandy beaches, a surrounding green lung of parks and gardens, and even on a lengthy visit you will only likely scrape the surface.

True, for all its go-ahead feel, Barcelona has its problems, not least a petty crime rate that occasionally makes the international news. But there's no need to be unduly paranoid and it would be a shame to stick solely to the main tourist sights, since you'll miss so much. Tapas bars hidden down alleys little changed for a century or two, designer boutiques in gentrified old town quarters, street opera singers belting out an aria, bargain lunches in workers' taverns, neighbourhood funicular rides, unmarked gourmet restaurants, craft workshops, restored medieval palaces, suburban walks and specialist galleries – all are just as much Barcelona as the Ramblas or the Sagrada Família.

Author picks

It's not all about Barcelona's big sights – Jules Brown has spent 25 years investigating the city, and the following hidden highlights make a great place to start...

Best boutique beds Barcelona must be the boutique-hotel capital of Europe – whether it's budget beauties like the *Market* (p.171) or straight-up style classics like the *Neri* (p.169).

Trusty tapas Move over new-wave pretenders – old-school *Cal Pep* (p.185) lets its peerless traditional tapas do all the talking.

Ice-cool bars *Resolis* (p.199) puts the razz into the Raval, while cool cats chill in Sant Pere's *Casa Paco* (p.200).

Over-the-top theatrics Forget a night at the opera – it's Catalan clowns, human beat-boxes and Goth-horror short films at quirky, crazy L'Antic Teatre (p.210).

> Our author recommendations don't end here. We've flagged up our favourite places throughout the guide – a stylish hotel, a classic tapas bar, a chic *coctelería* – with the ★ symbol.

What to see

Despite its size Barcelona is a pretty easy place to find your way around. In effect, it's a series of self-contained quarters or neighbourhoods (known as *barris*) stretching out from the harbour, flanked by parks, hills and woodland. Much of what there is to see in the city centre – Gothic cathedral, Picasso museum, markets, Gaudí buildings and art galleries – can be reached on foot, while a fast, cheap, integrated public transport system takes you directly to the peripheral attractions and suburbs.

This guide starts, as nearly everyone does, with the **Ramblas**, a kilometre-long, tree-lined avenue of pavement cafés, performance artists and kiosks that splits the old town in two. On the eastern side of the Ramblas is the **Barri Gòtic** (Gothic Quarter), the medieval nucleus of the city – a labyrinth of twisting streets and historic buildings, including La Seu (the cathedral) and the palaces and museums around Plaça del Rei. Further east lies **Sant Pere**, set around its terrific market, which adjoins the fashionable boutique-and-bar quarter of **La Ribera** to the south, home to the Picasso museum. Over on the western side of the Ramblas is the edgier, artier neighbourhood of **El Raval**, containing both the flagship museum of contemporary art (MACBA) and the pick of the city's coolest bars and restaurants.

BARCELONA ON A PLATE

In a town where lunch can go on until 5pm, and tapas isn't your dinner, but what you eat *before* dinner, dining out in Barcelona is a big deal. Word gets around quick if there's a hot new restaurant or bar on the scene, and city gourmets are pretty discerning customers – not for them the Ramblas tourist traps or fast-food chains. Embrace the local tastes and current trends and a whole new world opens up in Barcelona, from earthy, nose-to-tail dining in **Casa Mari y Rufo** (p.186) to cutting-edge "Mediterrasian" bar snacks at **Dos Palillos** (p.182). Above all, if it's fresh, seasonal and straight from the market – that's Barcelona on a plate.

At the bottom of the Ramblas is the waterfront, whose spruced-up harbour area is known as **Port Vell** (Old Port). Walking east from here takes you past the aquarium and marina, through the old fishing and restaurant quarter of **Barceloneta**, past the **Parc de la Ciutadella** and out along the promenade to the cafés and restaurants of the **Port Olímpic**. This whole area is where Barcelona is most like a resort, with city beaches all along the waterfront from Barceloneta as far as the conference and leisure zone of Parc del Fòrum at **Diagonal Mar**. Art- and garden-lovers, meanwhile, aim for the fortress-topped hill of **Montjuïc** to the southwest, where Catalunya's national art gallery (MNAC), the Miró museum, botanic garden and main Olympic stadium are sited, among a host of other cultural attractions.

At the top of the Ramblas, Plaça de Catalunya marks the start of the gridded nineteenth-century extension of the city, known as the **Eixample**, a symbol of the thrusting expansionism of Barcelona's early industrial age. This is where some of Europe's most extraordinary architecture – including Gaudí's **Sagrada Família** – is located. Beyond the Eixample lie the northern suburbs, notably **Gràcia**, with its small squares and lively bars, and the nearby **Parc Güell**, while you'll also come out this way to see the famous **Camp Nou** FC Barcelona stadium or the city's applied art museums at the **Palau Reial**. It's worth making for the hills, too, where you can join the crowds at Barcelona's famous **Tibidabo** amusement park – or escape them with a walk through the woods in the peaceful **Parc de Collserola**.

The good public transport links also make it easy to head further out of the city. The mountain-top monastery of **Montserrat** makes the most obvious day-trip, not least for the extraordinary ride up to the monastic eyrie by cable car or mountain railway. **Sitges** is the local beach town *par excellence*, while with more time you can follow various trails around the local **wine country**, head south to the Roman town of **Tarragona** or Gaudí's birthplace of **Reus**, or north to medieval **Girona** or the Dalí museum in **Figueres**.

ABOVE DOS PALILLOS **RIGHT** LAS RAMBLAS

When to go

Barcelona is an established city-break destination with a year-round tourist, business and convention trade. Different seasons have different attractions, from summer music festivals to Christmas markets, but there's always something going on. As far as the weather is concerned, the best times to visit are late **spring** and early **autumn**, when the weather is still comfortably warm (around 21–25°C) and walking the streets isn't a chore. There might be a chill in the air in the evening, but Barcelona in these seasons is sometimes nigh on perfect. However, in **summer** the city can be unbearably hot and humid, with temperatures averaging 28°C (but often a lot more). August, especially, is a month to be avoided, since the climate is at its most unwelcoming and many shops, bars and restaurants close as local inhabitants head out of the city in droves. It's worth considering a **winter** break, as long as you don't mind the prospect of occasional rain. It's generally still warm enough to sit out at a café, even in December, when the temperature hovers around 13°C. For a chart showing the average monthly temperatures in the city, see p.34.

Out of Barcelona, the weather varies enormously from region to region. On the coast it's best – naturally enough – in summer, though from June to September tourist resorts like **Sitges** are packed. **Tarragona**, too, can be extremely hot and busy in summer, though it's worth knowing that **Girona** is considered to have a much more equable summer climate, and escaping from the coast for a few cool days is easy.

23

things not to miss

It's not possible to see everything that Barcelona has to offer in one trip – and we don't suggest you try. What follows, in no particular order, is a selective taste of the region's highlights, including beautiful beaches, outstanding national parks, fascinating wildlife encounters and unforgettable urban experiences. All highlights have a page reference to take you straight into the guide, where you can find out more.

1 LA PEDRERA
Page 109

Is it an apartment building or a work of art? Both, when the building in question – the undulating Pedrera, or "Stone Quarry" – is designed by Antoni Gaudí.

2 CITY BEACHES
Page 84

Barcelona has a golden seafront, with 5km of sandy beaches stretching from Barceloneta to Diagonal Mar.

3 A TAPAS TOUR
Page 181

Hopping from bar to bar, sampling the specialities, is the best way to experience some of Barcelona's finest food.

4 CAMP NOU
Pages 131 & 223

The magnificent Camp Nou stadium is the home of FC Barcelona, one of the world's premier sides, with a cabinet full of trophies to prove it.

5

6

7

8

9

10

11

12 **MUSEU NACIONAL D'ART DE CATALUNYA (MNAC)**
Page 92
The National Museum of Art celebrates the grandeur of Romanesque and Gothic art, two periods in which Catalunya artists were pre-eminent in Spain.

13 **PARC GÜELL**
Page 127
The city's most extraordinary park is a fantasy land born of Antoni Gaudí's fertile imagination.

14 **MUSEU PICASSO**
Page 69
Trace the genesis of the artist's genius in the city that Picasso liked to call home.

15 **LA SEU**
Page 45
Marvel at the soaring spaces in one of the greatest Gothic cathedrals in Spain.

16 **MONTSERRAT**
Page 147
For centuries this mountain and monastery have been a place of pilgrimage – and now make a great day-trip from the city.

17 **LA BOQUERIA**
Page 40
The city's best-known market presents an extraordinary range of fresh produce.

18

19

20

21

EATRE DEL LICEU

22

23

TRAMVIA BLAU

Basics

Getting there

It's easy to reach Barcelona by air, with a variety of budget airlines from regional UK and European airports competing with the Spanish national carrier Iberia to get you directly to the city, quickly and cheaply. There's also a fair amount of choice from North America, though you may have to fly there via Madrid or another European city to get the best fare.

To get the very cheapest fares advertised by the budget airlines you'll need to book weeks, if not months, in advance. Flights with Iberia and other major airlines tend to be more expensive and seasonal, with the highest fares from June to September, at Christmas, New Year and Easter, and at weekends all year.

Most airlines prefer you to book tickets **online** these days and you can turn up some great deals, but always check the small print as most budget airline tickets are non-changeable and non-refundable. Another option is to contact a general flight or **travel agent** – these have similar deals on flights and services, and some are particularly geared towards youth, student and independent travel. Other specialist **tour operators** can book you onto a variety of city breaks or themed tours in Barcelona and Catalunya.

Travelling to Barcelona from elsewhere in Europe by **train** or **bus** inevitably takes much longer than flying and usually works out more expensive given the travelling time involved. However, if Barcelona and Spain are part of a longer European trip it can be an interesting proposition, and is an increasingly popular, green alternative to flying. **Driving** to Barcelona is also something of an undertaking and, with motorway tolls in France and Spain, fuel costs, cross-Channel ferry and Eurotunnel fares, it's certainly not a cheap option.

Flights from the UK and Ireland

Flying time to Barcelona from the UK or Ireland is between two and two and a half hours, depending on your departure airport.

A whole host of budget **no-frills airlines** compete on the Barcelona route from the UK and Ireland, notably easyJet (**W** easyjet.com), Monarch (**W** monarch.co.uk), Jet2 (**W** jet2.com), bmibaby (**W** bmibaby.com) and Aer Lingus (**W** aerlingus.com), with daily departures throughout the year from around a dozen regional airports, including all the London airports, plus Belfast, Birmingham, Bristol,

Dublin, East Midlands, Leeds-Bradford, Liverpool, Manchester and Newcastle. The earlier you book, the cheaper your flight will be – and special offers can even mean the seats are free, or virtually free, with just the taxes to pay (from £20 each way). Even Iberia (**W** iberia.com) is forced to compete, with good-value promotional fares – however, their more flexible tickets (allowing cancellation and/or date changes) are considerably more expensive and can rise to £200 (€240) return or more in peak season.

There's a second gateway to the city at **Girona**, 90km north of Barcelona, which is used almost exclusively by no-frills airline Ryanair (**W** ryanair.com), which flies there from around sixty British, Irish and European airports, including smaller UK airports like Bournemouth and Bristol. The other regional airport is at **Reus**, 110km south of Barcelona, near Tarragona, served by Ryanair from half a dozen UK airports and from Dublin and Cork. You've over an hour's journey from either airport to the centre of Barcelona, but there are reliable connecting bus services.

Flights from the USA and Canada

Most **direct scheduled services** to Spain from North America are to Madrid, but the Spanish national airline Iberia (**W** iberia.com) and Continental (**W** continental.com) and American Airlines (**W** aa.com), have year-round nonstop Barcelona services daily from New York; meanwhile Delta (**W** delta.com) flies direct from both New York and Atlanta. European-based airlines (like Air France, British Airways, Lufthansa, KLM and TAP) can also get you to Barcelona, though you'll be routed via their respective European hubs. Flying time from New York is around seven hours to Madrid, eight to Barcelona direct, though with an onward connection it can take up to eleven hours to reach Barcelona.

Return **fares** are as much as US$1000 in summer, though outside peak periods you should be able to fly for under US$600. Special promotional deals sometimes undercut these prices, or it might even pay you to buy a cheap flight to the UK and travel on to Barcelona from there with a budget airline (see "Flights from the UK and Ireland").

Flights from Australia, New Zealand and South Africa

There are no direct **flights** to Spain from Australia or New Zealand. However, a number of airlines do fly to Barcelona with a stopover elsewhere in Europe or Asia (flights via Asia are generally the cheaper option).

Another possibility is to fly to Madrid, from where you can pick up a connecting flight or train. It's best to discuss your route and preferences with a flight and travel agent like Flight Centre (W flightcentre.com.au or W flightcentre.co.nz) or STA Travel (W statravel.com .au or W statravel.co.nz), especially if your visit to Barcelona is part of a wider Spanish trip – in which case, you might be better off buying a **Round-The-World** (RTW) ticket.

From **South Africa**, there are direct flights with Iberia (W iberia.com) from Johannesburg to Madrid (for onward connections to Barcelona), which take around ten hours; or it's around fifteen hours if you fly via London.

City breaks and tours

Three-night **city breaks** to Barcelona start from as little as £200 (€240) per person flying from London, Manchester or Dublin. For this price, accommodation is most likely in a two-star hotel, and sometimes on a room-only basis. For three nights' bed-and-breakfast in a three- or four-star hotel you can usually expect to pay more like £300–400 (€360–480). The bigger US operators, such as American Express and Delta Vacations, can also easily organize short city breaks to Spain on a flight-and-hotel basis. From Australia, Iberian specialist Ibertours can arrange two- or three-night packages in most Spanish cities, including Barcelona.

A few British and Spanish operators offer rather more **specialist holidays** in and around Barcelona, concentrating on things like art and architecture, cooking classes, wine tours or rural Catalunya. Prices vary wildly, according to the standard of accommodation and services provided, from say £100 (€120) for a fully catered day out to several thousand pounds/euros for an all-inclusive luxury holiday. North American **tour companies** also tend to include a couple of days in Barcelona as part of a whirlwind escorted itinerary around Spain, starting from around US$1500–2000 for a standard two-week tour.

UK

Martin Randall Travel ☎ 020 8742 3355, **W** martinrandall .com. Experts lead small groups on annual, all-inclusive quality tours to Spain – tours and themes change each year, though a typical gastronomic tour of Catalunya might cost around £3000/€3600 for eight nights' wining and dining.

SPAIN

Madrid & Beyond ☎ 917 580 063, **W** madridandbeyond.com. Classy, customized holidays and special experiences, from private gallery tours to expert-led walks through Gaudí's Barcelona.

A Taste of Spain ☎ 856 079 626 or **☎** 934 170 716, **W** www .tasteofspain.com. Interesting food-based tours from a company with offices in Barcelona and Madrid – from lunch and olive-oil tasting (€200) to a four-day gourmet tour (land-only, €1175).

USA

Olé Spain ☎ 1 888 869 7156, **W** olespain.com. Eight-day cultural walking tours in Catalunya (US$3795), beginning and ending in Barcelona, with time to explore the city.

Petrabax ☎ 1 800 634 1188, **W** petrabax.com. City breaks, escorted Catalunya tours or self-drive Spanish holidays, plus independent travel services such as accommodation bookings and car rental.

Saranjan Tours ☎ 1 800 858 9594, **W** saranjan.com. Upscale, fully guided, customized tours concentrating on Barcelona and its nearby wine country.

AUSTRALIA

Ibertours ☎ 1 800 500 016, **W** ibertours.com.au. Specialist tour operator, which can arrange an organized visit to Barcelona, and sort out your accommodation, guided tours and car rental.

By rail

Travelling **by train** to Barcelona can't compete in price with the cheapest budget-airline fares – but it can be a real adventure. First stop should be **W seat61.com**, an amazingly useful website that provides route, ticket, timetable and contact information for all European train services.

The quickest and most straightforward option from the UK is to take the **Eurostar** service (W eurostar.com; from £69 return) from London St Pancras International via the Channel Tunnel to Paris, and then the overnight **Paris–Barcelona "train-hotel"**, which arrives in Barcelona at around 8.30am (total journey time around 16hr). This is a sleeper service (with restaurant and café), with various levels of comfort available – the cheapest ticket is in a four-berth compartment, currently from £135 return, depending on availability; you have to book well in advance to get the lowest prices.

There are other alternatives, but they take longer, can be more complicated to arrange and sometimes work out more expensive. For example, you can use the cross-Channel ferries and Seacats and local trains to Paris instead of Eurostar, and instead of the overnight "train-hotel" there are regular daytime services through France and Spain.

You can **book the whole journey online** with one of the specialist rail agents listed below. If you're booking from outside the UK, you can get Eurostar and "train-hotel" tickets through the websites **W** raileurope.com, **W** raileurope.ca and **W** raileurope .com.au.

If you plan to travel extensively in Europe by train, a **rail pass** might prove a good investment. However, if you're just headed for Barcelona, Inter-Rail (ⓦinterrailnet.com) and Eurail (ⓦeurail.com) aren't a good deal, and even if you intend to travel around Catalunya by train, rail travel in that part of Spain is fairly limited (and quite cheap), so you probably won't get your money's worth.

RAIL CONTACTS

Ffestiniog Travel ☎ 01766 772050, ⓦ ffestiniogtravel.co.uk.
Rail Europe ☎ 0844 848 4064, ⓦ raileurope.co.uk.
Spanish Rail Service ☎ 020 7725 7063, ⓦ spanish-rail.co.uk.

By bus

Eurolines (ⓦ www.eurolines.co.uk) operates a year-round bus service twice a week to Barcelona from London, which takes up to 28 hours. It usually costs around £125 return, though there are advance deals and special offers – it's always cheapest to book online. Eurolines also sells Barcelona tickets and transport to London at all UK National Express bus terminals.

Driving to Barcelona

It's about 1600km from London to Barcelona, which, with stops, takes almost two full days to drive. To plan your route, try motoring organizations such as AA (ⓦtheaa.com) or the RAC (ⓦrac.co.uk), which also provide advice on insurance requirements, documentation matters and how to avoid toll roads. If you're bringing your own car, carry your licence, vehicle registration and insurance documents with you; you should also have two warning triangles and a fluorescent vest in case of breakdown. For more details about driving conditions in the city itself, turn to "City transport" (see p.24).

Many people use the conventional **cross-Channel ferry** links, principally Dover–Calais, though services to Brittany or Normandy might be more convenient. However, the quickest way of crossing the Channel is to go via the **Eurotunnel** service (☎0844 335 3535, ⓦeurotunnel.com), which operates drive-on-drive-off shuttle trains between Folkestone and Calais/Coquelles. The 24-hour service runs every twenty minutes throughout the day and, though you can just turn up, booking is advised, especially at weekends and in summer holidays.

Alternatively, Brittany Ferries (ⓦbrittany-ferries .co.uk) operates car and passenger ferry services from Portsmouth and Plymouth to **Santander** (3 weekly;

20–24hr) or **Bilbao** (up to 5 weekly; 24hr). From Santander, it's about nine hours' drive to Barcelona, via Bilbao and Zaragoza. Fares start at £195 return per person (includes the car), but it costs significantly more in summer, particularly August.

Any ferry company or travel agent can supply up-to-date schedules and ticket information, or you can consult the encyclopedic ⓦdirectferries.com, which has details about, and links to, every European ferry service.

Arrival and departure

In most cases, you can be off the plane, train or bus and in your central Barcelona hotel room within the hour. Note that Ryanair flights (and some others) to Barcelona are actually to Girona (90km north) or Reus (110km south), and though there are reliable connecting bus and train services, this means up to a 90-minute journey from either airport to Barcelona city centre.

By air

Barcelona airport (☎902 404 704, ⓦaena.es) is 18km southwest of the city centre at El Prat de Llobregat. There are tourist offices in the terminals handling hotel bookings, as well as ATMs, exchange facilities and car-rental offices.

A metered **taxi** from the airport to the city centre costs up to €30, including the airport surcharge (plus other surcharges for travel after 9pm and at weekends, and for any luggage that goes in the boot).

Far cheaper is the **airport train service** (daily 5.42am–11.38pm; journey time 19min; €3.15; info on ☎902 320 320), which runs every thirty minutes to Barcelona Sants station (the main train station) and Passeig de Gràcia (best stop for Eixample, Plaça de Catalunya and the Ramblas). It departs from Terminal T2 – there's a free shuttle-bus to the station from T1 which takes around ten minutes. Trains back to the airport run from Barcelona Sants on a similar half-hourly schedule (daily 5.13am–11.14pm). Zone 1 city travel passes (*targetes*) and the Barcelona Card are valid on the airport train service.

Alternatively, the **Aerobús** service (daily 6am–5am; €5.30 one-way, €9.15 return; departures every 5–10min; ⓦaerobusbcn.com) from T1 and T2 stops in the city at Plaça d'Espanya, Plaça Universitat, Plaça de Catalunya and Passeig de Gràcia. It takes around 35–40 minutes to reach Plaça de Catalunya, though allow longer in the rush hour. Aerobús departures to the airport from Plaça de Catalunya leave from in front of El Corte Inglés department store (daily 5.30am–12.30am); note that Terminal T1 and T2 are served by separate services.

Ryanair arrivals at **Girona airport**, 90km north of Barcelona, can take the connecting Barcelona Bus service (☎902 361 550, ☻barcelonabus.com), which runs to Girona train station (for hourly trains to Barcelona Sants; 1hr 15min–1hr 30min) or direct to Barcelona Nord bus station (€12 one-way, €21 return; journey time 1hr 15min). From **Reus airport**, 110km south of Barcelona, there's a connecting Hispano Igualadina bus (☎902 292 900, ☻igualadina.com) to Barcelona Sants (€12 one-way, €20 return; 1hr 30min).

The return buses to Girona or Reus all connect with the relevant Ryanair and other airline departures. Note that there are also direct buses linking Barcelona airport with Sitges, Reus, Tarragona and Girona.

By train

The main station for domestic and international arrivals is **Barcelona Sants**, 3km west of the city centre. There is a tourist office here (with an accommodation booking service), as well as ATMs, an exchange office, car-rental outlets, a police station and left-luggage facilities. The metro station (accessed from inside Barcelona Sants) is called Ⓜ Sants Estació – line 3 from here runs direct to Liceu (for the Ramblas), Catalunya (for Plaça de Catalunya) and Passeig de Gràcia, while line 5 runs to Diagonal.

Some Spanish intercity services and international trains also stop at **Estació de França**, 1km east of the Ramblas and close to Ⓜ Barceloneta. Other possible arrival points by train are **Plaça de Catalunya**, at the top of the Ramblas (for trains from coastal towns north of the city), and **Passeig de Gràcia** (Catalunya provincial destinations).

The high-speed **AVE line** (Alta Velocidad Española) between Barcelona and Madrid (via Tarragona and Zaragoza) has cut journey times in half between the two cities (2hr 45min to 3hr 25min, depending on the service). Arrivals and departures are at Barcelona Sants, though a second high-speed station is currently being built at **La Sagrera**, east of the centre beyond Glòries (completion date estimated 2013).

For information about the local rail network in and around the city, see "City transport".

TRAIN INFORMATION

RENFE ☎902 320 320, ☻renfe.com. For all national rail enquiries, sales and reservations. At Barcelona Sants station (Pl. dels Països Catalans, Sants; Ⓜ Sants Estació) there are train information desks and advance ticket booking counters, some with English speakers.

By bus

The main bus terminal, used by international, long-distance and provincial buses, is **Barcelona Nord** on c/d'Ali-Bei (☎902 260 606, ☻barcelonanord .com; Ⓜ Arc de Triomf), four blocks north of Parc de la Ciutadella. There's a bus information desk on the ground floor (daily 7am–9pm), plus a tourist office (daily 9am–3pm), accommodation agency, ATMs, shops and luggage lockers. Various companies operate services across Catalunya, Spain and Europe – it's a good idea to reserve a ticket in advance on long-distance routes (a day before at the station is usually fine, or buy online).

Some intercity and international Eurolines services also make a stop at the bus terminal behind Barcelona Sants station on c/de Viriat (Ⓜ Sants Estació). Either way, you're only a short metro ride from the city centre.

By car

Driving into Barcelona is reasonably straightforward, with traffic only slow in the morning and evening rush hours. Parking, however, is a different matter altogether – rarely easy and not cheap. If your trip is just to the city and its surroundings, our advice is not to bother with a car at all, but you'll find some useful pointers in any case in the "City transport" section.

Coming into Barcelona along any one of the motorways (autopistes), head for the Ronda Litoral, the southern half of the city's ring road. Following signs for "Port Vell" will take you towards the main exit for the old town, though there are also exits for Gran Via de les Corts Catalanes and Avinguda Diagonal if uptown Barcelona is your destination.

City transport

Barcelona's excellent integrated transport system comprises the metro, buses, trams and local trains, plus a network of funiculars and cable cars. The local transport authority, Transport Metropolitans de Barcelona (TMB, ☻tmb.cat), has a useful website (English-language available) with full timetable and ticket information.

There are also TMB customer service centres at Barcelona Sants station, and at Universitat, Diagonal and Sagrada Família metro stations, where you'll be able to pick up a free public transport map. The map and ticket information is also posted at major bus stops and all metro and tram stations. Our public transport map can be found at the back of the book.

Tickets and travel passes

A transit plan divides the province into six zones, but as the entire metropolitan area of Barcelona (including the airport) falls within **Zone 1**, that's the only one you'll need to worry about on a day-to-day basis.

On all the city's public transport (including night buses and funiculars) you can buy a single ticket every time you ride (€1.45), but if you're staying for a few days it's much cheaper to buy a *targeta* – a **discount ticket** strip which you pass through the box on top of the metro or train barrier, or slot in the machine on the bus, tram or funicular. The *targetes* are available at metro, train and tram stations, but not on the buses.

The best general ticket is the **T-10** ("tay day-oo" in Catalan) *targeta* (€8.25), valid for ten separate journeys, with changes between methods of transport allowed within 75 minutes. The ticket can also be used by more than one person at a time – just make sure you punch it the same number of times as there are people travelling. It's also available at newsstands and tobacconists.

Other useful (single-person) *targetes* for Zone 1 include the **T-Dia** ("tay dee-ah"; one day's unlimited travel; €6.20), plus combinations up to the 5-Dies (five days; €25); the **T-50/30** (fifty trips within a thirty-day period; €33.50); or the **T-Mes** (one month; €51) – for the latter, the station ticket office will need to see some form of ID (driving licence or passport). The Barcelona Card (see box, p.27) also offers free city transport between two and five days.

Heading for Sitges, Montserrat or further **out of town**, you'll need to buy a specific ticket or relevant-zoned *targeta* as the Zone 1 *targetes* outlined above don't run that far. Anyone caught without a valid ticket anywhere on the system is liable to an on-the-spot fine of €50.

The metro

The quickest way of getting around Barcelona is by **metro**, which runs on eight lines (with major extensions across the city centre and out to the airport currently under construction). Metro entrances are marked with a red diamond sign with an "M". Its **hours of operation** are Monday to Thursday, plus Sunday and public holidays, 5am to midnight; Friday, 5am to 2am; Saturday and the day before a public holiday, 24hr service. There's a metro map at the back of this book, or you can pick up a little foldout one at metro stations (ask for *una guia del metro*).

The system is perfectly safe, though many of the train carriages are heavily graffitied. Buskers and beggars are common, moving from one carriage to the next at stations.

Buses

Most buses operate daily, roughly from 4 or 5am until 10.30pm, though some lines stop earlier and some run until after midnight. Night bus (*Nit bus*) services fill in the gaps on all the main routes, with services every twenty to sixty minutes from around 10pm to 4am. Many bus routes (including all night buses) stop in or near Plaça de Catalunya, but the full route is marked at each bus stop, along with a timetable – useful bus routes are detailed in the text.

Trams

The tram system (@www.trambcn.com) runs on six lines, with departures every eight to twenty minutes throughout the day from 5am to midnight. **Lines T1, T2 and T3** depart from Plaça Francesc Macià and run along the uptown part of Avinguda Diagonal to suburban destinations in the northwest – useful tourist stops are at L'Illa shopping centre

---

TOP 5 BUS RIDES

Here's our pick of the most scenic city routes; timetables, route maps and other information can be found on @tmb.cat.
Bus #7, all the way along Av. Diagonal, from Diagonal Mar to Zona Universitaria.
Bus #28, from Plaça de Catalunya, through Gràcia to Parc de la Creueta del Coll.
Bus #40, from Port Vell, through the old town, to Parc de la Ciutadella.
Bus #64, from Port Vell and Paral.lel, through the Eixample to Pedralbes.
Bus #193, from Plaça d'Espanya on a circular route through Montjuïc.

UP AND AWAY – FUNICULARS AND CABLE CARS

Several **funicular rail lines** still operate in the city, up the hills to Montjuïc park, Tibidabo funfair and the suburban village of Vallvidrera. Summer and year-round weekend visits to Tibidabo also combine a funicular trip with a fun ride on the clanking antique tram, the **Tramvia Blau**. There are also two dramatic **cable-car** (*telefèric*) rides: from Barceloneta right across the harbour to Montjuïc, and then from the top station of the Montjuïc funicular all the way up to the castle. These are both great experiences, worth doing just for the views alone. Ticket and service details for all funiculars and cable cars are given in the relevant sections of the text.

and the Maria Cristina and Palau Reial metro stations. **Line T4** operates from Ciutadella-Vila Olímpica (where there's also a metro station) and runs up past the zoo and TNC (the National Theatre) to Glòries before running down Avinguda Diagonal to Diagonal Mar and the Parc del Fòrum. You're unlikely to use suburban lines T5 and T6.

Trains

The city has a cheap and efficient commuter train line, the **Ferrocarrils de la Generalitat de Catalunya** (FGC; ☎ 932 051 515, ⓦ fgc.cat), with its main stations at Plaça de Catalunya and Plaça d'Espanya. These go to places like Sarrià, Vallvidrera, Tibidabo, Sant Cugat, Terrassa and Montserrat, and details are given in the text where appropriate. The Zone 1 *targeta* is valid as far as the city limits, which in practice is everywhere you're likely to want to go except for Montserrat, Colònia Güell, Sant Cugat and Terrassa.

The national rail service, operated by **RENFE** (☎ 902 320 320, ⓦ renfe.com), runs all the other services out of Barcelona, with local lines – north to the Costa Maresme and south to Sitges – designated as **Rodiales/Cercanías**. The hub is Barcelona Sants station, with services also passing through Plaça de Catalunya (heading north) and Passeig de Gràcia (south). Arrive in plenty of time to buy a ticket, as queues are often horrendous, though for all destinations you can use the automatic vending machines instead (they take credit cards as well as cash).

Taxis

Black-and-yellow taxis (with a green roof-light on when available for hire) are relatively inexpensive – most short journeys across town run to around €9. There's a minimum charge of €2 and after that it's €0.90 per kilometre (€1.15 after 8pm, and on Sat, Sun & hols), with surcharges for baggage and picking up from Barcelona Sants station and the airport. The taxis have meters so charges are transparent – if not,

asking for a receipt (*rebut* in Catalan, *recibo* in Spanish) should ensure that the price is fair (and current rates are posted on ⓦ taxibarcelona.cat). Many taxis take credit-card payment.

There are taxi ranks outside major train and metro stations, in main squares, near large hotels and along the main avenues. You can call a taxi in advance, but few of the cab company operators speak English – you'll also be charged an extra €3–4 on top of the fare for calling a cab.

TAXI COMPANIES

Barna Taxis ☎ 933 577 755; **Radio Taxi** ☎ 933 033 033; **Servi-Taxi** ☎ 933 300 300; **Taxi Amic** ☎ 934 208 088.

Driving

You don't need a car to get around Barcelona, but you may want to rent one if you plan to see anything else of the region. However, in summer the coastal roads in particular are a nightmare, so if all you aim to do is zip to the beach or wine region for the day, it's far better to stick to the local trains. Driving in the city itself is not for the faint-hearted either, parking is notoriously difficult, and vehicle crime is rampant – never leave anything visible in the car.

Most foreign **driving licences** are honoured in Spain – including all EU, US and Canadian ones. Remember that you drive on the right in Spain, and away from main roads you yield to vehicles approaching from the right. Speed limits are posted – maximum on urban roads is 60kph, other roads 90kph, motorways 120kph. Wearing seatbelts is compulsory.

Parking

Indoor **car parks** in the city centre are linked to display boards that indicate where there are free spaces. Central locations include Plaça de Catalunya, Plaça Urquinaona, Arc de Triomf, Passeig de Gràcia, Plaça dels Angels/MACBA and Avinguda Paral.lel, and though parking in one of these is convenient it's also pretty expensive (1hr from around €3, 24hr from €25).

FOLLOW THAT TRIXI

A fun way to get around the old town, port area and beaches is by **trixi** (W trixi .com), a kind of love-bug-style bicycle-rickshaw. They tout for business between noon and 8pm outside La Seu (cathedral) in the Barri Gòtic, though you can also flag them down if one cruises by or make an advance reservation. Fares are fixed (€15 for 30min, €25 for 1hr, longer tours available) and the *trixistas* are an amiable, multilingual bunch for the most part. As they say, "It's transportainment!".

There are cheaper BSM (Barcelona Serveis Municipals, W bsmsa.cat) **long-term car parks** for residents and visitors, with the best option being the large Plaça del Fòrum car park at Diagonal Mar (Pl. d'Ernest Lluch i Martin; M El Maresme-Fòrum or tram T4). Parking for between one and five days costs €33.75, plus €7 for each additional day. Closer to the centre, the 24-hour BSM car park at Barcelona Nord bus station (c/d'Ali-Bei 54; M Arc de Triomf) costs €16.85 per day.

Street parking is permitted in most areas, but it can be tough to find spaces, especially in the old town and Gràcia, where it's nearly all either restricted access or residents' parking only. The ubiquitous residents' **Área Verda meter-zones** (W areaverda .bsmsa.cat) throughout the city allow pay-and-display parking for visitors, for €2.94 per hour, with either a one- or two-hour maximum stay. Elsewhere, don't be tempted to double-park, leave your car in loading zones or otherwise park illegally – the **towing fee** is €150, plus a daily €20 charge, and no mercy is shown to tourists or foreign-plated vehicles.

Vehicle rental

Car rental is cheapest arranged in advance through one of the large multinational agencies. In Barcelona, the major chains have outlets at the airport and at, or near, Barcelona Sants station. Inclusive rates start from around €40 per day for an economy car (less by the week, and often with good rates for a three-day weekend rental, around €150). Drivers need to be at least 21 (23 with some companies) and to have been driving for at least a year. It's essential to take out fully comprehensive insurance and pay for Collision Damage Waiver, otherwise you'll be liable for every scratch.

Some of the local Barcelona rental outlets – like Motissimo (T 934 908 401, W motissimo.es) and Vanguard (T 934 393 880, W vanguardrent.com) –

have **mopeds and motorcycles** available, though given the traffic conditions (and the good public transport system) it's not really recommended as a means of getting around the city.

Cycling

The city council has embraced cycling as a means of transport, and is investing heavily in cycle lanes and bike schemes, notably the **Bicing** pick-up and drop-off scheme (W bicing.com), which is touted as Barcelona's new public transport system. You'll see the red bikes and bike stations all over the city, but Bicing is not aimed at tourists, rather at locals who are encouraged to use the bikes for short trips. Users can register online or at the **Oficina del Bicing**, Pl. Pi i Sunyer 8–10, Barri Gòtic, between c/de la Canuda and c/de Duran i Bas (Mon–Fri 8.30am–5.30pm).

In any case, there are plenty of **bike-rental outfits** more geared to tourist requirements. Rental costs around €20 a day with companies all over town (two recommended ones are listed below), while many bike tour companies (see "City tours") can also fix you up with a rental bike. For more on bike lanes, off-road paths and cycling, see "Sports and outdoor activities" (see p.223).

BIKE RENTAL

Biciclot Pg. Marítim 33–35, Port Olímpic M Ciutadella-Vila Olímpica T 932 219 778, W biciclot.net.

Un Coxte Menys/Bicicleta Barcelona c/de l'Esparteria 3, La Ribera M Barceloneta T 932 682 105, W bicicletabarcelona.com.

City tours

The number of available tours is bewildering, and you can see the sights on anything from a Segway to a hot-air balloon. Bike tours in particular are hugely popular – at times it seems as if every tourist in the city is playing follow-my-leader down the same old-town alley – while other operators offer tapas-bar crawls, party nights and out-of-town excursions. Highest profile are the open-top sightseeing bus tours, whose board-at-will services can drop you outside every attraction in the city. Otherwise, Barcelona has some parti-cularly good walking tours, showing you parts of the old town you might not find otherwise, while sightseeing boats offer a different view of the city.

BIKE TOURS

Bike Tours Barcelona ☎ 932 682 105, ⓦ biketoursbarcelona .com. Find the red-T-shirted guides in Pl. de Sant Jaume in the Barri Gòtic, outside the tourist office (top of c/de la Ciutat) – tours last 3hr (daily 11am, plus April–Sept Fri–Mon 4.30pm; €22), no reservations required.

BUS TOURS

Barcelona City Tour ⓦ barcelonatours.es. The red buses make a circular sweep through the city on two routes, east and west, from Pl. de Catalunya (daily 9am–8pm, departures every 10–20min). Tickets available on board and online: one-day €22, two-day €29 (under-14s €14/18 respectively, under-4s free).

Bus Turístic ⓦ barcelonabusturistic.cat. The main official sightseeing service (departures every 5–25min) with over forty stops on three combined routes, linking all the main tourist sights. Northern (red) and southern (blue) routes depart from Pl. de Catalunya (daily 9am–7pm, April–Sept 9am–8pm), and a full circuit on either route takes 2hr. The green Forùm route (daily April–Sept 9.30am–8pm) runs from Port Olímpic to Diagonal Mar and back via the beaches, and takes 40min. Tickets (valid for all routes) cost €23 for one day, €30 for two days (children aged 4–12 €14/18 respectively, under-4s free). The ticket also gives discounts at various sights, attractions, shops and restaurants. Buy online, or on board the bus, at any tourist office, Sants station and TMB customer centres.

WALKING TOURS

Barcelona Walking Tours ☎ 932 853 832, ⓦ barcelonaturisme .com. The Pl. de Catalunya tourist office coordinates a popular series of walks and tours, including a 90min historical walking tour of the Barri Gòtic (daily 10am; €13). There are also 90min Picasso walking tours (Tues, Thurs & Sat at 4pm; €19.50, includes entry to Picasso Museum), a 2hr Modernisme tour (Fri & Sat, May–Oct at 3pm, June–Sept at 6pm; €13) and 2hr Gourmet and Cuisine tour (Fri & Sat 10am; €20, includes tastings). Times given are for the current English-language tours; advance booking essential (discounts for online bookings, and reductions for children/seniors).

Follow the Baldie ⓦ followthebaldie.com. Follow erudite, self-professed baldie tour guide and longtime Barcelona resident, Trevor, on walks around anarchist Barcelona or over the hills to Tibidabo, tracking tarantulas near Sitges or staggering from bar to bar in rural Catalunya. These are not your normal tours, as a perusal of the website soon shows. Trips from €35 per person.

My Favourite Things ☎ 637 265 405, ⓦ myft.net. Highly individual tours which reveal the city in a new light – whether it's where and what the locals eat, Art Nouveau discoveries or eco-friendly Barcelona. Tours (in English) cost €26 per person and last around 4hr, and there's always time for anecdotes, diversions, workshop visits and café visits. Tour numbers are limited to ten, and advance bookings are essential – call or email for latest information or tailor-made requests.

Spanish Civil War Tour ✉ nick.iberianature@gmail.com. Engrossing English-language tours on Barcelona and the Spanish Civil War, bringing to life the city that George Orwell knew so well. Tours are under the auspices of a local history society and led by Civil War enthusiast Nick Lloyd. Three-hour walks around the old town cost €20 per person, or there are all-day tours (€40) including lunch and a trip up to Montjuïc, both with a minimum of three people.

WATER TOURS

Catamaran Orsom ☎ 934 410 537, ⓦ barcelona-orsom.com. Afternoon catamaran trips around the port (€12.95) and evening jazz cruises (€14.90), with departures Easter week & June–Sept daily, May & Oct daily except Tues & Wed. There's a ticket kiosk at the quayside opposite the Columbus statue, at the bottom of the Ramblas (ⓜ Drassanes), but you should call in advance to be certain of departures.

Las Golondrinas ☎ 934 423 106, ⓦ lasgolondrinas.com. Daily sightseeing boats depart from Pl. Portal de la Pau, behind the Columbus monument (ⓜ Drassanes) – trips are either around the port (35min; €6.80, under-10s €2.60, under-4s free), or port and coast including the Port Olímpic and Diagonal Mar (90min; €14, under-10s €5, under-4s free). Departures are at least hourly June–Sept, less frequently Oct–May but still daily.

Information

The city tourist board, Turisme de Barcelona (ⓦ barcelonaturisme.com), is the best first stop for information about Barcelona, with a really useful English-language website and offices at the airport, Barcelona Sants station, Plaça de Catalunya and Plaça de Sant Jaume.

There are also **staffed kiosks** in main tourist areas, such as on the Ramblas, outside the Sagrada Família and at Plaça d'Espanya, which dispense information and sell a large array of discount passes and entrance tickets for popular attractions. You can also **buy tickets online** for most city museums and attractions from ⓦ barcelonaturisme.com at a five-to ten-percent discount.

For information about the wider province of Catalunya, you need the Generalitat's information centre (Centre d'Informació de Catalunya) at **Palau Robert**, while events, concerts, exhibitions, festivals and other cultural diversions are covered in full at the Institut de Cultura in the **Palau de la Virreina** on the Ramblas.

For anything else you might need to know, you can try the city's 24-hour **☎010 telephone enquiries service**. They'll be able to help with questions about transport, public services and other matters, and there are English-speaking staff available.

The city hall (Ajuntament; ⓦ bcn.cat) and regional government (Generalitat; ⓦ gencat.cat) **websites** are absolute mines of information about every aspect of cultural, social and working life in Barcelona, from museum opening hours and festival dates to local politics and council office locations; they both have English-language versions. Also useful is **ⓦ barcelona-online.com**, with punchy

DISCOUNT CARDS AND PACKAGES

If you're going to do a lot of sightseeing, you can save yourself money by buying one of the widely available discount cards.

- **Barcelona Card** (2 days €27.50, 3 days €33.50, 4 days €38 or 5 days €45, full details on ⓦ barcelonaturisme.com). Free public transport, plus big discounts at museums, venues, shops, theatres and restaurants. It's available at points of arrival, tourist offices and kiosks and other outlets, though there's a ten-percent discount if you buy online.
- **Articket** (€22, valid six months, ⓦ articketbcn.org). Free admission into seven major art centres and galleries (MNAC, MACBA, CCCB, Museu Picasso, Fundació Antoni Tàpies, Fundació Joan Miró and Centre Cultural Caixa Catalunya at La Pedrera). Buy at participating galleries, at Barcelona tourist offices and kiosks or online.
- **Arqueoticket** (€14, valid calendar year). In the same vein as Articket, offers free entry into five historical museums (Museu d'Arqueologia de Catalunya, Barbier-Mueller, Egipci, Historia de Barcelona and Marítim). Available at participating museums and tourist offices.
- **Ruta del Modernisme** (€12, valid one year, ⓦ rutadelmodernisme.com). An excellent English-language guidebook, map and discount-voucher package that covers 115 *modernista* buildings in Barcelona and other Catalan towns, offering discounts of up to fifty percent on admission fees, tours and purchases. It's also packaged with *Let's Go Out*, a guide to *modernista* bars and restaurants (total package €18), with both available from the Centre del Modernisme desk at the main Plaça de Catalunya tourist office.

reviews in English of all things Barcelona plus links to scores of other websites.

For arts and events listings, the websites of the local newspapers and magazines (see "The media" below) are also very useful.

INFORMATION OFFICES

Turisme de Barcelona ☎ 807 117 222 if calling from within Spain, ☎ 932 853 834 if calling from abroad, ⓦ barcelonaturisme .com. Main office, Pl. de Catalunya 17, Ⓜ Catalunya (daily 8.30am–8.30pm); also at Pl. de Sant Jaume, entrance at c/de la Ciutat 2, Barri Gòtic, Ⓜ Jaume I (Mon–Fri 8.30am–8.30pm, Sat 9am–7pm, Sun & hols 9am–2pm); Airport Terminals 1 & 2 (daily 9am–9pm); and Barcelona Sants, Pl. dels Països Catalans, Ⓜ Sants Estació (daily 8am–8pm). The main Pl. de Catalunya office is down the steps in the southeast corner of the square, opposite El Corte Inglés. It's always busy and can be frustrating if you just want a quick answer to a question. There's also a money exchange service, separate accommodation desk, tour and ticket sales and a gift shop.

Institut de Cultura Palau de la Virreina, Ramblas 99 ☎ 933 161 000, ⓦ bcn.cat/cultura, Ⓜ Liceu (daily 10am–8.30pm). Cultural information office, with advance information on everything that's happening in the city, from events and concerts to exhibitions and festivals; you can also buy tickets here. The website portal has daily updated cultural news and web TV previews, or pick up the free "Cultural Agenda" (in English), a useful free monthly what's-on listings guide.

Centre del Modernisme ☎ 933 177 652, ⓦ rutadel modernisme.com. Offices inside the Turisme de Barcelona tourist office at Pl. de Catalunya, Ⓜ Catalunya (Mon–Sat 10am–7pm, Sun & hols 10am–2pm); at Hospital de la Santa Creu i Sant Pau, c/de Sant Antoni Maria Claret 167, Eixample, Ⓜ Hospital de Sant Pau (daily

9.30am–1.30pm); and Pavellons Güell, Av. de Pedralbes 7, Pedralbes, Ⓜ Palau Reial (Sat & Sun 10am–2pm). The staffed information desks provide details of visits to the city's *modernista* buildings and monuments, and sell the Ruta del Modernisme package.

Centre d'Informació de Catalunya Palau Robert, Pg. de Gràcia 107, Eixample ☎ 932 388 091 or ☎ 012, ⓦ gencat.cat /palaurobert; Ⓜ Diagonal (Mon–Sat 10am–7pm, Sun & hols 10am–2.30pm). Has information about travel in Catalunya and provides maps, guides, details of how to get around and lists of places to stay. Also exhibitions and events relating to all matters Catalan.

Barcelona Informació (Oficina d'Atenció Ciutadana) Pl. de Sant Miquel, Barri Gòtic ☎ 010, ⓦ bcn.cat; Ⓜ Jaume I (Mon–Sat 8.30am–8pm, except Aug Sat 9am–2pm). Citizens' information office, around the back of the Ajuntament in the new building. It's not really for tourists, but is invariably helpful about all aspects of living in Barcelona (though you can't count on English being spoken).

The media

You can buy foreign newspapers at the stalls down the Ramblas, and around Plaça de Catalunya, on Passeig de Gràcia, on Rambla de Catalunya and at Barcelona Sants station. The same stalls often sell international magazines and trade papers too, but if you can't find what you're looking for, try FNAC at El Triangle on Plaça de Catalunya (Ⓜ Catalunya), which has an excellent ground-floor magazine section.

Newspapers and magazines

Best of the **local newspapers** is the Barcelona edition of the liberal *El País* (Welpais.es), which has a daily Catalunya supplement and is good on entertainment and the arts. The conservative Barcelona paper *La Vanguardia* (Wlavanguardia.es) also has a good arts and culture listings section on Friday, while *El Periódico* (Welperiodico.com) is more tabloid in style; it also comes in a Catalan edition. *Avui* (Wavui.cat) is the chief nationalist paper, printed in Catalan. For wall-to-wall coverage of sport (for which, in Barcelona, read FC Barcelona), buy the specialist dailies *Mundo Deportivo* (Welmundo deportivo.es) or *Sport* (Wsport.es).

The two most useful weekly **city listings publications** are *Guía del Ocio* (Wguiadelociobcn.es), a small paperback-book-sized magazine (in Spanish), and the magazine-format *Time Out Barcelona* (Wtimeout.cat; in Catalan), both available at kiosks all over the city and also online.

English-language publications

Barcelona Metropolitan (Wbarcelona-metro politan.com) is a free monthly magazine for English-speakers living in Barcelona, and there's also the free monthly **Barcelona Connect** (Wbarcelona connect.com), containing an idiosyncratic mixture of news, views, reviews and classified ads. You'll find these and other free mags in hotels, hostels, bars and other outlets; the online versions are pretty comprehensive too. For the style scene look in newsagents for **b-guided** (Wb-guided.com), a painfully cool quarterly magazine, while the excellent Wlecool.com/barcelona is a hip cultural agenda and city guide, available online or as a weekly e-magazine.

Television

In Catalunya you can pick up two **national TV channels**, TVE1 and TVE2 (La 2), a couple of **Catalan-language channels**, TV3 and Canal 33, and the private Antena 3, Cuatro (ie, Four), Tele 5 and La Sexta (The Sixth) channels. In Barcelona you can also get the city-run **Barcelona Televisió** (Wbtv.cat), which is useful for information about local events, and news programmes on the otherwise subscriber-only Digital Plus channel. TVs in most pensions and small hotels tend to offer these stations, with cable and satellite channels available in higher-rated hotels.

Travel essentials

Admission charges

Admission charges for city attractions vary between €3 and €18, though most museums and galleries cost around €6 or €7. Many offer free admission on the first or last Sunday of every month, and most museums are free on the saints' days of February 12, April 23 and September 24, plus May 18 (international museum day). There's usually a reduction or free entrance if you show a student, youth or senior citizen card. Several discount cards are also available (see box, p.27), that give heavily reduced admission to Barcelona's museums and galleries – worth considering if you're planning to see everything that the city has to offer.

Costs

Barcelona is not a particularly cheap place to visit and it's more expensive on the whole than other major cities in Spain. However, it still rates as pretty good value when compared with the cost of visiting cities in Britain, France or Germany, especially when it comes to dining out or getting around on public transport. Hotel prices are the main drain on the budget, and they have increased considerably over the last few years. Realistically, you'll be paying from €70 a night for a room in a simple pension, and from €110 for a three-star or budget boutique hotel. Still, once you're there, a one-day public transport pass gives you the freedom of the city for €6.20, and most museums and galleries cost €6–7 (though a few of

ADDRESSES

Addresses are written as: c/Picasso 2 4° – which means Picasso street (*carrer*) number two, fourth floor. You may also see *esquerra*, meaning "left-hand" (apartment or office); *dreta* is right; *centro* centre. C/Picasso s/n means the building has no number (*sense numero*). In the gridded streets of the Eixample, building numbers run from south to north (ie lower numbers at the Plaça de Catalunya end) and from west to east (lower numbers at Plaça d'Espanya).

The main address abbreviations used in this book are: Av. (for Avinguda, avenue); Bxda. (for Baixada, alley); c/ (for Carrer, street); Pg. (for Passeig, more a boulevard than a street); Pl. (for Plaça, square); and Ptge. (for Passatge, passage).

BUDGET BARCELONA

Boutique hotels, designer stores, gourmet restaurants and hip bars – life in Barcelona can get pretty pricey at times. But here's how to keep costs to a minimum while still having a great time.

- **Cafés and restaurants** Eat your main meal of the day at lunchtime, when the *menú del dia* offers fantastic value. Also note that there's usually a surcharge for terrace service.
- **Public transport** Buy a public transport travel pass, which will save you around forty percent on every ride.
- **Discount cards** There are several useful city discount cards or packages, while you should bring along any student, youth or senior citizen card you're entitled to carry, as they often attract discounts on museum, gallery and attraction charges.
- **Special offers** Take advantage of the discount nights at the cinema (Mon & sometimes Wed), and at the theatre (Tues), and visit Tiquet Rambles in the Palau de la Virreina for half-price last-minute theatre and show tickets.
- **Museums and galleries** At many museums and galleries, admission is usually free one day a month, and most museums are free on saints' days (see "Admission charges", opposite).
- **See the sights for free** Go to the Ramblas, Boqueria market, La Seu, Santa María del Mar, Ajuntament and Generalitat, Parc de la Ciutadella, Parc de Collserola, Port Vell, Port Olímpic, city beaches, Els Encants flea market, Diagonal Mar/Fòrum, Caixa Fórum and Parc Güell – all free.

the showpiece attractions have much higher entry fees). A set three-course lunch goes for €10–15, and dinner from around €25, though of course the Michelin-starred destination restaurants are much pricier – even so, at around €100 a head, they're still a far better deal than the equivalent places in London or Paris.

Crime and personal safety

Catalunya has its own autonomous police force, the **Mossos d'Esquadra** (🅦 gencat.net/mossos), in navy-blue uniforms with red trim. They have gradually taken over most of the local duties traditionally carried out by the other police services in Spain, namely the **Policía Nacional** (🅦 policia.es) – the national police, in uniforms resembling blue combat gear – and the **Guàrdia Urbana** (🅦 bcn.cat /guardiaurbana), municipal police in blue shirts and high-visibility jackets. There's also the **Guàrdia Civil**, a national paramilitary force in green uniforms, seen guarding some public buildings, and at airports and border crossings.

In theory you're supposed to carry some kind of **identification** at all times, and the police can stop

you in the street and demand to see it. In practice they're rarely bothered if you're clearly a tourist – and a photocopy of your passport or a photo-driving licence should suffice.

If you're robbed, you need to go to the police to report it, not least because your insurance company will require a police report. Don't expect a great deal of concern if your loss is relatively small – but do expect the process of completing forms and formalities to take ages.

The easiest place to report a crime is at the **Guàrdia Urbana station** at Ramblas 43, opposite Pl. Reial, 🅜 Liceu ☎ 932 562 430 (24hr; English spoken), though there's a Guàrdia Urbana office in each city district (see their website).

However, to get a police report for your insurance you need to go to the **Mossos d'Esquadra station** at c/Nou de la Rambla 76–80, El Raval, 🅜 Paral.lel (☎ 933 062 300). You can fill in a report online (under "Serveis", then "Denúncies per internet" on the website, English option available), but you'll still have to go to the office within 72hr to sign the document.

In an **emergency**, contact the police on the following numbers: Mossos d'Esquadra ☎ 088, Policía Nacional ☎ 091, Guàrdia Urbana ☎ 092.

EMERGENCY SERVICES

In an emergency, dial: ☎ 112 for ambulance, police and fire services; ☎ 061 for ambulance; ☎ 080 for fire service; ☎ 091 for national police. For local police numbers see "Crime and personal safety".

Electricity

The electricity supply is 220v and plugs come with two round pins – bring an adaptor (and transformer) to use UK and US laptops, cellphone chargers, etc.

STAYING SAFE

Barcelona has a reputation as a city plagued by petty crime, but you don't need to be unduly paranoid. Take all reasonable precautions, and your trip should be a safe one. Sling **bags** across your body, not off one shoulder; don't carry wallets in back pockets; and don't hang bags on the back of a café chair. Make photocopies of your **passport**, leaving the original and any tickets in the hotel safe. Be on your guard when on **public transport**, or on the crowded Ramblas and the medieval streets to either side – at night, avoid unlit streets and dark alleys. While you can take many **beggars** at face value, you should beware of people directly accosting you or who in any other manner try to distract you – like the "helpful" person pointing out bird shit (shaving cream or something similar) on your jacket while someone relieves you of your money.

Embassies and consulates

Most countries have their embassies in Madrid and maintain a consulate in Barcelona. You'll need to contact them if you lose your passport or need other assistance. Most consulates are open to the public for enquiries Mon–Fri, usually 9am–1pm & 3–5pm, though the morning shift is the most reliable.

FOREIGN CONSULATES IN BARCELONA

Australia Av. Diagonal 458, Esquerra de l'Eixample ☎ 934 909 013, Ⓦ spain.embassy.gov.au; Ⓜ Diagonal.
Canada c/d'Elisenda de Pinós 10, Sarrià ☎ 932 042 700, Ⓦ canadainternational.gc.ca; FGC Reina Elisenda.
New Zealand Trav. de Gràcia 64, Gràcia ☎ 932 090 399, Ⓦ nzembassy.com; FGC Gràcia.
Republic of Ireland Gran Via Carles III 94, Les Corts ☎ 934 915 021; Ⓜ Maria Cristina/Les Corts.
UK Av. Diagonal 477, Esquerra de l'Eixample ☎ 933 666 200, Ⓦ ukinspain.fco.gov.uk; Ⓜ Hospital Clínic.
USA Pg. de la Reina Elisenda 23, Sàrria ☎ 932 802 227, Ⓦ barcelona.usconsulate.gov; FGC Reina Elisenda.

Entry requirements

EU citizens need only a **valid national identity card or passport** to enter Spain. Other Europeans, and citizens of the United States, Canada, Australia and New Zealand, require a passport but no visa and can stay as a tourist for up to ninety days. Other nationalities (including South Africans) will need to get a **visa** from a Spanish embassy or consulate before departure. Visa requirements do change and it's always advisable to check the current situation before leaving home.

Most EU citizens who want to stay in Spain for longer than three months, rather than just visit as a tourist, need to register at the **Oficina de Extranjeros** (foreigners' office), c/de Balmes 192, Ⓜ Diagonal (Mon–Fri 9am–2pm), where they'll be issued with a residence certificate. You don't need the certificate if you're an EU citizen living and working legally in Barcelona, or if you're legally self-employed or a student. US citizens can apply for one ninety-day extension, showing proof of funds, but this must be done from outside Spain. Other nationalities wishing to extend their stay will need to get a special visa from a Spanish embassy or consulate before departure.

Anyone planning to stay and live in Barcelona will also need a **Numero de Identidade de Extranjeros** (NIE), an ID number that's essential if you're to open a bank account, sign a utilities, job or accommodation contract, and for many other financial transactions.

As well as the Oficina de Extranjeros, there's also a telephone helpline on ☎ 012 (Mon–Fri 9am–5pm) that deals with all aspects of **residency and immigration**, and you'll find more information at Ⓦ gencat.cat.

Health

The **European Health Insurance Card** gives EU citizens access to Spanish state public health services under reciprocal agreements. While this will provide free or reduced-cost medical care in the event of minor injuries and emergencies, it won't cover every eventuality – and it only applies to EU citizens in possession of the card – so travel insurance (see opposite) is essential.

For minor health complaints look for the green cross of a **pharmacy** (farmàcia), where highly trained staff can give advice (often in English), and are able to dispense many drugs (including some antibiotics) available only on prescription in other countries. Usual hours are weekdays 9am–1pm & 4–8pm. At least one in each neighbourhood is open daily 24hr (and marked as such), or phone ☎ 010 for information on those open out of hours – Farmacia Clapies, Ramblas 98, Ⓜ Liceu (☎ 933 012 843, Ⓦ farmacia clapes.com) is a convenient 24hr pharmacy. A list of out-of-hours pharmacies can also be found in the window of each pharmacy store.

Any local **health-care centre** (Centre d'Atenció Primària, CAP) can provide non-emergency assistance. In the old town, there's one at Ptge. Pau 1, Barri Gòtic, Ⓜ Drassanes (☎ 933 425 549), and another at c/del Rec Comtal 24, Sant Pere, Ⓜ Arc de Triomf (☎ 933 101 421); both are open Mon–Fri 9am–8pm, Sat 9am–5pm. Alternatively, call ☎ 010 or consult Ⓦ bcn.cat for a full list.

For emergency hospital treatment, call ☎ 061 or go to one of the following **central hospitals**, which have 24hr accident and emergency (*urgències*) services.

HOSPITALS

Centre Perecamps Av. Drassanes 13–15, El Raval ☎ 934 410 600; Ⓜ Drassanes.
Hospital Clínic i Provincial c/de Villaroel 170, Eixample ☎ 932 275 400; Ⓜ Hospital Clínic.
Hospital del Mar Pg. Marítim 25–29, Vila Olímpica ☎ 932 483 000; Ⓜ Ciutadella-Vila Olímpica.
Hospital de la Santa Creu i Sant Pau c/de Sant Antoni Maria Claret, Eixample ☎ 932 919 000; Ⓜ Hospital de Sant Pau.

Insurance

You should take out a comprehensive **insurance policy** before travelling to Barcelona, to cover against loss, theft, illness or injury. A typical policy will provide cover for loss of baggage, tickets and – up to a certain limit – cash or travellers' cheques, as well as cancellation or curtailment of your journey. With medical coverage you should ascertain whether benefits will be paid as treatment proceeds or only after you return home, and whether there is a 24-hour medical emergency number. When securing baggage cover, make sure that the per-article limit will cover your most valuable possession. Most policies exclude so-called dangerous sports unless an extra premium is paid: in Spain this can mean most watersports are excluded, though probably not things like bike tours or hiking.

If you need to make a claim, you should keep receipts for medicines and medical treatment, and in the event you have anything stolen you must obtain an official statement from the police (see p.29).

Internet

There are internet shops and cybercafés all over Barcelona, and competition has driven prices down to around €2 an hour. A stroll down the Ramblas, or through the Barri Gòtic, La Ribera, El Raval and Gràcia will reveal a host of possibilities. Most youth hostels and many small pensions provide cheap or free internet access for their guests, but hotel business centres or hotel bedrooms wired for access tend to be far more expensive than going out on the street to an internet place. **Wi-fi** (pronounced "wee-fee" in Barcelona) is widespread in cafés, bars and hotels, while the city council operates Spain's largest free public wi-fi network (Ⓦ bcn.cat/barcelonawifi). If you take your own laptop or mobile device make sure you've got insurance cover and all the relevant plugs and adaptors for recharging.

Language schools

The Generalitat (the government of Catalonia) offers low-cost **Catalan classes** for non-Spanish speakers through the Consorci per a la Normalització Lingüística (Ⓦ cpnl.cat; call ☎ 010 for information). Otherwise, the cheapest **Spanish** or Catalan classes in Barcelona are at the Escola Oficial d'Idiomes, Av. Drassanes 14, El Raval, Ⓜ Drassanes (☎ 933 249 330, Ⓦ eoibd.cat) – expect queues when you sign on. Language courses for beginners are also offered at Barcelona University, Gran Via de les Corts Catalanes 585, Eixample, Ⓜ Universitat (☎ 934 021 100, Ⓦ ub .es). There's a basic Spanish and Catalan primer in our "Language" section (see p.262).

Laundry

There are inexpensive laundry services in most of the youth hostels and some pensions; hotels will

---

ROUGH GUIDES TRAVEL INSURANCE

Rough Guides has teamed up with **WorldNomads.com** to offer great travel insurance deals. Policies are available to residents of over 150 countries, with cover for a wide range of adventure sports, 24hr emergency assistance, high levels of medical and evacuation cover and a stream of travel safety information. Roughguides.com users can take advantage of their policies online 24/7, from anywhere in the world – even if you're already travelling. And since plans often change when you're on the road, you can extend your policy and even claim online. Roughguides.com users who buy travel insurance with WorldNomads.com can also leave a positive footprint and donate to a community development project. For more information go to Ⓦ roughguides.com/shop.

charge considerably more. Self-service laundries include Lavomatic, at Pl. Joaquim Xirau 1, Barri Gòtic, ⓂDrassanes ☎933 425 119, and c/del Consolat del Mar 43–45, Pl. del Palau, La Ribera, ⓂBarceloneta ☎932 684 768 (both open Mon–Sat 9am–9pm); and LavaExpress, at nine city locations, including c/de Ferlandina 34, El Raval, ⓂUniversitat ☎933 183 018, Ⓦlavaxpres.com (daily 8am–11pm). At La Lavanderia de Ana, c/del Carme 63, El Raval, ⓂLiceu ☎639 957 046, Ⓦlalavanderiadeana.com (Mon–Sat 9am–8pm) you can leave your laundry for a standard wash-and-dry (from around €8).

Left luggage

At Barcelona Sants the left-luggage office (*consigna*) is open daily 7am–11pm and costs €3–4.50 a day. There are also lockers at Estació de França, Passeig de Gràcia station and Barcelona Nord bus station (all 6am–11.30pm; €3–4.50).

Libraries

The **British Council**, c/d'Amigó 83, Sant Gervasi, FGC Muntaner ☎932 419 700, Ⓦbritishcouncil.es, has the only English-language lending library in Barcelona. There's also a full arts and events programme here.

The Catalan national library, the **Biblioteca de Catalunya**, is at c/de l'Hospital 56, El Raval, ⓂLiceu ☎932 702 300, Ⓦbnc.cat (Mon–Fri 9am–8pm, Sat 9am–2pm). A letter of academic reference is required, though there is the **Biblioteca Sant Pau-Santa Creu** (public library) in the same building (Tues, Thurs & Sat 10am–2pm, plus Mon–Fri 3.30–8pm). You can find all Barcelona's other public libraries listed on Ⓦbcn.cat – they've all got internet and wireless access, and some have English-language books, international press, etc.

The **Mediateca** library at the Caixa Fórum arts centre, Av. Francesc Ferrer i Guàrdia 6–8, Montjuïc ⓂEspanya (☎934 768 651, Ⓦmediatecaonline.net), is an open-access library for arts and culture books, music, magazines and reference material.

Lost property

Anything recovered by the police, or left on public transport, is sent to the **Oficina de Troballes** (municipal lost property office), at Pl. Carles Pi i Sunyer 8–10, Barri Gòtic, ⓂJaume I/Catalunya (Mon–Fri 9am–2pm; ☎010). Most items are kept for three months. You could also try the TMB (public transport) customer service centre at Universitat metro station.

Mail

The main **post office** in Barcelona is near the harbour in the old town, while each city neighbourhood also has a post office, though these have far less comprehensive opening hours and services. If all you need are **stamps**, however, it's usually quicker to visit a tobacconist (look for the brown-and-yellow *tabac* sign), found on virtually every street. These can also weigh letters and small parcels, advise about postal rates and send express mail (*urgente*). Use the yellow on-street postboxes and put your mail in the flap marked *províncies i estranger* or *altres destins*. Letters or cards take around three to four days to European countries, five days to a week to North America.

POSTAL SERVICES

Main post office (Correus) Pl. d'Antoni López, at the eastern end of Pg. de Colom, Barri Gòtic ☎934 868 302, Ⓦcorreos.es; ⓂBarceloneta/Jaume I (Mon–Fri 8.30am–9.30pm, Sat 8.30am–2pm). There's a poste restante/general delivery service here (*llista de correus*), plus express post, fax service, mobile phone top-ups, phonecard sales and bill payments.

Postal Transfer Pl. Urquinaona at c/de Roger de Lluria, Eixample; ⓂUrquinaona (Mon–Fri 10am–11pm, Sat 11am–midnight, Sun noon–11pm). Offers after-hours postal services plus money exchange, fax, photocopying and phonecard sales.

Maps

The city tourist offices and kiosks charge €1 for their maps – you can pick up a good free one instead from the information desk on the ground floor of El Corte Inglés department store, right outside the main tourist office. With that, and the maps in this book, you'll easily find your way around. You can also check the location of any building or address on the city council's extremely useful **interactive street plan** at Ⓦbcn.cat (click on "Plànol BCN", or "BCN map" in the English-language version).

You'll find a good selection of regional and national Spanish maps in most bookshops and at street newspaper kiosks or petrol stations. Map and travel shops in your home country should also be able to supply road maps of Catalunya or northern Spain (by Michelin, Firestone or Rand McNally). Alternatively, try mail order from Ⓦamazon.com or a map specialist like Ⓦstanfords.co.uk or Ⓦrandmcnally.com.

Money

Spain's **currency** is the euro (€), with notes issued in denominations of 5, 10, 20, 50, 100, 200 and 500

CATALAN NAMES

Traditionally, a person gets two surnames, one from dad and one from mum. They are not always used, but it explains why many of the names given in this book may be longer than those you are used to seeing. Thus, Antoni Gaudí i Cornet took Gaudí from his father and Cornet from his mother (the "i" simply means "and").

euros, and coins in denominations of 1, 2, 5, 10, 20 and 50 cents, and 1 and 2 euros.

By far the easiest way to get money is to use your bank debit card to withdraw cash from an **ATM**, found all over the city, including the airport and major train stations. You can usually withdraw up to €300 a day and instructions are offered in English once you insert your card. Make sure you have a personal identification number (PIN) that's designed to work overseas, and take a note of your bank's emergency contact number in case the machine swallows the card. Some European debit cards can also be used directly in shops to pay for purchases; you'll need to check first with your bank.

All major **credit cards** are accepted in hotels, restaurants and shops, and for tours, tickets and transport, though don't count on being able to use them in every small hotel or backstreet café. You can also use your credit card in an ATM to withdraw cash.

Spanish **banks** (*bancos*) and savings banks (*caixas*) have branches throughout Barcelona, with concentrations down the Ramblas and around Plaça de Catalunya. Normal banking hours are Monday to Friday from 8.30am to 2pm, although from October until May most institutions also open Thursday 4pm to 6.30pm (savings banks) or Saturday 9am to 1pm (banks).

For out-of-hours banking you can use bureaux de change or a **foreign-exchange office** (*canvi, cambio*), found down the Ramblas (often open until midnight); at Barcelona Sants (daily 8am–8pm); El Corte Inglés department store, Pl. de Catalunya (Mon–Sat 10am–9.30pm); or the Turisme de Catalunya tourist office, Pl. de Catalunya 17 (Mon–Sat 9am–9pm, Sun 9am–2pm). Exchange offices don't always charge commission, though their rates aren't usually as good as the banks.

Opening hours and public holidays

Basic **working hours** are Monday to Saturday 9.30 or 10am to 1.30pm and 4.30 to 8 or 9pm, though many offices and shops don't open on Saturday afternoons. Local cafés, bars and markets open from around 7am, while shopping centres, major stores and large supermarkets tend to remain open all day from 10am to 9pm, with some even open on Sunday. In the lazy days of summer everything becomes a bit more relaxed, with offices working until around 3pm and many shops and restaurants closing for part or the whole of August.

Most of the showpiece **museums and galleries** in Barcelona open all day, from 10am to 8pm, though some of the smaller collections and attractions close over lunchtime between 1 and 4pm. On Sundays most open in the morning only and on Mondays most are closed all day. On public holidays, most museums and galleries have Sunday opening hours, while pretty much everything is closed on Christmas Day, New Year's Day and January 6.

Apart from the cathedral (La Seu) and the Sagrada Família – the two churches you're most likely to visit, which have tourist-friendly opening hours – most other **churches** are often only open for worship in the early morning (around 7–9am) and the evening (around 6–9pm).

Not all **public and bank holidays** in Spain are observed in Catalunya, and vice versa. On the days listed below, and during the many local festivals, you'll find most shops closed, though bars and restaurants tend to stay open.

BARCELONA'S PUBLIC HOLIDAYS

January 1 Cap d'Any, New Year's Day
January 6 Epifanía, Epiphany
Variable Good Friday & Easter Monday
May 1 Día del Treball, May Day/Labour Day
June 24 Día de Sant Joan, St John's Day
August 15 L'Assumpció, Assumption of the Virgin
September 11 Diada Nacional, Catalan National Day
September 24 Festa de la Mercè, Our Lady of Mercy (Barcelona's patron saint)
October 12 Día de la Hispanidad, Spanish National Day
November 1 Tots Sants, All Saints' Day
December 6 Día de la Constitució, Constitution Day
December 8 La Imaculada, Immaculate Conception
December 25 Nadal, Christmas Day
December 26 Sant Esteve, St Stephen's Day

Smoking

Since 2006 smoking in public places in Spain has been regulated by law, and tougher restrictions introduced in 2011 mean that it's now forbidden to smoke in all public buildings and transport facilities, plus bars, restaurants, clubs and cafés. Compared to

AVERAGE MONTHLY TEMPERATURES

	Jan	Feb	Mar	Apr	May	Jun	Jul	Aug	Sep	Oct	Nov	Dec
Max/min (°C)	13/6	14/7	16/9	18/11	21/16	25/18	28/21	28/21	25/19	21/15	16/11	13/8
Max/min (°F)	56/42	58/44	61/48	65/52	70/61	77/64	82/70	82/70	77/66	70/59	61/52	56/46

other countries with smoking restrictions in force, you'll find there's still an awful lot of puffing going on, though the ban is generally observed.

Taxes

Local sales tax, **IVA**, is eight percent in hotels and restaurants, and eighteen percent in shops. It's usually included in the price though not always, so some hotel or restaurant bills can come as a bit of a surprise. Quoted prices should however always make it clear whether or not tax is included.

Telephones

Spanish **telephone numbers** have nine digits, and in Barcelona the first two digits of all landline phone numbers are 93 (the regional prefix), which you dial even when calling from within the city. Spanish mobile numbers begin with a 6 or 7, freephone numbers begin 900, while other 90-plus- and 80-plus-digit numbers are nationwide standard-rate or special-rate services. To **call Barcelona from abroad**, dial your international access number + 34 (Spain country code) + nine-digit number.

Most European **mobile phones** will work in Barcelona, though it's worth checking with your provider whether you need to get international access switched on and whether there are any extra charges involved. Even though prices are coming down, it's still expensive to use your own mobile

CALLING HOME FROM ABROAD

Note that the initial zero is omitted from the area code when dialing the UK, Ireland, Australia and New Zealand from abroad.
Australia international access code + 61
New Zealand international access code + 64
UK international access code + 44
US and Canada international access code + 1
Ireland international access code + 353
South Africa international access code + 27

extensively while abroad, and you will pay for receiving incoming calls for example.

Public telephones in Barcelona have instructions in English, and accept coins, credit cards and phonecards. Phonecards (*targetes/tarjetas*) with discounted rates for calls are available in tobacconists, newsagents and post offices, issued in various denominations either by Telefónica (the dominant operator) or one of its rivals. Credit cards are not recommended for local and national calls, since most have a minimum charge which is far more than a normal call is likely to cost. It's also best to avoid making calls from the phone in your hotel room, as even local calls will be slapped with a heavy surcharge.

You can make **international calls** from any public payphone, but it's cheaper to go to one of the ubiquitous **phone centres**, or *locutorios*, which specialize in discounted overseas connections. If the rates to the country that you want to call are not posted, just ask. You'll then be assigned a cabin to make your calls, and afterwards you pay in cash. For reverse-charge calls, dial the **international operator** (☎ 1008 Europe, ☎ 1005 rest of the world).

Ticket agencies

You can buy concert, sporting, exhibition and tourist attraction tickets with a credit card using the **Servi-Caixa** (ⓦ servicaixa.com) automatic dispensing machines in branches of La Caixa savings bank. You can also order tickets online through ServiCaixa or **TelEntrada** (ⓦ telentrada.com). Both websites have English-language versions. In addition, there's a concert ticket desk in the **FNAC store**, El Triangle, Plaça de Catalunya, while for advance tickets for all city council (Ajuntament)-sponsored concerts and events visit the **Palau de la Virreina**, Ramblas 99. The official tourist office website ⓦ **barcelonaturisme .com** also offers online ticket purchase for most city museums and attractions (click on "BCNShop"), and gives a five- to ten-percent discount as well.

Time

Barcelona is one hour ahead of the UK, six hours ahead of Eastern Standard Time, nine hours ahead of Pacific Standard Time, eight hours behind Australia, ten hours behind New Zealand and in the same time zone as South Africa. In Spain, the clocks go forward in the last week in March and back again in the last week in October.

Tipping

In most **restaurants and bars** service is considered to be included in the price of meals and drinks (hence the premium you pay for sitting at a terrace). Tipping is more a recognition that service was good or exceptional than an expected part of the server's wage. Locals leave only a few cents or round up the change for a coffee or a drink, and a euro or two for most meals, though fancier restaurants will expect ten to fifteen percent. **Taxi drivers** usually get around five percent, more if they have helped you with bags or been similarly useful, while **hotel porters** should be tipped a euro or two for their assistance.

Toilets

Public toilets are few and far between, and only averagely clean. Bars and restaurants are more likely to have proper (and cleaner) toilets, though you can't guarantee it – even in the poshest of places. Ask for *toaleta* or *serveis* (*lavabo* or *servicios* in Spanish). Dones or Damas (Ladies) and Homes/ Hombres or Caballeros (Gentlemen) are the usual signs.

Travellers with disabilities

The local tourist office has plenty of useful information on its website (W barcelonaturisme.com; click on "Accessible Barcelona", including a full guide to accessible sights and facilities in the city. Barcelona's city information line (T 010, English spoken) also has accessibility information for sights and services.

Barcelona's **airport** and **Aerobús** are fully accessible to travellers in wheelchairs, though the bus gets very busy and can be difficult if you have lots of luggage. At **Barcelona Sants** there are no access ramps for the trains themselves, and the steps and escalators are fairly steep, but there are access ramps at Estació de França and a lift to the platforms at Plaça de Catalunya's FGC station. Using the **metro** is also problematic, though improvements are ongoing – at present, only lines 1, 2 and 11 are fully accessible, with elevators at major stations (including Plaça de Catalunya, Universitat, Paral.lel, Passeig de Gràcia and Sagrada Família)

from the street to the platforms. However, all **city buses** have been adapted for wheelchair use, with automatic ramps/steps and a designated wheelchair space inside; simply ring the bell on the bus door. All trams and night buses are also wheelchair-accessible, as is the sightseeing Bus Turístic. The Transports Metropolitans de Barcelona (TMB) website (W tmb.net, English version available) lets you view all adapted metro stations and bus routes (look under "Transport for everyone"). If you need a **wheelchair-accessible taxi** call Taxi Amic (T 934 208 088, W taxi-amic-adaptat.com, English rarely spoken).

Out on the streets, the number of acoustic traffic-light signals is slowly growing, while dropped kerbs are being put in place across the city. However, most old-town attractions, including the Museu Picasso, have steps, cobbles or other impediments to access. Fully accessible **sights and attractions** include MNAC, Fundacío Antoni Tàpies, Fundacío Joan Miró, La Pedrera (though not the roof terrace), Caixa Forum, CosmoCaixa, Museu d'Història de Catalunya and the Palau de la Música Catalana.

USEFUL CONTACTS

Institut Municipal de Persones amb Discapacitat Av. Diagonal 233, 1°, Eixample T 934 132 775, W bcn.cat/accessible; M Glòries. Has information (some in English) on most aspects of life and travel in the city for disabled residents and visitors.

Water

Water from the tap is safe to drink, but it doesn't taste very nice. You'll always be given bottled mineral water in a bar or restaurant.

Women's Barcelona

Ca la Dona, c/de Casp 38, Eixample, M Urquinaona (T 934 127 161, W caladona.org), is a women's centre hosting meetings for women's groups, and with a library and bar. The Ajuntament's official women's resource centre, the **Centre Municipal d'Informació i Recursos per a les Dones** (CIRD), c/de les Camèlies 36–38, Gràcia, M Alfons X (T 932 850 357, W www.cird.bcn.cat), publishes a monthly calendar of events and news (see the website). **Llibreria Pròleg**, c/de Sant Pere Més Alt 46, Sant Pere, M Urquinaona (T 933 192 425, W llibreria proleg.com), is a bookshop specializing in women's issues. The **Barcelona Women's Network** (W bcn womensnetwork.com) is a social, business and networking club for English-speaking women living and working in the city.

The Ramblas

It is a telling comment on Barcelona's character that one can recommend a single street – the Ramblas (*Rambles* in Catalan) – as a highlight. No day in the city seems complete without a stroll down at least part of what, for Spanish poet Federico García Lorca, was "the only street in the world which I wish would never end". Lined with cafés, restaurants, souvenir shops, flower stalls and newspaper kiosks, and thronged by tourists, locals, buskers and performance artists, it's at the heart of Barcelona's life and self-image. There are important buildings and sights along the way, not least the Liceu opera house and the acclaimed Boqueria food market, but undoubtedly it's the vibrant street life that is the greatest attraction along Spain's most famous thoroughfare.

The Ramblas derives its name from the Arabic *ramla* (sand), which refers to the bed of a seasonal stream that was paved over in medieval times. In the nineteenth century, benches and decorative trees were added, overlooked by stately balconied buildings, and today – in a city choked with traffic – this wide tree-lined swath is still given over to pedestrians, with cars forced up the narrow strips of road on either side. There are **metro stops** at Catalunya (top of the Ramblas), Liceu (middle) and Drassanes (bottom), or you can walk the entire length in about twenty minutes.

The Ramblas splits the old town areas of Barcelona in half, with the Barri Gòtic on the east flank of the avenue and El Raval on the west. It also actually comprises **five separate sections** strung head to tail – from north to south, Rambla Canaletes, Estudis, Sant Josep, Caputxins and Santa Mònica – though it's rare to hear them referred to as such. However, you will notice changes as you walk down the Ramblas, primarily that the streets on either side become a little less polished – even seedy – as you get closer to the harbour. The businesses meanwhile, reflect the mixed clientele, from patisseries to pizza takeaways, and stores selling handcrafted jewellery to shops full of sombreros, bullfight posters ("your name here") and football shirts. On the central avenue under the plane trees you'll find stallholders peddling pet canaries, rabbits, tropical fish, flowers, plants, postcards and books. You can have your palm read and your portrait painted, or while away time with the buskers and human statues (though if you play cards or dice for money with a man on a street, you've only yourself to blame if you get ripped off). Drag yourself home with the dawn, and you'll rub shoulders with the street cleaners, watchful policemen and bleary-eyed stallholders. It's a never-ending show, of which visitors and locals alike rarely tire.

Plaça de Catalunya

Ⓜ Catalunya

The huge **Plaça de Catalunya** square at the top of the Ramblas stands right at the heart of the city, with the old town and port below it, and the planned Eixample district above and beyond. It was laid out in its present form in the 1920s, centred on a formal arrangement of statues, circular fountains and trees, and is the focal point for local events and demonstrations – notably the mass gathering here on New Year's Eve. The most prominent monument is the towering angular slab and bust dedicated to **Francesc Macià**, leader of the Republican Left, parliamentary deputy for Barcelona and first president of the Generalitat, who died in office in 1933. It was commissioned from the pioneer of Catalan avant-garde sculpture, Josep María Subirachs, perhaps best known for his continuing work on the Sagrada Família cathedral.

For visitors, an initial orientation point is the white-faced **El Corte Inglés** department store on the eastern side of the square, whose ninth-floor cafeteria has some stupendous views. The main tourist office is just across from here, while on the southwest side, over

---

THE RAMBLAS STATUES

You can't move for human statues on the Ramblas, standing on their little home-made plinths. Classical figures and movie characters have always formed part of the parade, but there's also some real wit and invention on display, like "Fruit Lady", a one-woman mobile market stall, or the twin "Bicycling Skeletons". Many are actors (or at least waiters who say they're actors), and others make a claim to art – how else to begin to explain the various men-without-heads or the kennel-dwelling "Human Dog"? Then there's just the plain weird, like "Lady Under Rock", crushed under a boulder, issuing plaintive shrieks at passers-by. And quite what demons drive "Man Sitting on Toilet", only he can say. They all put in long hours on the Ramblas, gratefully receiving small change, though tourists or no tourists, many of them would probably just turn up anyway, lock the bicycle, put down the battered suitcase and strike the pose. What else is a statue going to do?

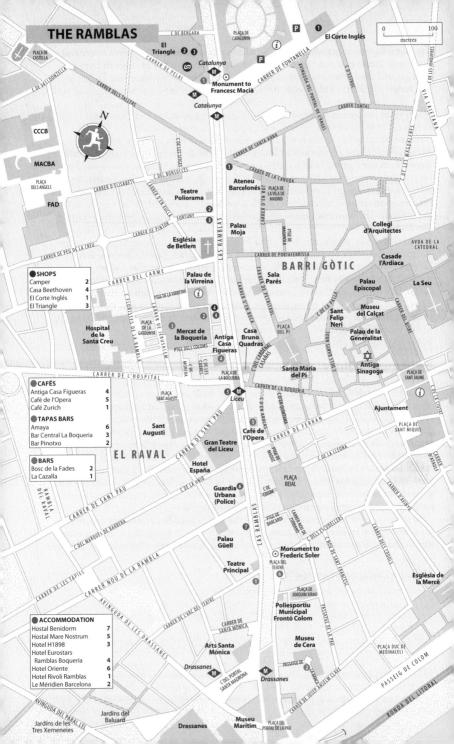

THE RAMBLAS

C. DE BERGARA
PLAÇA DE CATALUNYA
El Corte Inglés

El Triangle ❷ ❸
Catalunya
Monument to Francesc Macià
Catalunya

C. DE PELAI
CARRER DELS TALLERS
CARRER DE VALLDONZELLA
PLAÇA DE CASTELLA

0 — 100
metres

CARRER DE FONTANELLA
AVINGUDA DEL PORTAL DE L'ÀNGEL
CARRER COMTAL
VIA LAIETANA
C. DE LES MAGDALENES
CARRER D'OSTRIC
C. DE LES JONQUERES

CCCB
MACBA
PLAÇA DELS ANGELS
FAD

C. DE'ESTUDIS
C. DEL BONSUCCES
CARRER DE SANTA ANNA
CARRER DE LA CANUDA

Ateneu Barcelonés
PLAÇA DE LA VILA DE MADRID

Teatre Poliorama
CARRER D'ELISABETS
CARRER DE'EN XUCLÀ
FORTUNY
Palau Moja
PTGE DE MAGAROLA
PTGE DE LA DUANA

Església de Betlem
CARRER DE PORTAFERRISSA

Palau de la Virreina
CARRER DEL CARME
PTGE DE LA VIRREINA

BARRI GÒTIC
Casa de l'Ardiaca
AVDA DE LA CATEDRAL

Sala Parés
Palau Episcopal
La Seu
Collegi d'Arquitectes
C. DE LA PALLA
Museu del Calçat
Palau de la Generalitat

● SHOPS
Camper	2
Casa Beethoven	4
El Corte Inglés	1
El Triangle	3

Hospital de la Santa Creu
CARRER DE L'HOSPITAL
CARRER DEL PINTOR
CARRER DE PEU DE LA CREU

Mercat de la Boqueria
Antiga Casa Figueras
Casa Bruno Quadras
PLAÇA DEL PI
Sant Felip Neri
Antiga Sinagoga
Santa Maria del Pi
PLAÇA DE SANT JAUME

PLAÇA DE LA GARDUNYA
PTGE DELS COLOMS
C. DE LES CABRES
C. DE MORERA

PLAÇA DE LA BOQUERIA
CARRER DE LA BOQUERIA
Liceu
CARRER DE FERRAN
Ajuntament
PLAÇA DE SANT MIQUEL

● CAFÉS
Antiga Casa Figueras	4
Café de l'Opera	5
Café Zurich	1

● TAPAS BARS
Amaya	6
Bar Central La Boqueria	3
Bar Pinotxo	2

● BARS
Bosc de les Fades	2
La Cazalla	1

PLAÇA SANT AGUSTÍ
Sant Augusti
EL RAVAL
CARRER DE SANT PAU
Gran Teatre del Liceu
Café de l'Opera
Hotel España
Guardia Urbana (Police)
Palau Güell
Teatre Principal
PLAÇA REIAL
C. DE COLOM
PTGE DE BARCINÓ
CARRER NOU DE L'ESTEL
Monument to Frederic Soler
PLAÇA DEL TEATRE
Església de la Mercé
PLAÇA DE JOAQUIM XIRAU

C. DE LA UNIÓ
RAMBLA DEL RAVAL
CARRER DE SANT PAU
CARRER DEL MARQUÈS DE BARBERÀ
CARRER DE LES TÀPIES
CARRER NOU DE LA RAMBLA
AVINGUDA DE LES DRASSANES
CARRER DE L'ARC DEL TEATRE

● ACCOMMODATION
Hostal Benidorm	7
Hostal Mare Nostrum	5
Hotel H1898	3
Hotel Eurostars Ramblas Boquería	4
Hotel Oriente	6
Hotel Rivoli Ramblas	1
Le Méridien Barcelona	2

Poliesportiu Municipal Frontó Colom
Arts Santa Mònica
Museu de Cera
PLAÇA DUC DE MEDINACELI
CARRER DE SANTA MÒNICA
Drassanes
PASSATGE DE LA PAU
PASSATGE DE
PASSEIG DE COLOM

AVINGUDA DEL PARAL·LEL
Jardins de les Tres Xemeneies
Jardins del Baluard
Drassanes
Museu Marítim
PLAÇA DEL PORTAL DE LA PAU
CARRER DE JOSEP ANSELM CLAVÉ
RONDA DEL LITORAL

the road from the top of the Ramblas, **El Triangle** shopping centre makes another landmark. Incorporated in its ground floor is the **Café Zurich**, a traditional Barcelona meeting place, whose ranks of outdoor tables – patrolled by supercilious waiters – are a day-long draw for beggars, buskers and pan-pipe bands.

Rambla Canaletes and Estudis

The top two stretches of the Ramblas are **Rambla Canaletes**, with its iron fountain (a drink from which supposedly means you'll never leave Barcelona), and **Rambla Estudis**, named after the university (L'Estudi General) that was sited here until the beginning of the eighteenth century. This part is also known locally as Rambla dels Ocells, as it contains a **bird market**, the little captives squawking away from a line of cages on either side of the street.

Teatre Poliorama

Ramblas 115 • ⓦ www.teatrepoliorama.com • Ⓜ Catalunya

It seems hard to believe now, but the Ramblas was a war zone during the Spanish Civil War as the city erupted into factionalism in 1937. George Orwell (see box, p.40) was caught in the crossfire between the *Café Moka* – the current café of the same name is a modern replacement – and the Poliorama cinema opposite, now the **Teatre Poliorama**. This was built in 1863 as the Royal Academy of Science and Arts, and restored as a theatre in 1985.

Església de Betlem

Ramblas 107 • Daily 8am–6pm • Ⓜ Liceu

The **Església de Betlem** was built in 1681 in Baroque style for the Jesuits, but was completely gutted during the Civil War as anarchists sacked the city's churches at will – an activity of which Orwell quietly approved. Consequently, the interior is plain in the extreme, though the main facade on c/del Carme sports a fine sculpted portal.

Palau Moja

Ramblas 188 • Bookshop Mon–Fri 9am–8pm, Sat 9am–2pm & 4–8pm Sala Palau Moja Tues–Sat 11am–8pm, Sun & hols 11am–3pm • Usually free • ☎ 933 162 740 • Ⓜ Liceu

Across the Ramblas from the Betlem church, the arcaded **Palau Moja** dates from the late eighteenth century and still retains an exterior staircase and elegant great hall. The ground floor of the building is now a cultural bookshop, while the palace's gallery, the **Sala Palau Moja**, is open for art and other exhibitions relating to all things Catalan – the gallery entrance is around the corner in c/de la Portaferrissa. Take a look, too, at the illustrated tiles above the **fountain** at the start of c/de la Portaferrissa, which show the medieval gate (the Porta Ferriça) and market that were once sited here.

Palau de la Virreina

Ramblas 99 • **Tiquet Rambles** daily 10am–8.30pm **Galleries** Tues–Sun noon–8pm • Usually free • ☎ 933 161 000, ⓦ bcn.cat /virreinacentredelaimatge • Ⓜ Liceu

The graceful eighteenth-century **Palau de la Virreina** is set back slightly from the Ramblas. Commissioned by a Peruvian viceroy, Manuel Amat, and named after the wife who survived him, its five Ramblas-facing bays are adorned with pilasters and Rococo windows. Today the palace is used by the city council's culture department, and has a useful ground-floor **information centre** called "Tiquet Rambles" where you can find out about upcoming events and buy tickets. Various galleries and studios also present an interesting mix of changing **exhibitions** highlighting La Virreina's role as the "Centre de la Imatge", with an emphasis on contemporary culture, social studies and photography.

1

GEORGE ORWELL IN BARCELONA

Barcelona is a town with a long history of street-fighting.   *Homage to Catalonia, 1938*

When he first arrived in Barcelona in December 1936, **George Orwell** was much taken with the egalitarian spirit he encountered, as loudspeakers on the Ramblas bellowed revolutionary songs, café waiters refused tips, brothels were collectivized and buildings draped in anarchist flags. After serving as a militiaman on the Aragonese front, Orwell returned on leave to Barcelona in April 1937 to find that everything had changed. Not only had the city lost its revolutionary zeal, but the various leftist parties fighting for the Republican cause had descended into a "miserable internecine scrap". From the **Hotel Continental** (Ramblas 138), where Orwell and his wife Eileen stayed, he observed the deteriorating situation with mounting despair, and when street-fighting broke out in May, Orwell was directly caught up in it. As a member of the Workers' Party of Marxist Unification (POUM), Orwell became a target when pro-Communist Assault Guards seized the city telephone exchange near Plaça de Catalunya and began to try to break up the workers' militias. Orwell left the hotel for the **POUM headquarters** (Ramblas 128) just down the street, sited in the building that's now the *Rivoli Ramblas* hotel – a plaque here by the "Banco Popular" sign honours murdered POUM leader Andrés Nin ("victim of Stalinism"). With the trams on the Ramblas abandoned by their drivers as the shooting started, and Assault Guards occupying the adjacent **Café Moka** (Ramblas 126), Orwell holed up with a rifle for three days in the rotunda of the **Teatre Poliorama** (Ramblas 115) opposite, in order to defend the POUM HQ if necessary. Breakfasting sparsely on goat's cheese bought from the Boqueria market (its stalls largely empty), concerned about Eileen and caught up in rumour and counter-rumour, Orwell considered it one of the most unbearable periods of his life.

When the fighting subsided, Orwell returned to the front, where he was shot through the throat by a fascist sniper. Yet that was only the start of his troubles. Recuperating in a sanatorium near Tibidabo, he learned that the POUM had been declared illegal, its members rounded up and imprisoned. He avoided arrest by sleeping out in gutted churches and derelict buildings and playing the part of a tourist by day, looking "as bourgeois as possible", while scrawling POUM graffiti in defiance on the walls of fancy restaurants. Eventually, with passports and papers arranged by the British consul, Orwell and Eileen escaped Barcelona by train – back to the "deep, deep sleep of England" and the writing of his passionate war memoir, *Homage to Catalonia*.

At the back of the palace courtyard are usually displayed the city's two official **Carnival giants** (*gegants vells*), representing the celebrated thirteenth-century Catalan king Jaume I and his wife Violant. The origin of Catalunya's outsized (five-metre-high) wood-and-plaster Carnival figures is unclear, though they probably once formed part of the entertainment at medieval travelling fairs. The first record of specific city giants is in 1601 – they were later used to entertain the city's orphans but are now an integral part of Barcelona's festival parades (see box, p.219).

Mercat de la Boqueria

Ramblas 91 • Mon–Sat 8am–8.30pm • ☎ 933 182 584, ⓦ boqueria.info • Ⓜ Liceu

Beyond the Palau de la Virreina starts **Rambla Sant Josep**, the switch in names marked by the sudden profusion of flower stalls – it's sometimes known as Rambla de les Flors. Here stands the city's glorious main food market, officially the Mercat Sant Josep though referred to locally as **La Boqueria**. While others might protest, the market really can claim to be the best in Spain. Built on the site of a former convent between 1836 and 1840, the cavernous hall stretches back from the high wrought-iron entrance arch facing the Ramblas. It's a riot of noise and colour, as popular with locals who come here to shop daily as with snap-happy tourists. Everything radiates out from the central fish and seafood stalls – bunches of herbs, pots of spices, baskets of wild mushrooms,

1

mounds of cheese and sausage, racks of bread, hanging hams and overloaded meat counters. Many get waylaid at the entrance by the eye-candy seasonal fruit cartons and squeezed juices, but the flagship fruit and veg stalls here are pricey. It's better value further in, particularly in the small outdoor square just beyond the north side of the market where the local allotment-holders and market gardeners gather. Everyone has a favourite market stall, but don't miss *Petras*, the wild mushroom and dried insect stall (it's at the back, by the market restaurant, *La Garduña*). If you really don't fancy chilli worms, ant candy and crunchy beetles, there are some excellent stand-up **tapas bars** in the market as well, open from dawn onwards for the traders – *Bar Pinotxo* is the most famous (see p.179).

Plaça de la Boqueria

Ⓜ Liceu

The halfway point of the Ramblas is marked by **Plaça de la Boqueria**, with its large round **mosaic by Joan Miró** in the middle of the pavement. It's one of a number of public works in Barcelona by the artist, who was born just a couple of minutes' walk off the Ramblas in the Barri Gòtic (there's a plaque to mark the building on Passatge del Crèdit, off c/de Ferran), and has become something of a symbol for the city. Close by, at Ramblas 82, Josep Vilaseca's **Casa Bruno Quadros** – the lower floor is now the Caixa Sabadell – was built in the 1890s to house an umbrella store. This explains its delightful facade, decorated with a green dragon and Oriental designs, and scattered with parasols. On the other side of the Ramblas at no. 83 there are more *modernista* flourishes on the **Antiga Casa Figueras** (1902), which overdoses on stained glass and mosaics, and sports a corner relief of a female reaper. It's now a renowned bakery-café.

Gran Teatre del Liceu

Ramblas 51–59 • Tours daily 10am, 11.30am, noon, 12.30pm & 1pm, English spoken • 10am tour €9, later tours €4.20 • ☎ 934 859 914, Ⓦ www.liceubarcelona.com • Ⓜ Liceu

Barcelona's celebrated opera house was first founded as a private theatre in 1847. It was rebuilt after a fire in 1861 to become Spain's grandest theatre, regarded as a bastion of the city's late nineteenth-century commercial and intellectual classes – it still has no royal box in a nod to its bourgeois antecedents. The Liceu was devastated again in 1893, when an anarchist, acting in revenge for the recent execution of a fellow anarchist assassin, threw two bombs into the stalls during a production of *William Tell* – twenty people died in the bombing. It then burned down for the third time in 1994, when a worker's blowtorch set fire to the scenery during last-minute alterations to an opera set. The latest restoration of the lavishly decorated interior took five years, and the opera house opened again in 1999. **Tours** depart from the modern extension, the **Espai Liceu**, which also houses a music and gift shop and café. Meanwhile, the traditional meeting place for post-performance refreshments for audience and performers alike is the famous **Café de l'Opera**, just across the Ramblas.

Inside the Liceu

You'll learn most on the more expensive, hour-long 10am guided tour; the other, cheaper tours are self-guided and last only twenty minutes. Highlights include the classically inspired **Saló dels Miralls** (Salon of Mirrors), unaffected by any of the fires and thus largely original in decor, and the impressive gilded auditorium containing almost 2300 seats – making it one of the world's largest opera houses. The 10am tour also visits the **Cercle del Liceu**, the opera house's private members' club, whose burnished rooms feature tiled floors and painted ceilings, and culminate in an extraordinary *modernista* games room, illuminated by a celebrated series of paintings by Ramon Casas representing Catalan music and dance. For most of its 160-year history

1

UNDER THE ARCH AND INTO THE SHADOWS

One early summer morning in 1945, ten-year-old Daniel Sempere and his father walk under the arch of c/de l'Arc del Teatre, "entering a vault of blue haze … until the glimmer of the Ramblas faded behind us". And behind a large, carved wooden door, Daniel is shown for the first time the "Cemetery of Forgotten Books", where he picks out an obscure book that will change his life. It is, of course, the beginning of the mega-successful novel **Shadow of the Wind**, by Carlos Ruiz Zafón (2002), a gripping mystery set in postwar Barcelona that uses the city's old town in particular to atmospheric effect. With copy in hand you can trace Daniel's early progress, from the street where he lives (c/de Santa Anna) to the house of the beautiful, blind Clara Barceló on Plaça Reial, as well as a score of other easily identifiable locations across the city, from the cathedral to Tibidabo – always keeping a wary eye out for a pursuing stranger with "a mask of black scarred skin, consumed by fire".

---

the Cercle membership was restricted to men, until challenged by **Montserrat Caballé** – Spain's greatest soprano, born in Barcelona in 1933 – who won a court battle to become one of the first women to join.

Teatre Principal and around

Ⓜ Drassanes

The bottom stretch of the Ramblas is the **Rambla de Santa Mònica**, historically a theatre and **red-light district** that still has a rough edge or two. Across from the Teatre Principal stands the lavish **monument to Frederic Soler** (1839–95), better known as Serafí Pitarra, the playwright, impresario and founder of modern Catalan theatre. For an earthier memorial to the old days, however, walk down the Ramblas a little further to the entrances to nos. 22 and 24 (by the *Amaya* restaurant), where the deep depressions in the marble stoops were worn away by the heels of decades of loitering prostitutes – the doorways now have protected city monument status. Back across the Ramblas, street-walkers and theatre-goers alike drank stand-up shots and coffee at **La Cazalla** (Ramblas 25), under the arch at the start of c/de l'Arc del Teatre, a famous hole-in-the-wall bar (really just a street counter), recently restored, that's straight out of sleaze-era central casting.

Arts Santa Mònica

Ramblas 7 · Tues–Sun & hols 11am–9pm · Free · ☎ 935 671 110, Ⓦ artssantamonica.cat · Ⓜ Drassanes

The Augustinian **convent of Santa Mònica** dates originally from 1626, making it the oldest building on the Ramblas. It was remodelled in the 1980s as a contemporary **arts centre**, and hosts regularly changing exhibitions in its grand, echoing galleries – it's an unusual gallery space dedicated to "artistic creation, science, thought and communication" so there's usually something worth seeing, from an offbeat art installation to a show of archive photographs. There's also a city events information office at the centre, and a café-bar upstairs with a *terrassa* overlooking the Ramblas. Outside the centre, on the Ramblas, pavement artists, caricaturists and palm readers set up stalls, augmented on weekend afternoons by a **street market** selling jewellery, beads, bags and ornaments.

Museu de Cera

Ramblas 4–6, entrance on Ptge. de Banca · July–Sept daily 10am–10pm; Oct–June Mon–Fri 10am–1.30pm & 4–7.30pm, Sat & Sun 11am–2pm & 4.30–8.30pm · €15 · ☎ 933 172 649, Ⓦ museocerabcn.com · Ⓜ Drassanes

Final stop at the bottom of the Ramblas is the city's wax museum, the **Museu de Cera**, in an impressive nineteenth-century bank building. You'd have to be hard-hearted indeed not to derive some pleasure from the ever more ludicrous series of tableaux presented in the building's cavernous salons and gloomy corridors, depicting recitals, meetings and parlour gatherings attended by an anachronistic – not to say perverse – collection of personalities, film characters, public figures, heroes, villains, artists and musicians. Thus Yasser Arafat lectures Churchill, Hitler and Bill Clinton, while a concert by Catalan cellist Pau Casals numbers Princess Diana and Mother Teresa among the audience, before the museum culminates in cheesy underwater tunnels and space capsules and an unpleasant "Terror" room. Needless to say, it's extremely ropey and enormously amusing, and you also won't want to miss the museum's extraordinary grotto-bar, the **Bosc de les Fades** (see p.197).

THREE GRACES FOUNTAIN, PLAÇA REIAL

Barri Gòtic

The Barri Gòtic, or Gothic Quarter, spreads east from the Ramblas and forms the very heart of the old town. Its buildings date principally from the fourteenth and fifteenth centuries, when Barcelona reached the height of her medieval commercial prosperity, and culminate in the extraordinary Gothic cathedral known as La Seu. It takes the best part of a day to see everything here, with particular highlights being the Roman remains at the Museu d'Història de Barcelona and the frankly unclassifiable collections of the Museu Frederic Marès. There are also plenty of other quirks and diversions, from exploring the old Jewish quarter to touring the grand salons of the Ajuntament. That said, sauntering through the narrow alleys, shopping for antiques, following the remains of the Roman walls, or simply sitting at a café table in one of the lovely squares is just as much an attraction.

The picture-postcard images of the Barri Gòtic are largely based on the streets north of c/de Ferran and c/de Jaume I, where tourists throng the boutiques, bars, restaurants, museums and galleries. South of here, from Plaça Reial and c/d'Avinyó to the harbour, the Barri Gòtic is rather less gentrified and sometimes just plain run-down. There are no specific sights or museums in this section, though there are plenty of great shops, cafés, tapas bars and restaurants – just take care at night in the poorly lit streets. For a walk through the neighbourhood, start at **metros** Liceu (west), Jaume I (east) or Drassanes (south).

2

La Seu

Pl. de la Seu • Mon–Fri 8am–12.45pm & 5.15–7.30pm, Sat 8am–12.45pm & 5.15–8pm, Sun 8am–1.45pm & 5.15–8pm • Cathedral and cloister free during general admission times, otherwise tourist admission charge (obligatory 1–5pm) €6, but includes entrance to all sections • ⓦ catedralbcn.org • Ⓜ Jaume I

Barcelona's mighty cathedral, **La Seu**, whose intricate, high facade and soaring towers dominate the very heart of the medieval quarter, is one of the great Gothic buildings of Spain. Located on a site previously occupied by a Roman temple and then an early Christian basilica, it was begun in 1298 and finished in 1448, save for the neo-Gothic principal facade, which was completed in the 1880s. The cathedral is dedicated to the city's second patroness, **Santa Eulàlia** (known as Laia in Barcelona), a young girl brutally martyred by the Romans in 304 AD for daring to prefer Christianity. Her remains were first placed in the original harbourside church of Santa María del Mar in La Ribera, which explains why she's also patron saint of local sailors and seafarers. In 874 Laia was re-interred in the basilica and her remains later placed in an ornate alabaster tomb that now rests in a crypt beneath the high altar.

Visit in the morning or late afternoon and admission to the church **interior** and **cloister** is free, though there are separate small charges to view certain other areas, including the cathedral **museum**, filled with glittering church treasure. To see everything, it's better to visit during 1pm and 5pm when the obligatory admission charge includes entry to all sections of the cathedral, including areas like the choir and various side-chapels that are not open to the public during the general admission times. Note that, unfortunately, the **roof terrace**, or *terrats,* is currently closed, as it and large parts of the facade remain swathed in scaffolding. If it does reopen, expect intimate views of the cathedral towers and surrounding Gothic buildings and spires. It's by no means the highest view in town, but nowhere else do you feel so at the heart of medieval Barcelona.

The interior

Inside the church, all eyes lead to the raised altar, beneath which steps descend to the gated **crypt** containing the venerated **tomb of Santa Eulàlia** – each year on her saint's day, February 12, the crypt is open for visits and a choir sings in her honour. La Seu is also known for the richness of its 29 **side-chapels**, many of which contain beautifully carved and painted tombs. Perhaps the finest are those reputedly belonging to Ramon Berenguer I (count of Barcelona from 1035 to 1076) and his wife Almodis; however, the tombs actually hold the remains of an earlier count and Petronila, the Aragonese princess whose betrothal to Ramon Berenguer IV united the crowns of Aragón and Barcelona.

The cloister

The most renowned part of the cathedral is its magnificent fourteenth-century **cloister**, which looks over a lush tropical garden complete with soaring palm trees and – more unusually – a gaggle of honking **geese**. If they disturb the tranquillity of the scene, they do so for a purpose: white geese have been kept here for over five hundred years, either (depending on which story you believe) to reflect the virginity of Santa Eulàlia, or as a reminder of the erstwhile Roman splendour of Barcelona, as geese were kept on the Capitoline Hill in Rome.

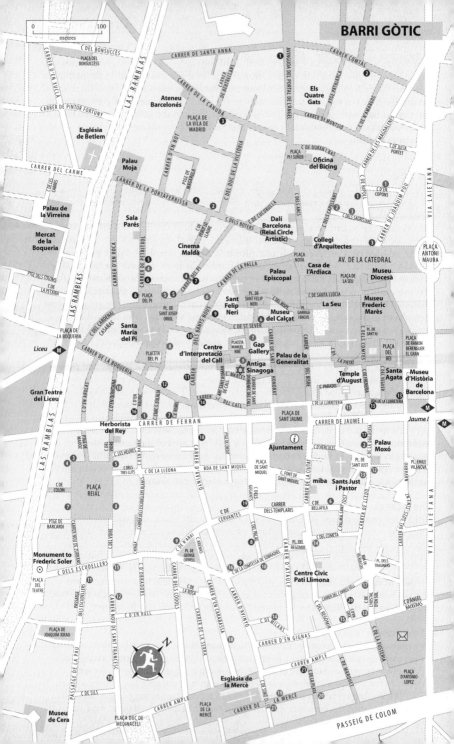

2

BOHO BARCELONA AND THE FOUR CATS

There's not much to see in the shopping zone north of the cathedral, but a century or so ago a tavern called **Els Quatre Gats** (The Four Cats; c/de Montsió 3, Ⓦ4gats.com) burned brightly and briefly as the epicentre of Barcelona's bohemian in-crowd. It was opened by Pere Romeu and other *modernista* artists in 1897 as a gathering place for their contemporaries, and the building itself is gloriously decorated inside and out in exuberant Catalan Art Nouveau style – it was the classy architect Josep Puig i Cadafalch's first commission. *Els Quatre Gats* soon thrived as the birthplace of *modernista* magazines, the scene of poetry readings and shadow-puppet theatre and the venue for cultural debate. A young Picasso designed the menu and, in 1901, the café was the setting for his first public exhibition. *Els Quatre Gats* has always traded on its reputation – a place where "accountants, dreamers and would-be geniuses shared tables with the spectres of Pablo Picasso, Isaac Albéniz, Federico García Lorca and Salvador Dalí" (*The Shadow of the Wind*, Carlos Ruiz Zafón). Today, a modern restoration displays something of its former glory, with the – frankly overpriced – bar-restaurant overseen by a copy of Ramon Casas' famous wall painting of himself and Pere Romeu on a tandem bicycle (the original is in MNAC).

Plaça de la Seu

Ⓜ Jaume I

The large cathedral square, **Plaça de la Seu**, is flanked by tourist cafés and generally awash with a milling crowd. The square is a regular weekly venue for the dancing of the *sardana*, the Catalan national dance (usually Sun at noon, plus Easter to Nov every Sat at 6pm) – anyone can join in, though you'd best read the feature on the *sardana* (see p.208) first. Meanwhile, in front of the cathedral, the wide, pedestrianized Avinguda de la Catedral hosts an **antiques market** every Thursday, and a **Christmas craft fair** every December.

Museu Diocesà

Av. de la Catedral 4 • Tues–Sat 10am–2pm & 5–8pm, Sun & hols 11am–2pm • €6 • ☏ 933 152 213 • Ⓜ Jaume I

Stand back to look at the cathedral buildings and it's easy to see the line of fortified Roman towers that stood originally on this spot, before being incorporated into the later medieval buildings. One such tower formed part of the cathedral almshouse (La Pia Almoina), now the **Museu Diocesà**, whose soaring spaces have been beautifully adapted to show an impressive collection of religious art and church treasures from around Barcelona. Most notably there's a series of frescoes of the Apocalypse (1122 AD) from Sant Salvador in Polinyà and several graphic retables, including one of St Bartholomew being skinned alive. The ticket also includes entrance into the temporary art and architecture exhibitions held here.

● SHOPS				● BARS	
Almacenes del Pilar	12	Drap	7	El Ingenio	16	L'Ascensor	6
L'Arca de l'Avia	9	Espácio de Creadores	2	Llibreria Quera	5	Café Milans	14
Artesania Catalunya	11	Espai Drap Art	20	La Manual Alpargatera	18	La Cerveteca	13
Cereria Subirà	13	Formatgeria La Seu	17	El Mercadillo	4	Glaciar	3
El Corte Inglés	1	Ganiveteria Roca	6	Obach Sombrería	14	Milk	15
Custo Barcelona	8	Germanes Garcia	10	Papabubble	21	Oviso	9
Decathlon	3	Gotham	19	Papirum	15	Pipa Club	4
						Schilling	1
● ACCOMMODATION		● CAFÉS		● RESTAURANTS		Zim	2
Hostal Fernando	7	Bar del Pi	5	Arc Café	18		
Hostal Rembrandt	2	Caelum	6	Bun Bo Viêtnam	2	● CLUBS AND LIVE MUSIC	
Hotel Cantón	10	Caj Chai	7	Café de l'Acadèmia	12	Fantástico	11
Hotel Colón	3	Dulcinea	4	Can Culleretes	10	Harlem Jazz Club	10
Hotel El Jardí	5	Mesón del Cafe	11	Los Caracoles	15	Jamboree	7
Hotel Racó del Pi	4			Koy Shunka	1	Karma	8
Itaca Hostel	1	● TAPAS BARS		Limbo	19	La Macarena	12
Neri Hotel	6	Bar Celta Pulperia	21	Matsuri	14	Sidecar	5
Pensió Alamar	9	Bodega La Plata	20	El Salón	17		
Pensión Mari-Luz	8	Ginger	13	Shunka	3	● FLAMENCO CLUB	
		Taller de Tapas	8	Venus Delicatessen	16	Tarantos	7
		La Viñatería del Call	9				

Casa de l'Ardiaca and Palau Episcopal

On the other flank of the cathedral are two more late-medieval buildings closely associated with it. The **Casa de l'Ardiaca** (once the archdeacon's residence, now the city archives) encloses a tiny cloistered and tiled courtyard with a small fountain. To the right of the badly worn Renaissance gateway on c/de Santa Llúcia look for the curious carved swallow-and-tortoise postbox.

The **Palau Episcopal**, just beyond at the western end of c/de Santa Llúcia, was the bishop's palace and built on a grander scale altogether. Though you're not allowed inside, you can go as far as the courtyard to see the fine outdoor stairway; there's a patio at the top with Romanesque wall paintings.

Plaça Nova

Ⓜ Jaume I

The large **Plaça Nova**, facing the cathedral, marks one of the medieval entrances to the old town – north of it, you're fast entering the wider streets and more regular contours of the modern city. Even if you're sticking with the Barri Gòtic for now, walk over to study the frieze surmounting the modern College of Architects, the **Collegi d'Arquitectes**, on the other side of the square. Designed in 1960 from sketches supplied by Picasso, it has a crude, almost graffiti-like quality, at odds with the more stately buildings to the side. Picasso himself refused to come to Spain to oversee the work, unwilling to return to his home country while Franco was still in power.

Real Circle Artístic and Dalí Barcelona

C/dels Arcs 5 · Daily 10am–10pm · €10 · ☎ 933 181 774, ⓦ dalibarcelona.com · Ⓜ Jaume I

Just a short walk from the cathedral, the handsome Gothic palace housing the **Real Circle Artístic** (Royal Artistic Circle) hosts various exhibitions and concerts, though the big draw is **Dalí Barcelona**, the collection of 44 wildly original bronze sculptures by Salvador Dalí. They were completed in the 1970s as a private commission for a wealthy Catalan businessman, and are significant in that they were made by Dalí himself, rather than to his designs, as was far more common. The sculptures, large and small, are theatrically displayed under Gothic arches, behind swags of red velvet curtain, and depict various themes that fascinated Dalí throughout his life: the sea, women, horses, mythology, religion and so on. From *Cosmic Elephant* to the *Seven Days of Creation*, the sculptures are arranged in groups alongside hundreds of drawings, sketches, watercolours and photographs by Dalí.

Plaça del Rei

Ⓜ Jaume I

The harmonious enclosed square of **Plaça del Rei**, behind the cathedral apse, was once the courtyard of the palace of the counts of Barcelona, later the residence of the count-kings of Aragón. The palace buildings themselves are steeped in history, and include the romantic Renaissance Torre del Rei Martí, the main hall, known as the Saló del Tinell, and the fourteenth-century **Santa Agata chapel** – there's no public access to the tower, though there's a fine view of it from the square, while the interiors of both hall and chapel can usually be seen during a visit to the Museu d'Història de Barcelona (see opposite). The square itself, meanwhile, was the scene of one of Barcelona's greatest historic set-pieces, since it was from the steps of the exterior stone staircase that Ferdinand and Isabella received Christopher Columbus on his triumphant return from his famous voyage of 1492. With the old-town streets packed, Columbus advanced in procession with the

A WALK AROUND THE ROMAN WALLS

The Barri Gòtic was once entirely enclosed by **Roman walls and towers**, dating from the fourth century AD, though they were largely pulled down in the nineteenth century to create more space for the expanding city. Parts of Roman Barcelona still exist, however, easily seen on an hour-long stroll – the city council has posted brown information boards showing the route at various points.

Outside the cathedral, in Plaça Nova, block metal letters a metre high spell out the word "Barcino" (the name of the Roman city), underneath a restored tower and a reconstructed part of the Roman **aqueduct**. There's more of the aqueduct on display north of here on c/de Duran i Bas (set into the facade of a building), while over on **Plaça de la Vila de Madrid** is a line of sunken Roman tombs. The line of the wall itself runs past the cathedral and the Museu Diocesà, with the next surviving section visible at **Plaça de Ramon Berenguer El Gran** (at Via Laietana). Some of the walls and towers here are over 13m high, and back onto the Capella de Santa Agata on Plaça del Rei. There's more wall to see down **c/del Sots-Tinent Navarro**, while the most romantic section is the truncated Roman tower in the sunken **Plaça dels Traginers**, planted with palms and a solitary olive tree. Along nearby **c/del Correu Vell** part of the wall and defence towers were incorporated into a medieval palace – you can see this section in the courtyard of a civic centre (through a gate, opposite c/d'en Groc.

A right turn after here, up c/del Regomir, leads to the **Centre Cívic Pati Llimona** (usually Mon–Fri 9am–2pm & 4.30–8pm, Sat 10am–2pm & 4–8pm; free), where lie the remains of one of the original gates through the Roman wall into inner Barcino. This and other remains are visible through a glass window from c/del Regomir, and if the centre is open you'll be able to go inside for a closer look. Then head up c/de Ciutat and cross Plaça de Sant Jaume for the **Temple d'August** on c/Paradís, where four impressive **Roman columns** and the architrave of a temple are preserved in the interior courtyard of the Centre Excursionista de Catalunya (c/Paradís 10; April–Sept Tues–Sun 10am–8pm, hols 10am–3pm; Oct–March Tues–Sat 10am–2pm & 4–7pm, Sun 10am–8pm, hols 10am–3pm; free). From here you're just a short walk from the cathedral again, though no Roman enthusiast should miss the nearby **Museu d'Història de Barcelona**, which features the underground excavations of Barcino itself.

monarchs to the palace, where he presented the queen with booty from the trip – exotic birds, sweet potatoes and six Indians (actually Haitians), taken on board during Columbus' return.

Museu d'Història de Barcelona (MUHBA)

Pl. del Rei, entrance on c/del Veguer • April–Sept Tues–Sun 10am–8pm; Oct–March Tues–Sat 10am–2pm & 4–7pm, Sun 10am–8pm; hols 10am–3pm • €7, includes entry to other MUHBA sites, Sun after 3pm free; sometimes an extra charge for special exhibitions held in the Saló del Tinell • ☎ 932 562 100, ⓦ www.museuhistoria.bcn.cat • Ⓜ Jaume I

The **Museu d'Història de Barcelona** (Barcelona History Museum) comprises half a dozen sites across the city, though its principal hub is what's known as the "Conjunt Monumental" (or monumental ensemble) at Plaça del Rei, whose crucial draw is its underground archeological section – nothing less than the extensive remains of the Roman city of Barcino. Descending in the lift (the floor indicator shows "12 BC"), you are deposited onto walkways running through excavations that extend for 4000 square metres, stretching under the surrounding streets as far as the cathedral. The remains date from the first century BC to the sixth century AD and reflect the transition from Roman to Visigothic rule – at the end of the sixth century, a church was erected on top of the old Roman salt-fish factory, the foundations of which are preserved down here almost in their entirety. Not much survives above chest height, but explanatory diagrams show the extent of the streets, walls and buildings – from lookout towers to laundries – while models, murals and displays of excavated goods help flesh out the reality of daily life in Barcino.

There's a good book and gift shop on site (entrance on c/de la Llibeteria), while the museum ticket is also valid for other MUHBA sites, notably the Poble Sec air raid shelter and Pedralbes monastery.

Saló del Tinell and Capella de Santa Agata

Plaça del Rei's **Saló del Tinell** and the beautiful **Capella de Santa Agata** are also part of the history museum, and are usually open for visits with your museum ticket. The hall is particularly impressive, being a fine example of secular Gothic architecture, with interior arches that span 17m. At one time the Spanish Inquisition met in the hall, taking full advantage of the popular belief that the walls would move if a lie was spoken.

2

Museu Frederic Marès

Museu Frederic Marès Pl. de Sant Iu 5–6, off c/dels Comtes • Tues–Sat 10am–7pm, Sun & hols 11am–8pm • €4.20, under-16s free, plus Sun after 3pm & first Sun of the month free • ☎ 932 563 500, ⓦ www.museumares.bcn.cat • **Café d'Estiu** April–Sept; closed Mon • ⓜ Jaume I

One of the old town's most fascinating museums, the **Museu Frederic Marès** occupies a wing of the old royal palace, behind Plaça del Rei. It celebrates the diverse passions of sculptor, painter and restorer Frederic Marès (1893–1991), whose beautifully presented collection of ancient and medieval sculpture does little to prepare visitors for Marès' true obsession, namely a kaleidoscopic array of curios and collectibles. The large arcaded courtyard, studded with orange trees, is one of the most romantic in the old town, and the summer café here, *Café d'Estiu*, makes a perfect place to take a break from sightseeing.

Sculpture collection

Frederic Marès trained as a sculptor at Barcelona's La Llotja (School of Fine Arts) and became known for his monumental sculpture, including grand works now on display in Plaça de Catalunya. His later focus, however, was on the restoration of Catalunya's decaying medieval treasures, many of which are now preserved in the galleries on the **ground** and **basement floors** of the museum. On display is essentially Marès' personal collection of medieval sculpture – an important body of work that includes a comprehensive series of wooden crucifixes showing the stylistic development of the form from the twelfth to the fifteenth century. There are also antiquities, from Roman busts to Hellenistic terracotta lamps, while the intricate craftsmanship of medieval masons is displayed in a stunning series of carved doorways, cloister fragments, sculpted capitals and alabaster tombs.

CORPUS CHRISTI AND THE DANCING EGG

One of the biggest religious festivals of the year in Barcelona is that of **Corpus Christi** (late May/early June), celebrated with the dancing of the *sardana*, parades of *gegants* (festival giants) and a big procession from the cathedral. These colourful events are all par for the course for any city festival, though unique to Corpus Christi is the far stranger *l'ou com balla*, the **dancing egg**, which bubbles atop fountain water-jets in flower-decorated cloisters, patios and courtyards across the old town. Records of *l'ou com balla* in Barcelona date back to the seventeenth century though its origins are obscure; nonetheless, it's possible to see that an egg (ie, a hollowed-out, weighted eggshell) gaily dancing on spurts of water represents not only the Eucharist but rebirth, renewal and even a celebration of spring. The city council publishes an annual programme for the Festa del Corpus which shows where you can see this oddity for yourself – most old-town courtyard fountains put on a show, including those of La Seu and the Museu Marès.

Collector's Cabinet

Marès was also an avid collector and the upper floors of the museum – the so-called **Collector's Cabinet** (Gabinet del Col.leccionista) – present an incredible retrospective jumble gathered during fifty years of travel. Entire rooms are devoted to keys and locks, pipes, cigarette cards and snuffboxes, fans, gloves and brooches, playing cards, draughtsmen's tools, walking sticks, dolls' houses, toy theatres, old gramophones and archaic bicycles, to list just a sample of what's on show. It's an absolute joy to spend an hour or so here, uncovering your own favourite piece of ephemera. In the **artist's library** on the second floor, meanwhile, some of Marès' own reclining nudes, penitent saints and bridling stags give an insight into his more orthodox work.

Església de Santa María del Pi and around

Ⓜ Liceu

With the cathedral area and Plaça del Rei sucking in every visitor at some point during the day, the third focus of attraction in the Barri Gòtic is to the west, around the church of Santa María del Pi – five minutes' walk from the cathedral or just two minutes from the Ramblas.

Església de Santa María del Pi

Pl. Sant Josep Oriol • Mon–Sat 9.30am–1pm & 5–8.30pm (Sat opens at 4pm), Sun 9.30am–2pm & 5–8.30pm • Ⓦ parroquiadelpi.com • Ⓜ Liceu

The fourteenth-century **Església de Santa María del Pi** stands at the heart of three delightful little squares. Burned out during the Civil War fighting in 1936, and restored in the 1960s, the church boasts a Romanesque door but is mainly Catalan-Gothic in style, with just a single nave with chapels between the buttresses. The rather plain interior only serves to set off some marvellous stained glass, the most impressive of which is contained within a ten-metre-wide rose window, often claimed (rather boldly) as the largest in the world.

Plaça Sant Josep Oriol and around

The Santa María del Pi church flanks **Plaça Sant Josep Oriol**, the prettiest of the three adjacent squares, an ideal place to take an outdoor coffee, listen to the buskers or browse the weekend **artists' market** (Sat 11am–8pm, Sun 11am–2pm). The statue here is of Àngel Guimerà, nineteenth-century Catalan playwright and poet, who had a house on the square. Meanwhile, off Plaça Sant Josep Oriol, the old town's **antiques trade** is concentrated in glittering galleries and stores along c/de la Palla and c/dels Banys Nous.

Plaça del Pi and Carrer de Petritxol

The church of Santa María del Pi is named – like the squares on either side, **Plaça del Pi** and Placeta del Pi – after the pine trees that once stood here (there's a solitary example still in Plaça del Pi). A **farmers' market** spills across Plaça del Pi on the last Saturday and Sunday of the month (Oct–May only), selling honey, cheese, cakes and other produce, while the characteristic cafés of narrow **Carrer de Petritxol** (off Plaça del Pi) are the places to head to for a cup of hot chocolate – *Dulcinea* at no. 2 is the traditional choice – and a browse around the street's commercial art galleries. The most famous is at c/de Petritxol 5, where the **Sala Pares** was already well established when Picasso and Miró were young.

Plaça Sant Felip Neri

Ⓜ Liceu

In the narrow streets close to the cathedral, behind the Palau Episcopal you'll stumble upon **Plaça Sant Felip Neri**, scarred by a bomb dropped during the Civil War and now used as a playground by the children at the square's school. Antoni Gaudí walked here every evening after work at the Sagrada Família to hear Mass at the eighteenth-century **Església de Sant Felip Neri**. Many of the other buildings that now hedge in the small square come from other parts in the city and have been reassembled here over the last fifty years. It's a charming spot and in summer you can eat outside at the restaurant of the boutique *Neri Hotel* (see p.169), which sets out candlelit tables in the square.

Museu del Calçat

Pl. Sant Felip Neri 5 • Tues–Sun & hols 11am–2pm • €2.50 • ☎ 933 014 533 • Ⓜ Liceu

One of the buildings flanking Plaça Sant Felip Neri – the former headquarters of the city's shoemakers' guild (founded in 1202) – now houses a quirky one-room footwear museum. The **Museu del Calçat** contains original footwear dating back to the 1600s, as well as oddities like the world's biggest shoe, made for the city's Columbus statue at the bottom of the Ramblas.

El Call Major and the Antiga Sinagoga

South of Plaça Sant Felip Neri you enter what was once the medieval **Jewish quarter** of Barcelona, centred on c/de Sant Domènec del Call. The city authorities have signposted some of the points of interest in what's known as **El Call Major** (*Call* is the Catalan word for a narrow passage).

Antiga Sinagoga

C/Marlet 5, corner with c/de Sant Domènec del Call • Mon–Fri 10.30am–5.30pm, Sat & Sun 10.30am–3pm, sometimes closed Sat for ceremonies • €2.50 • ☎ 933 170 790, Ⓦ calldebarcelona.org • Ⓜ Liceu

The Jewish quarter's most notable extant landmark is the main synagogue, the **Antiga Sinagoga**. A synagogue existed here, on the edge of the Roman forum, from the third century AD until the pogrom of 1391, but even after that date the building survived in various guises – the sunken dye vats from a family business of fifteenth-century New Christian (forcibly converted Jews) dyers are still visible, alongside some original Roman walling. Not many people stop by the synagogue – if you do, you'll get a personalized tour of the small room by a member of the local Jewish community.

Centre d'Interpretació del Call

Pl. Manuel Ribé • Wed–Fri & Sun & hols 11am–2pm, Sat 11am–6pm • Free • ☎ 932 562 100, Ⓦ www.museuhistoria.bcn.cat • Ⓜ Liceu

Aside from the Antiga Sinagoga, most local Jewish buildings were destroyed, though a plaque further down c/Marlet (junction with c/Arc Sant Ramon del Call) marks the site of the former **rabbi's house**, while in Plaçeta Manuel Ribé another house originally

---

JEWISH BARCELONA

There were Jews living in Barcelona as early as the ninth century, and a Jewish district was documented in the city by the eleventh. Later, as elsewhere in Spain, Barcelona's **medieval Jewish quarter** lay nestled in the shadow of the cathedral; under the Church's careful scrutiny. In the thirteenth and early fourteenth centuries some of the realm's greatest and most powerful administrators, tax collectors and ambassadors hailed from here, but reactionary trends sparked persecution and led to the closing off of the community in these narrow, dark alleys. Nevertheless, a prosperous settlement persisted until the pogrom and forced conversion of 1391 and exile of 1492 (see box, p.250). Today little except the street name and the synagogue survives as a reminder of the Jewish presence – after their expulsion, most of the buildings used by the Jews were torn down and used for construction elsewhere in the city. With the demise of the Franco regime, a small community was again established in Barcelona, and in recent years there has been a revival in interest in Barcelona's Jewish heritage. As well as the synagogue, the sites of the butchers', bakers', fishmongers' and Jewish baths have all been identified, while over on the eastern side of Montjuïc (ie, Jewish Mountain) was the Jewish cemetery – the castle at Montjuïc displays around thirty tombstones recovered from the cemetery in the early twentieth century.

belonging to a veil-maker now serves as a small museum, the **Centre d'Interpretació del Call.** Informative storyboards (in English) shed more light on Barcelona's fascinating Jewish heritage, while the centre also coordinates various historical tours and activities.

Plaça de Sant Jaume

Ⓜ Jaume I

Plaça de Sant Jaume marks the very centre of the Barri Gòtic. This spacious square at the end of the main c/de Ferran was once the site of Barcelona's Roman forum and marketplace; now it's at the heart of city and regional government business, containing two of the Barcelona's most significant buildings, the **Ajuntament**, or City Hall, and the **Palau de la Generalitat**. Whistle-happy local police try to keep things moving in the *plaça*, while taxis and bike-tour groups weave between the pedestrians. The square is also the traditional site of demonstrations, gatherings and local festivals.

Ajuntament de Barcelona

Pl. de Sant Jaume • Public admitted Sun 10am–2pm, entrance on c/Font de Sant Miquel • Free, English-language leaflet provided • ☎ 934 027 000, Ⓦ bcn.cat • Ⓜ Jaume I

On the south side of Plaça de Sant Jaume stands Barcelona's City Hall, the **Ajuntament**, parts of which date from as early as 1373, though the Neoclassical facade was added in the nineteenth century when the square was laid out. You get a much better idea of the grandeur of the original structure by nipping around the corner, down c/de la Ciutat, for a view of the former main entrance. It's a typically exuberant Catalan-Gothic facade, but was badly damaged during nineteenth-century renovations. On Sundays you're allowed into the building for a self-guided tour around the rather splendid marble halls, galleries and staircases. The highlights are the magnificent restored fourteenth-century council chamber, known as the **Saló de Cent**, and the dramatic historical murals by Josep Maria Sert in the **Saló de les Cròniques** (Hall of Chronicles), while the ground-floor courtyard features sculptural works by some of the most famous Catalan artists.

Palau de la Generalitat

Pl. de Sant Jaume, entrance on c/de Sant Honorat • 1hr tours on second & fourth Sun of the month (except Aug), every 30min–1hr, 10am–2pm (only 1 or 2 each day in English), also April 23, and Sept 11 & 24 • Free, ID required • ☎ 934 024 600, Ⓦ gencat.cat • Ⓜ Jaume I

Opposite the Ajuntament stands the **Palau de la Generalitat**, traditional home of the Catalan government, from where the short-lived Catalan Republic was proclaimed in April 1931. Begun in 1418, the oldest part of the building is the fifteenth-century facade on c/del Bisbe which has a spirited medallion portraying St George and the Dragon. (Incidentally, the enclosed Gothic bridge across the narrow street – the so-called **Bridge of Sighs** – is an anachronism, added in 1928, though it features on many a postcard of the "Gothic" quarter. It connects the Generalitat with the former canons' houses across c/del Bispe, now used as the official residence of the president.) Inside the palace, there's a beautiful first-floor cloister with superb coffered ceilings, while opening off this are the intricately worked chapel and salon of Sant Jordi (St George, patron saint of Catalunya as well as England), as well as an upper courtyard planted with orange trees and peppered with presidential busts.

Aside from the guided tours on alternate Sundays, the Generalitat is also open to the public on **Dia de Sant Jordi**, or Saint George's Day (April 23; expect a 2hr wait).

Plaça de Sant Just

Ⓜ Jaume I

Near the Ajuntament, down c/d'Hercules, **Plaça de Sant Just** is a handsome little corner of the old town, and a particularly nice spot for an alfresco lunch at the excellent *Café* *de l'Acadèmia*, which puts out dining tables on the square. The square sports a medieval **church** and restored fourteenth-century fountain, while one of the flanking Baroque palaces – the remarkable **Palau Moxó** – is now open for visits.

Església dels Sants Just i Pastor

Enter from the back, at c/de la Ciutat; the main doors on Pl. de Sant Just are open less often • Open for Mass Mon–Sat 7.30pm, Sun at noon, and occasional other times • Ⓜ Jaume I

The very plain stone facade of the **Església dels Sants Just i Pastor** belies the rich stained glass and elaborate chapel decoration within. The name commemorates the city's earliest Christian martyrs, and it's claimed that this is the oldest parish church site in Barcelona, held to have first supported a foundation at the beginning of the ninth century; the restored interior, though, dates from the mid-fourteenth century.

Palau Moxó

Pl. de Sant Just 4 • Guided tours (45min) Fri noon, English spoken, €10; Thurs concerts 8pm, €20; reservations essential for tours and concerts • ☎ 933 152 238, ⓦ palaumoxo.com • Ⓜ Jaume I

Built in 1770 for a wealthy land-owning family, the **Palau Moxó** has been in the hands of the Moxó family ever since, which makes it unique in Barcelona – doubly so, in fact, since most of the city's other palatial Baroque residences were destroyed during the Spanish Civil War. Family members still live here, but certain of the public and private rooms are open for guided tours each week, during which you'll see grand salons and intimate chambers that offer a fascinating perspective on city-centre living, Baroque style. The family is an interesting one too, with links to the Güell family, patrons of Antoni Gaudí, while Thursday evening **concerts** in the piano room – with a glass of cava on the charming inner patio – provide another way to soak up something of the noble life.

miba

C/de la Ciutat 7 • Tues–Fri 10am–7pm, Sat 10am–8pm, Sun & hols 10am–2pm • €7, under-12s €5, under-4s free • ☎ 933 327 930, ⓦ mibamuseum.com • Ⓜ Jaume I

The impressive buildings of the Barri Gòtic have many grand entrances, from exterior stone staircases to courtyards into which you can drive a coach-and-four – but there's only one where you get to peek in first through a periscope and then slide down an enclosed steel chute, water-park style, into the vaulted bowels of the building. There's also a regular entrance and staircase for access to Catalan inventor Pep Torres' brain-boggling Barcelona Museum of Ideas and Inventions, known as **miba**, which presents a mixture of his own inventions and those of budding and established creative inventors worldwide. Lots are very worthy, world-saving devices, from portable water-purifiers to sun-seeking plant-pots, and others are frankly bonkers – like shoe-umbrellas or karaoke mop-microphones. All sorts of gadgets are also available in the shop, but mostly, especially if you're under 10, you're going to be begging for just one more go on the chute.

Plaça Reial and around

Ⓜ Liceu

Of all the old-town squares, the most popular with visitors is the elegant nineteenth-century **Plaça Reial**, hidden behind an archway, just off the Ramblas. Laid out in around 1850, the Italianate square is studded with tall palm trees and decorated iron lamps (made by the young Antoni Gaudí), bordered by high, pastel-coloured arcaded buildings, and centred on a fountain depicting the Three Graces. Taking in the sun at one of the benches puts you in very mixed company – bikers, buskers, eccentrics and tramps, not to mention bemused tourists drinking a coffee at one of the pavement cafés. It used to be a bit dodgy in Plaça Reial, but most of the really unsavoury characters have been driven off over the years and predatory, menu-toting waiters are usually the biggest nuisance these days. The surrounding bars and restaurants are becoming increasingly more upmarket, but don't expect to see too many locals until night falls.

On Sunday morning Plaça Reial hosts a long-standing **coin and stamp market** (10am–2pm). Otherwise, the arcaded passageways connecting the square with the surrounding streets throw up a few interesting sights, like the quirky **Herborista del Rey** (c/del Vidre; closed Mon), an early nineteenth-century herbalist's shop, which stocks more than 250 medicinal herbs designed to combat all complaints.

Carrer dels Escudellers and Plaça George Orwell

The alleys on the south side of Plaça Reial emerge on c/dels Escudellers, where the turning spits of grilled chicken at **Los Caracoles** restaurant make a good photograph. **Carrer dels Escudellers** itself was once a thriving red-light street, and still has a late-night seediness about it, but it teeters on the edge of respectability. Bars and restaurants around here attract a youthful clientele, nowhere more so than those flanking **Plaça de George Orwell**, at the eastern end of c/dels Escudellers. The wedge-shaped square was created by levelling an old-town block – a favoured tactic in Barcelona to let in a bit of light – and it has quickly become a hangout for the grunge crowd.

Carrer d'Avinyó

Ⓜ Liceu

Carrer d'Avinyó, running south from c/de Ferran towards the harbour, cuts through the most atmospheric part of the southern Barri Gòtic. It used to be a red-light district of some renown, littered with brothels and bars, and frequented by the young Picasso, whose family moved into the area in 1895. It still looks the part – a narrow thoroughfare lined with dark overhanging buildings – but the funky cafés, streetwear shops and boutiques tell the story of its creeping gentrification. The locals aren't overly enamoured of the influx of bar-crawling fun-seekers – banners and notices along the length of this and neighbouring streets plead with visitors to keep the noise down.

La Mercè

Ⓜ Drassanes

In the eighteenth century, the harbourside neighbourhood known as **La Mercè** was home to the nobles and merchants enriched by Barcelona's maritime trade. Most took the opportunity to move north to the more fashionable Eixample later in the nineteenth century, and the streets of La Mercè took on an earthier hue. Since then, Carrer de la Mercè and the surrounding streets (particularly Ample, d'en Gignas and Regomir) have been home to a series of old-style **taverns** known as *tascas* or *bodegas* – a glass of wine from the barrel in *Bodega la Plata*, or a similar joint, is one of the old town's more authentic experiences.

Església de la Mercè

Pl. de la Mercè • Mon–Sat 10am–1pm & 6–8pm, Sun 10am–1.45pm & 6.30–7.45pm • Ⓜ Drassanes

The eighteenth-century **Església de la Mercè** is the focus of the city's biggest annual celebration, the Festes de la Mercè every September, dedicated to the co-patroness of Barcelona, the Virgin of Mercè, whose image is paraded from here. It's an excuse for a week of intense merrymaking, culminating in spectacular fireworks along the seafront. The church itself was burned out in 1936, but the gilt side-chapels, stained-glass medallions and apse murals have been authentically restored, while the statue of Virgin and Child sits behind glass above the altar – a staircase allows you a closer look.

El Raval

The old-town area west of the Ramblas is known as El Raval (from the Arabic word for "suburb") and has always formed a world apart from nobler Barri Gòtic. In medieval times it was the site of hospitals, churches, monasteries and various noxious trades, while later it acquired a reputation as the city's main red-light area, known to all (for obscure reasons) as the Barri Xinès – China Town. Over the last two decades, however, El Raval has changed markedly, particularly in the "upper Raval" around Barcelona's contemporary art museum, MACBA. Cutting-edge galleries, designer restaurants and fashionable bars are all part of the scene these days, while in the occasionally edgy "lower Raval" are found the neighbourhood's two other outstanding buildings, namely Gaudí's Palau Güell and the church of Sant Pau del Camp, one of the city's oldest churches.

According to the Barcelona writer Manuel Vázquez Montalbán, El Raval once housed "theatrical homosexuals and anarcho-syndicalist, revolutionary meeting places; women's prisons ... condom shops and brothels which smelled of liquor and groins". Even today in the backstreets between c/de Sant Pau and c/Nou de la Rambla visitors may run the gauntlet of cat-calling prostitutes and petty drug dealers, while a handful of atmospheric old bars trade on their former reputations as bohemian hangouts. Yet the 1992 Olympics and then European Union funding achieved what Franco never could, and cleaned up large parts of the neighbourhood almost overnight. North of c/de l'Hospital, in the "upper Raval", the development of MACBA, the adjacent CCCB culture centre and new university faculty buildings have seen entire city blocks demolished and remodelled. To the south, in the "lower Raval" between c/de l'Hospital and c/de Sant Pau, a new boulevard – the **Rambla de Raval** – was gouged through the former tenements and alleys, providing a huge new pedestrianized area. At the same time the area's older, traditional residents have gradually been supplanted by a more affluent, arty population, while there's also been a growing influx of immigrants from the Indian subcontinent and North Africa. Alongside the surviving spit-and-sawdust bars, and new restaurants, galleries and boutiques, you'll find specialist grocery stores, curry houses, halal butchers and hole-in-the-wall telephone offices advertising cheap international calls.

You'd hesitate to call El Raval gentrified, as it clearly still has its rough edges. You needn't be unduly concerned during the day as you make your way around, but it's as well to keep your wits about you at night, particularly in the southernmost streets.

Museu d'Art Contemporani de Barcelona (MACBA)

Pl. dels Àngels 1 • Mon & Wed–Fri 11am–7.30pm (mid-June mid-Sept till 8pm), Sat 10am–8pm, Sun & hols 10am–3pm; closed Tues all year • €6 or €7.50, depending on exhibition, one-year pass €12, under-14s free • Tours of the permanent collection in English Mon & Wed–Sat 4pm, included in admission fee • ☎ 934 120 810, ⓦ macba.cat • Ⓜ Catalunya

Anchoring the upper reaches of El Raval is the iconic **Museu d'Art Contemporani de Barcelona**, which opened in 1995. The contrast between the huge, white, almost luminous, structure of the museum and the buildings around it couldn't be more stark. The aim of the architect, American Richard Meier, was to make as much use of natural light as possible and to "create a dialogue" between the museum and its surroundings; this is reflected in the front of the building, which is constructed entirely of glass. Once inside, you go from the ground to the fourth floor up a series of swooping ramps which afford continuous views of the square below – usually full of careering skateboarders.

Inside the museum

The museum **collection** represents the main movements in contemporary art since 1945, mainly (but not exclusively) in Catalunya and Spain. Periodically changing themed exhibitions highlight selected works from the permanent collection, while there are always two or three other exhibitions and installations on too, so, depending on when you visit, you may catch works by major names such as Joan Miró, Antoni Tàpies or Eduardo Chillida. Joan Brossa, leading light of the Catalan Dau al Set group of the 1950s, also has work here, as do contemporary multimedia and installation artists like Antoni Muntadas and Francesc Torres. Probably the best way to acquaint yourself with the collection is to take the free **guided tour**. There's also a good museum **shop** selling everything from designer espresso cups to art books, and a **café-bar** around the back that's part of the CCCB (Contemporary Culture Centre).

Centre de Cultura Contemporània de Barcelona (CCCB)

C/de Montalegre 5 · CCCB Tues–Sun 11am–8pm, Thurs until 10pm; C3 café-bar Mon–Fri 9am–9pm; Sat & Sun 11am–9pm; · €5 or €7 depending on exhibition, under-16s free, reduced entry €3/5 on Wed & on Thurs after 8pm, free on Sun after 3pm · ☎ 933 064 100, Ⓦ cccb.org · Ⓜ Catalunya

Adjoining MACBA is the **Centre de Cultura Contemporània de Barcelona**, which hosts some really good art and city-related exhibitions (ranging from photography to architecture) and supports a varied cinema, concert and festival programme. The imaginatively restored building is a prime example of the juxtaposition of old and new; originally built in 1714 on the site of an Augustinian convent, it was once an infamous workhouse and lunatic asylum. The main courtyard (now called the Plaça de les Dones) still retains its old tile panels and presiding statue of Sant Jordi (patron saint of Catalunya). At the back of the building, the *C3* **café-bar** has a sunny *terrassa* on the modern square joining the CCCB to the MACBA.

Foment de les Arts i del Disseny (FAD)

Pl. dels Àngels 5–6 · Exhibitions Mon–Sat 11am–8pm · Free · ☎ 934 437 520, Ⓦ fad.cat · Ⓜ Catalunya

Across the open expanse from MACBA, part of the former Convent dels Àngels now houses the headquarters of the **Foment de les Arts i del Disseny** (Fostering Art and Design), a decorative art and design organization founded in 1903. Their exhibition spaces (including the former convent chapel) are dedicated to industrial and graphic design, arts, crafts, architecture, contemporary jewellery and fashion – drop by to see the latest temporary exhibitions.

Plaça de Vincenç Martorell and around

Ⓜ Catalunya

The Raval's nicest traffic-free square lies just a few minutes' walk from MACBA. In the arcaded **Plaça de Vicenç Martorell** there's a first-rate café, the *Kasparo*, whose tables overlook a popular children's playground. Meanwhile, around the corner, the narrow Carrer del Bonsuccés, Carrer de les Sitges and Carrer dels Tallers house a concentrated selection of the city's best independent **music stores** and urban and streetwear shops.

Hospital de la Santa Creu

Entrances on c/del Carme and c/de l'Hospital · **Garden** Daily 10am–dusk · Free · **La Capella** c/de l'Hospital 56 · Exhibition information on Ⓦ bcn.cat/lacapella · Ⓜ Liceu

The neighbourhood's most historic relic is the **Hospital de la Santa Creu**, which occupies a large site between c/del Carme and c/de l'Hospital. The attractive complex of Gothic buildings was founded as the city's main hospital in 1402, a role that it assumed for over 500 years. Antoni Gaudí, knocked down by a tram in 1926, was brought here for treatment but died three days later. The hospital shifted site to Domènech i Montaner's new creation in the Eixample in 1930 and the spacious fifteenth-century wards were subsequently converted for cultural and educational use; they now hold the Royal Academy of Medicine, an art and design school and two libraries, including the Catalan national library, the Biblioteca de Catalunya. Visitors can wander freely through the charming medieval cloistered **garden** (access from either street), while inside the c/del Carme entrance (on the right) are some superb seventeenth-century decorative tiles of various religious scenes. There's also the rather nice open-air *El Jardí* **café** in the garden at the c/de l'Hospital side (see p.182), while the hospital's former chapel, **La Capella** (entered separately from c/de l'Hospital) is an exhibition space for new contemporary artists.

EL RAVAL

● ACCOMMODATION

Barceló Raval	9
Hostal Cèntric	1
Hostal Gat Raval	5
Hostal Gat Xino	6
Hosteria Grau	4
Hotel Curious	7
Hotel España	11
Hotel Peninsular	10
Hotel Sant Agustí	8
Market Hotel	3
Mesón Castilla	2

● CAFÉS

Café de les Delícies	17
Federal	9
Granja M. Viader	8
El Jardí	12
Kasparo	1
Mendizábal	13

C. MARQUES DE CAMPO SAGRADO

TAPAS BARS
Dos Palillos	3
Mam i Teca	5
Sesamo	4

RESTAURANTS
Anima	7
Bar Ra	10
Biblioteca	14
Biocenter	6
Elisabets	2
Mesón David	16
Moti Mahal	19
Pollo Rico	18
Romesco	15
La Verónica	11

SHOPS
La Central del Raval	5
Discos Castelló	4
Etnomusic	2
Fantastik	6
Holalal Plaza	1
Indio	10
Lailo	11
Museu d'Art Contemporani de Barcelona	3
Naifa	9
Ras	8
Taller Textil Teranyina	7
Wah Wah Discos	12

BARS
Almirall	2
Betty Ford's	1
La Confitería	9
London Bar	10
Marmalade	8
Marsella	4
Muy Buenas	6
Resolís	7
Zelig	5

CLUBS & LIVE MUSIC
La Concha	11
Jazz Sí Club	3
Moog	12

0   100
metres

Reial Acadèmia de Medicina

Hospital de la Santa Creu, c/del Carme entrance • Wed only 10am–noon • Free • ⓦ ramc.cat • Ⓜ Liceu

You may need to ring the bell at the door of the Royal Academy of Medicine for admittance to the remarkable eighteenth-century anatomical theatre within. The chamber has been beautifully preserved, with carved wooden seats under a gilded dome, centred on a marble dissecting table.

Rambla de Raval and around

Ⓜ Liceu

The most obvious manifestation of the changing character of El Raval is the **Rambla de Raval**, a palm-lined boulevard driven right through the centre of the district between c/ de l'Hospital and c/de Sant Pau. The *rambla* has a distinct character that's all its own, mixing kebab joints and grocery stores with an increasing number of fashionable cafés and bars. Signature building, halfway down, is the glow-in-the-dark designer **Barceló Raval hotel**, while children find it hard to resist a clamber on the massive, bulbous cat sculpture. A Saturday **street market** (selling anything from samosas to hammocks) adds a bit more character, while the two extremes of the *rambla* offer a snapshot of the changing neighbourhood. At the bottom end, off **c/de Sant Pau**, the *barri*'s remaining prostitutes accost passers-by as they head back towards the Liceu and the Ramblas. The top end, meanwhile, leads you straight into the streets of the "upper Raval", flush with boutiques, bars and galleries.

Carrer de la Riera Baixa

Just off the top of Rambla de Raval, the narrow **Carrer de la Riera Baixa** is at the centre of the city's secondhand and vintage clothing scene. A dozen funky little independent clothes shops provide the scope for an hour's browsing, with funky *Resolis* bar (no. 22) the best place to take a break in between.

Plaça del Pedro and Carrer d'en Botella

In **Plaça del Pedro** (junction of c/del Carme and c/de l'Hospital) a cherished statue of Santa Eulàlia (co-patron of the city) stands on the site of her supposed crucifixion, facing the surviving apse of a Romanesque chapel. Carrer d'en Botella, just off the square, is unremarkable, save for the plaque at no. 11 which records the **birthplace of Manuel Vásquez Montalbán**, probably the city's most famous writer, whose likes and prejudices found expression in his favourite character, detective Pepe Carvalho.

SNOOPING AROUND THE RAVAL

Barcelona-born author, journalist, critic and poet, **Manuel Vásquez Montalbán** (1939–2003) was one of Spain's most popular writers, whose shabby, fast-living fictional detective **Pepe Carvalho** – ex-Communist and CIA agent – investigated foul deeds in the city in a series of terrific novels spanning thirty years. It was hardly an accident that Montalbán's own passions – for Barcelona itself, and for politics, markets, cooking, food and drink – all rubbed off on his detective, and Pepe Carvalho's cases took him around easily identifiable parts of the city, particularly the earthy streets of the Raval. With an office on the Ramblas, the gourmand detective is often picking out groceries in the Boqueria market or grabbing a bite at *Pinotxo*, the classic stand-up market bar, while in the *Casa Leopoldo* restaurant (c/Sant Rafael 24, off Rambla de Raval, ⓦ casaleopoldo.com) both Montalbán and Carvalho found their spiritual home. The remodelled square nearby, by the *Barceló Raval* hotel, has been named by the city in honour of the author, while an annual crime fiction prize established in 2005 (previous winners include Henning Mankell and Ian Rankin) bears the name of his celebrated detective.

HIGH SOCIETY AT THE HOTEL ESPAÑA

There's a hidden gem tucked around the back of the Liceu opera house, on the otherwise fairly shabby c/de Sant Pau. Here, in the lower reaches of the Raval, some of the most influential names in Catalan architecture and design came together at the beginning of the twentieth century to transform the **Hotel España** (c/de Sant Pau 9–11, Ⓦwww.hotelespanya .com; ⓂLiceu) – originally built as a simple boarding house in 1860 – into one of the city's most lavish addresses (see p.170). With a wonderfully tiled dining room designed by Lluís Domènech i Montaner, a bar with an amazing marble fireplace by Eusebi Arnau and a bathing area with glass roof (now the breakfast room) whose marine murals were executed by Ramon Casas, the hotel was the fashionable sensation of its day. A century later it's back in vogue, since a remarkable contemporary restoration has highlighted the classy *modernista* public spaces and brought the rooms up to scratch. Lunch or dinner here is a real in-the-know treat, with the original *modernista* dining room (known as the Fonda España) now under the helm of Michelin-starred Basque chef Martín Berasategui, while the classy bar welcomes passing visitors.

Palau Güell

C/Nou de la Rambla 3–5 · Tues–Sun & hols 10am–8pm (Nov–March until 5.30pm) · €10 · ☎933 173 974, Ⓦpalauguell.cat · ⓂLiceu

El Raval's outstanding building is the **Palau Güell**, an extraordinary townhouse designed (1886–90) by the young Antoni Gaudí for wealthy shipowner and industrialist Eusebi Güell i Bacigalupi. It was commissioned as an extension of the Güell family's house located on the Ramblas, and was later the first modern building to be declared a World Heritage Site by UNESCO. A painstaking restoration has returned the building, with its famous roof terrace, to its original state, and it's one of Barcelona's most popular attractions – numbers are limited and your ticket will be for a specific time-slot for a one-hour visit.

At a time when architects sought to conceal the iron supports within buildings, Gaudí turned them to his advantage, displaying them as decorative features in the grand rooms on the **main floor**, which are lined with dark marble hewn from the Güell family quarries. Columns, arches and ceilings are all shaped, carved and twisted in an elaborate style that was to become the hallmark of Gaudí's later works. Even the basement **stables** bear Gaudí's distinct touch, a forest of brick capitals and arches that with a touch of imagination become mushrooms and palms. Meanwhile the **roof terrace** culminates in a fantastical series of chimneys decorated with swirling patterns made from fragments of glazed tile, glass and earthenware. The family rarely ventured up here – it was the servants instead who were exposed to the fullest flight of Gaudí's fantasy as they hung the washing out on lines strung from chimney to chimney.

Església de Sant Pau del Camp

C/de Sant Pau 101 · Under restoration, hours not reliable, but officially Mon 5–8pm, Tues–Fri 10am–1.30pm & 5–8pm, Sat 10am–1.30pm · Admission to cloister €3 · ☎934 410 001 · ⓂParal.lel

Carrer de Sant Pau cuts west through the Raval to the church of **Sant Pau del Camp**, its name – St Paul of the Field – a graphic reminder that it once stood in open fields beyond the city walls. One of the most interesting churches in Barcelona, Sant Pau was a Benedictine foundation of the tenth century, built after its predecessor was destroyed in a Muslim raid of 985 AD and constructed on a Greek cross plan. It was renovated again at the end of the thirteenth century; the curious, primitive carvings of fish, birds and faces above the main entrance are from that period, while other animal forms adorn the twin capitals of the charming twelfth-century cloister. Inside, the church is dark and rather plain, enlivened only by tiny arrow-slit windows and small stained-glass circles high up in the central dome.

Mercat de Sant Antoni

C/del Comte d'Urgell 1 • Mon–Thurs 7am–2.30pm & 5.30–8.30pm, Fri & Sat 7am–8.30pm • ⓦ mercatsbcn.cat • Ⓜ Sant Antoni

The Raval's western edge is defined by the Ronda de Sant Pau and the Ronda de Sant Antoni, and where the two meet stands the handsome **Mercat de Sant Antoni**, the neighbourhood's major produce market, dating from 1876. Come on Sunday and there's a **book and coin market** (9am–2pm) here instead, with collectors and enthusiasts arriving early to pick through the best bargains, while kids and their shepherding parents stand on the sidelines swapping Panini and Pokémon cards.

Most of Barcelona's old markets are being revamped, as the nineteenth-century engineering starts to fail, and Sant Antoni is no exception: it's been remodelled entirely (for completion in 2012), though its external character has been retained – a temporary market on Ronda de Sant Antoni continues to operate while works continue (though the book and coin market still takes place around the perimeter of the original market building). Meanwhile, the traditional place to take a break from shopping is *Els Tres Tombs,* the restaurant-bar across the road on the corner of Ronda de Sant Antoni. You wouldn't make a special trip out here for it, but it's a handy place for the market, open from 6am – the far better local café is the nearby *Federal* (see p.182).

3

DESIGNER SHOES IN THE PASSEIG DEL BORN

Sant Pere, La Ribera and Ciutadella

The two easternmost old-town neighbourhoods of Sant Pere and La Ribera sit one on top of another, divided by Carrer de la Princesa. They are both medieval in origin, and are often thought of as one district, but each has a distinct character. Sant Pere – perhaps the least visited part of the old town – has two remarkable buildings, the *modernista* concert hall known as the Palau de la Música Catalana and the stylishly designed market, the Mercat Santa Caterina. By way of contrast, the old artisans' quarter of La Ribera has always been a big draw, by virtue of the presence of the graceful church of Santa María del Mar, the city's most perfect expression of the Catalan-Gothic style, and the Museu Picasso, Barcelona's biggest single tourist attraction. Meanwhile, for time out from the old town's labyrinthine alleys, retreat to the city's favourite park, Parc de la Ciutadella, on La Ribera's eastern edge.

Both neighbourhoods have seen a fair amount of regeneration in recent years, particularly Sant Pere, where new boulevards and community projects sit alongside DJ bars and designer shops. La Ribera's cramped, narrow streets, on the other hand, were at the heart of medieval industry and commerce, and it's still the location of choice for many contemporary designers, craftspeople and artists. Galleries and applied art museums occupy the mansions of Carrer de Montcada – the neighbourhood's most handsome street – while the *barri* is at its most hip in the area around the **Passeig del Born**, whose cafés, restaurants and bars make it one of the city's premier nightlife centres.

ARRIVAL AND DEPARTURE

By metro To walk through both neighbourhoods you can start at Ⓜ Urquinaona, close to the Palau de la Música Catalana, or Ⓜ Arc de Triomf over to the east, while Ⓜ Jaume I marks both the southern end of Sant Pere and the most direct access point to La Ribera.

Palau de la Música Catalana

C/de Sant Pere Més Alt · Guided tours (in English on the hour) daily 10am–3.30pm, plus Easter week & Aug 10am–6pm · €12 · Tour tickets available by phone, online or at the box office, up to a week in advance · ☎ 902 475 485, Ⓦ palaumusica.org · Ⓜ Urquinaona

Stumble upon *modernista* architect Lluís Domènech i Montaner's stupendous **Palau de la Música Catalana** from narrow c/de Sant Pere Més Alt and it barely seems to have enough space to breathe. The extraordinary concert hall was built in 1908 for the Orfeó Català choral group (it's still privately owned) and made an immediate statement of nationalistic intent. Smothered in tiles and mosaics typical of *modernisme*, the highly elaborate facade rests on three great columns, like elephant's legs, while the corner sculpture represents Catalan popular song, its allegorical figures protected by a strident Sant Jordi (St George). Domènech i Montaner strove to make the interior of his concert hall a veritable "box of light", which he achieved by capping the second-storey auditorium with a mighty bulbous stained-glass skylight – contemporary critics claimed it to be an engineering impossibility.

4

Numbers are limited on the very popular fifty-minute **guided tours** of the interior, so it's best to buy a ticket in advance. Or, of course, you can always come to a performance – the **concert season** here runs from October until June (see p.207).

Touring the concert hall

Tours start with a short video extolling the virtues of the building, followed by a close-up look at the decorated facade columns and a brief visit to the two floors of the main concert hall. Sculptures of the Muses ring the main stage, while allegorical decoration is everywhere, from the sculpted red and white roses in the colours of the Catalan flag to the representations of music and nature in the glistening stained glass. Successive extensions and interior remodelling have opened up the rest of the original site – the **Petit Palau** offers a smaller auditorium space, while to the side an enveloping glass facade provides the main public access to the box office, terrace restaurant and foyer bar.

Plaça de Sant Pere

Ⓜ Arc de Triomf/Urquinaona

Sant Pere neighbourhood extends around three parallel medieval streets, carrers de Sant Pere de Més Baix (lower), Mitja (middle) and Alt (upper), which contain the bulk of the district's most characteristic buildings and shops – a mixture of boutiques, textile firms, groceries and old family businesses. The streets all converge upon the original neighbourhood square, **Plaça de Sant Pere**, whose foursquare **Església de Sant Pere de les Puelles** flanks one side, overlooking a flamboyant iron drinking fountain and a few cafés that put out tables on the square. The church is actually one of the oldest in the city, rebuilt in 1147 on tenth-century foundations, though it's been destroyed and burned too many times since to retain any interior interest – the high-walled facade, although it looks medieval, is a twentieth-century renovation.

Mercat Santa Caterina

Av. de Francesc Cambó 16 • Mon 7.30am–2pm, Tues, Wed & Sat 7.30am–3.30pm, Thurs & Fri 7.30am–8.30pm; July & Aug 7.30am–3.30pm only • ☎ 933 195 740, ⓦ mercatsantacaterina.net • Ⓜ Jaume I

At the very heart of Sant Pere is the eye-catching **Mercat Santa Caterina**, whose splendid restoration has retained its original nineteenth-century balustraded market walls and added slatted wooden doors and windows and a dramatic multicoloured wave roof. It's one of the best places in the city to shop for food, and its market restaurant and bar are definitely

worth a visit in any case. During the renovation work, the foundations of a medieval convent were discovered here – the excavations are visible at the rear of the market.

Plaça de Sant Agusti Vell and around

Ⓜ Jaume I

The pretty, tree-shaded **Plaça de Sant Agusti Vell** sits at the centre of Sant Pere's most ambitious regeneration project, which has transformed previously crowded alleys into landscaped boulevards. To the north locals tend organic allotments in the middle of the **Pou de la Figuera** *rambla*, while south down **Carrer de l'Allada Vermell** are overarching trees, a children's playground and a series of outdoor cafés and bars. Meanwhile, running down from Plaça de Sant Agusti Vell, **Carrer dels Carders** – once "ropemakers' street" – is now a funky retail quarter mixing grocery stores and cafés with shops selling streetwear, African and Asian arts and crafts and contemporary jewellery. The little Romanesque chapel at the end of the street is the **Capella d'en Marcus** (usually locked), dating back to the twelfth century, though otherwise stripped of interest during the Civil War.

Centre Cívic Convent de Sant Agustí

C/del Comerç 36, entrance on c/d'en Tantarantana • Mon–Fri 9am–10pm, Sat 10am–2pm & 4–9pm • Admission charges vary, some events free • ☎ 932 103 732, Ⓦ bcn.cat/centrecivicsantagusti • Ⓜ Jaume I/Arc de Triomf

Driving many of the neighbourhood improvements in Sant Pere is the community centre installed inside the revamped **Convent de Sant Agustí**, whose thirteenth-century cloister provides a unique performance space. There's a full cultural programme here, from workshops to concerts, with a particular emphasis on electronic and experimental music and art, and don't miss the excellent convent café, with seats in the cloister, which is a good lunch destination if you're touring the neighbourhood (see p.184).

Museu de la Xocolata

C/del Comerç 36 • Mon & Wed–Sat 10am–7pm, Sun 10am–3pm • €4.30, under-7s free • ☎ 932 687 878, Ⓦ pastisseria.com • Ⓜ Jaume I/ Arc de Triomf

Another part of the Convent de Sant Agustí houses the city's **Museu de la Xocolata**, which presents a rather uninspiring plod through the history of chocolate all the way back to its origins as a sacred and medicinal product of prehistoric Central America. It's a topic with some local relevance, in that the Bourbon army, which was once quartered in this building, demanded the provision of chocolate for its sweet-toothed troops. Whether you go in or not probably depends on how keen you are to see models of Gaudí buildings or religious icons sculpted from chocolate. Nonetheless, there's a glittering counter of chocs to buy, while at the adjacent Escola de Pastisseria, glass windows allow you to look onto the students learning their craft in the kitchens. There are also chocolate workshops, tastings and children's days organized on a regular basis – enquire at the museum.

Museu Picasso

C/de Montcada 15–23 • Tues–Sun & hols 10am–8pm • €10, exhibitions €6, under-16s free, plus Sun after 3pm & first Sun of month free • Free guided tours in English (Tues 4.30pm & Thurs 5.30pm); advance bookings essential, by phone or by email through the website • ☎ 932 563 000, Ⓦ museupicasso.bcn.cat • Ⓜ Jaume I

The celebrated **Museu Picasso** is one of the most important collections of Picasso's work in the world, but even so some visitors are disappointed since the museum contains none of his best-known pictures, and few in the Cubist style. But there are almost four thousand works in the permanent collection – housed in five adjoining medieval

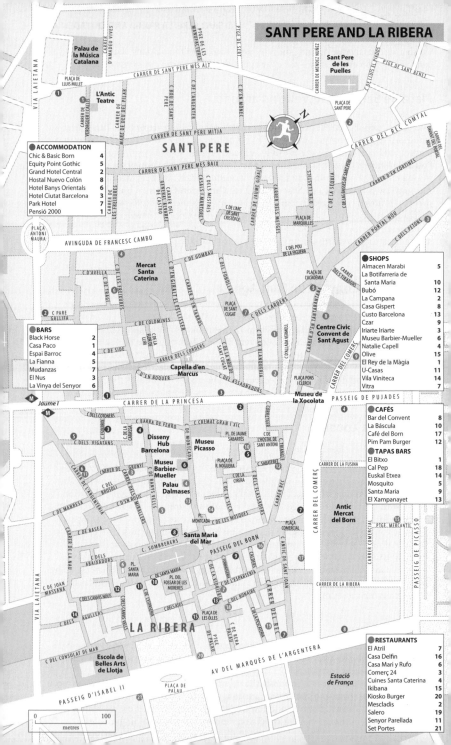

SANT PERE AND LA RIBERA

Palau de la Música Catalana

Sant Pere de les Puelles

L'Antic Teatre

SANT PERE

Mercat Santa Caterina

Capella d'en Marcus

Centre Civic Convent de Sant Agust

Museu de la Xocolata

Disseny Hub Barcelona

Museu Picasso

Museu Barbier-Mueller

Palau Dalmases

Santa Maria del Mar

PASSEIG DEL BORN

Antic Mercat del Born

LA RIBERA

Escola de Belles Arts de Llotja

Estació de França

0   100
metres

PICASSO IN BARCELONA

Although born in Málaga, **Pablo Picasso** (1881–1973) spent much of his youth – from the age of 14 to 23 – in Barcelona. He maintained close links with the city and his Catalan friends even when he left for Paris in 1904, and is said to have always thought of himself as Catalan rather than *andaluz*. The time Picasso spent in Barcelona encompassed the whole of his Blue Period (1901–04) and provided many of the formative influences on his art.

Apart from the Museu Picasso, there are echoes of the great artist at various sites throughout the old town. Not too far from the museum, you can still see many of the buildings in which Picasso lived and worked, notably the **Escola de Belles Arts de Llotja** (c/Consolat del Mar, near Estació de França), where his father taught drawing and where Picasso himself absorbed an academic training. The **apartments** where the family lived when they first arrived in Barcelona – Pg. d'Isabel II 4 and c/Reina Cristina 3, both near the Escola – can also be seen, though only from the outside, while Picasso's first real **studio** (in 1896) was located over on c/de la Plata at no. 4. A few years later, many of his Blue Period works were finished at a studio at c/del Comerç 28. His first **public exhibition** was in 1901 at *Els Quatre Gats* tavern (see box, p.47). The other place to retain a link with Picasso is **c/d'Avinyó** in the Barri Gòtic, which cuts south from c/de Ferran to c/Ample. Large houses along here were converted into brothels at the end of the nineteenth century, and Picasso used to haunt the street sketching what he saw. Some accounts of his life – based on Picasso's own testimony, it has to be said – claim that he had his first sexual experience here at the age of 14, and certainly the women at one of the brothels inspired his seminal Cubist work, *Les Demoiselles d'Avignon*.

palaces – which provide a fascinating opportunity to trace Picasso's development from his early paintings as a young boy to the major works of later years. It might often seem as if every visitor to Barcelona is trying to get into the place at the same time, but you can hardly come to the city and not make the effort. Arriving when it opens is a good way to beat the worst of the crowds. A **café** with a *terrassa* in one of the palace courtyards offers refreshments, and there is of course a **shop**, stuffed full of Picasso-related gifts.

The collection

The museum opened in 1963 with a collection based largely on the donations of Jaime Sabartes, longtime friend and former secretary to the artist. On Sabartes' death in 1968, Picasso himself added a large number of works – above all, the works of the Meninas series – and in 1970 he donated a further vast number of watercolours, drawings, prints and paintings.

The works on show are extremely well laid out, as they follow the artist's development chronologically, with the early periods by far the best represented.

Early works and Blue Period

The **early drawings**, particularly, are fascinating, in which Picasso – still signing with his full name, Pablo Ruiz Picasso – attempted to copy the nature paintings in which his father specialized. Works from his **art school** days in Barcelona (1895–97) show tantalizing glimpses of the city that the young Picasso was beginning to know well – the Gothic old town, the cloisters of Sant Paul del Camp, Barceloneta beach – and even at the ages of 15 and 16 he was producing serious works, including knowing self-portraits and a closely observed study of his mother from 1896. Works in the style of Toulouse-Lautrec, like the menu Picasso did for *Els Quatre Gats* tavern in 1900, reflect his burgeoning interest in Parisian art at the turn of the century, while other sketches, drawings and illustrations (many undertaken for competitions and magazines) clearly show Picasso's development of his own unique personal style. His paintings from the famous **Blue Period** (1901–04) burst upon you – whether its moody Barcelona rooftops or the cold face of *La Dona Morta* – and subsequent galleries trace the Pink Period (1905–06), though with the barest nod to his Cubist (1907–20) and Neoclassical (1920–25) stages.

Las Meninas

The large gaps in the main collection (for example, nothing after the early Pink Period works of 1905 until the celebrated *Harlequin* of 1917) only underline Picasso's extraordinary changes of style and mood. This is best illustrated by the large jump to 1957, a year represented by his 44 interpretations of Velázquez's masterpiece, **Las Meninas**, completed in just four months between August and December. In these, Picasso brilliantly deconstructed the individual portraits and compositions that make up Velázquez's work; in addition, and neatly juxtaposed, are displayed nine more donated works by Picasso, gorgeous light-filled Mediterranean scenes inspired by the pigeons and dovecotes of his Cannes studio.

Other works, ceramics and prints

The museum also addresses Picasso as **ceramicist**, highlighting the vibrantly decorated dishes and jugs given to the museum by his wife, Jacqueline. There are various portraits of Jacqueline here, too, though it's the deep friendship Picasso shared with Jaime Sabartes for almost seventy years that provokes the clearest expression of endearment, in a separate room of mature portraits, character studies and jokey sketches by one friend of another. Finally, separate rooms display annually changing exhibitions of Picasso's **prints**, culled from the 1500 or so engravings and lithographs that the museum possesses.

Along Carrer de Montcada

Ⓜ Jaume I

The street on which the Museu Picasso stands – **Carrer de Montcada** – is one of the best-looking in the city. It was laid out in the fourteenth century and, until the Eixample was planned almost five hundred years later, was home to most of the city's leading citizens. They occupied spacious mansions built around central courtyards, from which external staircases climbed to the living rooms on the first floor; the facades facing the street were all endowed with huge gated doors that could be swung open to allow coaches access to the interior. Today, almost all the mansions and palaces along La Ribera's showpiece street serve instead as museums, private galleries and craft and gift shops, sucking up the trade from Picasso-bound visitors.

Disseny Hub Barcelona (DHUB)

C/de Montcada 12 • Tues–Fri 11am–7pm, Sat, Sun & hols 11am–8pm • Some exhibitions free, otherwise €5, under-16s free, plus Sun after 3pm & first Sun of the month free • ☎ 932 562 300, ⓦ dhub-bcn.cat • Ⓜ Jaume I

The city's unparalleled design (*disseny*) and applied art collections are currently on display at the Palau Reial at Pedralbes pending the construction of the new Design Centre at Glòries. In the meantime, the umbrella organization, known as **Disseny Hub Barcelona**, hosts thought-provoking temporary exhibitions at **DHUB Montcada**, in the fourteenth-century palace that used to be the old Textile Museum building and covering anything from aspects of *modernista* design to 3D printing techniques. The ticket is also valid for the Palau Reial collections, and there's a handy courtyard café here too.

Museu Barbier-Mueller

C/de Montcada 14 • Tues–Fri 11am–7pm, Sat & Sun 11am–8pm, hols 11am–3pm • €3.50, first Sun of month free • ☎ 933 104 516, ⓦ barbier-mueller.ch • Ⓜ Jaume I

The sixteenth-century Palau Nadal houses a fascinating collection of pre-Columbian art at the **Museu Barbier-Mueller**. Temporary exhibitions – all beautifully presented – highlight wide-ranging themes, and draw on a peerless collection of sculpture, pottery, jewellery, textiles and everyday items, with some pieces dating back as far as the third century BC. Depending on the exhibition, you're as likely to see decorated

Mongolian belt-buckles as carved African furniture – there's nothing restrictive about the term "pre-Columbian" – and the shop, with a wide range of artefacts for sale, is also worth a browse.

Església de Santa María del Mar and around

Pl. de Santa María • Mon–Sat 9am–1.30pm & 4.30–8pm, Sun 9.30am–1.45pm & 4.30–8.45pm; choral Mass Sun at 1pm • ⓜ Jaume I

La Ribera's flagship church of **Santa María del Mar** is the city's most exquisite example of pure Catalan-Gothic architecture – much dearer to the heart of the average local than the overpowering cathedral, La Seu, the only other church in Barcelona with which it compares. Conceived as thanks for the Catalan conquest of Sardinia in 1324, work on the church began in 1329 and was finished in just over half a century, which explains its consistency of style. It's not obvious today, but Santa María *del Mar* (ie, of the sea) was also built on what was the seashore in the fourteenth century (hence the title of Ildefonso Falcone's medieval blockbuster novel *Cathedral of the Sea*, which relates its construction). The church – dedicated to Catalan maritime glories – stood foursquare at the heart of Barcelona's trading district (nearby c/de l'Argenteria, for example, is named after the silversmiths who once worked there), and indeed came to embody the commercial supremacy of the Crown of Aragón, of which the city was capital. Its wide nave, narrow aisles, massive buttresses and octagonal, flat-topped towers are all typically Catalan-Gothic features, while it's probably all to the good that its later Baroque trappings were destroyed during the Civil War. Subsequent long-term restoration work has concentrated on showing off the simple bare spaces of the interior, and the stained glass is especially beautiful.

Plaça del Fossar de les Moreres

To the south of the church is the modern brick-lined square known as **Placa del Fossar de les Moreres**, which was formally opened in 1989 to mark the spot where, following the defeat of Barcelona on September 11, 1714, Catalan martyrs fighting for independence against the king of Spain, Felipe V, were executed. A red steel scimitar with an eternal flame commemorates the fallen.

Passeig del Born

ⓜ Jaume I/Barceloneta

Fronting the church of Santa María del Mar is the fashionable **Passeig del Born**, once the site of medieval fairs and tournaments (*born* means tournament) and now an avenue lined with a parade of plane trees shading a host of classy bars, delis and shops. At night the Born becomes one of Barcelona's biggest bar zones, as spirited locals frequent the drinking haunts, from old-style cocktail lounges to thumping music bars. Shoppers and browsers, meanwhile, scour the narrow, vaulted medieval alleys on either side of the *passeig* for boutiques and craft workshops – carrers Flassaders, Vidreria and Rec in particular are noted for clothes, shoes, jewellery and design galleries.

Antic Mercat del Born

Pl. Comercial 12, at Pg. del Born • ⓜ Jaume I/Barceloneta

The handsome **Antic Mercat del Born** (1873–76) was the biggest of Barcelona's nineteenth-century market halls. It was the city's main wholesale fruit and veg market until 1971, and was then due to be demolished but was saved by local protest. It remained empty for decades, but while work is now under way to turn the building into a neighbourhood cultural centre, it's been a long drawn-out business. Partly, this is because it soon became apparent that the market stood directly on top of the remains of eighteenth-century shops, factories, houses and taverns, dating from before the huge

4

works associated with the building of the nearby Ciutadella fortress and the Barceloneta district. It's a fascinating archeological discovery that the city is keen to preserve, and the remodelled interior (due to be completed by 2013) will incorporate a viewing area and exhibition about the excavations.

Parc de la Ciutadella

Daily 8am–dusk • Park entrance free • park entrances on Pg. de Picasso (Ⓜ Barceloneta, or a short walk from La Ribera) and Pg. de Pujades (Ⓜ Arc de Triomf); use Ⓜ Ciutadella-Vila Olímpica for direct access to the zoo

While you might escape to Montjuïc or the Collserola hills for the air, there's no beating the city's green lung, **Parc de la Ciutadella**, for a quick break from the downtown bustle. The park holds a full set of attractions – Catalunya's legislative

PARC DE LA CIUTADELLA

assembly, the **Parlament** (not open to the public), plant houses, natural science buildings and zoo (see p.76) – though on lazy summer days there's little incentive to do much more than stroll the garden paths and pilot rowboats across the ornamental lake. The name of the park recalls the Bourbon citadel that once stood here, erected by Felipe V to quell the local population after Barcelona's spirited resistance during the War of the Spanish Succession. A great part of La Ribera neighbourhood was brutally destroyed to make way for the fortress, and this symbol of authority survived uneasily until 1869, when the military moved base (the only surviving portion of the citadel, the much-altered Arsenal, has since 1980 housed the Catalan parliament building). The surrounding area was subsequently made into a park, which was chosen as the site of the 1888 **Universal Exhibition** – from which period dates a series of eye-catching buildings and monuments by the city's pioneering *modernista* architects.

Arc de Triomf

Pg. de Lluís Companys • ⓜ Arc de Triomf

The giant brick **Arc de Triomf**, Roman in scale, announces the architectural splendours to come in the park itself. Conceived as a bold statement of Catalan intent, it's studded with ceramic figures and motifs, and topped by two pairs of bulbous domes. The reliefs on the main facade show the city of Barcelona welcoming visitors to the 1888 Universal Exhibition.

Cascada

Parc de la Ciutadella • ⓜ Arc de Triomf

The first of the major projects undertaken inside the park was the **Cascada**, the monumental fountain in the northeast corner. It was designed by Josep Fontseré i Mestrès, the architect chosen to oversee the conversion of the former citadel grounds into a park, and his assistant in the work was the young Antoni Gaudí, then a student. The Baroque extravagance of the Cascada is suggestive of the flamboyant decoration that was later to become Gaudí's trademark. The best place to contemplate the fountain's tiers and swirls is from the small open-air **café-kiosk**. Near here you'll also find a lake, where you can **rent a rowboat** and paddle about among the ducks. Incidentally, Gaudí is also thought to have had a hand in the design of the Ciutadella's iron park gates.

Museu de Ciències Naturals

Pg. de Picasso • ⓦ museuciencies.bcn.cat • ⓜ Arc de Triomf

The city's Natural Science Museum has its public showcase, the Museu Blau, over at the Diagonal Mar Fòrum site (see p.87), but its genesis lies in two interesting buildings in Ciutadella park that are currently undergoing major renovation (completion expected in 2012). The Neoclassical **Museu Martorell**, which opened in 1882, was actually the first public museum to be built in the city, designed by leading architect of the day Antoni Rovira i Trias. For decades this housed the city's geological collections; the new permanent exhibition here will concentrate on the development of the natural sciences in Barcelona. The other building has always been a city favourite, a whimsical red-brick confection that was long the zoology museum. It's universally known as the **Castell dels Tres Dragons** (Three Dragons Castle), designed by *modernista* architect Lluís Domènech i Montaner and originally intended for use as the café-restaurant for the 1888 Universal Exhibition. It's going to become the research, study and conservation centre for the Natural Science Museum's geology and zoology collections.

Umbracle and Hivernacle

Pg. de Picasso • Both daily 8am–dusk • Free • ⓜ Arc de Triomf

The two real unsung glories of Ciutadella are its plant houses, arranged either side of the Museu Martorell. The imposing **Umbracle** (palm house) is a handsome structure with a barrelled wood-slat roof supported by cast-iron pillars, which allows shafts of light to play across the palms and ferns. Both materials and concept are echoed in the larger **Hivernacle** (conservatory), whose enclosed greenhouses are separated by a soaring glass-roofed terrace.

Parc Zoològic

Main entrance on c/de Wellington · Daily: March–May & Oct 10am–6pm; June–Sept 10am–7pm; Nov–Feb 10am–5pm · €16.50, under-12s €9.90, under-3s free · ☎ 932 256 780, ⓦ zoobarcelona.cat · Signposted from ⓂCiutadellaVila Olímpica, or tram T4 stops outside

The city zoo, the **Parc Zoològic**, takes up most of the southeastern part of Ciutadella park. It boasts 7500 animals from over four hundred different species – which is simply too many for a zoo that is still essentially nineteenth-century in character, confined to the formal grounds of a public park. Nonetheless, it's hugely popular with families, as there are mini-train and pony rides, a petting zoo and daily dolphin shows alongside the main animal attractions. The many endangered species on show include the Iberian wolf and big cats such as the Sri Lankan leopard, snow leopard and the Sumatran tiger. However, the zoo's days in its current form are numbered, since there's been a belated recognition that it needs to modernize. Over the next few years its animal areas and habitats will be completely remodelled as the zoo attempts to expand its education, conservation and research facilities, and there are advanced plans to move the marine animals to a new coastal zoo and wetlands area at the Diagonal Mar seashore.

Museu de Carrosses Fúnebres

C/de Sancho de Ávila 2 · Mon–Fri 10am–1pm & 4–6pm, Sat, Sun & hols 10am–1pm · Free · ☎ 934 841 700 · Ⓜ Marina, or a 15min walk from Ciutadella park

One of the city's more esoteric attractions – the **Museu de Carrosses Fúnebres** (Funerary Carriage Museum) – is located out on a limb, across the far side of Parc de la Ciutadella from La Ribera. You need to present yourself at the front desk of the Serveis Funeraris (funerary services) de Barcelona, a few metres along c/de Sancho de Ávila from Avinguda Meridiana (by the blue "Banc Sabadell" sign), from where you'll be escorted into the bowels of the building. The lights are thrown on to reveal a staggering set of 22 funerary carriages, each parked on its own cobbled stage, complete with ghostly attendants, horses and riders suspended in frozen animation. Used for city funeral processions from the end of the nineteenth century until the service was mechanized in the 1950s, when the silver Buick, also on display, came into use, most of the carriages and hearses are extravagantly decorated in gilt, black or white. Old photographs show some of them in use in the city's streets, while showcases highlight antique uniforms, mourning wear and formal riding gear.

PORT VELL

The waterfront

Perhaps the greatest recent transformation in the city has been along the waterfront, where harbour and ocean have once again been placed at the heart of Barcelona. Dramatic changes over the last two decades have shifted the cargo and container trade away to the south, opened up the old docksides as promenades and entertainment areas and landscaped the city's beaches to the north – it's as if a theatre curtain has been lifted to reveal that, all along, Barcelona had an urban waterfront of which it could be proud. The glistening harbourside merges seamlessly with the old town, with the museums and attractions of Port Vell just steps from the bottom of the Ramblas. No visit to the city, meanwhile, is complete without a seafood meal in the eighteenth-century fishing quarter of Barceloneta, followed by a stroll along the beachfront promenade as far as the showpiece Port Olímpic.

5

The city's **beaches** extend for 5km along the Barcelona waterfront, from Barceloneta in the city centre out to the River Besòs, which defines the northeastern city limits. Locals have taken to the sands in a big way – jogging, cycling and skating their length, and descending in force at the weekend for a leisurely lunch or late drink in one of scores of restaurants and bars. Though the main development is around the Port Olímpic, there are also spruced-up beaches further north, on either side of the old working-class neighbourhood of **Poble Nou**, whose pretty *rambla* makes for an offbeat diversion. Beyond here, the **Diagonal Mar** exhibition district might appear to be a journey too far for most visitors, but its bold urban scale is definitely worth seeing, especially since the opening of the Museu Blau, the Natural Science Museum's flagship attraction.

Plaça del Portal de la Pau

Ⓜ Drassanes

The Ramblas ends at **Plaça del Portal de la Pau**, coming up hard against the teeming traffic that runs along the harbourside road. The landmark Columbus monument is straight ahead in the middle of the traffic circle, with the quayside square beyond flanked by the **Port de Barcelona** (Port Authority) and **Duana** (Customs House) buildings. Away to the south is the **Moll de Barcelona**, a landscaped wharf leading to the Torre de Jaume I **cable-car station** and the **Estació Marítima**, where ferries leave for the Balearics. The large, bulbous building perched in the centre of the wharf is the city's **World Trade Centre**, housing a deluxe hotel, plus offices, convention halls, shops and restaurants.

Mirador de Colón

Pl. del Portal de la Pau · Daily 8.30am–8.30pm · €4, under-12s €3, under-4s free · Ⓜ Drassanes

Inaugurated just before the Universal Exhibition of 1888, the striking **Mirador de Colón** commemorates the visit made by Christopher Columbus (known locally as Cristóbal Colón) to Barcelona in June 1493. The explorer tops a grandiose, iron column, 52m high, guarded by lions at the base, around which unfold reliefs telling the story of his life and travels – here, if nowhere else, the old mercenary is still the "discoverer of America". A lift whisks you up to the enclosed *mirador* at Columbus's feet for terrific 360-degree city views – the narrow viewing platform, which tilts perceptibly outwards and downwards, is emphatically not for anyone without a head for heights.

Museu Marítim

Av. de les Drassanes · Daily 10am–8pm · Reduced admission during renovation works €2.50, under-7s free, plus free on Sun after 3pm · ☎ 933 429 920, Ⓦ mmb.cat · Ⓜ Drassanes

Barcelona's medieval shipyards, or **Drassanes**, were in continuous use – fitting and arming Catalunya's war fleet or trading vessels – until well into the eighteenth century.

ANOTHER WRONG TURN FOR COLUMBUS?

When the Italian-born navigator, **Christopher Columbus**, sailed into Barcelona harbour in 1493, he was received in style by the Catholic monarchs of Spain, Ferdinand and Isabella. In a bid for new and profitable trading routes, they had financed his voyage of exploration a year earlier, when Columbus had set out to chart a passage west to the Orient. He famously failed in this, as he failed also to reach the North American mainland (instead "discovering" the Bahamas, Cuba and Haiti), but Columbus did enough to enhance his reputation and by 1504 had made three more exploratory voyages. Later, nineteenth-century Catalan nationalists took the navigator to their hearts – if he wasn't exactly Catalan, he was the closest they had to a local Vasco da Gama – and so they put him on the pedestal that they thought he deserved. Awkwardly for the locals, the statue is actually pointing in the general direction of Libya, not North America, but as historian Robert Hughes puts it, at least "the sea is Catalan".

CONSELL DE CENT
DIPUTACIÓ
PASSEIG DE SANT JOAN
GRAN VIA DE LES CORTS CATALANES
NÁPOLS
PLAÇA DE TETUÁN
RONDA DE SANT PERE
AUSIAS MARC

PASSEIG DE LES CORTS CATALANES
MARINA
IBIZA
ZAMORA
AVINGUDA DE MERIDIANA

Marina Ⓜ

Museu de
Carrosses
Fúnebres

Barcelona
Nord
(Bus Station)

Bogatell Ⓜ

ALMOGÀVERS
PERE IV
PUJADES
LLULL
RAMON TURRÓ
DR. TRUETA
PAMPLONA
D'ICARIA

Llacuna Ⓜ

RAMBLA DE POBLENOU
BAC DE RODA

POBLE NOU

Cementiri
de Poble Nou

Diagonal Mar

PASSEIG DE CALVELL

Bogatell

Arc de Triomf Ⓜ

Arc de
Triomf

Palau de
Justicia

Parc
de la
Ciutadella

Castell dels
Tres Dragons

Hivernacle
Museu
Martorell

Museu
Picasso

VIA LAIETANA
MÉTODRÓ

Antic
Mercat
del Born

Jaume I Ⓜ

VIA LAIETANA

Santa
Maria
del Mar

Parc
Zoològic

Parlament de
Catalunya

PASSEIG DE PICASSO
COMERÇ
PASSEIG CIRCUMVALLACIÓ

Estació de
França

BARRI
GÒTIC

Palau
del Mar

Drassanes Ⓜ
AV. DE LES
DRASSANES

Mirador de Colón

PLAÇA
PORTAL
DE LA PAU

Drassanes
(Museu
Marítim)

Trasbordador Aeri

World
Trade
Centre

MOLL DE BARCELONA

PORT
VELL

IMAX

L'Aquàrium

Maremàgnum

PASSEIG DE COLOM

PASSEIG MARÍTIM

Barceloneta Ⓜ

MAQUINISTA

PL.
BARCELONETA

BARCELONETA

JOAN DE BORBÓ

ADMIRAL
AIXADA

Torre Sant
Sebastià

Club Natació
Atlètic Barceloneta

MOLL DE PONIENTE

PASSEIG MARÍTIM

Sant Sebastià

SEE 'PORT VELL AND BARCELONETA' MAP

PORT OLÍMPIC

AVINGUDA

Torre
Mapfre

Hotel
Arts

Ciutadella-
Vila Olímpica Ⓜ

RONDA LITORAL

ⓘ

Barceloneta

SEE 'PORT OLÍMPIC AND POBLE NOU' MAP

MOLL DE MESTRAL

MOLL DE GREGAL

Port
Olímpic

Nova Icaria

MAR MEDITERRÁNEO

N

● ACCOMMODATION
W Barcelona   1

0   500
metres

THE WATERFRONT

5

HARBOURSIDE RIDES BY SKY AND SEA

The most thrilling ride in the city centre is across the inner harbour on the cable car, the **Trasbordador Aeri** (departures every 15min, daily 10.30am–6pm, June–Sept until 8pm; €10 one-way, €15 return; ☎ 932 414 820), which sweeps right across the water from the Torre de Sant Sebastiá, at the foot of Barceloneta, to Montjuïc. There's normally a stop in the middle at Torre de Jaume I, in front of the World Trade Centre in Port Vell, but this is currently closed for long-term repairs. Expect queues for the cable car in summer and at weekends as the cars only carry about twenty people at a time. Note that strong winds can also close the ride.

From the quayside just beyond the foot of the Mirador de Colón, **Las Golondrinas** sightseeing boats and the Catamaran Orsom depart on regular trips throughout the year around the inner harbour (see p.26).

The unique stone-vaulted buildings make a fitting home for the city's **Museu Marítim** (Maritime Museum), though ongoing renovations (probably until 2013) currently limit access to one or two changing exhibitions that draw on the museum collections, and the shop, café and **Santa Eulàlia** exhibit.

Santa Eulàlia

Tues–Fri noon–5.30pm, Sat, Sun & hols 10am–5.30pm • €1, free with Museu Marítim ticket

Moored over on the Moll de la Fusta (beyond the harbour's swing bridge), the **Santa Eulàlia** is one of the Maritime Museum's showpiece exhibits. Dating from 1908, and previously named the *Carmen Flores*, the three-masted ocean schooner once made the run between Barcelona and Cuba. It's been fully restored since being acquired by the museum, and a short tour lets you walk the deck and view the interior. It still sails occasionally, too, on short harbour and coastal jaunts, with future tour dates posted on the museum website.

Port Vell

Ⓜ Drassanes/Barceloneta

Barcelona's remodelled inner harbour, known as **Port Vell** (Old Port), has its local critics – it's undoubtedly tourist-oriented, showy and expensive – but there's no denying the improvement made to what was formerly a decaying harbourside. The city's old timber wharf, for example, the **Moll de la Fusta**, re-emerged as a landscaped promenade with a note of humour injected by the addition of a giant fibreglass crayfish by Catalan designer Xavier Mariscal and, further on, the Roy Lichtenstein totem-pole sculpture known as *Barcelona Head*. From the Columbus statue end of the wharf, the wooden **Rambla de Mar** swing bridge strides across to the **Moll d'Espanya**, whose main features are the **Maremàgnum** mall and leisure complex, aquarium and IMAX cinema. From here, it's only a ten-minute walk down the wharf and around the **marina** to the **Palau de Mar** and the Catalan history museum.

Maremàgnum

Moll d'Espanya • Daily 10am–10pm • Ⓦ maremagnum.es • Ⓜ Drassanes

Maremàgnum is a typically bold piece of Catalan design, the soaring glass lines of the complex tempered by the surrounding undulating wooden walkways. Inside are two floors of gift shops and boutiques, plus a range of cafés and fast-food outlets; outside, benches and park areas provide fantastic views back across the harbour to the city.

L'Aquàrium

Moll d'Espanya • Daily: July & Aug 9.30am–11pm; Sept–June 9.30am–9pm, until 9.30pm at weekends • €18, under-12s €13, under-4s free, online discounts available • ☎ 932 217 474, Ⓦ aquariumbcn.com • Ⓜ Drassanes/Barceloneta

Anchoring Moll d'Espanya, **L'Aquàrium** drags in families and school parties throughout the year to see "a magical world, full of mystery". Or, to be more precise, to see eleven

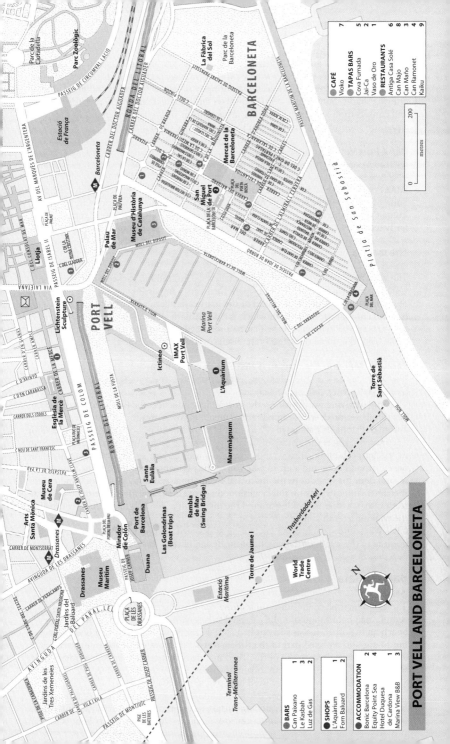

PORT VELL AND BARCELONETA

BARS
Can Paixano 1
Le Kasbah 3
Luz de Gas 2

SHOPS
L'Aquárium 1
Fom Baluard 2

ACCOMMODATION
Bonic Barcelona 2
Equity Point Sea 4
Hotel Duquesa
de Cardona 1
Marina View B&B 3

CAFÉ
Vioko 7

TAPAS BARS
Cova Fumada 5
Jai-Ca 2
Vaso de Oro 1

RESTAURANTS
Antiga Casa Solé 6
Can Majó 8
Can Maño 3
Can Ramonet 4
Kaiku 9

0   200
metres

Parc de la Ciutadella
Parc Zoològic
La Fàbrica del Sol
Parc de la Barceloneta

BARCELONETA

Estació de França

Barceloneta

Mercat de la Barceloneta

San Miquel del Port

Museu d'Història de Catalunya

Palau de Mar

Llotja

Lichtenstein Sculpture

PORT VELL

Marina Port Vell

Ictineo

IMAX Port Vell

L'Aquàrium

Platja de San Sebastià

Torre de Sant Sebastià

Església de la Mercè

Museu de Cera

Arts Santa Mònica

Drassanes

Museu Marítim

Mirador de Colón

Duana

Port de Barcelona

Las Golondrinas (Boat trips)

Rambla de Mar (Swing Bridge)

Santa Eulàlia

Maremàgnum

Torre de Jaume I

World Trade Centre

Estació Marítima

Transbordador Aeri

Terminal Trans-Mediterránea

N

5

thousand fish and sea creatures in 35 themed tanks representing underwater caves, tidal areas, tropical reefs and other maritime habitats. It's vastly overpriced and, despite the claims of excellence, it offers few new experiences, save perhaps the eighty-metre-long walk-through underwater tunnel which brings you face to face with gliding rays and cruising sharks. Some child-centred displays and activities and a nod towards ecology and conservation matters pad out the attractions before you're tipped out in the aquarium shop so they can part you from even more of your money.

IMAX Port Vell

Moll d'Espanya • Screenings daily 11am–10pm, later at weekends • From €8.70, or €12.20 for 2 films • ☎ 932 251 111, ⓦ imaxportvell.com • ⓂDrassanes/Barceloneta

IMAX Port Vell stands next to the aquarium, with three screens showing films virtually hourly in 3D or giant screen format. The themes are familiar – the mysteries of the human body, forces of nature, heroic exploration, alien adventure, etc – and tickets are fairly reasonably priced, but the films are in Spanish or Catalan only.

The marina

ⓂBarceloneta

The walk from Port Vell to Barceloneta takes you around the packed **marina**, where Catalans park their yachts like they park their cars – impossibly tightly and with plenty of gesticulation. A boat at the head of the marina has been converted into a floating bar, the *Luz de Gas* (see p.200), which is a particularly good place for a sundowner. Hawkers spread blankets on the marina promenade, selling jewellery and sunglasses, while behind is a line of seafood restaurants overlooking the water.

Palau de Mar and the Museu d'Història de Catalunya

Pl. de Pau Vila 3 • Tues–Sat 10am–7pm (Wed until 8pm), Sun & hols 10am–2.30pm • €4, under-18s €3, under-7s free, plus first Sun of month free • ☎ 932 254 700, ⓦ mhcat.net • ⓂBarceloneta

The only surviving warehouse on the Port Vell harbourside, the **Palau de Mar**, has been beautifully restored, with seafood restaurants in its lower arcade and the enterprising **Museu d'Història de Catalunya** (Catalunya History Museum) occupying the upper floors. The museum traces the history of Catalunya from the Stone Age to the present day, with its spacious exhibition areas wrapped around a wide atrium – there are **temporary shows** on the ground floor and a lift to take you to the **permanent displays** on the upper floors: second floor for year dot to the Industrial Revolution, and third for periods and events thereafter. You can pick up full English notes at the desk, and there's plenty to get your teeth into, whether it's poking around the interior of a Roman grain ship or comparing the rival nineteenth-century architectural plans for the Eixample. There's a dramatic Civil War section, while other fascinating asides shed light on matters as diverse as housing in the 1960s or the origins of the design of the Catalan flag.

Barceloneta

ⓂBarceloneta

There's no finer place for lunch on a sunny day than **Barceloneta**, an eighteenth-century neighbourhood of tightly packed streets with the harbour on one side and a **beach** on the other. It was laid out in 1755, where previously there had been only mud-flats, and replaced part of the Ribera district that was destroyed to make way for the Ciutadella fortress to the north. The long, narrow streets are broken at intervals by small squares and lined with abundantly windowed houses designed to give the sailors and fishing folk who originally lived here plenty of sun and fresh air.

Some original houses feature a decorative flourish, a sculpted balcony or a carved lintel, while in **Plaça de la Barceloneta** survives an eighteenth-century fountain and the Neoclassical church of **Sant Miquel del Port**. A block over in Plaça de la Font is the

5

MONTURIOL AND THE CATALAN SUBMARINE

Close to IMAX Port Vell, you can't fail to notice the full-sized replica of the fish-shaped submarine, the **Ictineo II** – the "fish-boat" – which was the work of self-taught scientist, engineer and inventor **Narcís Monturiol i Estarriol** (1819–85). Monturiol was born in Figueres in northeastern Catalunya but studied in Barcelona, soon falling in with radicals and revolutionaries. He set up a publishing company in 1846, espousing his beliefs in feminism, pacifism and utopian communism – radical ideas that saw Monturiol forced briefly into exile in the heady revolutionary days of 1848. This was a period in which scientific progress and social justice appeared as two sides of the same coin to utopians like Monturiol – indeed, his friend, the civil engineer Ildefons Cerdà, would later mastermind the building of Barcelona's Eixample on socially useful grounds.

Inspired by the harsh conditions in which Catalan coral fishermen worked, Monturiol conceived the idea of a **man-powered submarine**, which made its maiden voyage in Barcelona harbour on June 28, 1859. At 7m long, the first **Ictineo** could carry four or five men, and came to make more than fifty dives at depths of up to 20m, before its destruction in an accident. The construction of a vessel with an improved design was started in 1862 – the seventeen-metre-long *Ictineo II*, which was intended to be propelled by up to sixteen men. When trials showed that human power wasn't sufficient for the job, Monturiol installed a steam engine and the world's first steam-powered submarine was launched on October 22, 1867, diving to depths of up to 30m on thirteen separate runs (the longest lasting for over seven hours). However, the sub never managed to pay its way and when Monturiol's financial backers withdrew their support, the *Ictineo II* was seized by creditors and sold for scrap – the engine ended up in a paper mill.

Undaunted, Monturiol continued to come up with new inventions. With the submarines he had pioneered the use of the double hull, a technique still used today, while he also made advances in the manufacture of glues and gums, copying documents, commercial cigarette production and steam engine efficiency. Even so, he died in relative obscurity in 1885 and was buried in Barcelona, though his remains were later transferred to his home town. There's a memorial to Monturiol on the main *rambla* in Figueres, while in Barcelona he is remembered by a simple plaque at the Cementiri de Poble Nou.

stylish local market, **Mercat de la Barceloneta** (open from 7am, closed Mon & Sat afternoons), beautifully refurbished in 2007 and boasting a couple of excellent bars and restaurants. Barceloneta's famous seafood restaurants are found right across the neighbourhood but most characteristically lined along the harbourside **Passeig Joan de Borbó**, where for most of the year you can sit outside and enjoy your meal.

La Fàbrica del Sol

C/de Ginebra 52 • Tues–Fri 10am–2pm & 4–8pm, Sat 10am–2pm & 4–7pm (Aug Tues–Fri 10am–2pm only) • Free • ☎ 932 564 430, ⓦ bcn.cat/mediambient • Ⓜ Barceloneta

Inside the yellow-painted, red-brick building on the edge of the Parc de la Barceloneta – once the city's gas works – the local council has established **La Fàbrica del Sol**, a pioneering sustainable eco-centre that takes a close look at green living in all its guises, from recycling to transport. There's an introductory film (in English) and you can borrow some English notes at the entrance, but the displays, gadgets and exhibits are all fairly self-explanatory – you've got to love the elevator that weighs its passengers so as to use only the exact amount of energy required to lift them up to the roof terrace to see the building's garden and solar thermal system. From here you also get a view of the park's other notable feature, its whimsical *modernista* water tower (1905), rising like a minaret above the palms.

Platja de Sant Sebastià and Passeig Marítim

Ⓜ Barceloneta

Barceloneta's beach, **Platja de Sant Sebastià** is the first in the series of sandy city beaches that stretches northeast from here along the coast as far as the River Besòs. It curves out

5

BEACH BUSINESS

On the boardwalk arcade, in front of the Hospital del Mar, the city council operates a beach visitor centre, the **Centre de la Platja** (March–May Sat 11am–1.30pm & 4–6.30pm, Sun & holidays 11am–1.30pm; June–Sept daily 10am–7pm; ☎ 932 210 348, ⓦ www.bcn.cat/platges), as a kind of one-stop shop for information and activities along the seafront. There's a programme of seafront walks and activities, a small summer lending library for beach reading and Frisbees, volleyball and beach tennis gear available for pick-up games on the sand.

---

past the indoor and outdoor swimming pools of the *Club Natació* (see p.224) to the landmark, sail-shaped **W Barcelona** hotel, designed by Catalan architect Ricardo Bofill. Meanwhile, at the Barceloneta end there are beach bars, outdoor cafés and public sculptures, while a double row of palms backs the **Passeig Marítim** esplanade that runs above the sands as far as the Port Olímpic (a 15min walk). Just before the port there rises the dramatic latticed funnel of wood and steel that is the **Parc Recerca Biomèdica de Barcelona** (PRBB), the city's biomedical research centre.

Port Olímpic

Ⓜ Ciutadella-Vila Olímpica

Approaching the Olympic port along the Passeig Marítim, the shimmering golden mirage above the promenade slowly reveals itself to be a **huge copper fish** (courtesy of Frank O. Gehry, architect of the Bilbao Guggenheim). It's the emblem of the huge seafront development constructed for the 1992 Olympics – site of many of the Olympic watersports events – and is backed by the city's two tallest buildings, the **Torre Mapfre** and the steel-framed **Hotel Arts Barcelona**, both 154m high. The bulk of the action is contained within two wharves: the **Moll de Mestral** has a lower deck by the marina lined with cafés, bars and *terrassas*, while the **Moll de Gregal** sports a double-decker tier of seafood restaurants. The whole zone turns into a full-on resort in summer, backed by a series of class-conscious clubs along Passeig Marítim that appeal to the local rich kids and A-list celebs.

City beaches

From Port Olímpic (Ⓜ Ciutadella-Vila Olímpica) it's a 15min walk along the promenade to Bogatell beach, or around 1hr all the way to Parc del Fòrum

Beyond the Port Olímpic, the city **beaches** continue right the way up to Parc del Fòrum and Diagonal Mar, split into separate named sections (Nova Icària, Bogatell, Mar Bella, Nova Mar Bella and Llevant), each with showers, playgrounds and open-air café-bars. It's a pretty extraordinary leisure facility to find so close to a city centre – the water might not be as clean as it could be, but the sands are regularly swept and replenished, while joggers, cyclists and bladers have one of the Med's best views for company.

Poble Nou

Ⓜ Poble Nou (found at the junction of c/Pujades and c/Bilbao, one block east of Rambla del Poble Nou), or bus #36 from Port Olímpic

The next neighbourhood along from the Port Olímpic is **Poble Nou** (New Village), a largely nineteenth-century industrial area that has been in the throes of redevelopment since the early 1990s. The authorities have given the regeneration area a suitably contemporary epithet, **22@Barcelona** (ⓦ 22barcelona.com), and are currently overseeing the transformation of 120 city blocks, straddling 200 hectares of land, into "the innovation district". The redevelopment of old factories and the like has already had a significant effect, as some of the city's hottest clubs, galleries and art spaces are now found here. You can come here directly on the metro, but it's far nicer to walk along the promenade from the Port Olímpic (15min) to Poble Nou's spruced-up **beaches** – Bogatell, Mar Bella and Nova Mar Bella – before crossing the main highway to reach the neighbourhood's main spine, Rambla del Poble Nou.

Rambla del Poble Nou

Ⓜ Poble Nou

Poble Nou may be in the throes of dramatic change, but the main avenue still ticks along largely unaffected. Pretty, tree-lined **Rambla del Poble Nou** remains entirely local in character – no cardsharps or human statues here – with a run of modest shops, cafés and restaurants, including the classic milk and juice bar of *El Tío Ché* (see p.189), which serves orange or lemon *granissat* (crushed ice) and their famous *orxata* (milky tiger-nut drink).

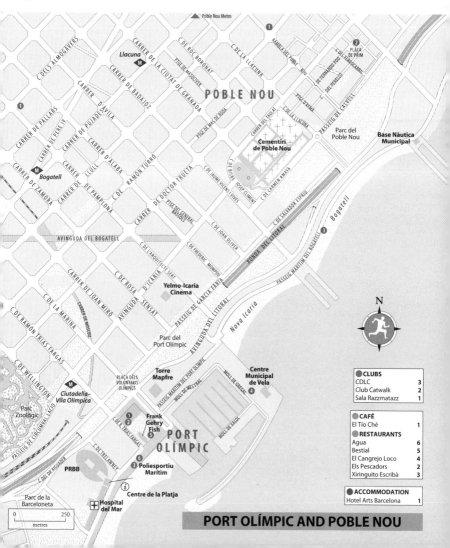

PORT OLÍMPIC AND POBLE NOU

5

Cementiri de Poble Nou

Av. d'Icaria • Daily 8am–6pm • Ⓜ Bogatell or bus #36 from Port Olímpic

The vast nineteenth-century **Cementiri de Poble Nou** has its tombs set in walls 7m high – the families that tend them have to climb great stepladders to reach the uppermost tiers. With traffic noise muted by the high walls, and birdsong accompanying a stroll around the flower-lined pavements, quiet courtyards, sculpted angels and tiny chapels, this village of the dead is a rare haven in contemporary Barcelona.

Diagonal Mar

Ⓜ El Maresme Fòrum, or tram T4 to Fòrum via Glòries and Av. Diagonal

The waterfront district north of Poble Nou was developed in the wake of the Universal Forum of Cultures Expo, held here in 2004. It's promoted as **Diagonal Mar**, anchored by the Diagonal Mar shopping mall, and with several classy hotels, convention centres and exhibition halls grouped nearby. Everything here is on a grand scale, starting with Jacques Herzog's dazzling blue biscuit tin of a building hovering – seemingly unsupported – above the ground. This houses the main exhibitions of the Natural Science Museum (the **Museu Blau**), while the vast, landscaped area beyond is one of the

city's showpiece urban leisure projects, the **Parc del Fòrum**. The district can still seem a bit soulless at times – hot as Hades in summer, buffeted by biting winter winds – but it's worth the metro ride if you're interested in heroic-scale public projects. The tram comes down here too, so you could always glide there or back via Avinguda Diagonal and Glòries to see more of Barcelona in transformation.

Museu Blau

Pl. Leonardo da Vinci 4–5, Parc del Fòrum • June–Sept Tues–Sun & hols 10am–9pm; Oct–May Tues–Fri 10am–7pm, Sat, Sun & hols 10am–8pm • €7, includes entrance to Jardí Botànic at Montjuïc, under-16s free, plus free first Sun of the month & every Sun after 3pm • ☎ 932 652 200, ⦿ museuciencies.bcn.cat • Ⓜ El Maresme Fòrum, or tram T4 to Fòrum

To unravel the mysteries of life, the universe and everything you need travel no further than the Natural Science Museum's bold reboot of its heritage collections, which were previously displayed in Ciutadella park. The million-strong collection of rocks, fossils, plants and animals – from the smallest microbe to a giant whale skeleton – have a state-of-the-art home in the visually stunning **Museu Blau** (Blue Museum), whose permanent exhibition – Planeta Vida (Planet Life) – plots a journey through the history of life on earth. It's heavily focused on evolutionary, whole-earth, Gaia principles, with plenty of entertaining, interactive bells and whistles to guide you through topics as diverse as sex and reproduction and conservation of the environment. There are also special exhibitions, a separate hands-on children's section (the Niu de Ciència, or "science nest", for under-6s) and regular family activities, plus shop, restaurant and a free-access media library – the latter the place where you can, for example, listen to birdsong, animal and habitat sounds stored in the fascinating Natura Sonora sound library.

Parc del Fòrum

Ⓜ El Maresme Fòrum, or tram T4 to Fòrum via Glòries and Av. Diagonal

The boast about Diagonal Mar's main open space, the **Parc del Fòrum**, is that it's the second largest square in the world (150,000 square metres) after Beijing's Tiananmen Square. This immense, undulating expanse spreads towards the sea, culminating in a giant solar-panelled canopy that overlooks the marina, beach and park areas. In summer, temporary bars, dancefloors, open-air cinema and chill-out zones are established, while the city authorities have shifted some of the bigger annual music festivals and events down here to inject a bit of life outside convention time.

Montjuïc

You'll need at least a day to see Montjuïc, the steep hill and park rising over the city to the southwest. It takes its name from the Jewish community that once settled on its slopes, and there's been a castle on the heights since the mid-seventeenth century. But it's as a cultural leisure park that contemporary Montjuïc is positioned, anchored around the heavyweight art collections in the Museu Nacional d'Art de Catalunya (MNAC). This unsurpassed national collection of Catalan art is supplemented by works in two other superb galleries, namely international contemporary art in the Caixa Forum and that of the famous Catalan artist Joan Miró in the Fundació Joan Miró. In addition, there are separate archeological, ethnological, military and theatrical museums, quite apart from the buildings and stadiums associated with the 1992 Olympics, which was centred on the heights of Montjuïc.

As late as the 1890s, the hill was nothing more than a collection of private farms and woodland on the edge of the old town, though some landscaping had already taken place by the time Montjuïc was chosen as the site of the **International Exhibition** of 1929. The slopes were then laid with gardens, terraces and fountains, while monumental Neoclassical buildings were added to the north side, many of them later adapted as museums. The famous **Poble Espanyol** (Spanish Village) – a hybrid park of collected Spanish buildings – is the most extraordinary relic of the Exhibition, while the various lush **gardens** still provide enjoyment and respite from the crowds. Above all, perhaps, there are the city and ocean views to savour from this most favoured of Barcelona's hills: from the steps in front of the Museu Nacional, from the castle ramparts, from the Olympic terraces or from the cable cars that zigzag up the steepest slopes of Montjuïc.

ARRIVAL AND GETTING AROUND

Metro For easy access to Caixa Forum, Poble Espanyol and the Museu Nacional d'Art de Catalunya (MNAC) use ⓜ Espanya (follow exit signs for "Fira/Exposició"). The Olympic area can then be reached by escalators behind MNAC.

Funicular The Funicular de Montjuïc (every 10min: April–Oct Mon–Fri 7.30am–10pm, Sat, Sun & hols 9am–10pm; Nov–March Mon–Fri 7.30am–8pm, Sat, Sun & hols 9am–8pm; €1.45, transport tickets and passes valid; ⓦ tmb.cat) departs from inside the station at ⓜ Paral.lel and takes a couple of minutes to ascend the hill. The upper station on Av. de Miramar is only a few minutes' walk from the Fundació Joan Miró, or you can switch to the Montjuïc cable car or bus services.

Cross-harbour cable car The Transbordador Aeri from Barceloneta (departures every 15min: daily 10.30am–6pm,

June–Sept until 8pm; €10 one way/€15 return; ☎ 932 414 820) drops you by the Jardins de Miramar, from where it's a 10min walk to the Montjuïc cable car and funicular stations, and another five to the Fundació Joan Miró.

Montjuïc cable car The Teleferic de Montjuïc (daily April, May & Oct 10am–7pm, June–Sept 10am–9pm, Nov–March 10am–6pm; €6.50 one way/€9.30 return, under-12s €5/6.70, under-4s free; ⓦ tmb.cat), from Av. de Miramar whisks you up to the castle and back in automated eight-seater gondolas.

Bus services City bus #193 (transport tickets and passes valid) covers a circular route around the main Montjuïc attractions, departing from a stop on Av. de la Reina Maria Cristina, outside ⓜ Espanya. The sightseeing, hop-on-hop-off Bus Turístic follows a similar route.

INFORMATION

Timing your visit Montjuïc covers a wide area, so if you're intent on covering everything it might be better to make two separate visits – MNAC, Poble Espanyol and the Olympic area on one day, and Fundació Joan Miró, the cable car and the castle on the other. From ⓜ Espanya, it takes a good hour to walk on the road around the hill, past Poble Espanyol, the Olympic area and Fundació Joan Miró to the cross-harbour cable-car station at the far end of Montjuïc. Escalators up the hill between MNAC and the Olympic area cut out the worst of the slog. Walking up the steep hill all the way to the castle is not advised in hot weather (though there are steps through the gardens and between the roads) – use the cable car.

Tickets The Barcelona Card, Articket and Arqueoticket (see p.27) and Bus Turístic pass (p.26) provide discounted entry into Montjuïc's museums, galleries and attractions.

Eating and drinking Places to eat are thin on the ground, though there are good cafés in Caixa Forum, Fundació Joan Miró and MNAC, outdoor snack bars at the castle and on the slopes below MNAC and a restaurant with outdoor terrace at the Font del Gat in the Jardins Laribal, below the Fundació Joan Miró. There are also plenty of decent restaurants and bars in the neighbouring *barri* of Poble Sec.

Plaça d'Espanya

ⓜ Espanya

Gateway to the 1929 International Exhibition was the vast **Plaça d'Espanya**, based on plans by noted architect Josep Puig i Cadafalch. Arranged around a huge Neoclassical fountain, the square is unlike any other in Barcelona, a radical departure from the *modernisme* that was so in vogue elsewhere in the city. It's ringed by landmarks, notably the majestic former bullring, now shopping and leisure centre Arenas de Barcelona (see p.115), and the striking twin towers, 47m high, that stand at the foot

6

FLYING THE FLAG

Simplest of architect Josep Puig i Cadafalch's ideas for the ceremonial gateway to Montjuïc at Plaça d'Espanya were **four 20m-high columns**, erected in 1919 on a raised site below the future Palau Nacional. Who could possibly object? The authoritarian government of General Primo de Rivera, as it happened, which knew perfectly well that noted Catalan nationalist Puig i Cadafalch meant the columns to represent the four stripes of the *senyera*, the Catalan flag. Down they came in 1928, to be replaced by the Magic Fountain, and not until 2010 were the columns (reconstructed using the original plans) to be seen again in public – erected (across from the fountain) by the city government as "an act of memory" and symbol of freedom and democracy.

---

of the imposing **Avinguda de la Reina Maria Cristina**. This avenue spears up towards Montjuïc, and is lined by huge exhibition halls used for trade fairs. At the end of the avenue is Plaça de Carles Buïgas, from where monumental steps (and modern escalators) ascend the hill to the Palau Nacional (home of MNAC), past water cascades and under the flanking walls of two grand Viennese-style pavilions. The higher you climb, the better the views, while a few café-kiosks put out seats on the way up to MNAC.

Font Màgica

Pl. de Carles Buïgas • May–Sept Thurs–Sun 9–11.30pm; Oct–April Fri & Sat only 7–9pm • Free

Things were certainly different in 1929, when mere whooshing water was enough to wow the crowds attending that year's International Exhibition. On selected evenings, the **Font Màgica** (Magic Fountain) at the foot of the Montjuïc steps still does its stuff, forming the centrepiece of what is now an impressive, if slightly kitsch, sound-and-light show, with sprays and sheets of brightly coloured water dancing to the strains of Holst and Abba. The fountain is also the site of a spectacular firework, music and laser show at the close of each year's Mercè festival in September.

Caixa Forum

Av. de Francesc Ferrer i Guàrdia 6–8 • Daily 10am–8pm (Sat until 10pm) • Free • ☎ 934 768 600, ⓦ fundacio.lacaixa.es • Ⓜ Espanya

Caixa Forum is a terrific arts and cultural centre set within the old *modernista* Casamarona textile factory, originally built in 1911 by Josep Puig i Cadafalch. The subsequent renovation and expansion under the auspices of the Fundació La Caixa has produced a remarkable building, entered beneath twin iron-and-glass canopies representing spreading trees. The exhibition halls were fashioned from the former factory buildings, whose external structure was left untouched – girders, pillars, brickwork and crenellated walls appear at every turn. The undulating roof (signposted "terrats") offers unique views, while the high Casamarona tower, etched in blue and yellow tiling, is as readily recognizable as the huge Miró starfish logos emblazoned across the building.

A permanent exhibition covers the history and design of the building, while other galleries are given over to the foundation's contemporary international **art collection**, which focuses on the period from the 1980s to the present – works are shown in partial rotation. In addition, there's an excellent free programme of changing **exhibitions** across all aspects of the arts – recent exhibitions have highlighted subjects as diverse as archeological treasures from Saudi Arabia and the films of Charlie Chaplin. There's also the Mediateca multimedia space, plus an arts bookshop, children's activities and a 400-seat auditorium for music, art and literary events. The **café** occupies a converted space within the old factory walls, and serves breakfast and light meals.

Pavelló Mies van der Rohe

Av. de Francesc Ferrer i Guàrdia 7, opposite Caixa Forum • Mon 4–8pm, Tues–Sun 10am–8pm • €4.60, under-18s free • ☎ 934 234 016, 🌐 miesbcn.com • Ⓜ Espanya

The German contribution to the 1929 International Exhibition was a pavilion designed by Ludwig Mies van der Rohe and reconstructed in 1986 by Catalan architects. Used as a reception room during the Exhibition, the **Pavelló Mies van der Rohe** is considered a major example of modern rationalist architecture. The pavilion has a startlingly beautiful conjunction of hard straight lines with watery surfaces, its dark-green polished onyx alternating with shining glass. It's open to visitors but unless there's an exhibition in place (a fairly regular occurrence), there is little to see inside save Mies van der Rohe's iconic tubular steel *Barcelona Chair*, though you can buy postcards and books from the small shop and debate quite how much you want a Mies mousepad or a "Less is More" T-shirt.

6

Poble Espanyol

Av. de Francesc Ferrer i Guàrdia 13 • Mon 9am–8pm, Tues–Thurs 9am–2am, Fri 9am–4am, Sat 9am–5am, Sun 9am–midnight; workshops daily 10am–6/8pm, depending on season • €9, under-4s free, family ticket €20, night ticket €5.50, combined ticket with MNAC €12 • ☎ 935 086 300, 🌐 poble-espanyol.com • Ⓜ Espanya and 800m walk, or bus #193 or #50 from Av. de la Reina Maria Cristina

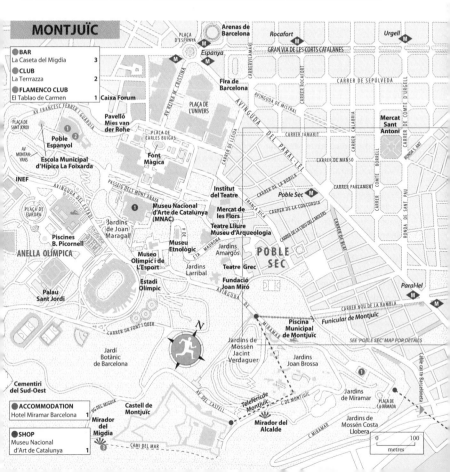

MONTJUÏC

● BAR
La Caseta del Migdia — 3
● CLUB
La Terrrazza — 2
● FLAMENCO CLUB
El Tablao de Carmen — 1

■ ACCOMMODATION
Hotel Miramar Barcelona — 1

■ SHOP
Museu Nacional d'Art de Catalunya — 1

The **Poble Espanyol**, or Spanish Village, was an inspired concept for the International Exhibition of 1929 – a complete village consisting of streets and squares with reconstructions of famous or characteristic buildings from all over Spain, such as the fairy-tale medieval walls of Ávila through which you enter. "Get to know Spain in one hour" is what's promised and it's nowhere near as cheesy as you might think. The echoing main square is lined with cafés, while the surrounding streets and alleys contain around forty workshops, where you can see engraving, weaving, pottery and other crafts. Inevitably, it's one huge shopping experience – castanets to Lladró porcelain, religious icons to Barcelona soccer shirts – and prices are inflated, but children will love it (they can run free as there's no traffic) and there are plenty of family activities.

Get to the village early to enjoy it in relatively crowd-free circumstances – once the tour groups arrive, it becomes a bit of a scrum. You could always come instead at the other end of the day, to venues like *Tablao de Carmen* for flamenco shows (see p.208) or *La Terrrazza* dance club (see p.201), when the village transforms into a vibrant centre of Barcelona nightlife.

Museu Nacional d'Art de Catalunya (MNAC)

Palau Nacional: Tues–Sat 10am–7pm, Sun & hols 10am–2.30pm • €8.50, ticket valid 48hr, annual pass €14, under-16s & first Sun of the month free; special exhibitions: varied charges apply • ☎ 936 220 376, ⓦ www.mnac.cat • Ⓜ Espanya, or bus #193 from Av. de la Reina Maria Cristina

The towering, domed **Palau Nacional**, set back on Montjuïc at the top of the long flight of steps from the fountains, was the flagship building of Barcelona's 1929 International Exhibition. Used for the opening ceremony, the palace was due to be demolished once the expo was over, but gained a reprieve and ultimately became home to one of Spain's great museums – the **Museu Nacional d'Art de Catalunya** (**MNAC**), showcasing a thousand years of Catalan art in stupendous surroundings.

The museum's scope is such that it can be difficult to know where to start, but if time is limited it's recommended you concentrate on the medieval collection. It's split into two main sections, one dedicated to **Romanesque** art and the other to **Gothic** – periods in which Catalunya's artists were pre-eminent in Spain. MNAC also has impressive holdings of European **Renaissance and Baroque** art, as well as an unsurpassed collection of **nineteenth- and twentieth-century Catalan art** (up until the 1940s; everything from the 1950s onwards is covered by MACBA in the Raval). In addition, there's a changing roster of blockbuster exhibitions and special shows based on the museum's archives. There's also a **café-bar**, gift shop and art **bookshop** in the gloriously restored oval hall, a bar service on the terrace and a separate museum restaurant with more extraordinary views over the city.

The Romanesque collection

From the eleventh century onwards, great numbers of sturdy Romanesque churches were built in the high Catalan Pyrenees as the Christian Reconquest spread. Medieval Catalan studios decorated the churches with extraordinary biblical frescoes, with even the most remote Pyrenean valleys boasting lavish masterpieces. However, by the nineteenth century many of these churches had been ruined by renovations or lay abandoned, and not until 1919 was a concerted effort made to preserve the frescoes for future generations, by removing them to a museum where they could be better displayed.

Today, they are imaginatively presented in reconstructions of the original interiors, so you can see exactly where the frescoes would have been placed in the church buildings. For the most part they have a vibrant, raw quality, best exemplified by those taken from churches in the Boí valley in the Catalan Pyrenees. In the apse of the early twelfth-century church of Sant Climent in Taüll, the so-called **Master of Taüll** painted an extraordinarily powerful *Christ in Majesty*, combining a Byzantine hierarchical

THE BRILLIANT FLOWERING OF CATALAN ART

Between about 1850 and 1940 Catalan art entered a modern golden age. Break-out artist was **Marià Fortuny i Marsal** – often regarded as the earliest *modernista* artist, and certainly the first Catalan painter known widely abroad, having exhibited to great acclaim in Paris and Rome. He specialized in minutely detailed pictures, often of exotic subjects – his set-piece *Battle of Tetuan*, for example, was based on a visit to Morocco in 1859 to observe the war there. The main name in contemporary Catalan Realism was **Ramon Martí i Alsina**, while the master of nineteenth-century Catalan landscape painting was **Joaquim Veyreda i Vila**, founder of the "Olot School" (Olot being a town in northern Catalunya), whose members were influenced both by the work of the early Impressionists and by the distinctive volcanic scenery of the Olot region.

However, it wasn't until the emergence of **Ramon Casas i Carbó** (whose famous picture of himself and Pere Romeu on a tandem once hung on the walls of *Els Quatre Gats*) and **Santiago Rusiñol i Prats** that Catalan art acquired its first contemporary art superstars, taking their cue from the very latest in European styles, whether the symbolism of Whistler or the vibrant social observation of Toulouse-Lautrec. Hot on their heels came a new generation of artists – Josep Maria Sert, Marià Pidelaserra i Brias, Ricard Canals i Llambí and others – who were strongly influenced by the scene in contemporary Paris. The two brightest stars of the period, though, were **Joaquim Mir i Trinxet**, whose highly charged landscapes tended towards the abstract, and **Isidre Nonell i Monturiol**, who from 1902 until his early death in 1911 painted sombre naturalistic studies of impoverished gypsy communities.

The other dominant contemporary trend was *noucentisme*, a style at once more classical and less consciously flamboyant than *modernisme* – witness the portraits and landscapes of **Joaquim Sunyer i Miró**, perhaps the best known *noucentista* artist, and the work of sculptors like **Pau Gargallo i Catalán**.

composition with the imposing colours and strong outlines of contemporary manuscript illuminators. Look out for details such as the leper, to the left of the Sant Climent altar, patiently allowing a dog to lick his sores. Frescoes from other churches explore a variety of themes, from heaven to hell, with the displays complemented by sculptures, altar panels, woodcarvings, religious objects and furniture retrieved from the mouldering churches themselves.

The Gothic collection

The evolution from the Romanesque to the Gothic period was marked by a move from murals to painting on wood, and by the depiction of more naturalistic figures in scenes showing the lives of the saints, and later in portraits of kings and patrons of the arts. In the early part of the period, the Catalan and Valencian schools particularly were influenced by contemporary Italian styles, and you'll see some outstanding altarpieces, tombs and church decoration. Later began the International Gothic or "1400" style in which the influences became more widespread; the important figures of this movement were the fifteenth-century artists **Jaume Huguet** and **Lluís Dalmau**. Works from the end of this period show the strong influence of contemporary Flemish painting, in the use of denser colours, the depiction of crowd scenes and a concern for perspective. The last Catalan artist of note here is the so-called **Master of La Seu d'Urgell**, represented by a number of works, including a fine series of six paintings (Christ, the Virgin Mary, Sts Peter, Paul and Sebastian, and Mary Magdalene) that once formed the covers of an organ.

The Renaissance and Baroque collections

Many of the **Renaissance** and **Baroque** works on display have come from private collections bequeathed to the museum, notably by conservative politician Francesc Cambó and Madrid's Thyssen-Bornemisza. Selections from these bequests rate their own rooms within the Renaissance and Baroque galleries, while the other rooms in this section trace artistic development from the early sixteenth to the eighteenth century.

Major European artists displayed include Peter Paul Rubens, Giovanni Battista Tiepolo, Jean Honoré Fragonard, Francisco de Goya, El Greco, Francisco de Zurbarán and Diego Velázquez, though the museum is of course keen to play up Catalan works of the period, which largely absorbed the prevailing European influences – thus Barcelona artist **Antoni Viladomat** (1678–1755), whose twenty paintings of St Francis, executed for a monastery, are shown here in their entirety. However, more familiar to most will be the masterpieces of the Spanish Golden Age, notably Velázquez's *Saint Paul* and Zurbarán's *Immaculate Conception*.

The modern art collection

MNAC ends on a high note with its unsurpassed **nineteenth- and twentieth-century Catalan art** collection, which is particularly good on *modernista* and *noucentista* painting and sculpture (see box, p.93), the two dominant schools of the period. Rooms highlight both individual artists and genres, shedding light on the development of art in an exciting period of Catalunya's history. The works provide a rich, varied experience, ranging from intricate Barcelona street scenes to *modernista* interior design (including furniture by Gaudí), while there are also fascinating diversions into avant-garde sculpture and historical photography.

Museu Etnològic

Pg. de Santa Madrona 16–22 • Tues–Sat 10am–6pm (Oct–May Tues, Thurs & Sat 10am–7pm, Wed & Fri 10am–2pm), Sun 10am–2pm & 3–8pm • €3.50, free Sun after 3pm • ☎ 934 246 807, ⓦ museuetnologic.bcn.cat • Ⓜ Espanya/Poble Sec, or bus #193 from Av. de la Reina Maria Cristina

The city's ethnological museum boasts extensive cultural collections from across the globe, particularly the Amazon region, Papua New Guinea, pre-Hispanic America, Australia, Morocco and Ethiopia. However, there are simply too many pieces to show at any one time, so the museum has rotating exhibitions, which usually last for a year or two and concentrate on a particular subject or geographical area. Refreshingly, Spain and its regions aren't neglected, which means that there's usually a focus on the minutiae of rural Spanish life or an examination of subjects like medieval carving or early industrialization. For these exhibits, the museum draws on the work of Spanish ethnographers such as Ramon Violant who spent much of the 1940s recording the daily routine of inhabitants of the Pyrenees.

Museu d'Arqueologia de Catalunya

Pg. de Santa Madrona 39–41 • Tues–Sat 9.30am–7pm, Sun & hols 10am–2.30pm • €3, under-16s & last Sun of the month free • ☎ 934 232 129, ⓦ www.mac.cat • Ⓜ Espanya/Poble Sec, or bus #193 from Av. de la Reina Maria Cristina

For the early and classical-era history of the land now known as Catalunya you shouldn't miss the **Museu d'Arqueologia de Catalunya**, whose rich archeological collection spans the centuries from the Stone Age to the time of the Visigoths. Dramatic finds from the most famous of the region's archeological sites are concentrated here, notably pieces from the Greek site at Empúries on the Costa Brava, including a replica of the renowned marble statue of Asclepius, Greek god of medicine, which dominates the central rotunda. The Second Punic War (218–201 BC) saw the Carthaginians expelled from Iberia by the Romans, who made their provincial capital at Tarragona (Tarraco), with a secondary outpost at Barcelona (Barcino). There's some fine Roman glassware and mosaic work on display, while an upper floor interprets life in **Barcino** itself through a collection of tombstones, statues, inscriptions and friezes, which were found all over the city. Some of the stonework is remarkably vivid, depicting the faces of some of Barcino's inhabitants as clearly as the day they were carved.

CLOCKWISE FROM TOP LEFT CASTELL DE MONTJUÏC (P.100); FONT MÀGICA (P.90); MONTJUÏC CABLE CAR (P.89) >

6

TEATRE GREC AND THE BARCELONA FESTIVAL

Montjuïc takes centre-stage each year during Barcelona's annual summer cultural festival (ⓦ barcelonafestival.com), known locally as the Grec, when arias soar from the open-air stage of the **Teatre Grec**, a Greek theatre cut into a former quarry on the Poble Sec side of the hill. Starting in late June (and running throughout July and August), the festival incorporates drama, music and dance, with the opening sessions and some of the most atmospheric events staged in the theatre, from Shakespearean productions to shows by avant-garde performance artists. These can be magical nights – a true Barcelona experience – though you'll need to be quick off the mark for tickets, which usually go on sale in May.

La Ciutat del Teatre

C/de Lleida · ⓜ Poble Sec

At the foot of Montjuïc, on the eastern slopes, the theatre area known as **La Ciutat del Teatre** occupies a back corner of the old working-class neighbourhood of Poble Sec. Passeig de Santa Madrona runs down here from MNAC, passing the ethnological and archeological museums, or there are more direct steps descending the hillside.

The theatre buildings that make up La Ciutat del Teatre sit in a tight huddle off c/de Lleida. Here you'll find the **Mercat de les Flores** – once a flower market, now a centre for dance and the "movement arts" – and progressive **Teatre Lliure** ("Free Theatre") occupying the spaghetti-western-style Palau de l'Agricultura premises built for the 1929 Exhibition. Walk through the terracotta arch from c/de Lleida, and off to the left is the far sleeker **Institut del Teatre**, with its sheer walls contrasting markedly with the neighbourhood's cheap housing, whose laundry is strung just metres away from the gleaming Theatre City. The institute brings together the city's major drama and dance schools, and various conservatories, libraries and study centres. Our "Theatre and cabaret" section has more details about performances, events and festivals at all these venues (see p.209).

Poble Sec

ⓜ Poble Sec/Paral.lel

Lying immediately below Montjuïc, confined by the hill on one side and the busy Avinguda del Paral.lel on the other, is the neighbourhood of **Poble Sec**, or "Dry Village", so called because it had no water supply until the nineteenth century. It's a complete contrast to the landscaped slopes behind it – a grid of contoured narrow streets, down-to-earth grocery stores, bakeries, local shops and good-value restaurants. Asian immigrants have stamped their mark on many of the neighbourhood stores and businesses, while Poble Sec is also emerging as an "off-Raval" nightlife destination, with its fashionable bars and music clubs – pedestrianized **Carrer de Blai** is the epicentre of the scene.

Refugi 307

C/Nou de la Rambla 169 · Guided visits Sat & Sun at 11am, noon & 1pm · €3 · ☎ 932 562 100, ⓦ museuhistoria.bcn.cat · ⓜ Paral.lel

Many visitors never set foot in Poble Sec, though the opening of one of the city's old Civil War air-raid shelters provides a compelling reason to make the short journey across town. **Refugi 307** was dug into the Montjuïc hillside by local people from 1936 onwards, and the 200m of tunnels could shelter up to two thousand people from Franco's bombing raids. With no radar to protect the city, they had two minutes from the first sound of the sirens to get underground. The tours are in Spanish or Catalan, though there is usually someone on hand who speaks English, and you can just turn up on the day. Photographic storyboards at the start of the tour give a bit of background, and then it's hard hat on to follow your guide into the labyrinth to the sound of screaming sirens and droning warplanes.

THE CITY UNDER SIEGE

During the Civil War years Poble Sec – like many inner-city neighbourhoods – suffered grievously from Nationalist bombing raids, a foretaste of what was to come in Europe during World War II. From 1936 onwards, the city authorities oversaw the building of a system of communal **air-raid shelters** and many had been excavated by the time that the first raids hit Barcelona in early 1937. Most were constructed in working-class areas (like Poble Sec, Barceloneta and Gràcia) where the locals hadn't been able to leave the city or couldn't reach the relative safety of either the metro tunnels or the Collserola hills. Altogether, around 1400 shelters were built in Barcelona (and another two thousand across Catalunya), some as simple as reinforced cellars, though many were larger collaborative efforts like Refugi 307, featuring vaulted brick-lined tunnels, ventilation, water supplies and even infirmaries and play areas for children. The raids were particularly savage in March 1938, and by the end of the war three thousand inhabitants had died in the bombings, with many more injured and thousands of buildings destroyed. Even so, the shelters undoubtedly saved many lives. In the wake of Republican defeat, after the war, many of the shelters were forgotten about, though the current city council is keen to raise their profile in the name of education and remembrance of Barcelona's often overlooked wartime history.

6

The Olympic area

Ⓜ Espanya, then either walk via the hillside escalators behind MNAC or take bus #193 or #50 from Av. de la Reina Maria Cristina

From Poble Espanyol, the main road through Montjuïc climbs around the hill and up to the city's principal Olympic area, sometimes known as the **Anella Olímpica** (Olympic Ring). The 1992 Olympics were the second planned for Montjuïc. The first, in 1936 – the "People's Olympics" – were organized as an alternative to the Nazis' infamous Berlin games of that year, but the day before the official opening, Franco's army revolt triggered the Civil War and scuppered the Barcelona games. Some of the 25,000 athletes and spectators who had turned up stayed on to join the Republican forces.

The Olympic stadium and other buildings

Estadi Olímpic Lluís Companys, Av. de l'Estadi 54 • No public access, except during events

The stadium at Montjuïc was built originally for the 1929 Exhibition, but it was refitted entirely for the 1992 Barcelona Olympics, while keeping its original Neoclassical facade. Seventy thousand spectators packed in for the opening and closing ceremonies, though the current stadium capacity is around 55,000. It's used for major sporting events (it hosted the 2010 European Athletics championships) and big concerts. It's also been officially renamed as the **Estadi Olímpic Lluís Companys**, after the Generalitat president who was executed at Montjuïc during the Spanish Civil War.

A vast *terrassa* on the west side of the stadium provides one of the finest vantage points in the city. Long water-fed troughs break up the concrete and marble expanse, while the confident, space-age curve of Santiago Calatrava's **communications tower** dominates the skyline. Rising above the terrace is the steel-and-glass **Palau Sant Jordi**, a 17,000-seater sports and concert hall, while other signature buildings in the Olympic area include Catalan architect Ricardo Bofill's **Institut Nacional d'Educació Física de Catalunya** (**INEF**; a sports university) and – one building you can visit as a general punter – the impressive **Piscines Bernat Picornell** (see p.224).

Museu Olímpic i de l'Esport

Av. de l'Estadi 60 • Tues–Sat 10am–8pm (Oct–March until 6pm), Sun & hols 10am–2.30pm • €4.50, under-14s free • ☎ 932 925 379, Ⓦ museuolimpicbcn.com • Ⓜ Espanya then 25min walk, or bus #193 or #50 from Av. de la Reina Maria Cristina

Just across the road from the Olympic stadium, the history of the Games themselves – and Barcelona's successful hosting – are covered in the **Museu Olímpic i de l'Esport**. It's a fully interactive experience, with lots of Olympic memorabilia and sports gear on display, plus sporting videos and an audiovisual presentation, but even so is probably one for hardcore sports fans only.

Fundació Joan Miró

Parc de Montjuïc • Tues–Sat 10am–7pm (July–Sept 10am–8pm), Thurs 10am–9.30pm, Sun & hols 10am–2.30pm • General admission to all areas €9, otherwise exhibitions €4, Espai 13 €4 • ☎ 934 439 470, ⓦ fundaciomiro-bcn.org • Ⓜ Paral.lel, then Funicular de Montjuïc and 5min walk, or bus #193 or #50 from Av. de la Reina Maria Cristina

Barcelona's most adventurous art museum, the **Fundació Joan Miró**, houses the life's work of the great Catalan artist Joan Miró (1893–1983), who established an international reputation while always retaining links with his homeland. The stark white modernist museum, designed by Miró's friend, the architect Josep-Luis Sert, is set in lovely gardens overlooking the city, and lies just a few minutes' walk from both the Olympic stadium and the Montjuïc funicular and cable-car stations.

Miró showed a childlike delight in colours and shapes and developed a free, highly decorative style – the paintings and drawings, in particular, are instantly recognizable, among the chief links between Surrealism and abstract art. Miró had his first exhibition

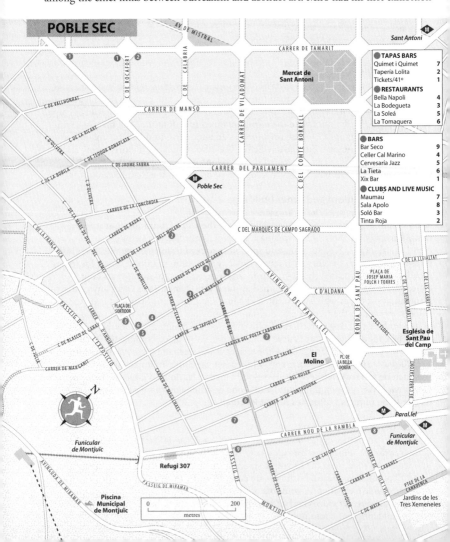

POBLE SEC

● TAPAS BARS	
Quimet i Quimet	7
Tapería Lolita	2
Tickets/41°	1
● RESTAURANTS	
Bella Napoli	4
La Bodegueta	3
La Soleá	5
La Tomaquera	6
● BARS	
Bar Seco	9
Celler Cal Marino	4
Cervesaría Jazz	4
La Tieta	6
Xix Bar	1
● CLUBS AND LIVE MUSIC	
Maumau	7
Sala Apolo	8
Soló Bar	3
Tinta Roja	2

in 1918 and subsequently spent his summers in Catalunya and the rest of the time in France, before moving to Mallorca in 1956, where he died.

The purpose-built museum contains a huge collection of paintings, graphics, tapestries and sculptures covering the period from 1914 to 1978, largely donated by Miró himself. Aside from the permanent displays, the Fundació sponsors excellent temporary exhibitions, film shows, lectures and children's theatre, while summer music nights (usually June and July) are a feature every year. Young experimental artists have their own space in the **Espai 13** gallery, while there's also a contemporary art **library**, a **bookshop** and a **café-restaurant** – you don't have to pay to get into the museum to use this.

Paintings and drawings

The works on display strongly emphasize Miró's later period, since the museum was only proposed (and works specifically set aside) in the 1960s, when Miró had already been painting for almost fifty years. But among over two hundred paintings in the collection there are early Realist works from before the mid-1920s, like the effervescent *Portrait of a Young Girl* (1919), while other gaps are filled by a collection later donated by Miró's widow, Pilar Juncosa, which demonstrates Miró's preoccupations in the 1930s and 1940s. During this period he began his **Constellations** series, in which first appeared the colours, themes and symbols that later came to define his work – reds and blues; women, birds and tears; the sun, moon and stars – all eventually pared down to the minimalist basics. The same period also saw the fifty black-and-white lithographs of the **Barcelona Series** (1939–44), executed in the immediate aftermath of the Civil War. They are a dark reflection of the turmoil of the period; snarling faces and great black shapes and shadows dominate. For a rapid appraisal of Miró's entire *oeuvre* look in on the museum's **Sala K**, whose 23 works are on long-term loan from a Japanese collector. Here, in a kind of potted retrospective, you can trace Miró's development as an artist, from his early Impressionist landscapes (1914) to the minimal renderings of the 1970s.

Works by other artists

Perhaps the most innovative section of the museum is that containing works by other artists in homage to Miró, including fine pieces by Henri Matisse, Henry Moore, Max Ernst, Richard Serra, Robert Motherwell and Eduardo Chillida. The single most compelling exhibit, however, has to be Alexander Calder's **Mercury Fountain**, which he built for the Republican pavilion at the Paris Universal Exhibition of 1936–37 – the same exhibition for which Picasso painted *Guernica*. Like *Guernica*, it's a tribute to a town, this time the mercury-mining town of Almáden – its name spelled out in dangling metal letters above the fountain – which saw saturation bombing during the Civil War.

Other exhibits

Other exhibits include Miró's enormous bright **tapestries** (he donated nine to the museum), pencil drawings (particularly of misshapen women and gawky ballerinas)

ON THE MIRÓ TRAIL

When you've seen one Miró, well, you start to see them everywhere in Barcelona, whether it's T-shirts for tourists or branding for businesses. There's the large ceramic mural on the facade of Terminal B at the **airport**, for a start, or the circular pavement mural at **Plaça de la Boqueria** that catches your attention every time you stroll down the Ramblas. He designed the starfish logo for the **Caixa de Pensions** savings bank (there's one splashed across the Caixa Forum arts centre on Montjuïc) and also the **España logo** on Spanish National Tourist Board publications. There's his towering *Dona i Ocell* (Woman and Bird) in the **Parc Joan Miró**, near Barcelona Sants train station, while a smaller *Dona* stands with other Catalan works in the courtyard of the **Ajuntament** (city hall). In many ways, Barcelona's a Miró city, whatever Picasso fans might think.

and **sculpture** outside in the gardens. All these started life in the form of **sketches and notes**, and the museum has retained five thousand separate examples, of which it usually displays a selection. From a doodle on a scrap of old newspaper or on the back of a postcard, it's possible to trace the development of shapes and themes that later evolved into full-blown works of art.

Castell de Montjuïc

Carretera de Montjuïc · Grounds open Tues–Sun 9am–7pm (April–Sept until 9pm) · Free · ☎ 932 564 445, ⓦ bcn.cat/castelldemontjuic · Direct access by Telefèric de Montjuïc, or bus #193 from Av. de la Reina Maria Cristina

Marking the top of Montjuïc and the end of the line is Barcelona's **castle**; the best way up is by the Telefèric de Montjuïc (see p.89), which tacks up the hillside, offering magnificent views on the way, before depositing you within the forbidding eighteenth-century walls. The fortress served as a military base and prison for decades, and was where the last president of the pre-war Generalitat, **Lluís Companys i Jover**, was executed on Franco's orders on October 15, 1940 – he had been in exile in Paris after the Civil War, but was handed over to Franco by the Germans upon their capture of the French capital (he's buried in the nearby Cementiri del Sud-Oest).

As an outpost of the Spanish state in fiercely proud Catalunya, the castle long remained a provocation to Barcelona's citizens but in 2008 it was symbolically handed over to the city, and restoration work is now transforming the site into a combined peace museum, memorial space and Montjuïc interpretation centre. The cable-car ride and dramatic location merit a visit in any case, while the ramparts and grounds are free to enter. You can also walk around the outer walls of the fortress, where the locals come at weekends to practise archery in the moat. There are open-air film screenings up here in summer too.

Santa Amàlia bastion

Exhibition, Baluard de Santa Amàlia · Sat 10am–2pm & 4–7pm, Sun & hols 10am–3pm · Free

The fortress defences comprise a series of angular concentric perimeters, designed for maximum security and artillery deflection. Something of its design and its brutal past are touched on in an **exhibition** in the Santa Amàlia bastion, in the inner keep, which also explains the future use to which the castle will be put.

Camí del Mar and Mirador del Migdia

Below the castle walls, a panoramic pathway – the **Camí del Mar** – has been cut from the cliff edge, providing magnificent views, first across to Port Olímpic and the northern beaches, and then southwest as the path swings around the castle. This is an unfamiliar view of the city, of the sprawling docks and container yards, and cruise ships and tankers are usually visible negotiating the busy sea lanes. The path is just over 1km long and ends at the back of the castle battlements near the **Mirador del Migdia**, where there's a great open-air chill-out bar, *La Caseta del Migdia* (see p.201). Down through the trees is the *mirador* itself, a balcony with extensive views over the Baixa Llobregat industrial area. You can see across to the Olympic stadium from here, while in the immediate foreground is the extraordinary **Cementiri del Sud-Oest**, stretching along the ridge below, whose tombs are stacked like apartment blocks on great conifer-lined avenues.

Jardí Botànic de Barcelona

C/Dr Font i Quer 2 · Daily: April, May & Sept 10am–7pm, June–Aug 10am–8pm; Oct–March 10am–6pm · €3.50, or €7 combined ticket with Museu Blau, under-16s free, plus free Sun after 3pm & last Sun of month · ☎ 932 564 160, ⓦ www.museuciencies.bcn.cat · Ⓜ Espanya, then 20min walk via escalators, or bus #193/PM or #50 from Av. de la Reina Maria Cristina.

Principal among Montjuïc's many gardens is the city's botanical garden, the **Jardí Botànic de Barcelona**, laid out on terraced slopes that offer fine views across the city.

THE GARDENS OF MONTJUÏC

Botanical gardens aside, there are plenty of places on Montjuïc where you can roll out a picnic rug or let the children scamper around safely.

Signposted off Avinguda de Miramar, west of (and below) the Fundació Joan Miró, the terraces, clipped hedges and grottoes of the **Jardins Laribal** (daily 10am–dusk; free) date from 1918. They surround the spring of **Font del Gat**, which has been a picnic site since the nineteenth century. Josep Puig i Cadafalch built a restaurant here of the same name for the 1929 International Exhibition, and it's open now for lunch (1–4pm; closed Mon & closed 3 weeks in Aug), with wonderful views from its terrace.

East of here, the Montjuïc cable car passes over the **Jardins de Mossèn Jacint Verdaguer** and adjacent **Jardins Joan Brossa** (both daily 10am–dusk; free), which tack up the hillside to the castle. Walking down through the gardens from the castle is a pleasant way to return to the lower slopes of Montjuïc, through what used to be the site of the old Montjuïc amusement park, though it's now fully landscaped, with children's play areas – halfway, there are sweeping city views from the **Mirador de l'Alcalde**.

Outside the upper cross-harbour cable-car station, are the formal **Jardins de Miramar** (always open; free), plus more fine views from the cable-car station café-*terrassa*. Steps lead down from a point close to the cable-car station into the precipitous cactus gardens of the **Jardins de Mossèn Costa i Llobera** (daily 10am–dusk; free), which look out over the port. The flourishing stands of Central and South American, Indian and African cacti, some over 6m high, make a dramatic scene experienced by few visitors to Montjuïc, though the people lounging on the steps and in the shade of the bigger specimens suggest it's something of an open secret among the locals.

6

Montjuïc buses run here directly, while the entrance is just a five-minute walk around the back of the Olympic stadium. It's a beautifully kept contemporary garden, where wide, easy-to-follow paths (fine for buggies – strollers – and wheelchairs) wind through landscaped zones representing the flora of the Mediterranean, Canary Islands, California, Chile, North and South Africa and Australia. Just don't come in the full heat of the summer day, as there's very little shade. Guided tours in Spanish/Catalan every weekend (except August) show you the highlights, but you get an English-language audio-guide and map included in the entry fee in any case.

CASA BATLLÓ

Dreta de l'Eixample

The nineteenth-century street grid north of Plaça de Catalunya is the city's main shopping and business district. It was designed as part of a revolutionary urban plan – the Eixample in Catalan (pronounced *aye-sham-pla*, the "Extension" or "Widening") – that divided districts into regular blocks, whose characteristic wide streets and shaved corners survive today. Two parallel avenues, Passeig de Gràcia and Rambla de Catalunya, are the backbone of the Eixample, with everything to the east known as the Dreta de l'Eixample (the right-hand side). It's here, above all, that the bulk of the city's famous *modernista* buildings are found, along with an array of classy galleries and fashionable hotels, shops and boutiques. It's not a neighbourhood as such – and you won't be able to see everything described in this chapter on a single outing – but the Dreta does contain many of the city's most stylish, show-stopping buildings.

In many ways the Dreta de l'Eixample acts as a sort of open-air museum, featuring the masterworks of a new class of **modernista architects**, who began to change the way Barcelona looked from around 1880 onwards. These extraordinary buildings – most notably by Antoni Gaudí i Cornet, Lluís Domènech i Montaner and Josep Puig i Cadafalch – were eagerly commissioned by status-conscious merchants and businessmen and, though most were originally built as private houses and apartments, many have subsequently been opened to the public. Most are found within the triangle formed by the Passeig de Gràcia, Avinguda Diagonal and the Gran Via de les Corts Catalanes, and all are within a few blocks of each other. The stand-out sights are Gaudí's **La Pedrera** apartment building, and the so-called **Mansana de la Discòrdia**, or "Block of Discord" (Passeig de Gràcia, between carrers del Consell de Cent and d'Aragó), which gets its name because the three adjacent houses, casas **Lleó Morera**, **Amatller** and **Batlló** – built within a decade of each other by three different architects – show off wildly varying manifestations of the *modernista* style and spirit. Also in the Dreta are not-to-miss **galleries** dedicated to Catalunya's most eminent postwar artist Antoni Tàpies, and his contemporary Joan Brossa, not to mention a great neighbourhood **market**.

7

Casa Lleó Morera

Pg. de Gràcia 35 · No public access · Ⓜ Passeig de Gràcia

The six-storey **Casa Lleó Morera** was designed by Lluís Domènech i Montaner and completed in 1906. It's the least extravagant of the buildings in the "Block of Discord", and has suffered more than the others from "improvements" wrought by subsequent owners, which included removing the ground-floor arches and sculptures. The luxury leather goods store Loewe occupies the whole of the ground floor, while the main entrance to the building is resolutely guarded to prevent more than a peek inside. This is a pity because it has a rich Art Nouveau interior, flush with ceramics and wood, as well as exquisite stained glass, while its semicircular jutting balconies are quite distinctive.

Museu del Perfum

Pg. de Gràcia 39 · Mon–Fri 10.30am–8pm, Sat 11am–2pm · €5 · ☎ 932 160 121, Ⓦ museodelperfume.com · Ⓜ Passeig de Gràcia

They may have to turn the lights on for you at the **Museu del Perfum**, sited at the back of the Regia perfume store, but there's no missing the exhibits as a rather cloying pong

---

DESIGN A CITY … DESIGNER CITY

As Barcelona grew more industrialized throughout the nineteenth century, the old town became overcrowded and unsanitary. In 1851 permission was given by the Spanish state to knock down the encircling walls so that the city could expand beyond its medieval limits.

When it came to building what amounted to an entire new town, Barcelona then, as now, didn't do things by halves. The city authorities championed a fan-shaped plan by popular municipal architect **Antoni Rovira i Trias**, whose design radiated out from the existing shape of the old town. (His statue, in Gràcia's Plaça Rovira i Trias, sits on a bench with his Eixample plan set in the ground beneath him.) However, much to local chagrin, Rovira's elegant if conventional plan was passed over by the Spanish government in favour of a revolutionary blueprint drawn up by utopian engineer and urban planner **Ildefons Cerdà i Sunyer**. This was defiantly modern in style and scale – a massive grid marching off to the north, intersected by broad avenues cut on the diagonal. Districts would be divided into wide, spacious blocks, with buildings limited in height, and central gardens, schools, markets, hospitals and other services provided for the inhabitants.

Cerdà eventually saw most of his more radical social proposals ignored, as the Eixample rapidly became a fashionable area in which to live and speculators developed buildings on the proposed open spaces. Even today though, the underlying fabric of his plan is always evident, while in certain quiet corners and gardens the original emphasis on social community within grand design lives on.

SHOPS

Antonio Miró	9
Armand Basi	7
Bulevard dels Antiquarius	6
Casa del Llibre	5
Colmado Quilez	8
Cubiña	2
Joaquín Berao	4
Laie	14
Mango	3 & 13
Mango Outlet	12
Purificación García	10
Vinçon	1
Zara	11

CAFÉS

Café del Centre	5
Forn de Sant Jaume	4

TAPAS BARS

La Bodegueta	3
Ciudad Condal	7
Tapas24	6

RESTAURANTS

Casa Calvet	8
El Japonés	1
Tragaluz	2

BAR

La Pedrera de Nit	1

CLUB

City Hall	2

GAY CLUB

Matinée	3

ACCOMMODATION

BCN Fashion House	12
Equity Point Centric	5
Hostal L'Antic Espai	7
Hostal Girona	9
Hostal Goya	8
Hostal San Remo	11
Hotel Claris	4
Hotel Condes de Barcelona	2
Hotel Majestic	3
Hotel Omm	1
Mandarin Oriental	6
the5rooms	10

exudes from the room. It's a private collection of over five thousand perfume and essence bottles from Egyptian times onwards, and there are some exquisite pieces displayed, including Turkish filigree-and-crystal ware and bronze and silver Indian elephant flasks. More modern times are represented by scents made for Brigitte Bardot, Grace Kelly and Elizabeth Taylor, and if you're diligent enough to scan all the shelves you might be able to track down the perfume bottle designed by Salvador Dalí.

Casa Amatller

Fundació Amatller, Pg. de Gràcia 41 • Guided tours €10; check website for current details; reservations essential, in person, by phone or email • ☎ 934 961 245, ✉ amatller@amatller.org, ⓦ amatller.org • Ⓜ Passeig de Gràcia

Josep Puig i Cadafalch's striking **Casa Amatller** apartment block (c.1900) was designed for Antoni Amatller, a Catalan chocolate manufacturer, art collector, photographer and traveller. It's a triumph of decorative detail, particularly the facade, which rises in steps

MODERNISME – WHO'S WHO AND WHAT'S WHAT

7

Modernisme – the Catalan offshoot of Art Nouveau – was the expression of a renewed upsurge in Catalan nationalism. Catalunya's economic recovery in the early nineteenth century provided the initial impetus, and the subsequent cultural renaissance – the Renaixença – led to fresh stirrings of a new Catalan awareness and identity (see box, p.93). Three architects in particular came to prominence in Barcelona and, in doing so, introduced a building style that has given the city a look like no other.

ANTONI GAUDÍ I CORNET

Born in Reus, near Tarragona, to a family of artisans, the work of **Antoni Gaudí i Cornet** (1852–1926) was never strictly *modernista* in style, but the imaginative impetus he provided was incalculable. Fantasy, spiritual symbolism and Catalan pride are evident in every building he designed, while his architectural influences were Moorish and Gothic, embellished with elements from the natural world. These themes are visible in projects as diverse as his extraordinary suburban industrial estate, Colònia Güell, and his masterpiece cathedral, the Sagrada Família. Yet Gaudí rarely wrote a word about the theory of his art, preferring to leave it to the buildings to provoke a reaction– no one stands mute in front of an Antoni Gaudí masterpiece.

Key buildings and works:
Colònia Güell See p.152 **Palau Güell** See p.64 **Parc Güell** See p.127
La Pedrera See p.109 **Sagrada Família** See p.116

LLUÍS DOMÈNECH I MONTANER

With Gaudí in a class of his own, it was **Lluís Domènech i Montaner** (1850–1923) who was perhaps the greatest pure *modernista* architect. Drawing on the rich Catalan Romanesque and Gothic traditions, his work combined traditional craft methods with modern technological experiments – with spectacularly innovative results.

Key buildings and works:
Castell del Tres Dragons **Hospital de la Santa Creu i** **Palau de la Música**
See p.75 **de Sant Pau** See p.120 **Catalana** See p.67

JOSEP PUIG I CADAFALCH

Like that of other *modernista* architects, the work of **Josep Puig i Cadafalch** (1867–1957) contains a wildly inventive use of ceramic tiles, ironwork, stained glass and stone carving. His first commission, the **Casa Martí**, housed the famous *Quatre Gats* tavern for the city's avant-garde artists and hangers-on, while in uptown mansions built for the newly enriched Barcelona bourgeoisie Puig i Cadafalch brought to bear distinct Gothic and medieval influences.

Key buildings and works:
Casa Amatller See above **Casa de les Punxes** See p.110 **Els Quatre Gats** See p.47

to a point, studded with ceramic tiles and heraldic sculptures, while inside the hallway twisted stone columns are interspersed with dragon lamps. The house is currently being restored as a *modernista* cultural centre, but it has kept much of its original Art Nouveau furniture and interior design, and **guided tours** continue to operate on various days, subject to the progress of the renovation works (the tours include a visit to Amatller's photographic studio and chocolate-tasting in the original kitchen). Temporary exhibitions at the house are usually worth a look, too, with some based on the collections amassed by Amatller or by his daughter Teresa, who established the Amatller Institute of Hispanic Art here in 1941. The institute promotes research into the history of Hispanic art, and maintains a photo library and archive in the house.

Casa Batlló

Pg. de Gràcia 43 · Daily 9am–8pm, access occasionally restricted due to private events · €18.15, under-18s €14.55, under-6s free; advance-purchase tickets advised, in person or by phone · ☎ 932 160 306, ⓦ casabatllo.es; ticket sales also from Barcelona Turisme (☎ 932 853 832, ⓦ barcelonaturisme.com) and TelEntrada (☎ 902 101 212, ⓦ telentrada.com) · Ⓜ Passeig de Gràcia

7

The most extraordinary creation on the "Block of Discord" is Antoni Gaudí's **Casa Batlló**, designed for the industrialist Josep Batlló. The original apartment building was considered dull by contemporaries, so Gaudí was hired to give it a face-lift, completing the work by 1907. He contrived to create an undulating facade that Salvador Dalí later compared to "the tranquil waters of a lake". There's an animal motif at work here, too: the stone facade hangs in folds, like skin, and from below, the twisted balcony railings resemble malevolent eyes. The higher part of the facade is pockmarked with circular ceramic buttons laid on a bright mosaic background, while on the rooftop sprout the celebrated mosaic chimneys and a little tower topped with a three-dimensional cross. Some see in the curving roof and chimneys the spine of the dragon killed by Sant Jordi (St George), with the cross representing the knight's lance, plunged into the dragon's back. Gaudí never made the theme explicit, but the sinuous house interior certainly resembles some great organism, complete with snakeskin-patterned walls, and window frames, fireplaces, doorways and staircases that display not a straight line between them.

Self-guided audio tours show you the main floor (including the salon overlooking Passeig de Gràcia), the patio and rear facade, the ribbed attic and the rooftop. Despite the steep admission price, this is a very popular attraction – be warned that the scrum of aimless visitors, audio-stick glued to their ears, can be a frustrating business at peak times.

Fundació Antoni Tàpies

C/d'Aragó 255 · Tues–Sun 10am–7pm · €7, under-16s €5.60 · ☎ 934 870 315, ⓦ fundaciotapies.org · Ⓜ Passeig de Gràcia

The definitive collection of the work of Catalan abstract artist **Antoni Tàpies** is housed in *modernista* architect Lluís Domènech i Montaner's first important building, the **Casa Montaner i Simon** (1880), which was originally constructed for the publishing firm of Montaner i Simon. It was converted in 1990 to house the **Fundació Antoni Tàpies** and it's hard to miss, since the foundation's building is capped by Tàpies's own striking sculpture, **Núvol i Cadira** ("Cloud and Chair"; 1990), a tangle of glass, wire and aluminium.

While the building is a beauty – one of Moorish-style flourishes, cast-iron columns and no dividing walls – Tàpies's work rather divides opinion. It's not immediately accessible (in the way of, say, Miró) and you're either going to love or hate the gallery. A selection of works from the permanent collection is on show, displayed chronologically, while three or four exhibitions a year highlight works and installations by other contemporary artists. The foundation also includes a peerless archive on Tàpies's work, held in the gorgeous **library** on the upper floor, which was fashioned from the original shelves of the publisher's warehouse.

ANTONI TÀPIES

Born in the city in 1923 (on c/de la Canuda in the Barri Gòtic), **Antoni Tàpies i Puig** initially studied law at the University of Barcelona, though he left before completing his degree. Drawn to art from an early age, and largely self-taught (though he studied briefly at Barcelona's Academia Valls), he became in 1948 a founding member of the influential Dau al Set ("Die at Seven"), a grouping of seven artists that produced a monthly avant-garde magazine of the same name which ran until 1956. His first major paintings date from as early as 1945, by which time he was already interested in collage (using newspaper, cardboard, silver wrapping, string and wire) and engraving techniques. In the Dau al Set period, after coming into contact with Miró, among others, he underwent a brief Surrealist phase. However, after a stay in Paris he found his feet with an **abstract style** that matured in the Fifties, a period during which he held his first major exhibitions, including shows in New York and Europe. Tàpies's large works are deceptively simple, though underlying messages and themes are signalled by the collage-like inclusion of everyday objects and a wide use of symbols on the canvas. He has also continually experimented with unusual materials, like oil paint mixed with crushed marble, or by employing sand, clay, cloth or straw in his collages. Tàpies's work became increasingly **political** during the Sixties and Seventies: *A la memòria de Salvador Puig Antich, 1974* ("In Memory of Salvador Puig Antich, 1974") commemorates a Catalan anarchist executed by Franco's regime, while slogans splashed across his works, or the frequent use of the red bars of the Catalan flag, leave no doubt about his affiliations. His most recent works are more sombre still, featuring recurring images of earth, shrouds and bodies, as echoes of civil war and conflict. Meanwhile, he has left a string of important outdoor works across the city, including the mysterious glass box that is his *Homenatge a Picasso* ("Homage to Picasso"; 1983), on Passeig de Picasso, outside the gates of the Parc de la Ciutadella.

Museu Egipci de Barcelona

C/de València 284 · Mon–Sat 10am–8pm, Sun 10am–2pm · €11 · Guided tours Sat at 11am (Catalan) & 5pm (Spanish) included in the entry price; for English-language tours, contact the museum in advance · ☎ 934 880 188, ⓦ museuegipci.com · Ⓜ Passeig de Gràcia

Half a block east of Passeig de Gràcia, the **Museu Egipci de Barcelona** is an exceptional private collection of artefacts from ancient Egypt – there's nothing else in Spain quite like it. It was founded by hotelier and antiquity collector Jordi Clos – whose deluxe *Hotel Claris*, a block away, still has its own private museum – and displays a remarkable gathering of over a thousand objects, ranging from amulets to sarcophagi. The emphasis is on exploring the shape and character of Egyptian society, and visitors are given a hugely detailed English-language guidebook, which enables you to nail down specific periods and descriptions, case by case, if you so wish. But the real pleasure here is a serendipitous wander, turning up items like a wood-and-leather bed of the First and Second Dynasties (2920–2649 BC), some examples of cat mummies of the Late Period (715–332 BC) or a rare figurine of a spoonbill (ibis) representing an Egyptian god (though archeologists aren't yet sure which). There are temporary exhibitions (extra charge sometimes levied), plus a good book- and gift shop on the lower floor and a terrace café upstairs. The museum also hosts a full programme of study sessions, children's activities and themed evening events, from Egyptian banquets to costumed guided visits.

Jardins de les Torres de les Aigües

C/de Roger de Llúria 56, between c/del Consell de Cent and c/de la Diputació · Daily 10am–dusk · Free · Ⓜ Girona

The original nineteenth-century Eixample urban plan was drawn up with local inhabitants very much in mind. Space, light and social community projects were part of the grand design, and something of the original municipal spirit can be seen in the **Jardins de les Torres de les Aigües**, an enclosed square (reached down a herringbone-brick tunnel) centred on a Moorish-style water tower. It has been handsomely restored by the city council, who turn it into a backyard family beach every summer, complete with sand and paddling pool. Another example of the old Eixample lies directly opposite, across c/Roger de Llúria, where the cobbled **Passatge del Permanyer** cuts across an Eixample block, lined by candy-coloured single-storey townhouses.

Mercat de la Concepció and around

Between c/de València and c/d'Aragó • Mon & Sat 8am–3pm, Tues–Fri 8am–8pm, July & Aug closes 3pm • ⓦ laconcepcio.com • Ⓜ Girona

The Dreta's finest neighbourhood market, the **Mercat de la Concepció**, was inaugurated in 1888, its iron-and-glass tram-shed structure reminiscent of others in the city. Flowers, shrubs, trees and plants are a Concepció speciality (the florists on c/de València are open 24 hours a day), and there are a couple of good snack bars inside the market and a few outdoor cafés to the side.

La Concepció

Entrance on c/de Roger de Llúria • Daily 8am–1pm & 5–9pm • Free • Ⓜ Girona

The market takes its name from the church of **La Concepció**, a block to the west, whose quiet cloister is a surprising haven of slender columns and orange trees. This was part of a fifteenth-century Gothic convent that once stood in the old town. It was abandoned in the early nineteenth century and then transferred here brick by brick in the 1870s, along with the Romanesque belfry from another old-town church.

Palau Montaner

C/de Mallorca 278 • Guided visits Sat at 10.30am in English, plus 11.30am & 12.30pm, Sun at 10.30am, 11.30am & 12.30pm in Spanish/Catalan • €6, under-18s €3 • ☎ 933 177 652, ⓦ rutadelmodernisme.com • Ⓜ Passeig de Gràcia

The **Palau Montaner** was built in 1896 for a member of the Montaner i Simon publishing family. After the original architect quit, *modernista* architect Lluís Domènech i Montaner took over halfway through construction, and the top half of the facade is clearly more elaborate than the lower part. Meanwhile, the period's most celebrated craftsmen were set to work on the interior, which sports rich mosaic floors, painted glass, carved woodwork and a monumental staircase. The building is now the seat of the Madrid government's delegation to Catalunya, but there are **guided tours** at the weekend that explain something of the house's history and show you the lavish public rooms, grand dining room and courtyard. It's unusual to be able to get inside a private *modernista* house of the period, so it's definitely worth the effort.

Fundació Joan Brossa

C/de Provença 318 • Tues–Thurs 10am–7pm, Fri 10am–6pm • Free • ☎ 934 676 952, ⓦ fundaciojoanbrossa.cat • Ⓜ Diagonal

Brossa's may not be a familiar name for most visitors to Barcelona, but a visit to the foundation that contains his life's work is time you're unlikely to regret. **Joan Brossa i Cuervo** (1919–98) was a most prolific and unusual poet and playwright, seeing poetry not just on the page or stage but also in everyday items and deconstructed words, which he incorporated into hundreds of installations, sculptures and posters. His fascinating "object" and "visual" poems continually broke down letters and words to make art both big and small – thus, tiny numbers and letters pouring out of a bottle of spilled ink, or the massive sculpture of the letter "A" above the Val d'Hebron cycling track ("A" being the start of everything for the wordsmith Brossa). The permanent exhibition at the **Fundació Joan Brossa** explores his work and traces Brossa's career as an early collaborator with Miró and co-founder of the Dau al Set Surrealist magazine. Meanwhile an English-language guidebook available from the foundation leads you around some of his more notable public works in Barcelona – like *Homenatge al Llibre* ("Homage to the Book") on Passeig de Gràcia (at Gran Via) or the letters spelling out the Roman name of the city, *Barcino*, outside La Seu in the Barri Gòtic.

La Pedrera

Pg. de Gràcia 92, tour entrance on c/de Provença • Daily: March–Oct 9am–8pm; Nov–Feb 9am–6.30pm, closed first week Jan • €11, or €15 with audio-guide, under-12s free • ☎ 902 400 973, Ⓦ lapedreraeducacio.org • Ⓜ Diagonal

Antoni Gaudí's weird and wonderful apartment building is simply not to be missed – though you can expect queues whenever you visit. Constructed as the Casa Milà between 1905 and 1911, but popularly known as **La Pedrera** – "The Stone Quarry" – it was declared a UNESCO World Heritage Site in 1984. Its hulking, rippled facade, curving around the street corner in one smooth sweep, is said to have been inspired by the mountain of Montserrat just outside Barcelona, while the apartments themselves, whose balconies of tangled metal drip over the facade, resemble eroded cave dwellings. Indeed, there's not a straight line to be seen – hence the contemporary joke that the new tenants would only be able to keep snakes as pets. The building, which Gaudí himself described as "more luminous than light", was his last secular commission but even here he was injecting religious motifs and sculptures into the building until told to remove them. A sculpture of the Virgin Mary was planned to complete the roof, but the building's owners demurred, having been alarmed by the anti-religious fervour of the "Tragic Week" in Barcelona in 1909, when anarchist-sponsored rioting destroyed churches and religious foundations. Gaudí, by now working full-time on the Sagrada Família, was appalled, and determined in future to use his skills only for religious purposes.

7

The roof terrace and attic

The self-guided visit includes a trip up to the extraordinary **terrat** (roof terrace) to see at close quarters the enigmatic chimneys – you should note that the roof terrace is often closed if it's raining. In addition, there's an excellent exhibition about Gaudí's life and work installed under the 270 curved brick arches of the **attic**.

The apartment

El Pis ("the apartment") on the building's fourth floor re-creates the design and style of a *modernista*-era bourgeois apartment in a series of extraordinarily light rooms that flow seamlessly from one to another. The apartment is filled with period furniture and effects, while the moulded door and window frames, and even the brass door handles, all follow Gaudí's sinuous building design.

Temporary exhibitions and events

Exhibition entrance at Pg. de Gràcia 92 • Daily 10am–8pm • Free • Ⓦ fundaciocaixacatalunya.org

Casa Milà itself is still split into private apartments, while the whole building is administered by the Fundació Caixa de Catalunya. Through the grand main entrance on Passeig de Gràcia there's access to the Fundació's **exhibition hall** which hosts temporary art shows of works by major international artists. There's also a full programme of children's and family activities, concerts and events, with booking details posted on the website.

A NIGHT ON THE TILES

Gaudí fans can get closer to the great man's work at two unique venues – and enjoy a night out in the process. At **La Pedrera de Nit** (see p.202), Gaudí's amazing ceramic-tiled rooftop at La Pedrera is the evening backdrop for a complimentary glass of cava and music from a mixed bunch of performers, from flamenco to folk. For a meal in glam surroundings, **Casa Calvet** (see p.191) – Gaudí's earliest commissioned townhouse building (1899), erected for a prominent local textile family – is now a fancy restaurant. Although fairly conventional in style, the Baroque inspiration on display in the sculpted facade and church-like lobby was to surface again in his later, more elaborate buildings on Passeig de Gràcia.

Casa Ramon Casas and Vinçon

Pg. de Gràcia 96 • Mon–Sat 10am–8.30pm • ☎ 932 156 050, Ⓦ vincon.com • Ⓜ Diagonal

Right next to La Pedrera, in the same block on Passeig de Gràcia, the **Casa Ramon Casas** (1899) was originally built as a house and studio for the wealthy Barcelona artist Ramon Casas i Carbó (1866–1932). He had found early success in Paris with friends Santiago Rusiñol and Miquel Utrillo, and the three of them were later involved in *Els Quatre Gats* tavern, which Casas largely financed. In 1941, the **Vinçon** store was established in the building, which emerged in the Sixties as the country's pre-eminent purveyor of furniture and design, a reputation today's department store still maintains. There are several street entrances, including separate sections for bedroom (Tinç Çon, c/del Rosselló 246) and kitchen (Kitchen Çon, c/de Pau Claris 179), while the extraordinary furniture floor gives access to a terrace with views of the interior of La Pedrera. The **Sala Vinçon** gallery, meanwhile (same hours as the store; admission free), located in Casas's original studio, puts on excellent shows of graphic and industrial design and contemporary furniture.

7

Palau Robert

Pg. de Gràcia 107 • Mon–Sat 10am–7pm, Sun 10am–2.30pm • Free • ☎ 932 388 091, Ⓦ gencat.cat/palaurobert • Ⓜ Diagonal

The information centre for the Catalunya region is installed inside the **Palau Robert**, right at the top of Passeig de Gràcia, and hosts changing **exhibitions** on all matters Catalan, from art to business. There are several exhibition spaces, both inside the main palace – built as a typical aristocratic residence in 1903 – and in the old coach house. The centre is also an important **concert venue** for recitals and orchestras, while the pretty gardens around the back are a popular meeting point for the local nannies and their charges.

Casa Àsia

Av. Diagonal 373 • Tues–Sat 10am–8pm, Sun 10am–2pm; café Mon–Fri 9am–9pm • Free • ☎ 933 680 836, Ⓦ casaasia.es • Ⓜ Diagonal

The beautifully detailed Palau Quadras (a Josep Puig i Cadafalch work from 1904) now serves as **Casa Àsia**, a cultural and arts centre for Asia and the Pacific region. You can check the website for current exhibitions, but it's always worth calling in anyway, if not for the café and multimedia library, then for the Jardí d'Orient **roof terrace** – take the elevator up for sparkling views of the neighbouring Casa de les Punxes and the Sagrada Família towers rising behind.

Casa de les Punxes

Av. Diagonal 416–420 • No public access • Ⓜ Verdaguer

Architect Josep Puig i Cadafalch's largest work, the soaring Casa Terrades, is more usually known as the **Casa de les Punxes** (House of Spikes) because of its red-tiled turrets and steep gables. Built in 1903 for three sisters, and converted from three separate houses spreading around an entire corner of a block, the crenellated structure is almost northern European in style, reminiscent of a Gothic castle.

UNIVERSITAT DE BARCELONA

Esquerra de l'Eixample

The long streets west of Rambla de Catalunya as far as Barcelona Sants train station – making up the Esquerra de l'Eixample – are perhaps the least visited by sightseers. With all the major architectural highlights found on the Eixample's right-hand side, the Esquerra (left-hand side) was intended by its nineteenth-century planners for public buildings, institutions and industrial concerns, many of which still stand. However, it does contain some cultural interest – not least two stand-out art galleries and an eye-catching public park or two – while over on the western fringes, the former Arenas bullring has been restyled as a spiffy leisure and shopping complex. This is also one of Barcelona's hottest night-out destinations, featuring both Michelin-starred restaurants and some of the city's best bars and clubs, particularly in the gay-friendly streets of the so-called Gaixample district, behind the university.

CONTEMPORARY ARCHITECTURE

It's easy to get sidetracked by the *modernista* architecture of the Eixample, and to forget that Barcelona also boasts plenty of contemporary wonders. Following the death of Franco, there was a feeling among architects that Barcelona had a lot of catching up to do, but subsequently the city has taken centre-stage in the matter of urban design and renewal. Now the world looks to Barcelona for inspiration.

Even in the Franco years, exciting work had taken place, particularly among the Rationalist school of architects working from the 1950s to the 1970s, like **José Antonio Coderch**. From the latter part of this period, too, dates the earliest work by the Catalan architects – among them **Oriol Bohigas**, **Carlos Buxadé, Joan Margarit, Ricardo Bofill** and **Frederic Correa** – who later transformed the very look and feel of the city. The impetus for change on a substantial level came from hosting the **1992 Olympics**. Nothing less than the redesign of whole city neighbourhoods would do, with decaying industrial areas either swept away or transformed. While Correa, Margarit and Buxadé worked on the refit of the **Estadi Olímpic**, Bofill was in charge of **INEF** (the Sports University) and had a hand in the airport refit. Down at the harbour, Bohigas and others were responsible for creating the visionary **Vila Olímpica** development, carving residential, commercial and leisure facilities out of abandoned industrial blackspots. New city landmarks appeared, like Norman Foster's **Torre de Collserola** tower at Tibidabo, and the twin towers of the *Hotel Arts* and **Torre Mapfre** at the Port Olímpic.

Attention later turned to other neglected areas, with signature buildings announcing a planned transformation of the local environment. Richard Meier's contemporary art museum, **MACBA**, in the Raval, and Helio Piñon and Alberto Viaplana's **Maremàgnum** complex at Port Vell, anchored those neighbourhoods' respective revivals. Ricardo Bofill's Greek-temple-style **Teatre Nacional de Catalunya** was an early indicator of change on the eastern side of the city, and it's here, around **Plaça de les Glòries**, that many of the biggest projects are currently under way. Anchored by the eye-catching 142-metre-high **Torre Agbar**, a giant glowing cigar of a building by Jean Nouvel, the area is undergoing radical restructuring as a public plaza. There are advanced plans for a new transport interchange, plus a **Centre del Disseny** (Design Centre) by MBM (architects Josep Martorell, Oriol Bohigas and David Mackay) that will bring together the city's applied art collections. Zaha Hadid has a "Cinema City" in the pipeline at nearby Plaça de les Arts, while to the northeast at **La Sagrera** work is under way on the city's second AVE (high-speed train) station, with the dramatic 34-storey Torre Sagrera by Frank O. Gehry to follow.

At the foot of Avinguda Diagonal, down on the shoreline, the former industrial area of Poble Nou was transformed by the works associated with the Universal Forum of Cultures held in 2004. **Diagonal Mar**, as the area is now known, sits at the heart of a new business and commercial district linking Barcelona with the once-desolate environs of the River Besòs. Meanwhile, on the other side of the city, Richard Rogers has revitalized the city's old bullring, at Plaça d'Espanya, now the **Arenas de Barcelona**, incorporating a domed promenade and viewing platform atop a shopping and leisure centre.

Universitat de Barcelona

Gran Via de les Corts Catalanes 585, at Pl. de la Universitat · ⓂUniversitat

Built in the 1860s, the grand Neoclassical main building of the **Universitat de Barcelona** is now largely used for ceremonies and administration purposes, but no one minds if you stroll through the doors. There's usually an exhibition in the echoing main hall, while beyond lie two fine arcaded courtyards and extensive gardens, providing a welcome escape from the traffic.

Fundació Francisco Godia

C/de la Diputació 250 · Daily except Tues 10am–8pm · €6.50 · Free guided tours of the collection Sat & Sun at noon · ☎ 932 723 180, Ⓦ fundaciofgodia.org · ⓂPasseig de Gràcia

Sited in a handsomely restored *modernista* mansion, the private art collection of the **Fundació Francisco Godia** spans eight centuries, showcasing an exquisite selection of medieval to modern Catalan art. The pieces were amassed by aesthete and 1950s'

ESQUERRA DE L'EIXAMPLE

● CAFÉ
Fast Vinic	10

● TAPAS BARS
Cerveseria Catalana	4
La Taverna del Clínic	2

● RESTAURANTS
Cinc Sentits	7
La Flauta	9
Gaig	8
Hanoi	6
Me	1
Out of China	5
El Racó d'en Balta	3

● ACCOMMODATION
Alternative Creative Youth Home	6
Gran Hotel Torre Catalunya	2
Hotel Axel	3
Hotel Inglaterra	7
Residencia Australia	5
Room Mate Emma	1
Somnio Barcelona	4

● SHOPS
Altair	6
Arenas de Barcelona	5
Come In	2
Jamonísimo	3
Jean-Pierre Bua	1
Kowasa	4

● BARS
Belchica	14
Danzarama	16
Dry Martini	5
Velódromo	2

● CLUBS
Antilla BCN Latin Club	7
Club Astoria	3
Luz de Gas	1
Quilombo	4

● GAY CAFÉS AND BARS
Aire	6
Atame	11
Bim Bam Bum Zeltas	9
Dietrich	10
People Lounge	13
Punto BCN	8

● GAY CLUBS
Arena Madre/Arena Classic	12
Arena VIP/Arena Dandy	15
Metro	17

racing driver, Francisco "Paco" Godia, an avid art collector in later life, and while not all of the collection can be shown at any one time, a representative selection is always on display – whether it's Romanesque carvings or Gothic art, the *modernista* paintings of Isidre Nonell, Santiago Rusiñol and Ramon Casas among others, or the varied selection of ceramics from most of the historically important production centres in Spain. Special exhibitions also run in tandem, for which there's usually no extra charge.

Museu del Modernisme Català

C/de Balmes 48 • Mon–Sat 10am–8pm, Sun & hols 10am–2pm • €10, under-16s €5, under-6s free • ☎ 932 722 896, ⓦ mmcat.cat • ⓜ Passeig de Gràcia

Barcelona's traditional "gallery district", around c/Consell de Cent, is a fitting location for the stupendous *modernista* collection housed in the **Museu del Modernisme Català**. It's the private enterprise of the celebrated Gothsland antiques gallery, and displays a collection forty years in the making – including the famous marble decorative vase by craftsman Eusebi Arnau that was the symbol of the Gothsland gallery for over thirty years. This is just one of 350 works on show across two exhibition floors in a restored building that was once a textile warehouse – the grand, vaulted basement contains paintings and sculpture while on the ground floor is *modernista* furniture, from screens to sofas. There are paintings and works by many famous names, from oils by Ramon Casa i Carbó to sinuous mirrors and tables by Antoni Gaudí (originally made for the casas Batlló and Calvet). But above all, this a rare opportunity to examine extraordinary Art Nouveau fixtures and fittings by artists you may not be familiar with – wonderful creations by pioneering cabinet-maker Joan Busquets i Jané, for example, the dramatic carved headboards of Gaspar Homar i Mezquida or the expressive terracotta sculptures of Lambert Escaler i Milà. As a crash course in the varied facets of Catalan *modernisme*, beyond the iconic buildings themselves, it's invaluable.

Mercat del Ninot and around

C/de Mallorca 133 • Mon–Fri 8am–9pm, Sat 8am–3pm • ☎ 934 536 512, ⓦ mercatdelninot.com • ⓜ Hospital Clinic

One of the oldest markets in the city (originally built in 1892), the **Mercat del Ninot** takes up a large area between carrers Villaroel and Casanova. It's currently undergoing a major refurbishment, but in the meantime there's a large temporary market building on c/Casanova, in front of the massive **Hospital Clinic**.

Escola Industrial

Corner of c/del Comte d'Urgell and c/del Rosselló • ⓜ Hospital Clinic

Around the back of the Hospital Clinic, it's worth having a look at the **Escola Industrial**, which was converted in 1908 from buildings of the former Batlló textile mill. It occupies four entire Eixample blocks, with later academic buildings added in the 1920s, including a chapel by Joan Rubió i Bellvér, who worked with Antoni Gaudí. Students usually fill the courtyards, and you're free to take a stroll through to view the highly decorative buildings.

Museu i Centre d'Estudis de l'Esport

C/de Buenos Aires 56–58 • June to mid-Sept Mon–Fri 8am–3pm; mid-Sept to May Mon–Fri 10am–2pm & 3–5pm • Free • ☎ 934 192 232 • ⓜ Hospital Clinic

Built as a private house in 1911 by Josep Puig i Cadafalch, the quirky **Museu i Centre d'Estudis de l'Esport** contains probably the most unassuming sporting "Hall of Fame" found anywhere in the world. In a couple of quiet, wood-panelled rooms photographs of 1920s Catalan rally drivers and footballers are displayed alongside a motley collection of memorabilia.

Parc de l'Espanya Industrial

C/de Sant Antoni • Daily 10am–dusk • Free • Ⓜ Sants-Estació

If you have time to kill at Barcelona Sants station, nip around the south side to Basque architect Luis Peña Ganchegui's urban park, the **Parc de l'Espanya Industrial**. Built on the site of an old textile factory, it has a line of red-and-yellow-striped lighthouses at the top of glaring white steps, with an incongruously classical Neptune in the water below. Altogether, six sculptors are represented here and, along with the boating lake, café-kiosk, playground and sports facilities provided, the park takes a decent stab at reconciling local interests with the mundane nature of the surroundings.

Parc Joan Miró

C/de Tarragona • Daily 10am–dusk • Free • Ⓜ Tarragona

Parc Joan Miró was laid out on the site of the nineteenth-century municipal slaughterhouse. It features a raised piazza whose only feature is Joan Miró's gigantic mosaic sculpture **Dona i Ocell** ("Woman and Bird"), towering above a shallow reflecting pool. It's a familiar symbol if you've studied Miró's other works, but the sculpture is known locally by several other names – all of them easy to guess when you consider its erect, helmeted shape. The rear of the park is given over to games areas and landscaped sections of palms and firs, with a kiosk café and some outdoor tables found in among the trees. The children's playground here is one of the best in the city, with a climbing frame and aerial runway as well as swings and slides.

Arenas de Barcelona

Gran Via de les Corts Catalanes 373–385, at Pl. d'Espanya • Daily 10am–10pm • ☎ 932 890 244, Ⓦ arenasdebarcelona.com • Ⓜ Espanya

Landmark building on the north side of Plaça d'Espanya is the fabulous Moorish-style bullring, the **Arenas de Barcelona**, originally built in 1900 but re-imagined as a swish shopping and leisure centre that opened in 2011. Conceived by architect Richard Rogers as a gateway to the city centre, and preserving the beautiful brick exterior, the various retail levels at Arenas are hung in sweeping, circular galleries, while right on top, outside, is a wide walk-around promenade circling the **dome** that offers 360-degree views of the western side of the city. An express elevator whisks you up here from street level, or take the glass lifts or escalators inside through four floors of shopping and entertainment that include a cinema, gym and health centre, various restaurants (some on the top-floor promenade) and a museum devoted to rock music.

Museu del Rock

4th Floor, Arenas de Barcelona • Tues & Wed 10am–10pm, Thurs & Fri 10am–4pm, €5, under-12s €3; Thurs & Fri 4–10pm, Sat & Sun 10am–10pm, €9, under-12s €5 • Ⓦ museudelrock.com • Ⓜ Espanya

The city's **Museu del Rock** is a "greatest hits" collection of gold records, musical instruments, stage clothes and music-history ephemera, from Spanish rockers and international superstars alike. We're talking Elvis, Beatles and the Rolling Stones, rather than any great coverage of the contemporary music scene, Still, if you ever wondered where Elton John's bathtub had got to…

Casa de la Papallona

C/de Llança 20 • No public access • Ⓜ Espanya

It's worth walking around the Arenas de Barcelona and craning your neck up to the top of the six-storey Casa Fajol, universally known as the **Casa de la Papallona** (1912). The work of architect Josep Graner i Prat (1844–1930), it's crowned by a huge ceramic butterfly (*papallona*) made using the favoured *modernista* technique of *trencadís*, or broken coloured tiles formed to make a picture.

8

Sagrada Família and Glòries

If there's one building in the city to which a visit is obligatory it's Antoni Gaudí's great church of the Sagrada Família, which lies in the eastern reaches of the Eixample. Most visitors make a special journey out by metro to see the church and then head straight back into the centre, but there are also a few lesser-known *modernista*-era buildings nearby, most notably the enchanting pavilions of the Hospital de la Santa Creu i de Sant Pau. A few blocks south of the Sagrada Família is the area known as Glòries, home to the city's main concert hall and music museum, and the flagship national theatre building. Glòries was originally conceived as the nucleus of the nineteenth-century city expansion plan, but while this never materialized, it is a neighbourhood destined for dramatic redevelopment as the city council continues to breathe new life into peripheral urban areas.

Sagrada Família

9

C/de Mallorca 401 • Daily: April–Sept 9am–8pm; Oct–March 9am–6pm • €12.50 (under-10s free) or €16.50 including guided tour or audioguide; combination ticket with Casa-Museu Gaudí at Parc Güell €14.50 • 1hr guided tours (no advance purchase) daily, in English at 11am, noon (Sat & Sun only Nov–May) & 1pm • ☎ 932 073 031, ⓦ sagradafamilia.cat, advance ticket sales through ⓦ servicaixa.com • Ⓜ Sagrada Família

Nothing – really, nothing – prepares you for the impact of the **Temple Expiatori de la Sagrada Família**, which occupies an entire city block between c/de Mallorca and c/de Provença, north of the Diagonal; the metro drops you right outside. In many ways the overpowering church of the "Sacred Family" has become a kind of symbol for the city, and was one of the few churches left untouched by the orgy of church-burning that accompanied both the 1909 "Tragic Week" rioting and the 1936 revolution. More than any other building, it speaks volumes about the Catalan urge to glorify uniqueness and endeavour. It is the most fantastic of the modern architectural creations in which Barcelona excels – even the coldest hearts will find the Sagrada Família inspirational in form and spirit.

Brief history

Initial work on the church was slow. It took four years to finish the crypt (1901), the first full plan of the building wasn't published until 1917 and by the time of Antoni Gaudí's death only one facade was complete. Although the building survived, Gaudí's plans and models were mostly destroyed during the Civil War – George Orwell (whose political sympathies were clear) remarking that the Sagrada Família was "one of the most hideous buildings in the world" and that the anarchists "showed bad taste in not blowing it up when they had the chance".

Work restarted in the late 1950s amid great controversy, and has continued ever since – as have the arguments. Some maintained that the Sagrada Família should be left incomplete as a memorial to Gaudí, others that the architect intended it to be the work of several generations. Construction is financed by private funding and ticket sales, not by government or church, and for many years the work has been overseen by chief architect Jordi Bonet, the son of one of Gaudí's assistants. His vision has attracted no little criticism for infringing Gaudí's original spirit, not least the work on the Passion facade, commissioned from sculptor Josep María Subirachs. Computer-aided design

---

ANTONI GAUDÍ: GOD'S ARCHITECT?

Begun in 1882 by public subscription, the **Sagrada Família** was originally intended by its progenitor, the Catalan publisher Josep Bocabella, to be an expiatory building that would atone for the city's increasingly revolutionary ideas. Bocabella appointed the architect Francesc de Paula Villar to the work, and his plan was for a modest church in an orthodox neo-Gothic style. Two years later, after arguments between the two men, **Antoni Gaudí** – only 31 years of age – took charge and changed the direction and scale of the project almost immediately, seeing in the Sagrada Família an opportunity to reflect his own deepening spiritual and nationalist feelings. He spent most of the rest of his life working on the church. Indeed, after he finished the Parc Güell in 1911, Gaudí vowed never to work again on secular projects, but to devote himself solely to the Sagrada Família, which became perhaps the most daring creation in all Art Nouveau. His church design displayed apparently lunatic flights of fantasy, yet it was always rooted in functionality and strict attention to detail – Gaudí himself, living in a workshop on site, carried on adapting the plans ceaselessly right up to his untimely death. Run over by a tram on the Gran Via on June 7, 1926, he died in hospital three days later – initially unrecognized, for he had become a virtual recluse, rarely leaving his small studio. His death was treated as a Catalan national disaster, and all of Barcelona turned out for his funeral procession. Following papal dispensation, he was buried in the Sagrada Família crypt, a fitting resting place for an architect whose masterpiece was designed (he said), to show "the religious realities of present and future life … man's origin, his end". Everything from the Creation to Heaven and Hell, in short, was included in his one magnificent sacred ensemble.

SAGRADA FAMÍLIA AND GLÒRIES

N

RAMBLA DE VOLART
PTGE GIRA-SOL
CARRER DEL TORRENT
CARRER DEL TROBADOR
C DE LA TORRE VÉLEZ
D'AMÈRICA
PASSATGE DE L'ALGUER
CARRER DEL BENEFICÈNCIA
CARRER DE CONCA

MUNTANYA
CARRER DE MARAGALL
PG DE MARAGALL
CARRER DEL
C.J. MASSANÉS
PLAÇA CAN
ROBACOLS
PISTO
C. INFANT
C DE FONTOVA
C DE SIBELIUS
C DE LLAGOSTERA
C DEL DEGÀ BAHÍ
CARRER DE ROGENT

PTGE DE ROMA
PTGE DE CATALUNYA
CARRER DE SANT QUINTÍ

CARRER DE JOAN DE PEGUERA
CARRER DEL COLL I VEHÍ

CARRER DEL FRESER
CARRER DE XIFRÉ
C DE SIBELIUS
C DE BASSOLS

Hospital de la Santa Creu i de Sant Pau

PTGE DOS DE MAIG
PTGE DE LA INDEPENDÈNCIA
Hospital de la Creu Roja
CARRER DE LA INDEPENDÈNCIA
Encants

Hospital de Sant Pau

CARRER DE CARTAGENA
CARRER DE CARTAGENA

PTGE DE CENTELLES
PTGE DE VILARET

CARRER DE LLORENÇ I BARBA
CARRER DE STA. CAROLINA
C DE ROSSÀLIA DE CASTRO
TRAVESSERA DE GRÀCIA

CARRER DELS CASTILLEJOS
CARRER DELS CASTILLEJOS

AVINGUDA DE GAUDÍ

CARRER DE PADILLA
CARRER DE PADILLA

C DE BERENGUER DE LAS CASAS

Mercat de la Sagrada Família

CARRER DE LEPANT
CARRER DE LEPANT

C DE TAXDIRT

CARRER DE LA MARINA
CARRER DE LA MARINA

Sagrada Família
PLAÇA DE GAUDÍ
Sagrada Família

CARRER DE SARDENYA

CARRER DE LA INDÚSTRIA
CARRER DE CÒRSEGA
PASSATGE DE SIMÓ
CARRER DEL ROSSELLÓ

Sagrada Família
PLAÇA DE LA SAGRADA FAMÍLIA
Sagrada Família

PTGE DE ROMANS
PTGE DE NOGUÉS
CARRER DE VENTALLÓ
C DE SETANTÍ
CARRER DE PARELLADA
C DE SECRETARI COLOMA

TRAVESSERA DE GRÀCIA
CARRER DE SANT ANTONI MARIA CLARET

PTGE DE LLAVALLOL
CARRER DE SICÍLIA

CARRER DE PROVENÇA
CARRER DE VALÈNCIA

Joanic
CARRER D'HIPÒLIT LÀZARO
DE JOAQUIM RUYRA

CARRER DE NÀPOLS
CARRER DE MALLORCA

Casa Planells

CARRER D'EN GRASSO

CARRER DE ROGER DE FLOR
PTGE D'ÀLIO

PASSEIG DE SANT JOAN

Casa Macaya

AVINGUDA DIAGONAL

Verdaguer

C DE L MINGO

CARRER DE BAILÈN

9

and high-tech construction techniques have also proved controversial, while tunnelling under the temple for the high-speed AVE train line kicked up a huge stink among critics who claim that the church will be put at risk (not so, say the tunnel engineers). All in all, though the project might be drawing inexorably towards completion (within the next twenty years, it's said), there's still plenty more time for argument.

The building

The size alone is startling – Gaudí's original plan was to build a church to seat over 10,000 people, while the iconic **towers** rise to over 100m high. A precise symbolism pervades the facades, each of which is divided into three porches devoted to Faith, Hope and Charity. Gaudí made extensive use of human, plant and animal models, as well as taking casts and photographs, in order to produce exactly the sculptural likenesses he sought – the spreading stone leaves of the roof in the church interior, for example, were inspired by the city's plane trees. The eastern **Nativity facade** (facing c/ de la Marina) was the first to be completed and is alive with fecund detail, its very columns resting on the backs of giant tortoises. Contrast this with the Cubist austerity of Subirachs' work on the western **Passion facade** (c/de Sardenya), where the brutal story of the Crucifixion is played out across the harsh mountain stone. Although parts of the interior still resemble a giant building site, and the **Glory façade** remains unfinished, the whole church will be roofed in due course, with a 170-metre-high central dome and tower to follow (which will then make the church the tallest building in Barcelona).

The towers and museum

Daily: April–Sept 9am–8pm; Oct–March 9am–6pm • Towers €2.50, timed elevator tickets available from main ticket office; museum free

There are eight **towers** at the Sagrada Família, four on each current facade, though following Gaudí's design there will eventually be eighteen – twelve symbolizing the apostles, four dedicated to the evangelists and one each for Mary and Jesus. They have been likened to everything from perforated cigars to celestial billiard cues. To see them at close quarters take one of the separate **elevators** that run up the Passion and Nativity facades, from where you'll be rewarded by partial views of the city through an extraordinary jumble of latticed stonework, ceramic decoration, carved buttresses and sculpture.

Your entrance ticket also gives you access to the **museum**, which traces the career of the architect and the history of the church. Models, sketches and photographs help to make some sense of the work going on around you, and you can see sculptors and model-makers at work in the plaster workshop.

Hospital de la Santa Creu i de Sant Pau

C/de Sant Antoni Maria Claret 167, at c/del Dos de Maig • Information point open daily 9.30am–1.30pm • Admission free, tours daily in English at 10am, 11am, noon & 1pm, plus others in Spanish/Catalan; €10, under-18s €5 • ☏ 933 177 652, ⓦ rutadelmodernisme.com • Ⓜ Hospital de Sant Pau

Lluís Domènech i Montaner's *modernista* public hospital, the **Hospital de la Santa Creu i de Sant Pau**, is possibly the one building in town that can rival the Sagrada Família for size and invention. The hospital has its own metro stop, but it's far better to walk up the four-block-long Avinguda de Gaudí from the church, which gives terrific views back over the spires of the Sagrada Família.

Work started in 1902, the brief being to replace the city's medieval hospital buildings in the Raval. The architect spent ten years working on the project and left his trademarks all over it: thumbing his nose at the city grid, he aligned the buildings diagonally to the Eixample, while whimsical pavilions, turrets and towers are covered with sculpture, mosaics, stained glass and ironwork. These days, the old buildings have

9

been superseded by the modern hospital of the same name behind, though a painstaking restoration of the *modernista* pavilions is currently under way. Informative hard-hat **tours** of the site tell you more about the six-hundred-year history of the hospital and the current renovation project; there's also a "Ruta del Modernisme" information point in the Sant Jordi pavilion, where you can see a documentary on the Art Nouveau period in Catalunya.

Casa Macaya

Pg. de Sant Joan 108 • No public access • Ⓜ Verdaguer

Four blocks west of the Sagrada Família, Josep Puig i Cadafalch's palatial **Casa Macaya** dates from 1898–1900. It's a superbly ornamental building with a Gothic-inspired courtyard and canopied staircase from which griffins spring. You might be able to poke your head inside for a look, since the house has been used in the past as a gallery run by the Fundació La Caixa, but even from the outside it's worth pausing to view the unusual exterior carvings by *modernista* craftsman Eusebi Arnau i Mascort – like the angel with a "box" Brownie camera or the sculptor himself on his way to work by bike.

Casa Planells

Av. Diagonal 332 • No public access • Ⓜ Monumental

Built in 1923–24, the **Casa Planells** apartment block – a sinuous solution to an acute-corner building – simplifies many of the themes that Gaudí exaggerated in his work. It's actually by Josep Maria Jujol i Gilbert, who was one of Gaudí's early collaborators, responsible not only for La Pedrera's iconic undulating balconies but also much of the famous mosaic work in Parc Güell.

Plaça de les Glòries Catalanes

Ⓜ Glòries

Barcelona's major avenues all meet at the **Plaça de les Glòries Catalanes**, a glorified roundabout dedicated to the "Catalan glories", from architecture to literature. It's now at the centre of the city's latest bout of regeneration, which plans to tunnel the traffic underground, thus opening up a grand pedestrianized park containing a design centre to house the city's applied art collections.

MODERNISM'S CRAFTY COLLABORATORS

Despite the overwhelming noise of the big-gun architects of the time, *modernisme* was often a true collaborative effort between the architects and their craftsmen and artisans. Lluís Domènech i Montaner, in particular, recognized the importance of ensemble working, and established a pioneering craft workshop in the building he designed initially as a restaurant for Barcelona's Universal Exhibition of 1888 (known as the *Castell dels Tres Dragons*). Antoni Gaudí, too, always worked with skilled craftsmen, including his longtime collaborator – and a master of mosaic decoration – **Josep Maria Jujol i Gilbert** (1879–1949). The other significant name is that of **Eusebi Arnau i Mascort** (1864–1933), who provided meticulous carvings for all the main *modernista* architects – much loved are his quirky figures adorning Josep Puig i Cadafalch's Casa Macaya and the tour-de-force carved fireplace in the Raval's *Hotel Espanya*. Some projects brought together the cream of craft talent, so at Domènech i Montaner's Palau de la Música Catalana, for example, the glorious stained glass by Antoni Rigalt and elaborate facade sculpture by Miquel Blay form an integral part of the whole. Meanwhile, the stunning private houses being built across Barcelona for wealthy captains of industry looked as good on the inside as they did on the outside, filled with furniture by *modernista* craftsmen like cabinet-maker extraordinaire **Joan Busquets i Jané** (1874–1949) and artist and interior designer **Gaspar Homar i Mezquida** (1870–1955).

9

TREASURE-HUNTING AT ELS ENCANTS VELLS

At the city's traditional open-air flea market, **Els Encants Vells** (c/del Dos de Maig; Mon, Wed, Fri & Sat 7am–3pm, plus same times Sun & hols Dec 1–Jan 5; Ⓦ encantsbcn.com; Ⓜ Encants/Glòries), you name it, you can buy it: old sewing machines, cheese graters, photograph albums, cutlery, lawnmowers, clothes, shoes, CDs, antiques, furniture and out-and-out junk. It's best in the early morning, and haggling for any "old charms" (*encants vells*) you might fancy is de rigueur, but you're up against experts. The market is due a new home with the completion of the Glòries renovations, so access, hours and location are subject to change over the next few years.

Glòries is already positioned as a gateway to the Diagonal Mar district, with **trams** running down Avinguda Diagonal to the district. Meanwhile, signature building on the roundabout is French architect Jean Nouvel's cigar-shaped **Torre Agbar** (142m), the headquarters of the local water company (Aigües de Barcelona), a highly distinctive aluminium-and-glass tower with no fewer than four thousand windows, its shape inspired by the rocky protuberances of Montserrat. A huge shopping mall lies across the Diagonal from here, while further across the Gran Via the park and play areas of **Parc del Clot** show what can be done in an urban setting within the remains of a razed factory site. Jean Nouvel also designed the **Parc del Centre del Poble Nou** further down the Diagonal (10min walk from Glòries or tram stop Pere IV), an eye-catching contemporary park set on another former industrial site – a surviving brick chimney stands in the centre, surrounded by willow trees.

Teatre Nacional de Catalunya

Pl. de les Arts 1 • Tours on the hour 10am–1pm; €5; reservations required • ☎ 933 065 700, Ⓦ tnc.cat • Ⓜ Glòries or tram T4

Off to the southwest of Glòries, the **Teatre Nacional de Catalunya** – Catalunya's national theatre – was designed by local architect Ricardo Bofill and auspiciously inaugurated on the Catalan national day, the *Diada* (September 11) in 1997. It presents the neighbourhood with a soaring glass box encased within a Greek temple on a raised dais, surrounded by manicured lawns. There are guided building and backstage **tours** for anyone interested in learning more, as well as a bar and restaurant that are open in the evening – a summer evening's drink on the open-air *terrassa* is a nice way to take in the grandiose surroundings.

L'Auditori and the Museu de la Música

L'Auditori c/de Lepant 150 • Ⓦ auditori.cat **Museu de la Música** c/de Padilla 155 • Mon & Wed–Sat 10am–6pm, Sun & hols 10am–8pm • €4, under-16s free, plus free first Sun of the month & every Sun after 3pm • ☎ 932 563 650, Ⓦ museumusica.bcn.cat • Ⓜ Glòries/Marina

Set a block over from the national theatre, and forming a sort of cultural enclave, **L'Auditori** is the city's contemporary city concert hall, built in 1999. Housed within it, on the c/de Padilla side, is the **Museu de la Música**, which displays a remarkable collection of instruments and musical devices, from seventeenth-century serpent horns to reel-to-reel cassette decks. It's all very impressive, with soaring glass-walled cases letting you view the pieces from all sides, and yet it struggles to engage, partly because of the sheer number and variety of instruments and partly because of the impenetrable commentary, with sections called things like "The humanist spirit and the predominance of polyphony". Make of that what you will, or the chronological "timeline" that runs from Pythagoras in the fifth century BC to 2007 when "the Rolling Stones continue to play". Still, there's a bit of big-screen Elvis here and African drumming there, and if you've ever wanted to pluck at a harp without anyone shouting at you, this is the place.

Gràcia, Parc Güell and Horta

Gràcia – the closest neighbourhood to the Eixample – was a village for much of its early existence before being annexed as a city suburb in the late nineteenth century. There's still a genuine small-town atmosphere here, very distinct from the old-town neighbourhoods, while Gràcia's vibrant cultural scene and nightlife counters the notion that Barcelona begins and ends on the Ramblas. The one unmissable attraction is just on the neighbourhood fringe, namely the surreal Parc Güell, by architectural genius Antoni Gaudí. Meanwhile in nearby Horta ("garden"), so called after the gardens and country estates that once characterized the area, two more distinctive parks attract the curious. That of Creueta del Coll is typical of the new urban projects that have revitalized forgotten corners of the city, while the Parc del Laberint and its renowned maze speak of more traditional times.

Gràcia

Still very much the liberal, almost bohemian, stronghold it was in the nineteenth century, the northern neighbourhood of **Gràcia** feels set apart from the city in many ways. Its traditional annual summer festival, the **Festa Major** every August – a week's worth of concerts, parades, fireworks and parties – has no peer in any other neighbourhood and although actual sights in Gràcia are few and far between, it's well known for its cinemas, bars and restaurants. Wander the narrow, gridded streets, park yourself on a bench under a plane tree, catch a film, grab a beer or otherwise take time out from the rigours of city-centre life – you'll soon get the feel of a neighbourhood that, unlike some in Barcelona, has a real soul.

10

ARRIVAL AND DEPARTURE · GRÀCIA

By bus Buses #22 or #24 from Plaça de Catalunya run to Gràcia, stopping on the main c/Gran de Gràcia.

By metro and train The most convenient metro stations are Ⓜ Diagonal (south), Ⓜ Fontana (north) or Ⓜ Joanic (east), or take the FGC train from Plaça de Catalunya to Gràcia station.

On foot Gràcia is a 30min walk from Plaça de Catalunya. From any of the neighbourhood stations, it's around a 500m walk to Gràcia's central squares.

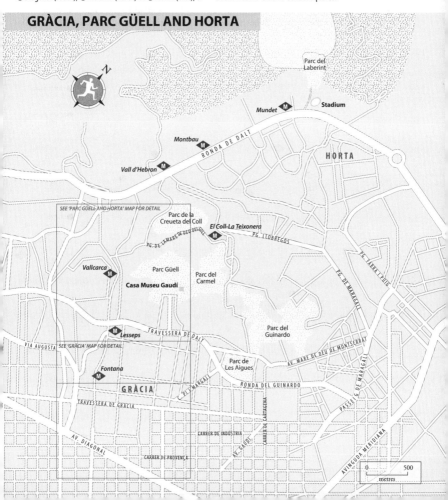

GRÀCIA, PARC GÜELL AND HORTA

10

Mercat de la Llibertat

Pl. Llibertat 27 • Mon–Fri 8am–8.30pm, Sat 8am–3pm • ☎ 932 170 995, ⊕ mercatsbcn.com • Ⓜ Fontana or FGC Gràcia

You may as well start where the locals start, first thing in the morning, shopping for bread and provisions in the **Mercat de la Llibertat**, a block west of c/Gran de Gràcia. The building was first revamped in 1893 by a former pupil of Gaudí, Francesc Berenguer i Mestrès, who sheltered its food stalls under a *modernista* wrought-iron roof. It's since been beautifully restored again and is always worth a walk through, especially if you fancy the breakfast of champions – oysters, grilled razor clams and a glass of cava – available from one of the classy stand-up café counters.

Casa Vicens

C/les Carolines 24 • No public access • Ⓜ Fontana

Antoni Gaudí's first major private commission, the **Casa Vicens** (1883–85), is on the northern edge of the neighbourhood. Here he took inspiration from the Moorish style, covering the facade in linear green-and-white tiles with a flower motif. The decorative iron railings are a reminder of Gaudí's early training as a metalsmith and, to further prove his versatility – and how Art Nouveau cuts across art forms – Gaudí also designed much of the mansion's furniture (though as it's a private house, unfortunately you can't get in to see it).

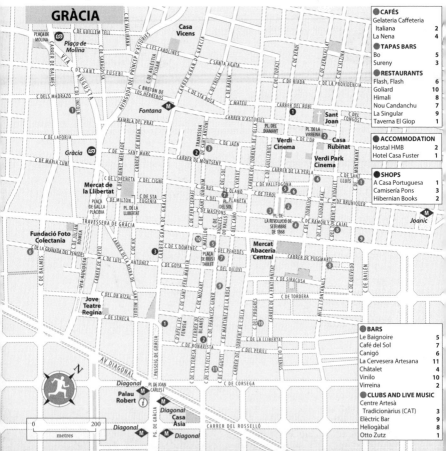

> **THE THREE SQUARES BAR CRAWL**
>
> Three squares tucked away in the middle of Gràcia (ⓂFontana/Diagonal), within a few blocks' walk of each other, contain many of the best neighbourhood cafés and bars. A night out in Gràcia invariably means passing through them at some point. Traditionally, **Plaça del Sol** has been the beating heart of the district's nightlife, though it was redesigned rather soullessly in the 1980s and is not quite so appealing during the day. Far more in keeping with Gràcia's overall village-like tenor is the mouthful that is **Plaça de la Revolució de Setembre de 1886**, just to the east of Plaça del Sol, and especially **Plaça Rius i Taulet**, to the south across Travessera de Gràcia. The thirty-metre-high clocktower in the latter was a rallying point for nineteenth-century radicals, whose twenty-first-century counterparts prefer to meet for brunch at the popular café *terrassas*.

10

Plaça de la Virreina
ⓂFontana

Pretty **Plaça de la Virreina**, backed by the parish church of Sant Joan, is one of Gràcia's favourite squares, with the *Virreina Bar* and others providing drinks and a place to rest and admire the handsome houses, most notably **Casa Rubinat** (1909), c/de l'Or 44, the last major work of Francesc Berenguer. Children and dogs, meanwhile, scamper around the small drinking fountain. Nearby streets, particularly **Carrer de Verdi**, contain many of the neighbourhood's most fashionable boutiques, galleries, cinemas and cafés.

Parc Güell

Antoni Gaudí's extraordinary urban park on the outskirts of Gràcia, **Parc Güell**, was his most ambitious project after the Sagrada Família. It was commissioned by Eusebi Güell (patron of Gaudí's Palau Güell, off the Ramblas) and was originally planned as a private housing estate of sixty dwellings, furnished with ornamental paths, recreational areas and decorative monuments. The idea was to build a "Garden City" of the type popular at the time in England – indeed, Gaudí's original plans used the English spelling "Park Güell". Gaudí worked on the project between 1900 and 1914 but in the end only two houses were actually built, and the park was officially opened to the public instead in 1922.

ARRIVAL AND DEPARTURE　　　　　　　　　　　　　　　　　　　　　　　**PARC GÜELL**

If you have a choice, it's best to visit Parc Güell during the week, as weekends can be very busy indeed. The park straddles a steep hill and however you get there will involve an ascent on foot of some kind to reach the main section. Leaving the park, you'll have to walk back down c/de Larrard to Travessera de Dalt for bus or metro connections back to the city, though taxis do hang about the main gates on c/d'Olot.

By bus The most direct route is on bus #24 from Plaça de Catalunya, Passeig de Gràcia or c/Gran de Gràcia, which drops you on Carretera del Carmel at the eastern side gate by the car park. The Bus Turístic stops at the bottom end of c/de Larrard on c/de la Mare de Deu de la Salut.
By metro From ⓂVallcarca walk a few hundred metres down Av. de Vallcarca until you see the mechanical escalators on your left, ascending Baixada de la Glória.

Follow these – and the short sections of stepped path in between – right to the western-side park entrance (15min), from where you wind down a path to the main terrace.
On foot Walking from Gràcia (ⓂLesseps), turn right along Travessera de Dalt and then left up steep c/de Larrard, which leads straight to the main entrance of the park on c/Olot (10min).

The park
Main entrance, c/d'Olot • Daily: March & Oct 10am–7pm; April & Sept 10am–8pm; May–Aug 10am–9pm; Nov–Feb 10am–6pm • Free

Laid out on a hill, which provides fabulous views back across the city, the park is an almost hallucinatory expression of the imagination. Pavilions of contorted stone, giant lizards, meandering rustic viaducts, a vast Hall of Columns (intended to be the estate's market), carved stone trees – all combine in one manic swirl of ideas and excesses. The

Hall of Columns, for example, was described by the art critic Sacheverell Sitwell (in *Spain*) as "at once a fun fair, a petrified forest, and the great temple of Amun at Karnak, itself drunk, and reeling in an eccentric earthquake". Perhaps the most famous element is the long, meandering **ceramic bench** that snakes along the edge of the terrace, entirely covered with a brightly coloured broken tile-and-glass mosaic (a method known as *trencadís*) that forms a dizzying sequence of abstract motifs, symbols, words and pictures. The ceramic mosaics and decorations found throughout the park were mostly the work of master craftsman Josep Maria Jujol i Gilbert, who assisted on several of Gaudí's projects.

There's a **café** with terrace seats in the park but to escape the milling crowds you'll need to climb up into the wooded, landscaped gardens. At the very highest point – follow signs for "**Turó de les Tres Creus**" – on the spot where Gaudí had planned to place a chapel, three stone crosses top a stepped tumulus. It's from here that a 360-degree city panorama unfolds in all its glory.

PARC GÜELL AND HORTA

Centre d'Interpretació

C/d'Olot • Daily: May–Sept 10am–8pm; Oct–April 10am–6pm • €2, combined ticket with Museu d'Història de Barcelona €7 • ☎ 932 562 122, ⓦ museuhistoria.bcn.cat

At the main entrance on c/d'Olot, the former porter's lodge – and never can a porter have had more whimsical lodgings – is now the **Centre d'Interpretació**, whose explanatory panels and displays offer a useful introduction to the park's history and design.

Casa Museu Gaudí

Inside Parc Güell • Daily: April–Sept 10am–8pm; Oct–March 10am–6pm • €5.50, combined ticket with Sagrada Família €14.50 • ☎ 932 193 811, ⓦ casamuseugaudi.org

10

One of Gaudí's collaborators, Francesc Berenguer, designed and built a turreted house within the park for the architect, where Gaudí was persuaded to live until he left to camp out at the Sagrada Família for good. In the **Casa Museu Gaudí**, his ascetic study and bedroom have been kept much as they were in his day – there's an inkling of his personality in the displayed religious texts and pictures, along with a silver coffee cup and his death mask, made at the Sant Pau hospital where he died. Other rooms display a diverting collection of furniture he designed for other projects – a typical mixture of wild originality and brilliant engineering – as well as plans and objects relating to the park and to Gaudí's life.

Parc de la Creueta del Coll

Pg. de la Mare de Deu del Coll 77 • Daily 10am–dusk • Free • Bus #28 from Pl. de Catalunya, via Pg. de Gràcia, stops 100m from the park, or walk from ⓜ Vallcarca in about 20min (there's a neighbourhood map at the metro station)

There couldn't be a greater contrast with Parc Güell than Horta's **Parc de la Creueta del Coll**, a contemporary urban park by Olympic architects Martorell and Mackay that was laid out on the site of an old quarry. You're greeted at the top of the park steps by an Ellsworth Kelly metal spike, while suspended by steel cables over a reflecting pool is a massive concrete claw by the Basque artist Eduardo Chillida. There's a stand of palm trees by a small artificial lake, which becomes a summer swimming pool, and concrete promenades and picnic areas under the sheer quarry walls.

Combining the park with a visit to Parc Güell is easy, too, though you'll need a keen sense of direction to find it from the rear exit of Parc Güell – it helps if you've climbed to the top of Güell's three-crosses hill and fixed in mind the quarry walls, which you can see across the valley. It's far easier to visit Parc de la Creueta del Coll first, then walk back down the main Passeig de la Mare de Deu del Coll until you see the signpost pointing down c/Balears (on your left) – from there, signposts guide you into Parc Güell the back way.

Parc del Laberint

Pg. dels Castanyers 1–17 • Daily 11am–dusk • €2.20, free Wed & Sun • ⓜ Mundet: use the Passeig Vall d'Hebron (Muntanya) exit, walk up the main road and against the traffic flow for 1min (past the sports pitches) and turn left into the grounds of the Velòdrom (cycle stadium)

Half a dozen stops further out on the metro from Gràcia, and confronted by the roaring traffic on the Passeig Vall d'Hebron, it seems inconceivable that there's any kind of sanctuary to hand, but just a couple of minutes' walk from Mundet metro puts you at the gates of the **Parc del Laberint**, sited behind the cycle stadium. The former estate mansion is now used by the city's parks and gardens department, while the late eighteenth-century gardens (the oldest in the city) are open for public visits and are an enchanting spectacle. A series of shady paths, terraces, pavilions and water features embrace the hillside, merging with the pine forest beyond. At the very heart of the park is the famed topiary maze, El Laberint, created by the Marquis de Llupià i Alfarràs and designed as an Enlightenment puzzle concerning the forms of love. A statue of Eros in the centre is the reward for successfully negotiating the maze. Near the park entrance are a drinks kiosk, picnic area and children's playground.

Les Corts, Pedralbes and Sarrià-Sant Gervasi

To the northwest of the city centre, what was once the village of Les Corts is now largely indistinguishable from the rest of the modern city, save for the hallowed precincts of Camp Nou, FC Barcelona's stupendous football stadium. Nearby, across Avinguda Diagonal, the Palau Reial de Pedralbes combines the city's applied art collections (of clothes and textiles, decorative arts and ceramics), while a half-day's excursion can be made by walking from the palace, past the Gaudí dragon gate at Pavellons Güell to the calm cloister at the Gothic monastery of Pedralbes. Complete the day by returning via Sarrià, to the east, with a pretty main street and market to explore. At night the focus shifts to the bars and restaurants of neighbouring Sant Gervasi, in the streets north of Plaça de Francesc Macià.

Uptown Avinguda Diagonal

Ⓜ Maria Cristina or tram T1, T2 or T3 from Pl. de Francesc Macià

The uptown section of **Avinguda Diagonal** runs through the heart of Barcelona's flashiest business and shopping district. The giant **L'Illa** shopping centre flanks the avenue – the stepped design is a prone echo of New York's Rockefeller Centre. Designer fashion stores are ubiquitous, particularly around **Plaça de Francesc Macià** and Avinguda de Pau Casals – at the top of the latter, **Turó Parc** (daily 10am–dusk) is a good place to rest weary feet, with a small children's playground and a café-kiosk. For picnic supplies, the traditional neighbourhood market, **Mercat de Galvany** (c/de Santaló 65; Mon–Sat 7am–2pm; ⓦmercatgalvany.com), is just three blocks to the east. Meanwhile, behind L'Illa, it's worth seeking out **Plaça de la Concordia**, another surprising survivor from the past amid the uptown tower blocks. The pretty little square is dominated by its church belltower and ringed by local businesses (florist, pharmacy, hairdresser), with an outdoor café or two for a quiet drink.

Camp Nou and FC Barcelona

11

Av. Arístides Maillol • ☎ 902 189 900 or ☎ 934 963 600, ⓦ fcbarcelona.com • Ⓜ Collblanc/Maria Cristina, then a 10min walk, or Bus Turístic stops outside the stadium

It's no exaggeration to say that football in Barcelona is a genuine obsession, with support for the local giants **FC (Futbol Club) Barcelona** raised to an art form. "More than just a club" is the proud boast, and certainly during the dictatorship years the club stood as a Catalan symbol around which people could rally. Arch-rivals Real Madrid, on the other hand, were always seen as Franco's club. The swashbuckling players in the famous "blaugrana" (claret and blue) shirts have transcended national barriers to become every football fan's second favourite team; indeed, the four-times European champions (most recently in 2011) – mercurial masters of the elegant *tiki-taka*, pass-and-move style – are often hailed as the world's best team.

There's no more invigorating introduction to Catalan passions than to take in a match at the magnificent **Camp Nou** ("New Ground") stadium, sited in the Les Corts neighbourhood, behind the university buildings. This was built in 1957, and enlarged for the 1982 World Cup semi-final to accommodate 98,000 people – a further remodelling (by architect Norman Foster) plans to update the stadium again over the next few years. The stadium provides one of the best football-watching experiences in the world and the matches can be an invigorating introduction to Catalan passions. The museum and stadium tour is a must, whether you get to a game or not (see p.223), while the stadium complex also hosts basketball, handball and hockey games with FC Barcelona's other professional teams. There's also a public ice rink, souvenir store and café.

Museum and stadium tour

Museu del Futbol, entrance on Av. Arístides Maillol, through gates (Accés) 7 and 9 • April–Oct Mon–Sat 10am–8pm (rest of the year until 6.30pm), Sun & hols 10am–2.30pm, last tour 1hr before closing, no tours on match days • €19, under-13s €15.50, under-5s free • ☎ 902 189 900 or ☎ 934 963 600, ⓦ fcbarcelona.com

Together, the stadium and museum – billed as the "**Camp Nou Experience**" – provide a magnificent celebration of Spain's national sport. The **self-guided tour**, complete with audio-guide, winds through the changing rooms and players' tunnel onto the pitch and up to the press gallery and directors' box for stunning views. The **museum** is jammed full of silverware and memorabilia, including the six cups won in 2009 alone, Barcelona's *annus mirabilis*, while a cracking multimedia zone profiles historic games and famous players and relives the match-day atmosphere. Finally, you're directed into the **FC Botiga** megastore, where you can buy anything from a replica shirt down to a branded bottle of wine.

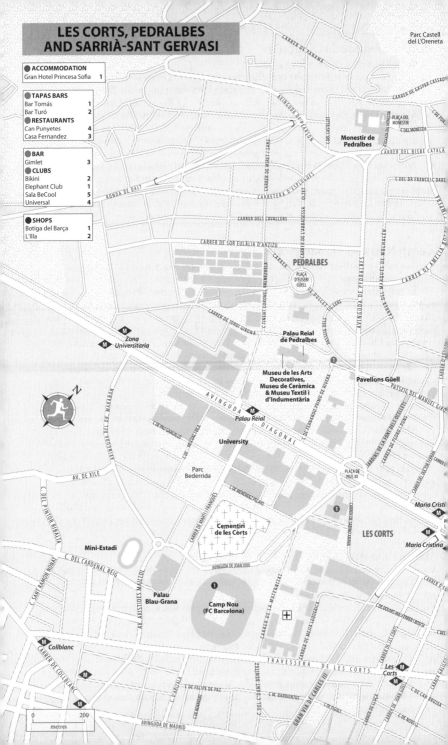

LES CORTS, PEDRALBES AND SARRIÀ-SANT GERVASI

● **ACCOMMODATION**
Gran Hotel Princesa Sofia   **1**

● **TAPAS BARS**
Bar Tomás   **1**
Bar Turó   **2**
● **RESTAURANTS**
Can Punyetes   **4**
Casa Fernandez   **3**

● **BAR**
Gimlet   **3**
● **CLUBS**
Bikini   **2**
Elephant Club   **1**
Sala BeCool   **5**
Universal   **4**

● **SHOPS**
Botiga del Barça   **1**
L'Illa   **2**

IT'S ONLY A GAME?

Some people believe football is a matter of life or death … I can assure you it is much, much more
important than that.
Bill Shankly

There isn't a Catalan football supporter who wouldn't agree with Liverpool legend and quip-meister Bill Shankly. These are fans who boo their own team if they think the performance isn't up to scratch, thousands of white handkerchiefs waving along in disapproval. A disappointing season is seen as a slur on the Catalan nation, and if success goes instead to bitter rivals Real Madrid, then the pain is almost too much to bear. When team figurehead and captain **Luis Figo** was transferred to Madrid in 2000 (one of only a handful to have played for both clubs), the outrage was almost comical in its ferocity – at a later match between the two sides, a pig's head was thrown onto the pitch as Figo prepared to take a corner. In recent years, though, there has been a lot more cheering than booing, as the team has played with a swagger rarely seen in modern club football. Under coach Josep **"Pep" Guardiola** – former Barça player and all-Catalan hero – Barcelona have evolved into a team of scintillating beauty, not only running rings around rivals from home and abroad but also providing the bulk of the side that won the World Cup for Spain for the first time in 2010. The Barcelona style – don't give the ball away, ever, period – is learned at **La Masia**, the club's own training centre and school for young footballers, most of whom are Catalan or come at an early age from elsewhere. Half the current team are graduates, including the peerless, best-in-the-world, Lionel Messi. Things change quickly in football – Madrid might start winning again, Messi or Guardiola might leave – but the production line at La Masia is the best guarantee that boos and white hankies will be absent from the Camp Nou for a while longer yet.

Palau Reial de Pedralbes

Av. Diagonal 686 • Gardens daily 10am–dusk; free • ⓜ Palau Reial or tram T1,T2 or T3

Opposite the university on Avinguda Diagonal, formal grounds stretch up to the Italianate **Palau Reial de Pedralbes** – basically a large villa with pretensions. It was built for the use of the royal family on their visits to Barcelona, with funds raised by public subscription, and received its first such visit in 1926. However, within five years the king had abdicated and the palace somewhat lost its role. Franco kept it on as a presidential residence and it later passed to the city, which now uses its rooms to show off its applied art collections. Until the projected Centre del Disseny (Design Centre) at Glòries is completed, the palace rooms contain separate **museums** of ceramics, the decorative arts and textiles and clothing, which can be visited on the same ticket (note that all are closed on Mondays, full details given below). The Decorative Arts Museum is probably the highlight for anyone with just a general interest in applied art, but you can easily whip around all three museums in an hour or two.

The **gardens**, meanwhile, are a calm oasis, where – hidden in a bamboo thicket, to the left-centre of the facade – is the "Hercules fountain" (1884), an early work by Antoni Gaudí.

Museu de Ceràmica

Palau Reial, Av. Diagonal 686 • Tues–Sun 10am–6pm • €5, ticket valid for other Palau Reial museums, free Sun after 3pm & free first Sun of the month • ☎ 932 563 465, ⓦ museuceramica.bcn.cat • ⓜ Palau Reial or tram T1,T2 or T3

In the **Museu de Ceràmica** (Ceramics Museum) is housed Spain's most significant collection of historic ceramics, which ranges from the thirteenth to the twentieth century. Temporary exhibitions focus on special themes or contemporary ceramic artists, though it's the historical exhibits in the permanent exhibition that often really grab your attention. These include a series of fifteenth- and sixteenth-century *socarrats* (decorated terracotta panels) depicting demons and erotic scenes, while from Catalunya's long ceramics tradition are displayed entire rooms of decorated water stoups, jars, dishes, plates and bowls. The collection is nothing if not diverse, whether it's a painted nineteenth-century ceramic Barcelona street sign or the vivid *azulejo* (ceramic tile) panel of 1710 showing the feasting and dancing taking place at a party centred on the craze of the period – hot-chocolate-drinking.

Museu de les Arts Decoratives

Palau Reial, Av. Diagonal 686 • Tues–Sun 10am–6pm • €5, ticket valid for other Palau Reial museums, free Sun after 3pm & free first Sun of the month • ☎ 932 563 465, ⓦ dhub-bcn.cat • Ⓜ Palau Reial or tram T1, T2 or T3

Arranged around the upper gallery of the Palau Reial's former throne room, the **Museu de les Arts Decoratives** (Decorative Arts Museum) provides a hugely enjoyable romp from Romanesque art through to contemporary Catalan design. Side rooms showcase the various periods under the spotlight, with displays of highly polished Baroque cabinets, Art Deco glassware and *modernista* furniture. A particular highlight is the four-metre-high stained-glass window of 1900, depicting the *sardana* (a circle dance) being performed in a scene that looks back to medieval times for its inspiration. The second half of the gallery traces the development of industrial design from the 1930s to the present day, which is actually an excuse to showcase an extraordinary range of Catalan *disseny* (design), from chairs to espresso machines, lighting to sink taps.

Museu Textil i d'Indumentaria

Palau Reial, Av. Diagonal 686 • Tues–Sun 10am–6pm • €5, ticket valid for other Palau Reial museums, free Sun after 3pm & free first Sun of the month • ☎ 932 563 465, ⓦ dhub-bcn.cat • Ⓜ Palau Reial or tram T1, T2 or T3

In "Dressing the Body" – the permanent exhibition at the **Museu Textil i d'Indumentaria** (Textile and Clothing Museum) – the city's extensive textile and clothing collection is put to work to explain how clothes have modified body image through the ages. It's basically a history of fashion and design from the sixteenth century onwards, from court gowns to Parisian silk stockings by way of 1930s cocktail dresses and contemporary *haute couture*. The museum's full collection actually extends far wider than the pieces shown in the selective permanent exhibition – some date back to Roman times – while additional special exhibitions might demonstrate the art and technique behind crafts like cloth-making, embroidery, lace or tapestry work.

Pavellons Güell

Av. de Pedralbes 7 • Guided visits Sat & Sun at 10.15am & 12.15pm in English, plus 11.15am & 1.15pm in Spanish/Catalan; visits also possible on Fri & Mon with advance reservation • €6, under-18s €3 • ☎ 933 177 652, ⓦ rutadelmodernisme.com • Ⓜ Palau Reial, then a 5min walk

As an early test of his capabilities, Antoni Gaudí was asked by his patron, Eusebi Güell, to rework the entrance, gatehouse and stables of the Güell summer residence, which was sited on a large working estate well away from the filth and unruly mobs of

---

HERE BE DRAGONS

The slavering beast on Gaudí's dragon gate at the Pavellons Güell is not the vanquished dragon of Sant Jordi (St George), the Catalan patron saint, but the one that appears in the **Labours of Hercules** myth, a familiar Catalan theme in the nineteenth century. Gaudí's design was based on a work by the Catalan renaissance poet **Jacint Verdaguer**, a friend of the Güell family, who had reworked the myth in his epic poem, *L'Atlàntida* – thus, the dragon guarding golden apples in the Gardens of Hesperides is here protecting instead an orange tree (considered a more Catalan fruit). Gaudí's gate indeed can be read as an homage to Verdaguer, with its stencilled roses representing those traditionally given to the winner of the Catalan poetry competition, the Jocs Floral, which the poet won in 1877.

downtown Barcelona. The summer house itself was later given to the royal family (and rebuilt as the Palau Reial), but the brick-and-tile stables and outbuildings – known as the **Pavellons Güell** – survive as Gaudí created them. They are frothy, whimsical affairs showing more than a Moorish touch to them, with minarets that display Gaudí's first experimentation with *trencadís* (broken tile mosaics), a technique he then used continually on his more famous projects.

However, it's the **gateway** that's the most famous element. An extraordinary winged dragon made of twisted iron snarls at the passers-by, its razor-toothed jaws spread wide in a fearsome roar: backing up to pose for a photograph suddenly doesn't seem like such a good idea. During the week you can't go any further than the gate, but guided visits show you the grounds and Gaudí's innovative stables, now used as a library by the university's historical architecture department.

Monestir de Pedralbes

11

Baixada del Monestir 9 • Tues–Sat 10am–2pm (April–Sept until 5pm), Sun 10am–8pm, hols 10am–3pm; church usually open 11am–1pm & 5–8pm • €7, includes entry to other Museu d'Història de Barcelona sites, free Sun after 3pm • ☎ 932 563 434, ⓦ museuhistoria .bcn.cat • ⓜ Palau Reial and 20min walk, or FGC Reina Elisenda (frequent trains from Pl. de Catalunya) and 10min walk, or bus #64 from Pl. Universitat

Founded in 1326 for the nuns of the Order of St Clare, the Gothic **Monestir de Pedralbes** is, in effect, an entire monastic village preserved on the outskirts of the city, within medieval walls that completely shut out the noise and clamour of the twenty-first century. It took medieval craftsmen a little over a year to prepare Pedralbes (from the Latin *petras albas*, "white stones") for its first community of nuns. The speed of the initial construction and the subsequent uninterrupted habitation by the order helps explain the extreme architectural harmony. After 600 years of isolation, the monastery was sequestered by the Generalitat during the Civil War and it later opened as a **museum** in 1983 – a new adjacent convent was built as part of the deal, where the Clare nuns still reside. The ensemble now forms part of the Barcelona History Museum.

The cloisters and monastery

The **cloisters** are the finest in the city, built on three levels and adorned by the slenderest of columns, with the only sound the tinkling water from the fountain. Side rooms and chambers give a clear impression of medieval convent life, from the chapter house and austere refectory to a fully equipped kitchen and infirmary. Alcoves and day cells display restored frescoes, religious artefacts, furniture and utensils, while in the nuns' former dormitory – now given a black marble floor and soaring oak-beamed ceiling – is a selection of the rarer **treasures**. While the nuns themselves eschewed personal trappings, the monastery acquired valuable art and other possessions over the centuries – including pieces of Gothic furniture, paintings by Flemish artists, an impressive series of so-called "factitious" altarpieces from the sixteenth century (made up of sections of different style and provenance), and some outstanding illuminated choirbooks.

The church

The monastic **church** is a simple, single-naved structure, which retains some of its original fourteenth-century stained glass. In the chancel, to the right of the altar, the foundation's sponsor, Elisenda de Montcada, wife of Jaume II, lies in a superb carved marble tomb. Widowed in 1327, six months after the inauguration of the monastery, Elisenda retired to an adjacent palace, where she lived until her death in 1364.

Sarrià

FGC Sarrià (take c/Mare de Deu de Núria exit), or bus #64 from Monestir de Pedralbes/Pl. Universitat

The **Sarrià** district was once an independent small town and still looks the part, with a narrow, traffic-free main street – c/Major de Sarrià – at the top of which stands the much-restored church of **Sant Vicenç**. The church flanks the main Passeig de la Reina Elisenda de Montcada, across which lies the neighbourhood market, **Mercat Sarrià**, housed in a 1911 *modernista* red-brick building. You'll find a few other surviving old-town squares down the main street, prettiest of which is **Plaça Sant Vicenç de Sarrià** (off c/Mañe i Flaquer), where there's a statue of the saint. If you make it this way, don't miss the *Bar Tomás*, just around the corner on c/Major de Sarrià (see p.194), for the world's best *patatas bravas*.

11

PERFORMERS AT THE PARC D'ATRACCIONS TIBIDABO

Tibidabo and Parc de Collserola

The views from the heights of Tibidabo (550m), the peak that signals the northwestern boundary of the city, are legendary. On a clear day you can see across to the Pyrenees and out to sea even as far as Mallorca. However, while many make the tram and funicular ride up to Tibidabo's wonderfully old-fashioned amusement park, few realize that beyond stretches the Parc de Collserola, an area of peaks, wooded river valleys and hiking paths – one of Barcelona's best-kept secrets. You can walk into the park from Tibidabo, but it's actually better to start from the park's information centre, across to the east, above the hilltop village of Vallvidrera, which can be reached by another funicular ride. Meanwhile, families won't want to miss CosmoCaixa, the city's excellent science museum, which can easily be seen on the way to or from Tibidabo.

CosmoCaixa

C/Teodor Roviralta 47–51 • Tues–Sun 10am–8pm • €3, first Sun of month free, under-18s €2, under-7s free, children's activities €2, planetarium €2 • ☎ 932 126 050, ⓦ cosmocaixa.com • FGC Avinguda del Tibidabo (trains from Pl. de Catalunya) and 10min walk, or Tramvia Blau (see p.140) or Bus Turístic stop close by

A dramatic refurbishment in 2005 transformed the city's science museum into a must-see attraction, certainly if you've got children in tow – it's an easy place to spend a couple of hours. Partly housed in a converted *modernista* hospice, **CosmoCaixa** retains the original building but has added a light-filled public concourse and a huge underground extension with four subterranean levels, where hands-on experiments and displays investigate life, the universe and everything, "from bacteria to Shakespeare". Many of the exhibits, and their densely worded explanations, require a very large thinking cap – younger children are soon going to be zooming around the open spaces. But there's no denying the overall pull of the two big draws, namely the 100 tonnes of "sliced" rock in the **Mur Geològic** (Geological Wall) and, best of all, the **Bosc Inundat**

– nothing less than a thousand square metres of real Amazonian rainforest, complete with croc-filled mangroves, anacondas and giant catfish.

Other levels of the museum are devoted to children's and family activities, such as **Toca Toca!** (Touch Touch!) – handling animals, insects and plants – **Clik** (ages 3–6) and **Flash** (7–10), where science games and experiments are presented in a fun way. These activities tend to be held at weekends and during school holidays – pick up a schedule when you arrive. There are also daily shows in the **planetarium** (in Spanish and Catalan only), a great gift shop and a café-restaurant with outdoor seating beneath the restored hospital facade.

Parc d'Atraccions Tibidabo

Pl. del Tibidabo • Days and hours vary, but basically June–Sept & hols Wed–Sun, rest of the year Sat, Sun & hols only, closed Jan & Feb; park open noon–7/11pm depending on season • Skywalk ticket €12, full admission €26, plus family/discount tickets • ☎ 932 117 942, ⓦ www.tibidabo.es

Barcelona's self-styled "magic mountain" amusement park – the **Parc d'Atraccions** – has been thrilling its citizens for over a century. It's a mix of traditional rides, plus an influx of high-tech roller-coasters and free-fall drops, laid out around several levels of the mountaintop, connected by landscaped paths and gardens. Some of the most famous historic attractions are grouped under the discounted "**Skywalk**" ticket, like the aeroplane – spinning since 1928 – the carousel and the quirky **Museu d'Autòmates**, a collection of coin-operated antique fairground machines in working order. Summer weekends finish with parades, concerts and a noisy *correfoc*, a theatrical **fireworks** display.

12

Sagrat Cor

Daily 10am–2pm & 3–7pm • €2

There are amazing views from everywhere in Tibidabo park, and they become even more extensive if you climb the shining steps of the neighbouring Templo Expiatorio de España, otherwise known as the **Sagrat Cor** (Sacred Heart), topped by a huge statue of Christ. Inside the church, an elevator (*ascensor*) climbs to a sensational viewing platform, from where the city, surrounding hills and sea shimmer in the distance.

ARRIVAL AND DEPARTURE   PARC D'ATRACCIONS TIBIDABO

Getting to Tibidabo can be a convoluted matter but it is also half the fun, since you'll need to combine several forms of transport. It takes up to an hour, all told, from the city centre.

By train, tram and funicular Take the FGC train (Tibidabo line 7) from Plaça de Catalunya station to Avinguda del Tibidabo (the last stop), where you cross the road to the tram/bus shelter. An antique tram service, the Tramvia Blau (departures every 15–30min: mid-June to mid-Sept daily 10am–8pm, rest of year weekends & hols, plus Christmas and Easter weeks 10am–6pm; €2.90 one-way, €4.50 return) then runs you up the hill to Plaça del Doctor Andreu; there's a bus service instead out of season during the week. By the tram and bus stop on Plaça Doctor Andreu (where there are several café-bars and restaurants),

you change to the Funicular del Tibidabo, with connections to Tibidabo at the top (every 15min; operates when the Parc d'Atraccions is open; €4 return, fare reimbursed with park admission).
By bus The Bus Turístic stops at Avinguda del Tibidabo, where you can change for the Tramvia Blau. Alternatively, the special Tibibus runs direct to Tibidabo from Plaça de Catalunya (from 10.30am every day that the park is open; €3, fare reimbursed with park admission). Local bus #111 runs on a circuit (every 30min; city passes and transport tickets valid) between Tibidao park and Vallvidrera village.

Torre de Collserola and Vallvidrera

Torre de Collserola, Carretera de Vallvidrera al Tibidabo • Easter week, July, Aug & Christmas Wed–Sun noon–2pm & 3.15–7/8pm, otherwise weekends & hols only noon–2pm & 3.15–6pm, closed Jan & Feb • €5, under-14s €3, under-3s free, combined ticket available with Parc d'Atraccions • ☎ 932 117 942, ⓦ www.tibidabo.es • Bus #111 from Tibidabo or Vallvidrera village

Follow the road from the Tibidabo car park and it's only a few minutes' walk to Norman Foster's **Torre de Collserola**, a soaring communications tower high above the tree line, with a glass lift that whisks you up ten floors (115m) for yet more stunning views – 70km, they claim, on a good day.

Afterwards, you could just head back to Tibidabo for the funicular-and-tram ride back to the city, but to complete a circular tour it's more interesting to follow the cobbled path near the tower's car park, which brings you out on the pine-clad edges of **Vallvidrera**, a well-to-do suburban village perched on the flank of the Collserola hills – a twenty-minute walk all told from Tibidabo. There's another **funicular** station here (6am–midnight; every 6–10min), connecting to Peu del Funicular, an FGC station on the Sabadell and Terrassa line from Plaça de Catalunya.

Vallvidrera's main square isn't obvious – if you turn left out of the funicular station and walk down the steep steps, Plaça de Vallvidrera is the traffic roundabout at the bottom.

Parc de Collserola

Centre d'Informació daily 9.30am–3pm • ☎ 932 803 552, ⓦ www.parcnaturalcollserola.cat • FGC Baixada de Vallvidrera (on the Sabadell or Terrassa line from Pl. de Catalunya; 15min)

Given a half-decent day, local bikers, hikers and outdoors enthusiasts all make a beeline for the city's ring of wooded hills beyond Tibidabo. The **park information centre** lies in oak and pinewoods, an easy, signposted ten-minute walk up through the trees from the FGC Baixada de Vallvidrera train station. There's a bar-restaurant here with an outdoor terrace, plus an exhibition on the park's history, flora and fauna, while the staff hand out English-language leaflets detailing the various walks, which range from a fifteen-minute stroll to the Vallvidrera dam to a couple of hours circling the hills.

Some of the park walks – like the oak-forest walk – soon gain height for marvellous views over the tree canopy, while others descend through the valley bottoms to springs and shaded picnic areas. Perhaps the nicest short walk from the information centre is to the **Font de la Budellera** (1hr 15min return), a landscaped spring deep in the woods. If you follow the signs from the *font* to the Torre de Collserola (another 20min), you can return to Barcelona instead via the funicular from Vallvidrera, or even take in the views from the Collserola tower or Tibidabo before heading back.

12

Museu-Casa Verdaguer

Villa Joana, Carretera de l'Església 4 • Sat, Sun & hols 10am–2pm • Free • ☎ 932 047 805, ⓦ museuhistoria.bcn.cat • FGC Baixada de Vallvidrera

If you're up at the Collserola park at the weekend, you might as well have a quick look inside the **Museu-Casa Verdaguer**, housed in the Villa Joana, which sits just below the park information centre. Jacint Verdaguer i Santaló (1845–1902), the Catalan Renaissance poet and priest, lived here briefly before his death, and the house has been preserved as an example of well-to-do nineteenth-century Catalan life. Extracts from his poetry enliven the climb up from the FGC station to the information centre and house.

STAINED GLASS, GAUDÍ'S CHURCH, COLÒNIA GÜELL

Out of the city

Barcelona is the capital of the wider province known as Catalunya, which stretches from the Mediterranean coast to the mountains of the Pyrenees. The region's excellent public transport links mean that even on a short trip you can easily see a contrasting set of destinations, from historic Catalan cities to rolling vineyards, and from ancient churches to seaside resorts. Most lie within an hour's journey from Barcelona by train – it really isn't worth renting a car unless you want to see a lot of Catalunya in a short time. The accounts in this chapter are geared towards day-trips, though you can always check with the local tourist offices about accommodation in their area and consult ⓦcatalunya.com, the region's official tourism website. You might also arrive at the regional airports of Girona or Reus on your visit to Barcelona, in which case you can visit some of the destinations en route to the city.

Although there are plenty of traditional coastal bolt-holes close to Barcelona, like Castelldefels to the south or the small towns of the Costa Maresme to the north, unquestionably the best local seaside destination is **Sitges**, half an hour to the south along the Costa Daurada. It's a charming resort with an international reputation, extremely popular with gay visitors and chic city-dwellers. Otherwise, the one essential excursion is to **Montserrat**, the extraordinary mountain and monastery 40km northwest of Barcelona, reached by a precipitous cable-car or mountain railway ride. However short your trip to the city, this is worth making time for, as it's a site of great significance for Catalans, not to mention being a terrific place for a hike in the hills.

If you enjoy Barcelona's varied church architecture, there's more to come, starting with Gaudí's inspired work at the **Colònia Güell**, a late nineteenth-century idealistic community established by the architect's patron Eusebi Güell. This is a half-day's outing, while a second half-day can be spent visiting the Benedictine monastery at **Sant Cugat del Vallès** and the complex of early medieval churches at **Terrassa**, all of them largely unsung and utterly fascinating. Another route out of the city, due west, leads through the wine-producing towns of **Sant Sadurní d'Anoia** and **Vilafranca del Penedès**, both of which can be seen in a day's excursion with enough time for a wine-tasting tour.

It's also straightforward to see something of Barcelona's neighbouring cities, all very different from the Catalan capital. To the south of Barcelona, beyond Sitges, lies **Tarragona**, with a compact old town and an amazing series of Roman remains. Nearby **Reus** was the birthplace of Antoni Gaudí and features an interpretative museum that's

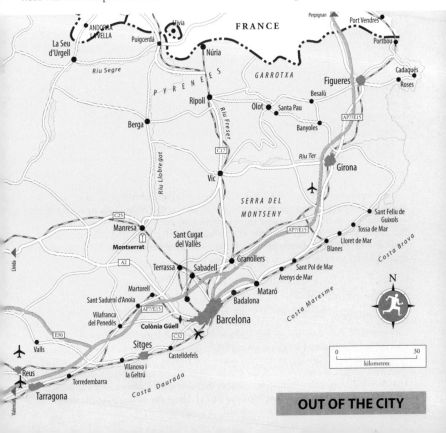

13

REGIONAL FESTIVALS

FEBRUARY–MARCH
Carnival Sitges has Catalunya's best Carnival celebrations (see p.146).

MARCH–APRIL
International jazz festival in Reus sees acts playing in clubs and old-town squares.

MAY
Third week Fires i Festes de la Santa Creu in Figueres, with processions and music. Also Trapezi, the international circus fair in Reus, with street performances and spectacle.
Corpus Christi (moveable feast, sometimes falls in early June): Festa de Corpus Christi in Sitges – big processions and streets decorated with flowers.

JUNE
24 Dia de Sant Joan celebrated everywhere; watch out for things shutting down for a day on either side.
Last week Annual festival at Sant Cugat del Vallès. Also Festa Major de Sant Pere in Reus, the town's biggest annual bash.

JULY
Second week Gay Pride Sitges (ⓦ gaypridesitges.com) sees several days of events, parties and street parades every July.

AUGUST
19 Festa de Sant Magi in Tarragona.
Last week Festa Major in Sitges, to honour the town's patron saint, Sant Bartolomeu.
29 & 30 Festa Major in Vilafranca del Penedès (ⓦ festamajor.info), dedicated to Sant Felix, with human towers, dancing and processions.

SEPTEMBER
Second Sunday Fira Gran in Sant Sadurní d'Anoia, the town's big annual festival.
23 Festa de Sant Tecla in Tarragona, with processions of *gegants* and human castles.

OCTOBER
Second week The Setmana del Cava – a sort of cava festival – is held in Sant Sadurní d'Anoia.
Early Oct Festival Internacional de Cinema Fantastic in Sitges (ⓦ sitgesfilmfestival.com), a celebrated sci-fi, horror and fantast fest, complete with film premieres and zombie walks.

the last word on the man and his work. To the north, inland from the coast, sits medieval **Girona**, perhaps the most beautiful of all Catalan cities, with its river, fortified walls and golden buildings. These three destinations are all an hour or so from Barcelona, and it's only the extreme northern town of **Figueres** that requires any lengthier a journey – entirely justified for anyone interested in seeing Catalunya's most extraordinary museum, the renowned **Museu Dalí**.

Sitges

The seaside town of **Sitges**, 36km south of Barcelona, is definitely the highlight of the local coast – the great weekend escape for young Barcelonans, who have created a resort very much in their own image. It's also a noted gay holiday destination, with an outrageous carnival and an ebullient nightlife to match – between June and September it seems like there's one nonstop party going on. During the heat of the day, though, the tempo drops as everyone hits the beach, while out of season Sitges is delightful: far less crowded, and with a temperate climate that encourages promenade strolls and old-town exploration. Note that Monday isn't the best day to come, as the three museums and many restaurants are closed.

13

The seafront

There are clean sand **beaches** on either side of the old-town headland, though these become extremely crowded in high season. For more space it's best to keep walking west along the promenade, past a series of eight interlinked beaches that runs a couple of kilometres down the coast as far as the *Hotel Terramar*. There are breakwaters, beach bars, restaurants, showers and watersports facilities along the way, with the more notorious gay nudist beaches found at the far end.

Scores of handsome **restored mansions** in town were built in the nineteenth century by successful local merchants (known as "Americanos") who returned from Cuba and Puerto Rico. A walk along the seafront promenade reveals the best of them, adorned with wrought-iron balconies, stained-glass windows and ceramic decoration.

The old town

The knoll overlooking the beaches and marina is topped by the landmark Baroque **Església Parroquial** (parish church) dedicated to Sant Bartolomeu, whose festival is celebrated in town in the last week of August. The views from the terrace sweep along the coast, while behind, in the narrow streets of the old town, you'll find a series of late-medieval whitewashed mansions as well as the brick **Mercat Vell** (Old Market), the latter now an exhibition hall. The pedestrianized shopping street, **Carrer Major**, is the best place for browsing boutiques.

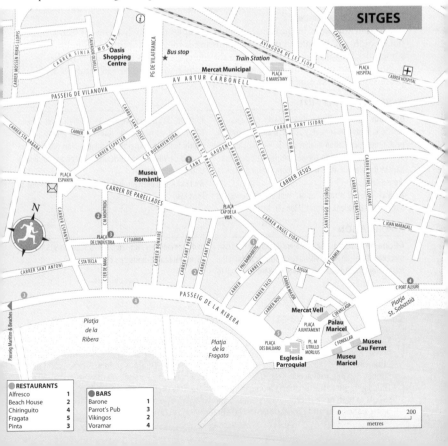

RESTAURANTS		BARS	
Alfresco	1	Barone	1
Beach House	2	Parrot's Pub	3
Chiringuito	4	Vikingos	2
Fragata	5	Voramar	4
Pinta	3		

13

Museu Cau Ferrat

C/Fonollar • Tues–Sat 9.30am–2pm & 3.30–6.30pm (July–Sept 4–7pm), Sun 10am–3pm • €3.50, combined ticket for all museums €6.50 • ☎ 938 940 364

One of the old-town mansions contains the **Museu Cau Ferrat**, set in the former house and workshop of the artist and writer **Santiago Rusiñol i Prats** (1861–1931), who moved here in 1891. Sitges flourished as an important *modernista* centre under his patronage – Rusiñol organized five *modernista* festivals between 1892 and 1899 – and the house contains a mixture of his own works and those by contemporaries, as well as various collected odds and ends, like the decorative ironwork Rusiñol brought back in bulk from the Pyrenees.

Museu Maricel

C/Fonollar • Tues–Sat 9.30am–2pm & 3.30–6.30pm (July–Sept 4–7pm), Sun 10am–3pm • €3.50, combined ticket for all museums €6.50 • ☎ 938 940 364

Next door to the Cau Ferrat museum, the **Museu Maricel** contains minor artworks, ceramics and sculpture. In July and August (usually two evenings a week) the main part of the mansion itself is open for guided tours, a short concert and drinks – ask at the tourist office for the current schedule.

Museu Romàntic

C/Sant Gaudenci 1 • Tues–Sat 9.30am–2pm & 3.30–6.30pm (July–Sept 4–7pm), Sun 10am–3pm • Tours hourly €3.50, combined ticket for all museums €6.50 • ☎ 938 942 969

The **Museu Romàntic**, in the centre of town, occupies the stately rooms of Can Llopis, a bourgeois home completed in 1793. Admission is by guided tour only (English sometimes spoken), which demonstrate the lifestyle of a rich Sitges family in the eighteenth and nineteenth centuries by displaying a wealth of period furniture and possessions, from divans to dolls.

ARRIVAL AND DEPARTURE
SITGES

By train Trains to Sitges leave Passeig de Gràcia or Barcelona Sants stations every 20min, more frequently at peak times (destination Vilanova or St Vicenç) and take 30–40min depending on the service. The last departure back to Barcelona is at around 10.30pm (starting again at around 5am).
By bus Mon-Bus (Ⓦ monbus.cat) runs a direct service to Sitges from Barcelona Airport (Mon–Fri hourly 7.40am–11.40pm, Sat & Sun every 2–3hr), which takes around 30min and stops near the tourist office. There's also an hourly nightbus (currently midnight–3am; 50min) from Passeig de Vilafranca, which drops passengers on Ronda Universitat in Barcelona.
By taxi A taxi between Barcelona and Sitges will cost at least €50.

INFORMATION

Oficina de Turisme c/Sinia Morera 1, behind the Oasis shopping centre, up Pg. de Vilafranca, a 5min walk from the station (mid-June to mid-Sept daily 9am–8pm; mid-Sept to mid-June Mon–Fri 9am–2pm & 4–6.30pm; ☎ 938 109 340, Ⓦ sitgestur.cat, Ⓦ bestsitges.cat).

CARNIVAL TIME

Carnival in Sitges (*Carnestoltes* in Catalan; Feb/March) is outrageous, thanks largely to the strong gay presence. It opens on the so-called Fat Thursday with the arrival of the Carnival King, following which there's a full programme of parades, masked balls, concerts, beach parties and sausage sizzles. The traditional *xatónada* gala dinners are named after the carnival dish, *xató*, a kind of salt-cod salad, which originates in Sitges. There's a children's procession on Sunday, while Carnival climaxes in Sunday night's Debauchery Parade and the even bigger Tuesday-night Extermination Parade, in which exquisitely dressed drag queens swan about the streets in high heels, twirling lacy parasols and coyly fanning themselves. Bar doors stand wide open, bands play and processions and celebrations go on until dawn.

EATING

Sitges has a huge array of restaurants, and the quality is largely very good, thanks to a discerning, upmarket tourist crowd and well-heeled locals. Every restaurant along the front does a paella with a promenade view, though some of the more interesting places are hidden away in the backstreets. For picnic supplies visit the **Mercat Municipal** (Mon–Thurs 8am–2pm, Fri & Sat 8am–2pm & 5.30–8.30pm), close to the train station on Av. Artur Carbonell, which is good for cured meats, olives, cheese, fresh bread and fruit.

Alfresco café c/Major 33 ☎ 938 113 307, restaurant c/Pau Barrabeitg 4 ☎ 938 940 600, ⓦ alfrescorestaurante.es. The café (on the main shopping street) is open for breakfast and light meals, while an associated restaurant (around the corner and down the steps) serves fancier Catalan cuisine (monkfish on white beans, gnocchi with wild mushrooms), with meals for €25–35. Café daily 10am–11pm, restaurant Tues–Sat 8.30pm–1am.

Beach House c/Sant Pau 34 ☎ 938 949 029, ⓦ beach housesitges.com. The Aussie owners have created a highly relaxed restaurant, offering a changing *table d'hôte* dinner menu (€25) of the best Asian-Med fusion food, from Thai fishcakes to seared tuna. It's a cocktail joint too (with happy hour 4–8pm), while the open-air terrace adds a touch of seaside romance. Easter–Oct: daily 4pm–2am.

Chiringuito Pg. de la Ribera ☎ 938 947 596. With a prime position on the prom, this claims to be Spain's oldest beach bar, serving grilled sardines, fried baby squid and calamari, sandwiches and tapas at reasonable prices (€5–15). Daily 10am–10pm, reduced hours in winter.

Fragata Pg. de la Ribera 1 ☎ 938 941 086, ⓦ restaurante fragata.com. *Fragata* is typical of the new wave of classy seafood places in town, where catch-of-the-day choices like grilled scallops or wild sea bass cost €17–28. Daily 1–4pm & 8–11pm.

Pinta Pg. de la Ribera 58–59 ☎ 938 947 871. The restaurants along the front all do their best to lure passers-by, and the *Pinta* pulls in many by virtue of its shady terrace and bargain lunchtime *menú del dia* (not available weekends). Otherwise, it's the usual enormous fish and seafood menu on offer from which you can eat à la carte for around €35. Daily 1–4pm & 8pm–midnight.

DRINKING AND NIGHTLIFE

The epicentre of local **nightlife** is c/Primer de Maig and c/Montroig, lined with café-*terrassas* that are busy in summer from morning to night. Call in at *Parrot's* for the lowdown on the gay scene and to find out which clubs are in this year.

Barone c/Sant Gaudenci 17 ☎ 938 942 279. Definitely not a style bar, but an old tavern that's a real slice of Sitges nonetheless. It's nowhere near the sea, so there's more of a down-to-earth local crowd. Daily 9pm–2am.

★ **Parrot's Pub** Pl. de l'Industria ☎ 938 947 881, ⓦ parrots-sitges.com. The stalwart of the gay bar scene in Sitges, with seats under shaded parasols. *Parrot's* also now has a stylish Mediterranean hotel and restaurant (dinner only) next door. Daily 9pm–2am.

Vikingos c/Marqués de Montroig 7–9 ☎ 938 949 687, ⓦ losvikingos.com. Long-standing party-zone bar with an enormous air-conditioned interior and streetside terrace. This and the similar *Montroig* next door serve drinks, snacks and meals from morning until night to a really mixed crowd. Daily 11am–1am (Fri & Sat until 2am).

Voramar c/Port Alegre 55 ☎ 938 944 404. Charismatic seafront bar, away from the main crowds, just right for an ice-cold beer or sundowner cocktail. It's a bit more pub-like than many in town, and generally attracts an older clientele. Daily 6pm–2am.

Montserrat

The mountain of **Montserrat**, with its rock crags, vast monastery and hermitage caves, stands just 40km northwest of Barcelona, off the road to Lleida. It's the most popular day-trip from the city, reached in around ninety minutes by train and then cable-car or mountain railway for a thrilling ride up to the monastery. Once there, you can visit the basilica and **monastery** buildings, and complete your day with a **walk** around the woods and crags, using the two funicular railways that depart from the monastery complex. There are cafés and restaurants at the monastery, but they are relatively pricey, none too inspiring and very busy at peak times – there's a lot to be said for taking your own picnic instead and striking off into the hills for an alfresco lunch.

Legends hang easily upon Montserrat. Fifty years after the birth of Christ, St Peter is said to have deposited an image of the Virgin (known as La Moreneta, the Black Virgin), carved by St Luke, in one of the mountain caves. The icon was lost in the early eighth century after being hidden during the Moorish invasion, but reappeared in 880,

13

accompanied by the customary visions and celestial music. A chapel was built to house it, and in 976 this was superseded by a Benedictine monastery, set at an altitude of nearly 1000m. Miracles abounded and the Virgin of Montserrat soon became the chief cult-image of Catalunya and a pilgrimage centre second in Spain only to Santiago de Compostela in Galicia with the main **pilgrimages** to Montserrat taking place on April 27 and September 8. In addition to the tourists, tens of thousands of newly married couples come here to seek La Moreneta's blessing, while Montserrat has also become something of an important nationalist symbol for Catalans.

The monastery

Basilica Daily 7.30am–8pm; access to La Moreneta 8–10.30am & noon–6.30pm • Free **Boys' choir** Mon–Fri at 1pm & 6.45pm, Sun at noon & 6.45pm, not Sat and not during school holidays at Christmas/New Year and from late June to mid-Aug • Free

The monastery's various outbuildings – including hotel and restaurant, post office, souvenir shop, self-service cafeteria and bar – fan out around an open square, and there are extraordinary mountain views from the terrace.

Of the religious buildings, only the Renaissance **Basilica**, dating largely from 1560 to 1592, is open to the public. **La Moreneta** stands above the high altar – reached from behind, by way of an entrance to the right of the basilica's main entrance. The approach to this beautiful icon reveals the enormous wealth of the monastery, as you queue along a corridor leading through the back of the basilica's rich side-chapels. Signs at head height command "SILENCE" in various languages, but nothing quietens the line which waits to kiss the image's hands and feet.

The best time to visit the basilica is when Montserrat's world-famous **boys' choir** sings. The boys belong to the Escolania, a choral school established in the fourteenth century and unchanged in musical style since its foundation.

Museu de Montserrat

Museu de Montserrat Daily 10am–5.30pm • €6.50 **Espai Audiovisual** Mon–Fri 9am–6pm, Sat & Sun 9am–6.45pm • €2

The **Museu de Montserrat** presents a few archeological finds brought back by travelling monks, together with paintings and sculpture dating from as early as the thirteenth century, including works by Old Masters, French Impressionists and Catalan *modernistas*. There's also a collection of Byzantine icons, though other religious items are in short supply, as most of the monastery's valuables were carried off by Napoleon's troops who sacked the complex in 1811. For more on the history, and to learn something of the life of a Benedictine community, visit the **Espai Audiovisual**, near the information office.

Mountain walks

Funicular departures every 20min, daily 10am–6pm, weekends only Oct–March • Santa Cova €3 return, Sant Joan €7.50 return, combination ticket €8.50

Following the mountain tracks to the nearby caves and hermitages, you can contemplate Goethe's observation of 1816: "Nowhere but in his own Montserrat will a man find happiness and peace." The going is pretty good on all the tracks and the signposting is clear, but you do need to remember that you're on a mountain – take a bottle of water and keep away from the edges. Two separate funiculars run from points close to the cable-car station, and a map with walking notes is available from the Montserrat tourist office.

One funicular drops to the path for **Santa Cova**, a seventeenth-century chapel built where the Moreneta icon is said to have been found. It's an easy walk there and back, which takes less than an hour.

The other funicular rises steeply to the hermitage of **Sant Joan**, from where it's a tougher 45-minute walk to the **Sant Jeroni** hermitage, and another fifteen minutes to the Sant Jeroni summit at 1236m. This is an excellent place to watch for peregrines, crag martins and black redstarts; in summer you may also spot alpine swifts, while Iberian wall lizards emerge from the crevices to bask on the rockfaces. Several other walks are also possible from the Sant Joan funicular, perhaps the nicest being the 45-minute circuit around the ridge that leads all the way back down to the monastery.

ARRIVAL AND DEPARTURE   MONTSERRAT

There are two ways to reach Montserrat by public transport – cable car and mountain railway – but in the first instance you need to take the **FGC train** (line R5, direction Manresa), which leaves Barcelona's Plaça d'Espanya (Ⓜ Espanya) daily at hourly intervals from 8.36am.

By cable car Get off at the train at Montserrat Aeri (52min) for the connecting cable car, the Aeri de Montserrat (every 15min; daily: March–Oct 9.40am–2pm & 2.30–7pm, Nov–Feb 10.10am–2pm & 2.30–5.45pm; ☎ 938 350 005, ⓦ aeridemontserrat.com). Queues are possible at busy times. Returning to Barcelona, the R5 trains depart hourly from Montserrat Aeri (from 9.37am).

By mountain railway The Montserrat mountain railway, the Cremallera de Montserrat (hourly; daily 8.48am–5.38pm, until 7.38pm at weekends April–Oct plus daily July–Sept; ☎ 902 312 020, ⓦ cremalleramontserrat.cat), departs from Monistrol de Montserrat (the next stop after Montserrat Aeri, another 4min), and takes 20min. Returning to Barcelona, the R5 trains depart hourly from Monistrol de Montserrat (from 9.33am).

Tickets An information desk at Plaça d'Espanya station details all the fare options, including return through-tickets from Barcelona (around €20) for either train/cable car or train/mountain railway. There are also two combination tickets available: the Trans Montserrat (€25), which includes all transport services, including unlimited use of the mountain funiculars, and entry to the audiovisual exhibit; and the Tot Montserrat (€40), which includes the same plus monastery museum entry and a cafeteria lunch. Both tickets are also available at the Plaça de Catalunya tourist office in Barcelona.

By car Take the A2 motorway as far as the Martorell exit, and then follow the N11 and C55 to the Montserrat turn-off – or park at either the cable-car or the mountain-railway station and take the rides up instead. All-in cable-car/Cremallera/Montserrat attraction combo tickets are available at the station for drivers who park and ride.

INFORMATION

Visitor Centre At the monastery (Mon–Fri 9am–5.45pm, Sat & Sun, plus daily July–Sept, 9am–6.45pm; ☎ 938 777 701, ⓦ montserratvisita.com). You can pick up maps of the complex and mountain, and they can also advise about accommodation, from camping to staying at the three-star *Abat Cisneros* hotel.

Sant Cugat and Terrassa

A series of remarkable churches lies on the commuter train line out of the city to the northwest, the first in the dormitory town of **Sant Cugat del Vallès** – just 25 minutes from Barcelona – and the second (actually a group of three) another fifteen minutes beyond in the industrial city of **Terrassa**. You can easily see all the churches in a

13

morning, but throw in lunch and this just about stretches to a day-trip, and it's not a bad ride in any case – after Sarrià, the train emerges from the city tunnels and chugs down the wooded valley into Sant Cugat.

Sant Cugat del Vallès

Reial Monestir Mon–Sat 9am–noon & 6–8pm, Sun open for Mass from 9am • Free **Museu de Sant Cugat** Jardins del Monestir • Tues–Sat 10am–1.30pm & 3–7pm (June–Sept until 8pm), Sun & hols 10am–2.30pm • €3, under-16s free • ☎ 936 759 951, ⓦ www .museu.santcugat.cat

At **Sant Cugat del Vallès**, the Benedictine **Reial Monestir** (Royal Monastery) was founded as far back as the ninth century, though most of the surviving buildings date from three or four hundred years later. Its fawn stone facade and triple-decker bell tower make a lovely sight as you approach from the square outside, through the gate, past the renovated Bishop's Palace and under a splendid rose window. Finest of all, though, is the beautiful twelfth-century Romanesque **cloister**, with noteworthy capital carvings of mythical beasts and biblical scenes. They have an unusual homogeneity, since they were all completed by a single sculptor, Arnau Gatell.

The main church is free to visit, but entrance to the cloister is to the side of the church, and forms part of the **Museu de Sant Cugat**, which also includes the restored dormitory, kitchen and refectory of the monastery, along with exhibitions about its history and monastic life. What were once the monastery's kitchen gardens lie across from the Bishop's Palace, though the formerly lush plots that sustained the brothers are now mere dusty gardens, albeit with views over the low walls to Tibidabo and the Collserola hills. Plaça Octavia, outside the monastery, has a weekly **market** every Thursday.

ARRIVAL AND DEPARTURE   SANT CUGAT

By train FGC trains from Barcelona (S1 line from Plaça de Catalunya; ⓦ fgc.cat) depart every 10–15min. In Sant Cugat, walk straight ahead out of the train station and down the pedestrianized c/Valldoreix, taking the first right and then the first left (it's still c/Valldoreix), and then keep straight along the shopping street (c/Santa Maria and then c/Santiago Rusiñol) until you see the monastery belltower (10min walk).

INFORMATION

Oficina de Turisme Sant Cugat del Vallès, Pl. Octavia, inside the main doorway of the monastery (June–Sept Tues–Sat 10am–1pm & 5–8pm, Sun & hols 10am–2pm; Oct–May Tues–Fri 10am–1.30pm & 4–6pm, Sat 10am–2pm & 4–6pm, Sun & hols 10am–2pm; ☎ 936 759 952, ⓦ turisme.santcugat.cat).

Terrassa

Terrassa, a large city with a population of 200,000 about 20km out of Barcelona, was an important textile producer in the nineteenth century, and retains many fine *modernista*-style factories, mills and warehouses that now enjoy protected status. But Terrassa has a much longer history to boast about, and on the edge of the city centre, built on the site of the former Roman town of Ègara, stand its true treasures – namely three pre-Romanesque churches, dating from the fifth to the tenth centuries.

La Seu d'Ègara

La Seu d'Ègara, Pl. del Rector Horns 1 • Tues–Sat 10am–1.30pm & 4–7pm, Sun & hols 11am–2pm • €3, under-6s free • ☎ 937 833 702, ⓦ seudegara.cat

Known as **La Seu d'Ègara**, Terrassa's ecclesiastical complex has been fully restored and is centred on its largest church, **Sant Pere**, which sports a badly faded Gothic mural and a tenth-century mosaic fragment within its walls. The church of **Santa Maria** is far better endowed, boasting a mosaic pavement outside and sunken baptismal font inside that both date from the fifth century. Much later Gothic (fourteenth- and fifteenth-century) murals and altarpieces – one by Catalan master Jaume Huguet – are also on display.

FROM TOP AQÜEDUCTE DE LES FERRERES, TARRAGONA (P.157); FREIXENET WINERY (P.154); SITGES BEACH (P.145) >

13

But it's the fifth-century baptistry of **Sant Miquel**, that's the most fascinating – a tiny, square building of rough masonry, steeped in gloom, with eight assorted columns supporting the dome, each with carved Roman or Visigothic capitals. Underneath sits the partially reconstructed baptismal bath, while steps lead down into a simple crypt.

ARRIVAL AND DEPARTURE   TERRASSA

By train FGC trains from Barcelona (S1 line from Plaça de Catalunya; wfgc.cat) depart every 10–15min – get off at Terrassa-Rambla, the last stop. The churches are a 20min walk from the station – turn right out of the station (Rambla d'Egara exit) and immediately right again into Plaça de Clavé, follow c/Major up to Plaça Vella, cross the square, turn up c/Gavatxons and follow c/Sant Pere, c/Nou de Sant Pere and c/de la Creu Gran, finally crossing a viaduct to arrive at the entrance. There is a more convenient Renfe mainline train station in Terrassa (direct trains from Barcelona Sants every 20min; wrenfe.com) – a straight 10min walk down c/del Mas Adel to the churches – but only the FGC line connects both Sant Cugat and Terrassa.

INFORMATION AND TOURS

Oficina de Turisme Raval de Montserrat 14 (Mon–Fri 9am–2pm & 5–7pm, Sat 10am–2pm & 5–7pm, Sun & hols 10am–2pm; t 937 397 019, w terrassa.org/turisme). Organizes guided tours of the city's industrial heritage.

Ruta del Modernisme Barcelona's Ruta del Modernisme package (w rutadelmodernisme) provides an "industrial and modernista route" through Terrassa (see p.27).

Colònia Güell

Before work at the Parc Güell got under way, Antoni Gaudí had already been charged with the design of parts of Eusebi Güell's earliest attempts to establish a Utopian industrial estate, or *colònia* (colony), on the western outskirts of Barcelona. The **Colònia Güell** at Santa Coloma de Cervelló was very much of its time – more than seventy similar colonies were established along Catalan rivers in the late nineteenth century, using water power to drive the textile mills. The concept was a familiar one in Britain, where enlightened Victorian entrepreneurs had long created idealistic towns (Saltaire, Bournville) to house their workers.

The Colònia Güell was begun in 1890, and by 1920 incorporated over one hundred houses and public buildings, plus the chapel and crypt for which Gaudí was responsible. The Güell company was taken over in 1945 and the whole complex closed as a going concern in 1973, though the buildings have since been restored – and, indeed, many are still lived in today. There are rows of terraced houses, with front gardens tended lovingly by the current inhabitants, while brick towers, ceramic panels and stained glass elevate many of the houses above the ordinary. It's a working village, so you'll also find a bank and pharmacy, as well as two or three cafés and restaurants.

Gaudí's church

May–Oct Mon–Sat 10am–2pm & 3–7pm, Sun 10am–3pm; Nov–April daily 10am–3pm; closed for visits during Mass on Sundays (11am & 1pm) • €5

Gaudí's **church** – built into the pine-clad hillside above the colony – is a masterpiece. While you can see the angular exterior from the outside for free, to see the far more dramatic interior you'll have to first buy a ticket at the visitor centre. The crypt was designed to carry the weight of the chapel above, its palm-tree-like columns supporting a brick vault, and the whole lot resembling a labyrinth of caves fashioned from a variety of different stone and brick. The more extraordinary features of Gaudí's flights of fancy presage his later work on the Sagrada Família – like the original scalloped pews, the conch shells used as water stoups, the vivid stained glass and the window that opens up like the wings of a butterfly. Despite appearances, the church was never actually finished – Gaudí stopped work on it in 1914 – and continuing restoration work aims to complete the outer walls, though Gaudí's planned forty-metre-high central dome is unlikely ever to be realized.

ARRIVAL AND DEPARTURE

By train Take the FGC train S8 (direction Martorell; departures every 15–20min; w fgc.cat) from Plaça d'Espanya to the small Colònia Güell station; the ride takes 20min. From the station, follow the painted blue footprints across the highway and into the *colònia* directly to the visitor centre (10min).

INFORMATION AND TOURS

Centre d'Acollida de Visitants (May–Oct Mon–Fri 10am–2pm & 3–7pm, Sat, Sun & hols 10am–3pm; Nov–April daily 10am–3pm. t 936 305 807, w elbaixllobregat. net/coloniaguell). The visitor centre has an exhibition (with English notes).

Guided tours Tours are available daily throughout the year, of either the church and estate or the church on its own, but call the visitor centre in advance since the service is usually only for groups.

EATING AND DRINKING

Ateneu Unió Pl. Joan Güell 5 t 936 613 111. The big, old-fashioned bar-restaurant on the quiet central square is good for sandwiches, tapas and a bargain €10 *menú del dia* served on the sunny *terrassa*. Daily 10am–midnight.

L'Alt Penedès wine region

L'Alt Penedès wine region (w altpenedes.net) lies roughly halfway between Barcelona and Tarragona. It's the largest Catalan producer of still and sparkling wines, which becomes increasingly clear the further the train heads into the region, with vines as far as the eye can see on both sides of the track. There are two main towns to visit, both of which can easily be seen in a single day: **Sant Sadurní d'Anoia**, the closer to Barcelona, is the self-styled "Capital del Cava", home to around fifty producers of sparkling wine; **Vilafranca del Penedès**, ten minutes down the line, is the region's administrative capital and produces mostly still wine, red and white.

If you're serious about **visiting vineyards** it's a trip better done by car, as many of the more interesting boutique producers lie out in the countryside. Either of the towns' tourist offices can provide a good map pinpointing all the local vineyards as well as the rural farmhouse restaurants that are a feature of this region. However, even by train you'll be able to visit a winery or two, including one of the most famous of Catalan wine names.

Sant Sadurní d'Anoia

The small town of **Sant Sadurní d'Anoia** (population 12,000), built on land watered by the Riu Noya, has been an important centre of wine production since the eighteenth century. When, at the end of the nineteenth century, French vineyards suffered heavily from philoxera, Sant Sadurní prospered, though later it too succumbed to the same wasting disease – something remembered still in the annual

---

CAVA

Cava is a naturally sparkling wine made using the *méthode champenoise,* the traditional method for making champagne. The basic **grape** varieties of L'Alt Penedès are *macabeu, xarel.lo* and *parellada*, which are fermented to produce a wine base and then mixed with sugar and yeast before being bottled: a process known as **tiratge**. The bottles are then sealed hermetically – the **tapat** – and laid flat in cellars – the **criança** – for up to nine months to ferment for a second time. The wine is later decanted to get rid of the sediment before being corked.

The cava is then **classified** according to the amount of sugar used in the fermentation: either Brut (less than 20g a litre) or Sec (20–30g); Semisec (30–50g) or Dolç (more than 50g). This is the first thing to take note of before buying or drinking: Brut and Sec are to most people's tastes and are excellent with almost any food, or as an aperitif; Semisec and Dolç are better consumed as dessert wines.

13

September festival by the parade of a representation of the feared philoxera parasite. The production of cava, for which the town is now famous, began only in the 1870s – an industry that went hand in hand with the Catalan cork business, established in the forests of the hinterland. Today, a hundred million bottles a year of cava are turned out by dozens of companies, many of which are only too happy to escort you around their premises, show you the fermentation process and let you taste a glass or two.

The wineries

Freixenet Daily tours and tastings, schedule varies, see website; reservations suggested • €6.10, under-18s €2.55, under-8s free • ☎ 938 917 000, ⓦ freixenet.es **Codorníu** Reservations required • ☎ 938 913 342, ⓦ codorniu.com

Most people never get any further than the most prominent and most famous company, **Freixenet**– producer of those distinctive black bottles – whose building is right outside the train station. Many other companies have similar arrangements, including the out-of-town **Codorníu** – the region's earliest cava producer – which has a fine building by *modernista* architect Josep Puig i Cadafalch as an added attraction. In addition, there are several dozen other *caves* or cellars in and around town, all shown on a map available at the Sant Sadurní tourist office.

Vilafranca del Penedès

As a town, **Vilafranca del Penedès** is rather more interesting than Sant Sadurní. Founded in the eleventh century in an attempt to attract settlers to land retaken from the expelled Moors, it became a prosperous market centre. This character is still in evidence today, with a compact old town at whose heart lie narrow streets and arcaded squares adorned with restored medieval mansions.

From the train station, walk up to the main Rambla de Nostra Senyora and cut to the right up c/de Sant Joan to the enclosed Plaça de Sant Joan, which has a small daily produce **market**. A rather larger affair takes place every Saturday, when the stalls also stock clothes, household goods, handicrafts and agricultural gear. The **Festa Major**, meanwhile, at the end of August and the first couple of days in September, brings the place to a standstill: dances and parades clog the streets, while the festival is most widely known for its display of *castellers* – teams of people competing to build human towers.

Vinseum

Pl. Jaume I 5 • Tues–Sat 10am–2pm & 4–7pm, Sun & hols 10am–2pm • €3 • ☎ 938 900 582, ⓦ vinseum.cat

The town museum is housed in a medieval mansion in the centre, and is the best place to get to grips with the region's wine industry. Exhibitions range far and wide – the emphasis is as much on local traditions and culture as wine – and the visit culminates with a tasting or two in the museum's own tavern.

The wineries

Torres Mon–Sat 9.15am–4.45pm, Sun & hols 9.15am–1pm • Tours €6.10, under-18s €3.55, under-8s free • ☎ 938 177 487, ⓦ torres.es **Jean Leon** Mon–Fri 9.30am–5pm, Sat, Sun & hols 9.30am–1pm, closed 2 weeks in July • Tours €10 • ☎ 938 995 512, ⓦ jeanleon.com

The vineyards of Vilafranca are all out of town, though the largest and best-known winery, **Torres**, is only a 3km taxi ride to the northwest, on the Sant Martí de Sarroca road. Also owned by Torres is boutique winemaker **Jean Leon** at Torrelavit, closer to Sant Sadurní, whose American-modernist-inspired visitor centre is set in particularly bucolic surroundings.

ARRIVAL AND DEPARTURE

L'ALT PENEDÈS

By train Renfe services from Pl. de Catalunya or Barcelona Sants (Mon–Fri every 30min, Sat & Sun every 1hr, ⓦ renfe .com) run west into L'Alt Penedès, calling at Sant Sadurní d'Anoia (40min) and Vilafranca del Penedès (50min).

13

INFORMATION AND TOURS

Spanish Trails Adventures (☎ 935 001 616, ⓦ spanish -trails.com) offers full-day, small-group escorted Penedès wine tours (from €95, transport and lunch included), including a cycling-wine tour option that lets you bike the quiet country lanes while visiting two or three wineries.

SANT SADURNÍ D'ANOIA

Oficina de Turisme c/Hospital 26 (Tues–Fri 10am–2pm & 4.30–6.30pm, Sat, Sun & hols 10am–2pm ☎ 938 913 188,

ⓦ santsadurni.cat). The office is in the centre of town, a 15min walk from the train station. You can rent bikes here too if you fancied cycling to some of the out-of-town producers.

VILAFRANCA DEL PENEDÈS

Oficina de Turisme c/Cort 14 (Mon 4–7pm, Tues–Fri 9am–1pm & 4–7pm, Sat 10am–1pm ☎ 938 181 254, ⓦ turismevilafranca.com).

EATING AND DRINKING

VILAFRANCA DEL PENEDÈS

L'Hereu c/del Casal 1 ☎ 938 902 217, ⓦ restauranthereu .com. Good lunchtime choice, serving big portions of country-style food with local wines (meals under €20). It's across the *rambla* from c/de Sant Joan, through the passageway. Mon–Thurs 1–4pm, Fri & Sat 1–4pm & 8–11pm.

Inziola c/de la Palma 21, off c/de Sant Joan ☎ 938 181 938, ⓦ inziola.com. The most agreeable place in town to wine-taste – a range of cavas and wines is sold by the glass, and there's a good wine shop attached. Mon 5–10pm, Tues–Sat 10am–2pm & 5–10pm.

Tarragona

Majestically sited on a rocky hill, 100km southwest of Barcelona and sited sheer above the sea, **Tarragona** is an ancient place: settled originally by Iberians and then Carthaginians, it was later used as the base for the Roman conquest of the peninsula, which began in 218 BC with Scipio's march south against Hannibal. The fortified city became an imperial resort and, under Augustus, "Tarraco" was the most elegant and cultured city of Roman Spain, boasting at its peak a quarter of a million inhabitants. It's still a very handsome city, especially the upper town, with the sweeping Rambla Nova at its heart, lined with cafés and restaurants. The parallel Rambla Vella marks the start of the old town, while to either side of the *ramblas* are scattered a profusion of relics and monuments from Tarragona's Roman past. Note that almost all Tarragona's sights and museums are **closed on Mondays**, though the old town and the exterior of some of the Roman remains can still be seen should you decide to visit then.

Catedral

Pl. de la Seu • Mon–Sat: mid-March to May 10am–6pm; June to mid-Oct 10am–7pm; mid-Oct to mid-Nov 10am–5pm; mid-Nov to mid-March 10am–2pm • €4, under-16s €1.20, under-7s free, includes entry to Museu Diocesà

Focal point of the medieval old town is the **Catedral**, a site of great antiquity since the Christian church was built over the site of the provincial Roman forum. Sitting at the top of a broad flight of steps, the main facade presents a soaring Gothic portal framed by Romanesque doors, surmounted by a cross and an elaborate rose window. Except for during services, entrance to the cathedral is through the lovely **cloisters** (*claustre*; signposted up a street to the left of the facade), where among several oddly sculpted capitals is one representing a cat's funeral being directed by rats. The ticket also gives access to the **Museu Diocesà**, piled high with ecclesiastical treasures.

Museu Nacional Arqueològic

Pl. del Rei 5 • Easter week & June–Sept Tues–Sat 9.30am–8pm, Sun 10am–2pm; Oct–May Tues–Sat 9.30am–6pm, Sun 10am–2pm • €2.40

Tarragona has several museums – dedicated among other things to modern art, old weapons, the port and harbour and the noble Castellarnau family – but the only essential visit is to the archeology museum, the **Museu Nacional Arqueològic**. The huge collection is a marvellous reflection of the richness of imperial Tarraco, with thematic displays on the various remains and buildings around the city, as well as whole rooms devoted to inscriptions, mosaics, sculpture, ceramics and jewellery.

13 Roman Tarragona: Museu d'Història de Tarragona

April–Sept Tues–Sat 9am–9pm; Sun & hols 9am–3pm; Oct–March Tues–Sat 9am–7pm, Sun & hols 10am–3pm • Each site €3, joint ticket to all €10, under-16s free • ⓦ museutgn.com

The local Roman sites are grouped together under the umbrella of the **Museu d'Història de Tarragona** (Tarragona History Museum) and all with the same opening hours and admission details. These start most spectacularly with the **Pretori i Circ Romans** (entered from Plaça del Rei), built at the end of the first century AD to hold chariot races. The

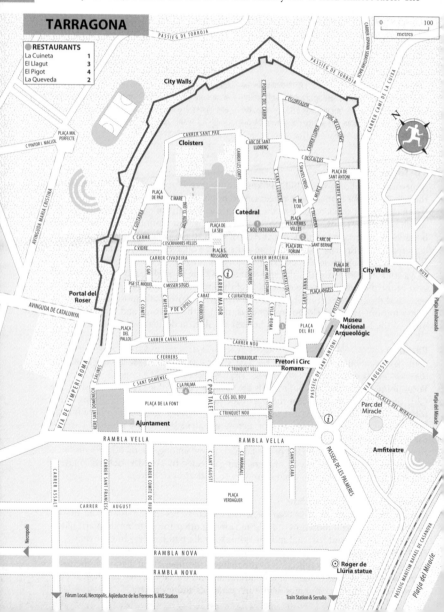

TARRAGONA

● **RESTAURANTS**	
La Cuineta	1
El Llagut	3
El Pigot	4
La Queveda	2

0   100
metres

13

vaults and chambers have been restored to spectacular effect, while a lift takes you up to the roof of the tower for the best view in Tarragona, looking down over the nearby **Amfiteatre**. There may only be scant remains of the ceremonial provincial forum (Plaça del Fòrum), but the **Fòrum Local** (c/Lleida, a short walk west of Rambla Nova, near the central market) is far more impressive, where the evocative remains of temple, shops, Roman road and house foundations can still be seen. Other remains lie further out, including those of the ancient **necropolis,** where both pagan and Christian tombs have been uncovered – this lies a twenty-minute walk from the centre, down Av. Ramon i Cajal, off Rambla Nova.

Aqüeducte de les Ferreres

Off N240, Lleida road • Open access • Free • Take the bus marked "Sant Salvador" (every 20min; 10min) from the stop outside Av. Prat de la Riba 11 (western end of Rambla Nova and off Av. Ramon i Cajal)

Perhaps the most remarkable of Tarragona's monuments stands 4km outside the original city walls, namely the **Roman aqueduct**, which brought water from the Riu Gayo, some 32km distant. The most impressive extant section, nearly 220m long and 26m high, lies in an overgrown valley, off the main road, in the middle of nowhere, and is popularly known as the *Pont del Diable* ("Devil's Bridge").

Local beaches

The rocky coastline below Tarragona conceals a couple of reasonable beaches. Closest to town is the long **Platja del Miracle**, over the rail lines below the amphitheatre, though nicer by far is **Platja Arrabassada**, a couple of kilometres further up the coast, reached by taking Via Augusta (off the end of Rambla Vella) and turning right at the *Hotel Astari* – a pleasant thirty-minute walk with gradually unfolding views of the beach and a few beach bars when you get there.

ARRIVAL AND DEPARTURE   **TARRAGONA**

By train Hourly AVE (high-speed) trains from Barcelona Sants take just 35min, but tickets are expensive and the Camp de Tarragona AVE station is a 10min drive from the centre of town, which adds on the price of a taxi. Otherwise, normal trains from Passeig de Gràcia and Barcelona Sants (every 30min, ⓦ renfe.com) take just over an hour: turn right out of the station, climb the steps ahead of you to reach Rambla Nova, by the statue of Roger de Llúria (10min).

INFORMATION

Oficina de Turisme c/Major 39 (July–Sept Mon–Sat 10am–8pm, Sun & hols 10am–2pm; Oct–June Mon–Sat 10am–6pm, Sun & hols 10am–2pm; ☎977 250 795, ⓦ tarragonaturisme.cat). The tourist office sells the Tarragona Card (valid 48hr; €15), which gives free admission to all city museums and monuments, a free guided tour and other discounts and benefits.

EATING AND DRINKING

The pretty old-town squares, like Plaça del Rei, Plaça del Fòrum and Plaça de la Font are the best places for outdoor drinks and meals. The latter in particular features more than a dozen **cafés**, **bars and restaurants** serving everything from *pintxos* to pizzas. Otherwise, a good place for lunch is down in **Serrallo**, Tarragona's so-called fishermen's quarter, a 15min walk west along the industrial harbourfront from the train station, where you'll get a tasty paella.

La Cuineta c/Nou Patriarca 2 ☎977 226 101. Stylish all-day café that has a big choice of breakfast sandwiches and pastries, followed by lunch from 1pm, where €15 gets you a good meal from a wide-ranging menu – grilled mussels to chicken with prunes. Mon–Sat 8.30am–5pm.

★ **El Llagut** c/Natzaret 10, at Pl. del Rei ☎977 228 938. The best place in the town centre for seafood and rice dishes, with a quiet *terrassa* opposite the archeological museum. There's a good lunch deal at around €12; otherwise à la carte meals for around €30. Tues–Sat 1–4pm & 8–11.30pm, Sun 1–4pm.

El Pigot Pl. de la Font 24 ☎977 217 766. Lunch menus around the town's nicest square are all similarly priced at around €12 but locals plump for the reliably good Catalan food at *El Pigot* – from summer salads to signature rice and

13

fideuà dishes. Main dishes otherwise cost around €11. And don't forget an ice cream afterwards from *Sirvent*, the well-known parlour just a few doors down the square. Daily 1–4pm & 8–11pm.

La Queveda Pl. del Fòrum 6 ☎977 235 419. The century-old bar by the sole standing wall of the Roman forum is a decent spot for a cheap lunch and a drink in the sun. Daily 10am–midnight.

Reus

Fourteen kilometres northwest of Tarragona, and 100km southwest of Barcelona, the small city of **Reus** was the birthplace in 1852 of architect Antoni Gaudí. There was little in his early life in Reus to indicate what was to come. He was born to a humble family of boilermakers and coppersmiths, and left for Barcelona when he was 16 years old. Consequently, there are no Gaudí buildings in Reus itself, but there is a fascinating interpretative centre dedicated to the city's most famous son that's essential viewing for anyone interested in his life and work. The Gaudí Centre itself forms part of the city's **Ruta del Modernisme**, a marked trail around the many buildings and mansions erected

CAFÉS AND RESTAURANTS	
Café de Reus	3
Cerveseria Ferreteria	1
GaudiR	4
La Glorieta del Castell	5
Restaurant Joan Urgellès	2

13

in the *modernista* style at the end of the nineteenth century and beginning of the twentieth. This was a period when Reus was Catalunya's second city (after Barcelona), with a merchant class made wealthy by the trade in wine and olive oil and, later, textiles, fabrics and ceramics. You can easily see all of Reus's sights in a day out from Barcelona – a charming city of 100,000, it's full of pretty squares, good restaurants and handsome pedestrianized shopping streets, with almost everything of note lying within a clearly defined circuit of boulevards.

Gaudí Centre

Pl. del Mercadal 3 • Mon–Sat 10am–2pm & 4–7pm (mid-June to mid-Sept 10am–8pm), Sun & hols 11am–2pm • €7, under-14s €4, under-7s free • ☎ 977 010 670, ⓦ gaudicentre.com

The **Gaudí Centre** is a gleaming box of a building that throws much light on the inspiration behind Gaudí's work. It's not really a museum as such, though there are exhibits including his former school reports, his only surviving manuscript notebook and a reproduction of the architect's study-workshop at the Sagrada Família. Instead, the centre cleverly investigates the architectural techniques pioneered by Gaudí, with hands-on demonstration models and audiovisual aids that show, for example, how he created wave roofs and spiral towers. If you ever wondered why none of Gaudí's door frames are straight, or what trees, ferns and snails have to do with architecture, the centre is undoubtedly the place to find out.

Casa Navàs

Pl. del Mercadal 5 • Tours every Sat, plus certain other times, check with Oficina de Turisme; reservations required • €10, under-14s €8, under-7s free, includes Gaudí Centre

Antoni Gaudí may never have built in Reus, but his contemporary, Lluís Domènech i Montaner did. His magnificently decorated **Casa Navàs** (1901), across Plaça del Mercadal from the Gaudí Centre, is considered Reus's finest townhouse – it's still privately owned, but is open for pre-booked tours of the virtually intact period interior, which you shuffle around in overshoes to protect the floor.

Sant Pere and around

Pl. Sant Pere • Daily 10.30am–12.30pm & 5–7pm • Free

Reus's main church is that of the city's patron saint, **Sant Pere**, a couple of minutes' walk from the Gaudí Centre. This is where Gaudí was baptized (there's a plaque by the baptismal chapel, to the left of the main entrance) and the church also boasts the heart of Reus's number-two son, *modernista* artist Marià Fortuny i Marsal (the plaque here reads "he gave his soul to heaven, his fame to the world, and his heart to his country"). Behind the church is an arcaded square with cafés, **Plaça de les Peixateries Velles**, that was once the fish market, while **Plaça del Mercadal** itself used to be the site of the general market – the numbers you can see etched in the square's paving indicated the position of the stalls.

Gaudí's birthplace

C/Sant Vicenç 4

You might as well divert the few minutes from the commercial centre to see **Gaudí's birthplace**. The house is not original, but a plaque marks the site while, just down the street, outside a school, is a rather touching sculpture of the young Gaudí playing marbles.

ARRIVAL AND DEPARTURE   **REUS**

By air Ryanair arrivals at Reus airport, 3km outside town, can catch connecting buses direct to Barcelona (see p.22), while local bus #50 runs hourly into town, via the train station.

By train There are hourly Renfe services (ⓦ renfe.com) to Reus (via Tarragona) from Passeig de Gràcia and Barcelona Sants, and the journey takes 1hr 40min. It's 15min from the train station into the centre (walk down Pg. Sunyer, turn left at Pl. de les Oques and follow c/Sant Joan to Pl. del Prim), or there are taxis outside the station.

13

INFORMATION

Oficina de Turisme Pl. del Mercadal, inside the Gaudí Centre (mid-June to mid-Sept Mon–Sat 10am–8pm, Sun & hols 11am–2pm; mid-Sept to mid-June Mon–Sat 10am–2pm & 4–7pm, Sun & hols 11am–2pm; ☎ 977 010 670 or ☎ 902 360 200, ⊕ reus.cat/turisme). You can pick up a good map of town here and ask about guided tours (not always in English).

EATING AND DRINKING

Restaurants are plentiful and surprisingly good value for the most part, with a particular concentration around Pl. del Mercadal and along nearby c/de Santa Anna. The daily market (Mon–Sat) takes place at the **Mercat Central** on c/Sant Joan, not far from the train station.

Café de Reus c/del Metge Fortuny ☎ 977 771 951. This classic café, just up a lane from the main square, is a reliable place for a good meal at a reasonable price, with seasonal menus available day and night for €12–15. In summer you can eat outside on the square. Daily 8am–midnight.

★ **Cerveseria Ferreteria** Pl. de la Farinera 10 ☎ 977 340 326, ⊕ laferreteriadereus.com. A popular place for tapas and grills (€2–10, weekday lunch menu €12.50) – the interesting interior is a converted nineteenth-century ironmonger's, with tools still in cabinets and bottles stacked on the old wooden shop shelves, while there's a pretty *terrassa* in the square outside. Daily noon–midnight.

GaudíR Gaudí Centre, top floor ☎ 977 127 702, ⊕ gaudi restaurant.com. Widely considered to be the best place in town, and especially good for fish and rice – the menu changes according to the catch, but expect prawn-stuffed calamari or a piquant stew of langoustine and monkfish.

There's a weekday lunch menu for around €20, otherwise mains at €20–30 and a tasting menu at €55. Reserve ahead for a terrace table. Mon 1.30–4pm, Tues–Sat 1.30–4pm & 8.30–11pm, Sun 1.30–4pm.

La Glorieta del Castell Pl. del Castell 2 ☎ 977 340 826. A traditional place, with market-led Catalan cuisine and good-value *menús del dia* day and night (€15–20, otherwise mains €10–20), serving things like grilled bream with artichokes, *fideuà* or lamb chops. Mon & Wed–Sat 1–4pm & 8–11.30pm, Sun 1–4pm.

Restaurant Joan Urgellès c/Aleus 7 ☎ 977 342 178. For fancier, contemporary cuisine – on the inventive, "Mediterrasian" side of things – where steak might come with a sweet-sour *salsa* or a good old Catalan *botifarra* sausage arrives on a compôte of apple and langoustine with a red-wine reduction. There are tasting menus at €30 and €50, otherwise mains mostly €15–20. Mon 8–11.30pm, Tues–Sat 1.30–4pm & 8–11.30pm.

Girona

The ancient walled city of **Girona** stands on a fortress-like hill, high above the Riu Onyar. It's been fought over in almost every century since it was the Roman fortress of Gerunda, and has been rebuilt and added to many times: following the Moorish conquest of Spain, Girona was an Arab town for over two centuries, and there was also a continuous Jewish presence here for six hundred years. The overall impression for the visitor is of an overwhelmingly beautiful medieval city, with old and new towns divided by the river, which is crisscrossed by footbridges, with pastel-coloured houses reflected in the waters below. The compact wedge of land that comprises the old town contains all the sights and monuments, and it takes only half an hour or so to walk from end to end – making historic Girona an easily manageable and very enjoyable day-trip from Barcelona.

Catedral

Pl. de la Catedral • Mon–Sat 10am–8pm (Nov–March 10am–7pm), Sun 10am–2pm • €5, includes visit to nave, treasury and cloister, Sun free & under-7s free • ⊕ catedraldegirona.org

Centrepiece of the old city is the **Catedral**, a mighty Gothic structure approached by a magnificent flight of seventeenth-century Baroque steps. Inside, there are no aisles, just one tremendous Gothic nave vault with a span of 22m. This emphasis on width and height is a feature of Catalan-Gothic, with its "hall churches", of which, unsurprisingly, Girona's is the ultimate example. The displayed treasures of the cathedral include the famous eleventh-century "Creation Tapestry" – the best piece of Romanesque textile in existence. But it's the exquisite Romanesque **cloisters** (1180–1210) that make the strongest impression, boasting minutely carved figures and scenes on double columns.

13

Banys Arabs

C/Ferran el Catòlic • April–Sept Mon–Sat 10am–7pm, Sun & hols 10am–2pm; Oct–March daily 10am–2pm • €2, under-16s €1 •
☎ 972 213 262, ⓦ banysarabs.cat

Through the twin-towered Portal de Sobreportas, below the cathedral, are the intact
remains of Girona's so-called **Banys Arabs**, the best-preserved ancient baths in Spain
after those at Granada. Probably designed by Moorish craftsmen in the thirteenth
century, a couple of hundred years after the Moors' occupation of Girona had ended,

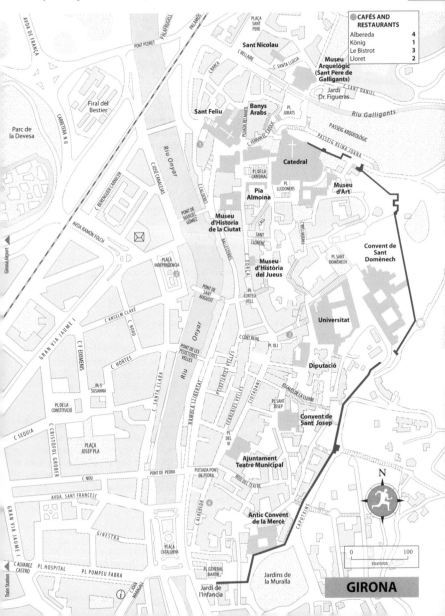

CAFÉS AND
RESTAURANTS
Albereda   4
König   1
Le Bistrot   3
Lloret   2

GIRONA

13

they feature three principal rooms for different temperatures, with an underfloor heating system.

Museu Arqueològic

Monestir de Sant Pere de Galligants, c/de Santa Llúcia 8 • June–Sept Tues–Sat 10.30am–1.30pm & 4–7pm, Sun 10am–2pm; Oct–May Tues–Sat 10am–2pm & 4–6pm, Sun 10am–2pm • €2.30, under-16s free • ☎ 972 202 632, ⓦ mac.cat

From the cathedral square, the main street, Pujada Rei Marti, leads downhill to the Riu Galligants, a small tributary of the Onyar. The **Museu Arqueològic** stands on the far bank in the former monastic church of Sant Pere de Galligants, a harmonious setting for displays of Roman statuary, sarcophagi and mosaics. The beautiful Romanesque cloisters contain heavier medieval relics, such as inscribed tablets and stones, including some bearing Jewish inscriptions.

Passeig Arqueològic

Daily 8am–10pm • Free

Near the archeological museum, steps up through landscaped grounds lead onto the walls of the old city. You can walk right around their perimeter on the **Passeig Arqueològic**, or archeological route, and enjoy views out over the rooftops and the cathedral. There are endless little diversions along the way, into old watchtowers, down blind dead ends and around crumpled sections of masonry.

The Jewish quarter

Quite apart from its Roman remains and Arab influences, Girona also contains one of the best-preserved **Jewish quarters** in western Europe, home at its height to around three hundred people who formed a sort of independent town within Girona, protected by the king in return for payment. From the eleventh century onwards, however, the Jewish community suffered systematic persecution and, until the expulsion of the Jews from Spain in 1492, the quarter was effectively a ghetto, its residents restricted to its limits and forced to wear distinguishing clothing if they did leave.

Museu d'Història dels Jueus

C/de la Força • July & Aug Mon–Sat 10am–8pm, Sun & hols 10am–2pm; Sept–June Mon–Sat 10am–2pm, Tues–Sat 10am–6pm, Sun & hols 10am–2pm • €2, free 1st Sun of the month • ☎ 972 216 761

For an impression of the cultural and social life of Girona's medieval Jewish community visit the **Museu d'Història dels Jueus**, sited just off c/de la Força up the skinniest of stepped streets. Amid the complex of rooms, staircases, courtyards and adjoining buildings were the synagogue, the butcher's shop, the baths and other community buildings and services.

ARRIVAL AND DEPARTURE   GIRONA

By air Regular bus services run from Girona airport, 13km south of the city, to Girona, Barcelona or the Costa Brava (see p.22).

By train Renfe trains (ⓦ renfe.com) run at least hourly to and from Barcelona Sants, calling at Passeig de Gràcia station, and take between 1hr 15min and 1hr 30min. When open, the new high-speed AVE service will cut times considerably, though tickets will be much more expensive than standard fares. Girona's train station lies across the river in the modern part of the city – walk down to the avenue, turn left and then take the second right off the avenue, down c/Alvarez de Castro, towards Plaça Catalunya and the river (10min walk). There's also a taxi rank at the station.

INFORMATION

Oficina de Turisme c/Joan Maragall 2 (April–Sept Mon–Fri 8am–8pm, Sat 8am–2pm & 4–8pm, Sun & hols 9am–2pm; Oct–March Mon–Sat 9am–5pm, Sun & hols 9am–2pm; ☎ 872 975 975, ⓦ girona.cat/turisme). They can give you a useful map and have bus and train timetables for all onward and return services.

EATING AND DRINKING

There are plenty of cafés and restaurants along Rambla de la Llibertat and on the parallel Pl. del Vi, and also a group of bars with lovely terraces sited at the opposite end of the old town, under Sant Feliu church. There are another dozen or so restaurants (from pizzerias to creative Catalan restaurants), all with alfresco terraces, just over the river in pretty Pl. Independencia.

Albereda c/Albereda 7 ☎972 226 002, ⓦrestaurant albereda.com. The glam choice in town for very fine Catalan dining – say milk-fed Pyrenean lamb or seafood rice cooked with monkfish and cuttlefish. Mains cost €20–30, though there's a weekday lunch menu at €30. Tues–Sun 1–4pm & 9–11pm.

König c/Calderes 16 ☎972 225 782, ⓦkonig.cat. With its pretty *terrassa* under the high walls of Sant Feliu church, this all-day café-bar makes a pleasant stop for a drink. Food (€3–7) is along the lines of salads, tapas, sandwiches and burgers. Daily 8am–midnight, food served 1–4.30pm & 8pm–midnight.

Le Bistrot Pujada de Sant Domènec ☎972 218 803. A good-value bistro that often puts out tables on the steps below the church. The food is straightforward Catalan, and a decent lunch will cost you €15–20. Daily noon–4pm & 8pm–midnight.

★ **Lloret** Pl. de la Independencia 14 ☎972 213 671. You won't score a cheaper *menú del dia* (€10 or €15, otherwise mains €5–15) than at this simple restaurant – the food's reasonable enough and there's outdoor dining, while the room upstairs has river and cathedral views. Daily 1–4pm & 8–11pm.

Figueres

Figueres, a provincial town in the north of Catalunya with a population of some thirty thousand, would pass almost unnoticed were it not for the Museu Dalí, installed by Salvador Dalí in a building as surreal as the exhibits within. It's a popular day-trip from Barcelona, though you should make a reasonably early start since – at 135km northeast of Barcelona – even the fastest trains take an hour and forty minutes to reach the town. The museum is very much the main event in town (it's signposted from just about everywhere), though it's easy to fill in the rest of the

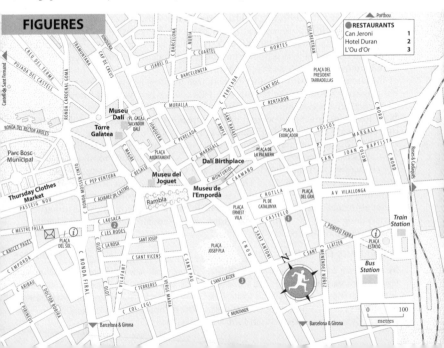

13

SURREAL SALVADOR

Salvador Dalí i Domènech (1904–89) was born in Figueres – you can see the exterior of his **birthplace** at c/Monturiol 6 (there's a plaque) and that of the next house in which the Dalí family lived (at no. 10). He gave his first exhibition in the town when he was just 14 and, after a stint at the Royal Academy of Art in Madrid (he was expelled), he made his way to Paris, where he established himself at the forefront of the Surrealist movement. A celebrity artist in the US in the 1940s and 1950s, he returned eventually to Europe where, among other projects, he set about reconstructing Figueres' old municipal theatre, where he had held his first boyhood exhibition. This opened as the Museu Dalí in 1974, which Dalí then fashioned into an inspired repository for some of his most bizarre works.

By 1980, Dalí was growing increasingly frail, particularly after he suffered severe burns in a fire in 1984 (following which he moved into the **Torre Galatea**, the tower adjacent to the museum), and controversy surrounded the artist's final years. Spanish government officials and friends feared that he was manipulated in his senile condition. In particular, it's alleged that he was made to sign blank canvases – and this has inevitably led to the questioning of the authenticity of some of his later works. Dalí died in Figueres on January 23, 1989. His body now lies behind a simple granite slab inside the museum.

day in the handsome centre. Pavement cafés line the tree-shaded *rambla*, while art galleries, clothes stores and gift shops line the pedestrianized streets and squares. On Tuesday, Thursday and Saturday, you'll coincide with the main **fruit, veg and flower market** – if you have a choice, Thursday is best since there's also a huge **clothes market** in town.

Museu Dalí

Pl. Gala i Salvador Dalí · July–Sept daily 9am–7.15pm, Aug also daily 10pm–12.30am; Oct–June Tues–Sun 9.30am–5.15pm · €12, under-9s free · ☎ 972 677 500, ⓦ salvador-dali.org

The **Museu Dalí** appeals to everyone's innate love of fantasy, absurdity and participation. The museum is not a collection of Dalí's greatest hits – those are scattered far and wide – but what you do get beggars description and is not to be missed.

The building (a former theatre) is an exhibit in itself, topped by a huge metallic dome and decorated with a line of luminous egg shapes. Outlandish sculptures and statues adorn the square and facade and it gets even crazier inside, where the walls of the circular courtyard are ringed by stylized mannequins preparing to dive from the heights – below sits the famous *Rainy Cadillac*, where you can water the snail-encrusted occupants of a steamy Cadillac by feeding it with coins. In the Mae West Room an unnerving portrait of the actress is revealed by peering through a mirror at giant nostrils, red lips and hanging tresses, while elsewhere there's a complete life-sized orchestra, some of Dalí's extraordinary furniture (like the fish-tail bed), and ranks of Surrealist paintings – including one room dominated by the ceiling fresco of the huge feet of Dalí and Gala (his Russian wife and muse). The museum also contains many of Dalí's collected works by other artists, from Catalan contemporaries to El Greco, and there are temporary exhibitions, too, while your ticket also allows admission to see the **Dalí-Joies** – a collection of extraordinary jewels, designed in the 1940s for an American millionaire and displayed here with Dalí's original drawings.

ARRIVAL AND DEPARTURE   FIGUERES

By train Renfe trains (ⓦ renfe.com) depart hourly from Barcelona Sants and Passeig de Gràcia and take up to 2hr to reach Figueres, depending on the service – for a day-trip, it's best to catch a train before 10am from Barcelona. Services on the new high-speed AVE line will be significantly faster, but tickets will be much pricier than standard fares. Figueres is just 30–40min by Renfe train from Girona. Arriving at the train station, you reach the centre of town by following the "Museu Dalí" signs (10min).

13

INFORMATION

Oficina de Turisme Pl. del Sol, in front of the post office building (July–Sept Mon–Sat 9am–8pm, Sun 9am–3pm; Oct–June Mon–Fri & Sun 10am–2pm, Sat 10am–2pm & 3–6pm; ☎ 972 503 155, ⓦ figueres.cat).

EATING AND DRINKING

A gaggle of largely avoidable tourist **restaurants** is crowded into the narrow streets around the Dalí museum, and there are more cafés and restaurants overlooking the *rambla*. Lunch menus everywhere go for €10–12, with the sunniest seats those at the top of the *rambla*. Elsewhere, there's a better selection of hidden-away restaurants that are more geared to locals, where the food tends to be more interesting and authentic.

Can Jeroni c/Castelló 36 ☎ 972 500 983. Locals like this tiled tavern opposite the market, where country-style dishes and grills (*torrades*, salads, steaks, chops, sausages) go for €6–15. Mon–Wed 1–3.30pm, Thurs–Sat 1–3.30pm & 8.30–10pm.

★ **Hotel Duran** c/Lausaca 5 ☎ 972 501 250, ⓦ hotelduran.com. The top choice in town, known for its excellent regional cuisine, including fresh fish landed daily from the nearby coast. It's fairly pricey (mains €13–26) though there is a reasonable lunchtime menu for €20 and a more elaborate tasting menu at €45. Daily 1–3.30pm & 8–11pm.

L'Ou d'Or c/Sant Llàtzer 16 ☎ 972 503 765, ⓦ loudor. com. An uncomplicated *menú del dia* is served here day and night – say hake, or trout with almonds, and there's always *tortilla* on the menu. The weekday lunch is around €12; otherwise it's weekend lunch or dinner every night for around €15. Mon–Sat 1–3.30pm & 8–11pm.

HOTEL ARTS BARCELONA, PORT OLÍMPIC

Accommodation

Finding a hotel vacancy in Barcelona at any time of year can be very difficult, so it's always best to book in advance. Prices are high for Spain but still pretty reasonable when compared to other big European cities, while stylish rooms on a moderate budget – in this designer style capital – are fairly easy to come by. There's a wide range of overnight options in the city, from youth hostels and budget pensions to glam five-star-plus resort hotels, housed in medieval mansions and modernista masterpieces alike. If you're looking for the home-from-home experience then Barcelona also has lots of self-contained apartments for rent, not to mention an increasing number of private "bed-and-breakfast" establishments – some simply the traditional room in someone's house, others very stylish and pricey boutique bolt-holes.

Places to stay go under various names – *pension, residencia, hostal, hotel* – though only **hotels and pensions** are recognized as official categories. These are all star-rated (hotels, one- to five-star; pensions, one- or two-star), but the rating is not necessarily a guide to cost or ambience. Some of the smaller, boutique-style pensions and hotels have services and facilities that belie their star rating; some four- and five-star hotels have disappointingly small rooms and an impersonal feel.

Apartment rentals are available by the night or week, and while prices compare well with mid-range hotels make sure you're happy with the location (some are out in the suburbs) and understand all the costs – cleaning charges, utility bills and taxes can all push up the attractive quoted figure. As for **youth hostels**, some traditional backpacker dives survive here and there, but they have largely been superseded by well-equipped, well-run modern hostels with en-suite dorm rooms as well as private rooms. For a more intimate experience there are plenty of **budget pensions** that also have dorms and shared accommodation. A youth hostel, incidentally, is an *albergue*; *hostal* is the word for a pension.

14

ESSENTIALS

ROOM RATES

Prices Rates given in our reviews reflect the usual cost of a double or twin room in high season (basically Easter to the end of October, plus Christmas/New Year, major trade fairs, festivals and other events). The cheapest rooms in a simple hotel, sharing a bathroom, cost around €50 (singles from €30), though for private facilities €70–80 a night is more realistic. Places with a bit of boutique styling start at around €100, while for Barcelona's most fashionable hotels, count on €250–400 a night. Studio apartments sleeping two start at around €100, while a hostel dorm bed costs between €15 and €30 a night, depending on the season.

Tax An eight-percent tax, IVA, is added to all accommodation bills, though it's sometimes included in the quoted price.

Discounts Book directly online through hotel websites for the best available rates. Some places offer discounts in the off-season months of January, February and November, while others have special rates in August (when business travel is scarce).

Breakfast While many hotels put on a lavish buffet spread, breakfast can be expensive (around €10–15 per person), so if all you want is coffee and a croissant it's better to go out to a café.

RESERVATIONS

Hotels You can reserve hotel accommodation online with the city tourist board (w barcelonaturisme.com) or make same-day bookings in person only at their tourist offices at Plaça de Catalunya, the airport, Sants train station and elsewhere.

Apartments For apartments, try Barcelona On-Line (w barcelona-on-line.es) or Inside-BCN (w inside-bcn .com), while Barcelona-based My Favourite Things (w myft .net) has an eye for offbeat rooms and apartments in private houses.

WHERE TO STAY

If you hanker after a **Ramblas** view, you'll pay for the privilege – generally speaking, there are much better deals to be had either side of the famous boulevard, often just a minute's walk away. Alongside some classy boutique choices, most of Barcelona's cheapest accommodation is found in the old town, principally the **Barri Gòtic** and **El Raval** neighbourhoods, which can both still have their rough edges – be careful (without being paranoid) when coming and going after dark. East of the Barri Gòtic, in **Sant Pere** and **La Ribera**, there are a number of safely sited budget, mid-range and boutique options, handy for the Picasso museum and the Born nightlife area. North of Plaça de Catalunya, the **Eixample** – split into Right (**Dreta**) and Left (**Esquerra**)– has some of the city's most fashionable hotels, often housed in converted palaces and mansions and located just a few minutes' walk from the *modernista* architectural masterpieces. Hotels near Sants station are convenient for **Montjuïc** and the metro system, and those further north in **Les Corts** for the Avinguda Diagonal shopping district. For waterfront views look at **Port Vell** at the end of the Ramblas, and at the **Port Olímpic** southeast of the old town – while new four- and five-stars abound much further out on the metro at the **Diagonal Mar** conference and events site. If you prefer neighbourhood living, then the northern district of **Gràcia** is the best base, as you're only ever a short walk away from its excellent bars, restaurants and clubs.

14

BALCONIES, VIEWS AND NOISE

Almost all hotels and pensions in Barcelona have at least some rooms with a **balcony** over the street or square. These tend to be the brightest rooms in the building and, because of the obvious inherent attraction, they usually cost more than the other rooms. However, it can't be stressed enough that rooms facing onto Barcelona's streets are often noisy. Traffic is a constant presence (including the dawn street-cleaners) and, in a city where people are just getting ready to go out at 10pm, you can be assured of a fair amount of pedestrian noise too, particularly in the old town, and especially at weekends. Soundproofed windows and double-glazing deal partly with the problem, but you tend not to have this luxury in cheaper pensions – where throwing open the windows may be the only way to get some air in the height of summer anyway. Bring earplugs if you're at all concerned about having a sleepless night.

Alternatively, ask for an **internal room** (*habitación interior*). It's true that most buildings are built around a central air or lift shaft, and your view could simply be a lime-green wall 1m away and someone's washing line. However, some places are built instead around an internal patio, so your room might overlook a pot-plant terrace or garden – and you shouldn't get any street noise.

Credit cards Although you may be asked for a credit card number to secure a room, at most hotels your card won't be charged until your stay. However, some smaller pensions may take a deposit or charge you in advance. Credit cards are accepted almost everywhere (though American Express isn't always).

INTERNET AND WI-FI

Pretty much every pension and hotel is now wired for access, but while you get cheap or free internet and wi-fi in budget hotels and hostels, swankier hotels tend to charge like a wounded bull – sometimes as much as €20 for 24 hours' worth of internet access. Always check the small print before you sign up.

THE RAMBLAS

★ **Hostal Benidorm** Ramblas 37 ☎933 022 054, ⓦhostalbenidorm.com; ⓂDrassanes; map p.38. Refurbished pension opposite Plaça Reial that offers real value for money, hence the tribes of young tourists. Plain rooms are available for one to five people, all with bathtubs or showers, and a balcony and Ramblas view if you're lucky (and prepared to pay a bit more). **€75**

Hostal Mare Nostrum Ramblas 67, entrance on c/de Sant Pau ☎933 185 340, ⓦhostalmarenostrum.com; ⓂLiceu; map p.38. A cheery Ramblas pension whose English-speaking management offers comfortable double, triple and family rooms with satellite TV and a/c. It's nothing flashy, but rooms are reasonably modern and double-glazed against the noise, and some come with balconies and street views – you'll pay €10 less for a room with a shared bathroom. **€95**

★ **Hotel H1898** Ramblas 109, entrance on c/de Pintor Fortuny ☎935 529 552, ⓦhotel1898.com; ⓂCatalunya; map p.38. The former HQ of the Philippines Tobacco Company got an eye-popping refit, adding four grades of rooms (the standard is "Classic") in deep red, green or black, plus sumptuous suites, some with their own private pool, jacuzzi and garden. Public areas are similarly dramatic, like the neo-colonial hall, lounge and bar, and the sleek *Xina* noodle bar, while other facilities include both outdoor and indoor pools, and a glam spa. Online deals can bring rates down as low as €160. **€255**

Hotel Eurostars Ramblas Boquería Ramblas 91–93 ☎933 435 461, ⓦeurostarsramblasboqueria.com; ⓂLiceu; map p.38. Snappy little boutique rooms in a small three-star hotel right outside the Boqueria market. There's not much space, but all you need is on the doorstep, and the sound-proofing is good so you get a street view without the racket. **€130**

Hotel Oriente Ramblas 45 ☎933 022 558, ⓦhotel husaoriente.com; ⓂLiceu; map p.38. For somewhere on the Ramblas that's traditional but not too pricey, this historic three-star is your best bet. Converted from a former convent, its grand public rooms and tastefully updated bedrooms display nineteenth-century style; some of the latter have Ramblas views (though the quieter ones face inwards). Special rates from €85. **€120**

Hotel Rivoli Ramblas Ramblas 128 ☎934 817 676, ⓦhotelrivoliramblas.com; ⓂCatalunya; map p.38. The elegant rooms in this stylish four-star hotel near the top of the avenue are imaginatively furnished (Art Deco to avant-garde), and all come with spacious marble bathrooms, while the front ones have floor-to-ceiling windows with classic Ramblas views. There's also a lovely rooftop terrace and bar. Special rates from €99. **€150**

Le Méridien Barcelona Ramblas 111 ☎933 186 200, ⓦlemeridienbarcelona.com; ⓂCatalunya; map p.38. A big-money makeover for the five-star *Méridien*, one of the high-end Ramblas stalwarts, has sharpened up both rooms and public areas, and as "deluxe" is the norm you can expect your bedroom to feature designer leather furniture, an iPod-dock and splash-proof TVs in the natural-toned marble bathroom. You pay a lot more for a Ramblas view or any kind of extra space (another €100 for example gets you

a "Mediterranean" suite with terrace and hammock), though things are surprisingly democratically priced in the flash *CentOnze* restaurant, which opens right onto the Ramblas. **€189**

BARRI GÒTIC

14

Hostal Fernando c/de Ferran 31 ☎ 933 017 993, ⓦ hfernando.com; ⓜ Liceu; map p.46. Rooms at these prices fill quickly around here (low-season dorms from just €17 and rooms from €55); that they're also light, modern and well kept by friendly people is a real bonus. All come with a/c and private bathroom (though some singles share facilities), while straightforward dorm accommodation is available in en-suite rooms that sleep four to eight. Dorms **€26**, rooms **€80**

★ **Hostal Rembrandt** c/de la Portaferrissa 23 ☎ 933 181 011, ⓦ hostalrembrandt.com; ⓜ Liceu; map p.46. A clean, safe, old-town budget pension that has been smartened up over the years by friendly English-speaking owners, who request "pin-drop silence" after 11pm. Simple tile-floored rooms (a bit cheaper without private bathroom) have a street-side balcony or little patio, while larger rooms – either here or in a nearby apartment building (€70–100) – are more versatile and can sleep up to four. **€85**

Hotel Cantón c/Nou de Sant Francesc 40 ☎ 933 173 019, ⓦ hotelcanton-bcn.com; ⓜ Drassanes; map p.46. A modest one-star hotel that's only two blocks off the Ramblas and close to the harbour and Port Vell. Forty rooms feature uniform blue-and-white trim curtains and bedspreads, central heating and a/c, fridge and wardrobe. A few rooms have balconies (though they don't have much of a view) – all are well insulated against street noise. A buffet continental breakfast is available, served in a stone-walled dining room, and room prices drop a good bit out of season. **€85**

Hotel Colón Av. de la Catedral 7 ☎ 933 011 404, ⓦ hotel colon.es; ⓜ Jaume I; map p.46. Before Barcelona went boutique, this is the kind of traditional four-star hotel where big-spenders splashed their cash – an old-money establishment, with faithful-retainer staff, huge public salons and rooms at the front that throw open their windows onto balconies overlooking La Seu (cathedral view from €30 extra). It's still a pretty privileged location, and while some rooms are too frilly and floral by half, others are more contemporary in style. **€130**

Hotel El Jardí Pl. Sant Josep Oriol 1 ☎ 933 015 900, ⓦ eljardi-barcelona.com; ⓜ Liceu; map p.46. The hotel's location, overlooking the charming Plaça del Pi, is what sells this place – and explains the steepish prices for quarters that can seem a bit bare and poky. But some rooms (the top ones have terraces or balconies, €10 extra) look directly onto the square, and there's a range of cheaper

internal rooms too. You can have breakfast at the hotel, but the *Bar del Pi* in the square below is nicer. **€85**

Hotel Racó del Pi c/del Pi 7 ☎ 933 426 190, ⓦ h10hotels.com; ⓜ Liceu; map p.46. A stylish little three-star hotel in a great location. Appealing rooms – some with balconies over the street – have wood floors and granite-and-mosaic bathrooms. There's a glass of cava on check-in, and free coffee and pastries during the day in the bar. **€95**

Itaca Hostel c/de Ripoll 21 ☎ 933 019 751, ⓦ itaca hostel.com; ⓜ Jaume I; map p.46. Bright and breezy converted house close to the cathedral, offering spacious hostel rooms (sleeping eight or twelve) with balconies. Dorms are mixed, though you can also reserve a private room or even an apartment (sleeps up to six; €150), and with a hostel capacity of only thirty it rarely feels overcrowded. There's a kitchen and book-exchange service, coffee and breakfast available and decent discounts in the low season. Dorms **€26**, rooms **€65**

★ **Neri Hotel** c/de Sant Sever 5 ☎ 933 040 655, ⓦ hotelneri.com; ⓜ Liceu/Jaume I; map p.46. Close to the cathedral, a delightful eighteenth-century palace houses this stunning boutique hotel of just 22 rooms and suites, featuring swags of flowing material, rescued timber, granite-toned bathrooms and lofty proportions. Catalan designers have created eye-catching effects, like a boa constrictor sofa and a tapestry that falls four floors through the central atrium, while a beamed library and stylish roof terrace provide a tranquil escape. Breakfast is served bento-box style, either out in the courtyard in summer or in chef Benito Iranzo's fine contemporary Mediterranean restaurant. **€285**

Pensió Alamar c/de la Comtessa de Sobradiel 1 ☎ 933 025 012, ⓦ pensioalamar.com; ⓜ Liceu/Jaume I; map p.46. If you don't mind sharing a bathroom then this simply furnished pension makes a convenient base. There are twelve rooms (including five singles), most with little balconies, and while space is tight, there's a friendly welcome, laundry service and use of a kitchen. Requests no

---

TOP 5 BOUTIQUE HOTELS

Abac See p.176
Grand Hotel Central See p.171
Hotel H1898 See opposite
Hotel España See p.170
Neri Hotel See above

14

TOP 5 OLD-WORLD CHARM
Gran Hotel Princesa Sofia See p.175
Hostal L'Antic Espai See p.173
Hotel Colón See p.169
Hotel Peninsular See below
Mesón Castilla See opposite

noise after midnight, so it suits early-birds and sightseers rather than partygoers. No credit cards. **€45**

★ **Pensión Mari-Luz** c/del Palau 4, 2º ☎ 933 173 463,

EL RAVAL

★ **Barceló Raval** Rambla de Raval 17–21 ☎ 933 201 490, Ⓦ www.barceloraval.com; Ⓜ Liceu/Sant Antoni; map pp.60–61. This glow-in-the-dark tower is the landmark of the neighbourhood; its USP is the 360-degree top-floor terrace with plunge pool and sensational city views. Sophisticated, open-plan rooms have a crisp, space-station-style sheen, plus iPod docks, espresso machines and other cool comforts, while the slinky lobby "B-lounge" is the place for everything from breakfast to cocktails. **€100**

Hostal Cèntric c/de Casanova 13 ☎ 934 267 573, Ⓦ hostalcentric.com; Ⓜ Universitat; map pp.60–61. A good upper-budget choice, a couple of minutes' walk from the Raval. Most rooms feature wood panelling and plenty of light; cheaper ones on the upper floors (no lift) share bathrooms, while some of the more expensive en-suite ones (€30 extra) also have a/c. There's a sunny terrace at the rear. **€49**

★ **Hostal Gat Raval** c/de Joaquín Costa 44, 2º ☎ 934 816 670, Ⓦ gatrooms.com; Ⓜ Universitat; map pp.60–61. At the boutique end of the budget market, the *Gat Raval* has done its fashionable best with a rambling townhouse. Lime green is a recurring theme, from doors to bedspreads, while each room is broken down to fundamentals – chair, basin, wall-mounted TV, fan and heating, and signature back-lit street photograph and artwork that doubles as a reading light. Only six of the 24 rooms are en suite (an extra €10), but communal facilities are good, and there are internal or street and MACBA views, and staff on duty 24/7. **€60**

Hostal Gat Xino c/de l'Hospital 149–155 ☎ 933 248 833, Ⓦ gatrooms.com; Ⓜ Sant Antoni; map pp.60–61. The sister hotel to the *Gat Raval* shares the same signature style, and 24hr staff and security, but all the rooms here are en suite and breakfast is included, served in an internal patio area. Four suites (from €85) have more space, bigger bathrooms and less street noise (and one has a terrace; from €100). **€75**

★ **Hosteria Grau** c/de les Ramelleres 27 ☎ 933 018 135, Ⓦ hostalgrau.com; Ⓜ Catalunya; map pp.60–61. A really friendly pension that's been updated and adapted over the years, with attractive, colour-coordinated rooms

Ⓦ pensionmariluz.com; Ⓜ Jaume I/Liceu; map p.46. This old mansion, on a quieter-than-usual Barri Gòtic street, offers inexpensive rooms (shared bathrooms) and small dorms, plus a more personal welcome than in many other places of its kind. Someone's been to IKEA for furniture and there are contemporary art prints on the walls, central heating and a/c, laundry facilities and a small kitchen. It can be a tight squeeze when full, but a dozen apartments (sleeping two to six, €65–125) a few minutes' walk away in the Raval offer more space. Rates drop in low season. Dorms **€24**, rooms **€65**

on several floors; you'll pay around €15 less for a room with shared facilities or €15 more for superior rooms with balconies and a touch of modern Catalan style. There's a buffet continental breakfast included, and an adjacent café-bar, while six small private apartments in the same building (sleeping two to four, available by the night; €100) offer a bit more independence. **€80**

Hotel Curious c/del Carme 25 ☎ 933 014 484, Ⓦ hotel curious.com; Ⓜ Liceu; map pp.60–61. Stylish budget digs that offer coordinated, elemental room colours and a huge Barcelona photo backdrop behind each bed. Aside from a free buffet breakfast and helpful staff, services are on the light side, but you're only a few steps from the Ramblas or from the Raval's restaurants and nightlife. **€105**

★ **Hotel España** c/de Sant Pau 9–11 ☎ 935 500 000, Ⓦ hotelespanya.com; Ⓜ Liceu; map pp.60–61. There's been no more eagerly awaited hotel opening in recent times than the re-vamp of the classic *Hotel España* (see box, p.64) as a four-star-plus. The *modernista* icon has been sumptuously restored, and the gem-like interior – colourful tiles, bright mosaics, sculpted marble, iron swirls and marine motifs – has no equal in Barcelona. While public areas reboot the *modernista* era, guest rooms are a perfectly judged boutique blend of earth tones and designer style, with rain-showers, iPod docks and the like. There's a plunge pool and chill-out deck on the roof terrace, while the handsome house restaurant – known as *Fonda España* – offers contemporary Catalan bistro dishes by hot chef Martín Berasategui. **€135**

Hotel Peninsular c/de Sant Pau 34 ☎ 933 023 138, Ⓦ hotelpeninsular.net; Ⓜ Liceu; map pp.60–61. This interesting old building originally belonged to a priestly order, which explains the slightly cell-like quality of the rooms. However, there's nothing spartan about the galleried inner courtyard (around which the rooms are ranged), hung with dozens of tumbling houseplants, while breakfast is served in the arcaded dining room. **€80**

Hotel Sant Agustí Pl. Sant Agusti 3 ☎ 933 181 658, Ⓦ hotelsa.com; Ⓜ Liceu; map pp.60–61. Barcelona's oldest hotel occupies a former seventeenth-century convent building, with balconies overlooking a restored square and church.

It's of three-star standard, with the best rooms located in the attic, from where there are rooftop views. **€100**

★ **Market Hotel** c/del Comte Borrell 68, at Ptge. Sant Antoni Abat ☎ 933 251 205, ⓦ markethotel.com.es; ⓜ Sant Antoni; map pp.60–61. The designer-budget *Market* makes a definite splash with its part-Japanese, part neo-colonial look – think jet-black rooms with hardwood floors and shutters, and boxy wardrobes topped with travel trunks. It's a feel that flows through the building and down into the impressive restaurant, where the food is exceptionally good value, while the hotel's vintage Asian-style *Bar Rosso* has become a bit of a local hipsters' haunt. **€100**

Mesón Castilla c/de Valldonzella 5 ☎ 933 182 182, ⓦ mesoncastilla.com; ⓜ Universitat; map pp.60–61.

TOP 5 STYLE ON A BUDGET

Chic & Basic Born See below
Hostal Gat Xino See opposite
Hostal Goya See p.173
Hotel Banys Orientals See below
Market Hotel See above

A curious throwback to 1950s rural Spain, every inch of this two-star hotel is carved, painted and stencilled, from the grandfather clock in reception to the wardrobe in your room. The large rooms (some with terraces; €20 extra) feature country-style furniture, there's a vast rustic dining room (buffet breakfast included) and – best of all – a lovely tiled rear patio on which to read in the sun. **€135**

14

SANT PERE AND LA RIBERA

★ **Chic & Basic Born** c/de la Princesa 50 ☎ 932 954 652, ⓦ chicandbasic.com; ⓜ Jaume I; map p.70. From the babbling blurb ("it's fresh, it's cool, it's fusion") to the open-plan, all-in-white decor, everything here is punchily boutique and in-your-face. The 31 rooms mix glamour and comfort with laugh-aloud conceits like adjustable mood-lighting, sashaying plastic curtains and mirrored walls; larger rooms cost €25 more. Chic, certainly; basic, not at all, though the concept eschews room service, mini-bars and hordes of staff at your beck and call. Meals are courtesy of the attached – also effortlessly cool – *La Burguesa* burger-and-cocktail joint. There are other *Chic & Basic* outlets in the Raval, one on c/Tallers (near Pl. Universitat) and the other off the bottom of the Ramblas, and some Barri Gòtic apartments too (details on the website). **€110**

Equity Point Gothic c/dels Vigatans 5, online bookings only ⓦ equity-point.com, hostel information ☎ 932 312 045; ⓜ Jaume I; map p.70. Of Barcelona's three Equity Point hostels, this is the most backpacker-orientated, which might or might not be a good thing, depending on your view, age and capacity for company. Multi-bunk rooms have an en-suite shower-bathroom, each bed has its own bedside cabinet and reading light, and there are lockers, left-luggage and tour services, and an old-town roof terrace. Winter prices go as low as €15. Open 24hr. Includes breakfast. Dorms **€25**

★ **Grand Hotel Central** Via Laietana 30 ☎ 932 957 900, ⓦ grandhotelcentral.com; ⓜ Jaume I; map p.70. It might be on one of the city's noisiest thoroughfares, but the soundproofing does its job handsomely in this wham-glam designer hotel beloved of all the style mags. Spacious, ever-so-lovely rooms hit all the right buttons – hardwood floors, massage-showers, MP3 players – and up on the roof there are amazing views from the sundeck and infinity pool. Meanwhile, the fab hotel restaurant and café, *Ávalon*, showcases the new-wave Catalan cooking of chef Ramón Freixa. **€200**

★ **Hostal Nuevo Colón** Av. del Marquès de l'Argentera 19, 1º ☎ 933 195 077, ⓦ hostalnuevocolon .com; ⓜ Barceloneta; map p.70. In the hands of the same friendly family for decades, this well-kept pension sports 32 spacious rooms, painted yellow and kitted out with directors' chairs and double-glazing. Sunny front rooms, lounge and terrace all have side views to Ciutadella park. You'll save around €20 in a room with shared facilities; there are also three self-catering apartments available (by the night; €155) in the same building, which sleep up to six. **€70**

Hotel Banys Orientals c/de l'Argenteria 37 ☎ 932 688 460, ⓦ hotelbanysorientals.com; ⓜ Jaume I; map p.70. Funky boutique hotel with 43 minimalist rooms, plus some more spacious duplex suites (€130) in a nearby building. Hardwood floors, crisp white sheets, sharp marble bathrooms and urban-chic decor – not to mention bargain prices for this sort of style – make it a hugely popular choice. The attached restaurant, *Senyor Parellada*, is a great find too. **€100**

Hotel Ciutat Barcelona c/de la Princesa 35 ☎ 932 697 475, ⓦ ciutatbarcelona.com; ⓜ Jaume I; map p.70. Contemporary elegance at three-star prices in a hotel that's well sited for old-town sightseeing and the Picasso museum. The stylish, colour-coordinated rooms are sound-proofed against street noise, if a bit tight on space. Up top there's a cute deck and small pool for lounging about, and a handsome restaurant below. **€125**

Park Hotel Av. del Marquès de l'Argentera 11 ☎ 933 196 000, ⓦ www.parkhotelbarcelona.com; ⓜ Barceloneta; map p.70. The classy update for this elegant, modernist 1950s building starts with the chic bar and lounge, and runs up the feature period stairway to rooms in fawn and chocolate-brown with parquet floors, marble bathrooms and beds with angular reading lights. It's a bit on the pricey side for a three-star, but there's real retro style here. **€150**

14

★ **Pensió 2000** c/de Sant Pere Més Alt 6, 1° ☎ 933 107 466, ⊛ pensio2000.com; Ⓜ Urquinaona; map p.70. As close to a traditional, family-style B&B as Barcelona gets – seven en-suite rooms (some overlooking the Palau de la Música Catalana, across the street) in a welcoming mansion

apartment strewn with books, plants and pictures. A third person could easily share most rooms (€20 supplement), and kids are welcome at knock-down prices. A choice of breakfasts (not included) is served either in your room or on the internal patio. Laundry service available. €80

PORT VELL AND BARCELONETA

★ **Bonic Barcelona** c/de Josep Anselm Clavé 9 ☎ 626 053 434, ⊛ www.bonic-barcelona.com; Ⓜ Drassanes; map p.81. Chic and charming "urban guesthouse", just a few steps from port and Ramblas, with Gothic-Moorish decor and gorgeous tile floors. Rooms are simply furnished, and the three bathrooms are shared, but a maximum of six guests at any one time ensures peace and privacy. Advance reservations essential; minimum two-night stay required. €90

Equity Point Sea Pl. del Mar 1–4, online bookings only ⊛ equity-point.com, hostel information ☎ 932 312 045; Ⓜ Barceloneta; map p.81. The budget beachside choice: neat little modern bunk rooms sleep six or seven, with an en-suite shower-bathroom in each one. The attached café, where you have breakfast (included), looks right out onto the boardwalk and palm trees. In low season prices fall steeply. Open 24hr. Dorms €26

Hotel Duquesa de Cardona Pg. de Colom 12 ☎ 932 689 090, ⊛ hduquesadecardona.com; Ⓜ Drassanes; map p.81. Step off the busy harbourfront highway into this soothing four-star haven, set in a remodelled sixteenth-century mansion. The rooms are calm and quiet, decorated in earth tones and immaculately appointed. Although not all of them have harbour views, everyone has access to the stylish roof-deck overlooking the harbour. It's

great for sundowner drinks and boasts (if that's the word) probably the city's smallest outdoor pool. €160

Marina View B&B Pg. de Colom ☎ 933 175 920 or ☎ 678 854 456, ⊛ marinaviewbcn.com; Ⓜ Drassanes; map p.81. A classy, personally run place in a great location – the two front rooms have terrific harbour views (€25 extra). There's far more of a hotel feel here than a simple B&B, with the six rooms featuring stylish linen, bold colours, excellent bathrooms and nice touches, from mini-bars with normal drinks prices to tea-and-coffee trays – then again, these aren't exactly run-of-the-mill B&B prices. Breakfast is included (served in the room); advance reservations essential (contact for directions); two-night minimum stay at weekends. €115

★ **W Barcelona** Pl. de la Rosa dels Vents ☎ 932 952 800, ⊛ w-barcelona.com; Ⓜ Barceloneta; map p.79. Signature building on the Barceloneta seafront is one of the city's most iconic structures – the stupendously cool, wave-shaped *W Barcelona*. Open-plan designer rooms have fantastic views through floor-to-ceiling windows, and facilities are first-rate: iPod docks to infinity pool, state-of-the-art spa to "whatever-you-want" concierge service. There's a hip, resort feel, with direct beach access, a chill-out lobby bar and see-and-be-seen rooftop lounge, while dining in *Bravo* is courtesy of creative Barcelona chef Carles Abellan. €245

PORT OLÍMPIC

Hotel Arts Barcelona c/Marina 19–21, Port Olímpic ☎ 932 211 000, ⊛ ritzcarlton.com/hotels/barcelona; Ⓜ Ciutadella-Vila Olímpica; map p.85. Still the city benchmark for five-star designer luxury, service and standards: effortlessly classy rooms feature enormous marble bathrooms and fabulous views, while stunning duplex apartments have their own perks (like 24hr butler

service and a personal Mini Cooper). You're only a hop from the beach, but seafront gardens encompass a swimming pool and hot tub. The jaw-dropping Six Senses spa occupies the top two floors, while dining options range from the open-air terrace restaurant to Michelin-starred chef Sergi Arola's contemporary tapas place, *Arola* (closed Mon & Tues). €385

MONTJUÏC

Hotel Miramar Barcelona Plaza Carlos Ibañez 3 ☎ 932 811 600, ⊛ hotelmiramarbarcelona.com; Ⓜ Paral.lel or Funicular de Montjuïc; map p.91. The remodelled *Miramar* – first built for the 1929 International Exhibition – has 75 super-stylish rooms wrapped around the kernel of the original building, all with views to knock your socks off. From the architecture books in the soaring lobby to the terrace-jacuzzi that comes with each room, it's clearly designer heaven; the room gadgets and stunning pool, garden and deck come as no surprise. True, you're not

in the city centre, but it's only a 10min taxi ride from most downtown destinations. €189

TOP 5 VIEWS

Barceló Raval See p.170
Gran Hotel La Florida See p.176
Hotel Casa Fuster See p.175
Hotel Majestic See opposite
Hotel Miramar Barcelona See above

DRETA DE L'EIXAMPLE

★ **BCN Fashion House** c/del Bruc 13 ✆ 637 904 044, ⓦ bcnfashionhouse.com; ⓜ Urquinaona; map p.104. Italian owners have added a touch of chic flair to what was formerly an *atelier* in Barcelona's "garment district", and the seven spacious, high-ceilinged rooms (some with veranda) are lightened with prints, sculptures and artefacts from their travels. The rooms share three bathrooms and a plant-strewn internal terrace, though a studio-suite (€130) has its own facilities, private terrace area and kitchenette. The buffet breakfast is optional, and off-season deals are good value. **€82**

★ **Equity Point Centric** Pg. de Gràcia 33, online bookings only ⓦ equity-point.com, hostel information ✆ 932 312 045; ⓜ Passeig de Gràcia; map p.104. Bills itself as "one of the most spectacular hostels in Europe" and it's hard to disagree, with around 450 beds spread across several floors of a refurbished *modernista* building in a swish midtown location. Dorms sleep up to twelve, while private rooms are also available (sleeping two to four, low-season rates from €80), all with lockers and en-suite shower room, and many with balcony and views. Facilities are first-rate, with bar, kitchen and laundry, and a roof terrace with yet more spectacular city views. Prices include continental breakfast. Dorms **€22**, rooms **€110**

Hostal L'Antic Espai Gran Via de les Corts Catalanes 660 ✆ 933 041 945, ⓦ www.lanticespai.com. ⓜ Passeig de Gràcia; map p.104. Camp and cosy, this beautifully ornate period piece springs a surprise in every room, from mosaic tile floors to antique pendants, with candles and flowers at every turn. Room 102 has an original glassed-in balcony, and 107 opens onto an internal terrace with a candelabra-topped table. Modern bathrooms and DVD players keep comforts up-to-date. **€120**

Hostal Girona c/de Girona 24, 1 ✆ 932 650 259, ⓦ hostalgirona.com; ⓜ Urquinaona; map p.104. Delightful, family-run pension with cosy, traditional rooms, plus corridors laid with rugs, polished wooden doors, antique paintings and restored furniture throughout. There's a whole range of rooms available (from as low as €60) – some share a bathroom, others have a shower or full bath, while the biggest and best rooms (€90) have a/c and balconies, though you can expect some noise. **€75**

★ **Hostal Goya** c/de Pau Claris 74, 1 ✆ 933 022 565, ⓦ hostalgoya.com; ⓜ Urquinaona; map p.104. Boutique-style pension that offers a dozen crisply furnished fabulous rooms on two floors of a mansion building. There's a fair range of options, with the best rooms opening onto a balcony or a terrace (€15 extra). Comfortable sitting areas, and free coffee and tea, are available on both floors, while two apartments (sleeping two to six; from €175 for two people) offer more space for groups and families. **€95**

Hostal San Remo c/d'Ausias Marc 19, 2 ✆ 933 021 989, ⓦ hostalsanremo.com; ⓜ Urquinaona; map p.104.

This basic pension's doubles aren't a bad size for the money and its small tiled bathrooms are pretty good for the price range. There's a/c and double-glazing, though you'll still get more peace at the back – that said, the internal rooms aren't nearly as appealing as those with balconies. The seven rooms include one decently priced single. **€65**

Hotel Claris c/de Pau Claris 150 ✆ 934 876 262, ⓦ derbyhotels.com; ⓜ Passeig de Gràcia; map p.104. Very select five-star-deluxe hotel, from the incense-scented marble lobby complete with authentic Roman mosaics to the hugely appealing rooms ranged around a soaring, water-washed atrium. It even has its own private antiquities museum. If there's a gripe, it's that there's not a lot of room space for your euro, but the staff couldn't be more accommodating and there's a swish rooftop terrace pool. The bar is a cool hangout in its own right, while the hotel restaurant, *East 47*, offers creative Mediterranean cuisine under the gaze of a line of Warhol self-portraits. **€200**

★ **Hotel Condes de Barcelona** Pg. de Gràcia 73–75 ✆ 934 450 000, ⓦ condesdebarcelona.com; ⓜ Passeig de Gràcia; map p.104. Straddling two sides of c/de Mallorca, the four-star *Condes* is fashioned from two former palaces: the north side has kept its interior marblework and wrought-iron balconies, but there's little difference between the rooms in either building. All are classily turned out in contemporary style, while some of the suites (from €260) have jacuzzi, balcony and private terrace with views of Gaudí's La Pedrera. There's also a pretty hotel roof terrace and plunge pool, while multi-Michelin-starred Basque chef Martín Berasategui offers fine dining in the hotel's acclaimed *Lasarte* restaurant (closed Sun & Mon) and a more informal bistro menu in *Loidi* (closed Sun). **€135**

Hotel Majestic Pg. de Gràcia 68 ✆ 934 881 717, ⓦ hotelmajestic.es; ⓜ Passeig de Gràcia; map p.104. This traditional *grand-dame* hotel, first opened in 1918, has been refitted in contemporary style and muted colours to provide a tranquil city-centre base. Big-ticket original art adorns the public areas (it's known for its art collection), and the rooms – larger than many in this price range – have been pleasantly refurbished. The absolute clincher is the rooftop spa, pool and deck, with amazing views over to the Sagrada Família. Meanwhile chef Fermí Puig's renowned *Drolma* restaurant (closed Sun) pulls in Michelin-star seekers. **€200**

14

TOP 5 MONEY NO OBJECT

Hotel Arts Barcelona See opposite
Hotel Omm See p.174
Le Méridien Barcelona See p.168
Mandarin Oriental See p.174
W Barcelona See opposite

14

TOP 5 B&BS
BCN Fashion House See p.173
Bonic Barcelona See p.172
Marina View B&B See p.172
Pensió 2000 See p.172
the5rooms See below

Hotel Omm c/del Rosselló 265 ☎934 454 000, ⊛hotelomm.es; Ⓜ Diagonal; map p.104. The glam designer experience that is *Omm* means minimalist, open-plan rooms, a studiously chic bar, the Roca brothers' sensational, Michelin-starred *Moo* restaurant (closed Sun & Aug), plus terrace, pool and Spaciomm "relaxation centre", not to mention fearsomely handsome staff. It's not to everyone's taste – it's probably fair to say that the less annoying you find the endless Omm/Moo tagging of services and facilities, the more you'll like the hotel. €220
Mandarin Oriental Pg. de Gràcia 38–40 ☎931 518 888, ⊛mandarinoriental.com/Barcelona; Ⓜ Passeig de Gràcia; map p.104. The latest designer addition to Barcelona's most prestigious avenue is the super-sleek *Mandarin Oriental*, which fills the premises of a former bank building with a soaring white atrium and a serene selection of gorgeously light rooms – the suites particularly, with their stunning bathrooms and private terraces, are among the finest in Barcelona. There's the obligatory superstar restaurant, *Moments* (under the direction of the world's most Michelin-starred female chef, Carme Ruscalleda), while bar, spa, mimosa garden and rooftop "dipping pool" combine oriental tranquillity and Euro cool. €300
★ **the5Rooms** c/de Pau Claris 72, 2 ☎933 427 880, ⊛thefiverooms.com; Ⓜ Urquinaona; map p.104. The impeccable taste and fashion background of owner Jessica is evident at *the5rooms*: gorgeous contemporary-styled B&B rooms are spacious and light-filled, with original artwork above each bed, exposed brick walls and terrific bathrooms. Despite the high-spec surroundings, the feel is house party rather than hotel – breakfast is served whenever you like, drinks are always available, and Jessica is happy to sit down and talk you through her favourite bars, restaurants and galleries. Suites and apartments are also available (from €175 for two). €145

ESQUERRA DE L'EIXAMPLE

★ **Alternative Creative Youth Home** Ronda de la Universitat 17 ☎635 669 021, ⊛www.alternative-barcelona.com; Ⓜ Universitat/Catalunya; map p.113. The hostel hangout for a self-selecting art crowd, who love the laidback vibe, projection lounge, cool music and city-savvy staff. The regular hostel stuff is well designed too, with a walk-in kitchen, lockers and laundry, and a maximum of 24 people spread across three small dorms. For much of the year rates fall to around €20, though peak summer sees them rise to €36. Dorms €30
★ **Gran Hotel Torre Catalunya** Av. de Roma 2–4 ☎936 006 999, ⊛torrecatalunya.com; Ⓜ Sants-Estació; map p.113. The landmark four-star-deluxe hotel outside Sants station towers over the surrounding buildings, which means that the large, light, elegant rooms have sweeping views from all sides (the pricier rooms – from €150 – above the twelfth floor are considered "superior"). Breakfast on the 23rd floor is a buzz; there's a panoramic restaurant, too, plus spa with indoor pool, while guests can also use the nearby *Expo* hotel's outdoor pool. €125
Hotel Axel c/d'Aribau 33 ☎933 239 393, ⊛axelhotels.com; Ⓜ Universitat; map p.113. Central to the self-image of the city's gay quarter, the Gaixample, the *Axel*'s snazzy "heterofriendly" boutique stylings are a real hit with gay visitors. It's a hip but relaxed space with designer rooms (featuring complimentary beauty products), a bar and restaurant that are part of the local scene, plus a fabulous terrace pool and "Skybar" for posing and preening, excellent spa and fitness facilities, and a full range of massage and other treatments available. €170
Hotel Inglaterra c/de Pelai 14 ☎935 051 100, ⊛www.hotel-inglaterra.com; Ⓜ Universitat; map p.113. The boutique little three-star sister to the Dreta's *Majestic* has an excellent location, harmoniously toned rooms and snazzy bathrooms. Space is at a premium, but some rooms have cute private terraces, others street-side balconies, while best of all is the romantic roof terrace. Guests are also welcome to use the *Majestic*'s rooftop pool and spa (see p.173). €139
Residencia Australia Ronda de la Universitat 11, 4 ☎933 174 177, ⊛residenciaustralia.com; Ⓜ Universitat; map p.113. A very welcoming budget pension, overseen by Thomas, fount of city knowledge, musician and cheery host. Three of the four rooms have basins and balconies, and share two nice bathrooms; the other is classed as a suite (€60–85, depending on season) with private bathroom, a/c, TV, fridge and kettle for tea and coffee. Just down the street in another building are some more similarly priced suites with kitchen facilities. €53
Room Mate Emma c/del Rosselló 205 ☎932 385 606, ⊛room-matehotels.com; Ⓜ Diagonal; map p.113. Ignore the tacky come-on ("would you like to sleep with me?" erm, no thanks, you're a marketing construct, not a real person), and get beyond the *Battlestar Galactica*-style lobby, and you're left with *Emma*'s undeniably appealing barebones-chic rooms and suites at realistic uptown prices. It's part of a Spanish chain with a fresh, fun vibe and an

accommodating air, from free fruit at reception to breakfast until noon. **€125**

★ **Somnio Barcelona** c/de la Diputació 251 ☎ 932 725 308, ⓦ www.somniohostels.com. ⓜ Passeig de Gràcia; map p.113. Sisters Lauren and Lee from Chicago bring their passion for Barcelona right into their upscale pension, dropping "tips for the day" into your room each morning. Simple but smart rooms with wood-block floors cater for singles, couples and friends (it's especially welcoming for women visitors), and there are two six-bed, single-sex dorms. You'll pay another €10 for an en-suite room, while there's more inexpensive shared budget

TOP 5 DORMS AND HOSTELS

Alternative Creative Youth Home
See opposite
Barcelona Urbany See p.175
Equity Point Centric See p.171
Pensión Mari-Luz See p.170
Somnio Barcelona See opposite

14

accommodation at their new sister hostel in the same district. Dorms **€26**, rooms **€78**

SAGRADA FAMÍLIA AND GLÒRIES

★ **Barcelona Urbany** Av. Meridiana 97 ☎ 932 458 414, ⓦ www.barcelonaurbany.com; ⓜ Clot; map pp.118–119. This huge steel-and-glass four hundred-bed hostel might be a bit off the beaten track, but it's handy for the metro (it's an easy ride in to Plaça de Catalunya) and airport train, and has terrific views of the landmark Torre Agbar. The rooms are like space-shuttle pods – boxy en-suites with pull-down beds (sleeping two to eight), power-showers and key-card lockers – that are just as viable for couples on a budget as backpackers. Rates vary according to season, but go as low as €15 for dorms and €50 for rooms. There's a bar and terrace, all sorts of tours

and offers available, plus free health club and pool entry in the same building. Breakfast included. Dorms **€30**, private rooms **€84**

Hotel Eurostars Gaudí c/del Consell de Cent 498–500 ☎ 932 320 288, ⓦ eurostarsgaudi.com; ⓜ Monumental; map pp.118–119. A good four-star choice within walking distance of the Sagrada Família; sharply styled, well-equipped standard rooms are real value for money, while the top-floor suites (from €200) boast a terrace with loungers and views of the Gaudí church and distant hills. **€120**

GRÀCIA

★ **Hostal HMB** c/de Bonavista 21 ☎ 933 682 013, ⓦ hostalhmb.com; ⓜ Diagonal; map p.126. Tucked away at the bottom of the neighbourhood is this chic little budget pension, with a range of rooms including some family and friends "suites" (ie, bigger rooms with a sofa bed), from €90. It's a safe, well-run, value-for-money choice if you prefer to stay uptown near Gràcia's nightlife – though add €10 per night for a weekend stay. **€60**

Hotel Casa Fuster Pg. de Gràcia 132 ☎ 932 553 000, ⓦ hotelcasafuster.com; ⓜ Diagonal; map p.126.

Modernista architect Lluís Domènech i Montaner's magnificent Casa Fuster (1908) is the backdrop for five-star-deluxe luxury with service to match. Rooms are in natural tones, with huge beds and gorgeous bathrooms, while public areas make full use of the architectural heritage, from the magnificent pillared lobby bar, *Café Vienés*, to the wonderful panoramic roof terrace and pool – summer nights see the terrace turned over to chill-out lounge bar *Blue View*. There's also a contemporary restaurant, *Galaxó*, plus fitness centre, sauna and 24hr room service. **€200**

PARC GÜELL

Alberg Mare de Déu de Montserrat Pg. de la Mare de Déu del Coll 41–51 ☎ 932 105 151, reservations on ☎ 934 838 363, ⓦ xanascat.cat; ⓜ Vallcarca (follow Av. de la República d'Argentina, c/Viaducte de Vallcarca and then signs) or bus #28 from Pl. de Catalunya, plus night buses, stop just across the street; map p.128. This popular hostel, owned by the regional government, is set in a converted mansion, with a tiled and stained-glass interior,

gardens, terrace and great city views – it's a long way out, but close to Parc Güell. Dorms sleep six, eight or twelve, and there are all the usual facilities plus meals are provided (or there's a local restaurant just around the corner). IYHF membership required; five-night maximum stay; reception open 8am–3pm & 4.30–11pm; main door closes at midnight, but opens every 30min thereafter. Includes breakfast. Dorms **€22**

LES CORTS, PEDRALBES AND SARRIÀ-SANT GERVASI

Gran Hotel Princesa Sofia Pl. de Pius XII 4 ☎ 935 081 000, ⓦ princesasofia.com; ⓜ Maria Cristina; map pp.132–133. Well placed for shoppers, this vintage classic – one of the first five-star hotels in town – also has

wide-ranging city views from the upper floors. It still exudes old-school charm (the concierges know everything) though the warm-toned rooms, massages and treatments in the Aqua Diagonal Wellness Centre, pool (with retractable roof) and superior club rooms (from €210) and lounges offer a more contemporary experience – the Barcelona football team stays and eats here before every home match. An immense buffet breakfast is served in the *Contraste* restaurant, which also features a pretty patio for summer dining. **€140**

TIBIDABO

★ **Abac** Av. Tibidabo 1 ☎ 933 196 600, ⓦ www.abac barcelona.com; FGC Avinguda del Tibidabo; map p.139. *The* chic address for intimate, uptown boutique style, the five-star-plus *Abac* showcases the Michelin-starred talents of chef Jordi Cruz in a gorgeous designer, glass-and-wood revamp of an old Tibidabo mansion. There are just fifteen rooms – cream and white decor, swishing drapes, sumptuous bathrooms with whirlpool baths and Hermes cosmetics – and services include a spa and lounge bar, though perhaps the measure of the place is the personal-shopper service available for guests. **€250**

Gran Hotel La Florida Carreterra Vallviderera a Tibidabo 83–93, 7km from the centre ☎ 932 593 000, ⓦ www.hotellaflorida.com; map p.139. Describing itself as an "urban resort", the five-star, hillside *Gran Hotel La Florida* re-creates the glory days of the 1950s, when it was at the centre of Barcelona high society. Its terraces and garden areas have amazing views, while some of the seventy rooms and suites have private gardens or terraces and jacuzzis. There's also an achingly lovely spa and pool, and Sunday brunch on the terrace at *L'Orangerie* restaurant is one of the city's great secrets. Special offers can slash the rate by half. **€300**

FLASH FLASH, GRÀCIA

Cafés, tapas bars and restaurants

If you step no further than the Ramblas or the streets of the Barri Gòtic, you are not going to experience the best of the city's cuisine – in the main tourist areas food and service can be indifferent and prices high. For the finest food the city has to offer, it pays to be a bit more adventurous and explore the backstreets of neighbourhoods like Sant Pere, La Ribera, El Raval and Poble Sec, where you'll find excellent restaurants, some little more than hole-in-the-wall taverns, others surprisingly funky and chic. Most, but not all, of the big-ticket, destination-dining restaurants are found in the Eixample. Gràcia, further out, is a nice village-like place to spend the evening, with plenty of good mid-range restaurants, while for fish and seafood you're best off in the harbourside Barceloneta district or at the Port Olímpic.

Barcelona's thousands of **cafés** keep the city fuelled from morning to night, and you're rarely more than a step away from a coffee fix or a quick sandwich. Many are classics of their kind – century-old establishments or unique neighbourhood haunts – while others specialize in certain types of food and drink. A **forn** is a bakery, a **pastisseria** a cake and pastry shop, a **xocolateria** specializes in chocolate, while a **granja** (milk bar) offers traditional delights like *orxata* (*horchata*, tiger-nut drink) and *granissat* (*granizado*, a flavoured crushed-ice drink).

The **tapas** boom, meanwhile, shows no sign of abating, with increasing numbers of bars and restaurants figuring that small is beautiful when it comes to designing new menus. Little dishes are all the rage, and while there are still plenty of old-style, hanging-ham and counter-display tapas bars in town, there's also a real sense of adventure in new-wave places that are deadly serious about their food. You're as likely to get shrimp tempura, a samosa or a yucca chip as a garlic mushroom these days, while a few stand-out places offer classy, restaurant-standard experiences that are still truly tapas at heart.

Traditional **Catalan and regional Spanish food** remains at the core of many **restaurant** menus, while the city has the usual range of pizza places, curry houses, fast-food joints and the like. But these are exciting times for foodies in Barcelona, as **contemporary Spanish cooking** continues to be a big deal. The minimalist, food-as-chemistry approach, pioneered by best-chef-in-the-world Ferran Adrià (of *El Bulli* fame), has spawned a thousand followers, many with restaurants in Barcelona (and a fair few now with Michelin stars). The best are reinterpreting classic Catalan dishes in innovative ways, and while prices in these gastro-temples are high there's a trend towards more economic, bistro-style dining even by the hottest chefs. Meanwhile, the current fad obsessing city restaurateurs is the fusion of Mediterranean and Asian flavours – a so-called **"Mediterrasian" cuisine** – that combines local, market-fresh ingredients with more exotic tastes. Sometimes this works (Catalan-Asian sushi-style tapas), sometimes this doesn't (erm, Catalan-Asian sushi-style tapas), but eating out in Barcelona has never been more interesting.

ESSENTIALS

COSTS AND RESERVATIONS

Prices Overall, eating out in Barcelona is still pretty good value, and you'll be able to dine in a huge variety of restaurants for around €25–30 a head, and around the same if you jump from tapas bar to tapas bar. In fancier, fashionable places you can double this, while "tasting menus" at the current dining hot-spots run from €70–120 a head, excluding drinks (still a lot cheaper than equivalents in, say, New York or London).

Getting a good deal Nearly all restaurants offer a weekday (ie Mon–Fri) three-course *menú del dia* (menu of the day) at lunchtime, with the cheapest starting at about €9, rising to €18–20 in fancier places. In many restaurants the price also includes a drink, so this can be a real bargain (at night, you might pay three or four times as much to eat dinner in the same restaurant).

Reservations and payment If there's somewhere you'd particularly like to eat – certainly at the more fashionable end of the market – you should reserve a table. Some places are booked solid for days, or weeks, in advance. Credit and debit cards are widely accepted in restaurants, though not necessarily in cheaper places, traditional tapas bars and the like. Finally, all restaurant menus should make

it clear whether the eight-percent IVA tax is included in the prices or not (it usually is).

OPENING HOURS AND CLOSING DAYS

Opening hours Most cafés are open from 7 or 8am until midnight, or much later – so whether it's coffee first thing or a late-night nibble, you'll find somewhere to cater for you. Restaurants are generally open 1 to 4pm and 8.30 to 11pm, though most locals don't eat lunch until at least 2pm and dinner after 9 or even 10pm. However, in tourist zones like the Ramblas and Port Olímpic, restaurants tend to stay open all day and serve on request, while many tapas bars are also open all day from morning until night.

Closing days and holidays Many restaurants close on Sundays or Mondays, and on public holidays, and lots close over Easter and throughout August – check the listings for specific details but expect changes, since many places imaginatively reinterpret their own posted opening days and times.

MENUS

Dishes and specialities To ask for a menu, request *la carta*, though be warned that some cheaper places

STARTING THE DAY

Unless you're staying somewhere with a decent buffet spread, you may as well pass up the overpriced coffee-and-croissant option in your hotel and join the locals for **breakfast** in one of the city's bars, cafés or patisseries. A few euros will get you a hot drink and a brioche, croissant or sandwich just about anywhere – *ensaimadas* (pastry spirals) are a popular choice, while *xocolata amb xurros* (*chocolate con churros* – long, fried tubular doughnuts with thick drinking chocolate) is a good cold-weather starter. The traditional country breakfast is *pa amb tomàquet* (*pan con tomate*) – bread rubbed with tomato, olive oil and garlic, perhaps topped with some cured ham or sliced cheese. Otherwise, breakfast sandwiches are whatever can be stuffed inside a *flauta* (thin baguette), from cured ham to a slice of *tortilla*.

might not have a written menu, with the waiter merely reeling off the day's dishes at bewildering speed. Turn to the "language" section for a menu reader (see p.266).

A warning Budget meals sometimes come in the form of a garishly photographed *plat combinat* (*plato combinado*, combined plate) of things like eggs, steak or calamari with fries and salad, but generally speaking, pictures of dishes on a menu is not an indicator of great cuisine – especially so in the case of the pre-prepared paellas advertised on boards outside tourist restaurants.

15

THE RAMBLAS

CAFÉS

Antiga Casa Figueras Ramblas 83 ☎ 933 016 027, ⊛ escriba.es; Ⓜ Liceu; map p.38. "We don't just make pastries, we create illusions", claims the renowned Escribà family business. Visit their classy, historic *modernista*-designed pastry shop near the Boqueria market and find out why many rate this as the best bakery in Barcelona. Mon–Sat 9am–3pm & 5–8.30pm.

★ **Café de l'Opera** Ramblas 74 ☎ 933 177 585, ⊛ cafeoperabcn.com; Ⓜ Liceu; map p.38. If you're going to pay through the nose for a Ramblas seat, it may as well be at one of the bank of sought-after pavement tables at this famous old café-bar opposite the opera house, which retains its *fin-de-siècle* feel. Surprisingly, it's not a complete tourist-fest, and locals pop in by day and night for drinks, cakes and tapas. Daily 8.30am–2.30am.

Café Zurich Pl. Catalunya 1 ☎ 933 179 153; Ⓜ Catalunya; map p.38. The most famous meet-and-greet café in town, right at the top of the Ramblas underneath El Triangle shopping centre. It's good for croissants and breakfast sandwiches and there's a huge pavement terrace, but sit inside if you don't want to be bothered by endless rounds of buskers and beggars. Mon–Fri 8am–11pm, Sat & Sun 10am–11pm (June–Sept open until 1am).

TAPAS BARS

Amaya Ramblas 20–24 ☎ 933 026 138 (bar), 933 021 037 (restaurant), ⊛ restauranteamaya.com; Ⓜ Drassanes;

map p.38. A Ramblas fixture since 1941 – restaurant on one side, tapas bar on the other, both serving Basque seafood specialities, from octopus to anchovies. The bar offers the cheapest and most enjoyable introduction to the cuisine; otherwise, main dishes in the restaurant cost €14–20. Bar daily 10am–12.30am; restaurant daily 1.30–4pm & 8.30pm–midnight.

Bar Central La Boqueria Mercat de la Boqueria, Ramblas 91 ☎ 933 011 098; Ⓜ Liceu; map p.38. This gleaming, chrome stand-up bar in the market's central aisle is the venue for ultra-fresh market produce, served by snazzy staff who work at a fair lick. Breakfast, snack or lunch, it's all the same to them – salmon cutlets, sardines, calamari, razor clams, hake fillets, sausages, pork steaks, asparagus spears and the rest, plunked on the griddle and sprinkled with salt. Breakfast costs just a few euros or it's €5–15 for some tapas or a main dish and a drink. Mon–Sat 6.30am–4pm.

★ **Bar Pinotxo** Mercat de la Boqueria, Ramblas 91 ☎ 933 171 731; Ⓜ Liceu; map p.38. The market's most renowned refuelling stop – just inside the main entrance on the right – attracts traders, chefs, tourists and celebs, who stand three deep at busy times. A coffee, a grilled sandwich and a glass of cava (no, really) is the local breakfast of choice, or let the cheery staff steer you towards the tapas and daily specials (€5–15) – anything from a slice of tortilla to fried baby squid. Mon–Sat 6am–5pm; closed Aug.

BARRI GÒTIC

CAFÉS

Bar del Pi Pl. de Sant Josep Oriol 1 ☎ 933 022 123; Ⓜ Liceu; map p.46. Located on one of Barcelona's prettiest squares, *Bar del Pi* is best known for its terrace tables.

Linger over drinks and sandwiches let the old town reveal its charms, especially during the weekend artists' market. Mon–Sat 9am–11pm, Sun 10am–10pm; closed 2 weeks in Jan, & Aug.

15

TOP 5 CLASSY CAFÉS

Bar del Convent See p.184
Café de les Delícies See p.182
Café de l'Opera See p.179
Caelum See below
Caj Chai See below

★ **Caelum** c/de la Palla 8 ☎ 933 026 993, ⓦ caelum barcelona.com; ⓜ Liceu; map p.46. The lovingly packaged confections in this upscale café-cum-deli (the name is Latin for "heaven") are made in convents and monasteries across Spain. Choose from *frutas de almendra* (marzipan sweeties) from Seville, Benedictine preserves or Cistercian cookies – or hunker down for cakes and coffee in the atmospheric basement crypt. Mon–Thurs 10.30am–8.30pm, Fri & Sat 10.30am–11.30pm, Sun 11.30am–8.30pm; closed 2 weeks in Aug.

★ **Caj Chai** c/de Sant Domènec del Call 12 ☎ 933 019 592, ⓦ cajchai.com; map p.46. This refined backstreet boudoir offers a menu of painstakingly prepared teas, from Moroccan mint to organic Nepalese *oolong*. Snacks are similarly delectable, along the lines of chocolate brownies, *baklava* and wholewheat sandwiches. Mon 3–10pm, Tues–Sun 10.30am–10pm.

Dulcinea c/de Petritxol 2 ☎ 932 311 756; ⓜ Liceu; map p.46. One of the old town's age-old treats is to come here for a thick hot chocolate, slathered in cream. Then if you've still got room, try one of their pastries or perhaps a dish of *mel i mato* (curd cheese with honey). It's a bygone-era kind of place, with dickie-bow-wearing waiters patrolling the beamed and panelled room bearing silver trays. Daily 9am–1pm & 5–9pm; closed Aug.

Mesón del Cafe c/de la Llibreteria 16 ☎ 933 150 754; ⓜ Jaume I; map p.46. Offbeat locals' café, great for quick coffees, pastries and (is-it-that-time-already?-oh-go-on-then-I'll-have-a-brandy) pick-me-ups. You'll probably have to stand, though there is a sort of cubbyhole at the back with a few tables. Mon–Sat 7am–9.30pm.

TAPAS BARS

Bar Celta Pulpería c/de la Mercè 16 ☎ 933 150 006; ⓜ Drassanes; map p.46. This brightly lit, no-nonsense Galician tapas bar specializes in typical dishes like octopus (*pop gallego*) and fried green *pimientos* (peppers), washed down with heady regional wine (dishes €3–10). You eat at the U-shaped bar or at tables in the back room, and while it's not one for a long, lazy meal, it's just right to kick off a bout of bar-hopping. Tues–Sat noon–midnight.

★ **Bodega La Plata** c/de la Mercè 28 ☎ 933 151 009; ⓜ Drassanes; map p.46. A classic taste of the old town, with a marble counter open to the street and dirt-cheap wine served straight from the barrel. It attracts an enthusiastic local crowd, from businessmen to pre-clubbers,

and for €5 or so you can get a couple of drinks and a dish of the speciality anchovies, either marinaded or deep-fried like whitebait. Daily 10am–4pm & 8–11pm.

Ginger c/Palma Sant Just 1 ☎ 933 105 309, ⓦ ginger.cat; ⓜ Jaume I; map p.46. Wine, cocktails and creative tapas in a slickly updated 1970s-style setting. It's a world away from *patatas bravas* and battered squid – think roast duck vinaigrette, tuna tartare and vegetarian satay for around €7–9 a pop. Tues–Sat 7pm–3am, kitchen open until 1am; closed 2 weeks in Aug.

Taller de Tapas Pl. de Sant Josep Oriol 9 ☎ 933 018 020, ⓦ tallerdetapas.com; ⓜ Liceu; map p.46. The fashionable "tapas workshop" sucks in tourists with its year-round outdoor terrace and pretty location by the church of Santa Maria del Pi. The open kitchen turns out reliable market-fresh tapas, with fish a speciality at dinner, from grilled langoustine to seared tuna (most tapas €4–12). There are several other branches around town, though this was the first and has the nicest location. Daily noon–midnight (Fri & Sat until 1am).

★ **La Viñatería del Call** c/de Sant Domènec del Call 9 ☎ 933 026 092, ⓦ lavinateriadelcall.com; ⓜ Jaume I; map p.46. The wood-table tavern is principally an eating place – with a long menu of cheese and ham platters, smoked fish, fried peppers and much more – but it's also a great late-night bar, with a serious wine list and jazz and flamenco sounds as a backdrop. If you want to eat, especially at weekends, it's best to reserve a table. Mon–Sat 8.30pm–1am.

RESTAURANTS

★ **Arc Café** c/d'enCarabassa 19 ☎ 933 025 204, ⓦ arc cafe.com; ⓜ Drassanes; map p.46. This chilled-out bistro-bar is a real neighbourhood stalwart. You can just drop by for a drink, but the kitchen is open all day, serving a good-value, seasonally changing menu (most mains around €10). There are hearty soups, Mediterranean salads, spring rolls, pastas and Thai curries (with Thurs & Fri nights designated Thai food nights). Mon–Thurs noon–1am, Fri & Sat noon–2am.

Bun Bo Viêtnam c/dels Sagristans 3 ☎ 933 011 378, ⓦ bunbovietnam.com; ⓜ Jaume I; map p.46. Set on a light street corner with a spacious terrace and big windows, there's a fresh and fun vibe at *Bun Bo*, from the frilly lanterns to the centre-stage cyclo-trike. The Vietnamese food might be a bit toned down for locals, but rice-paper rolls, pho soups, steamed fish and clay-pot pork are all realistically priced (mains €8–11), there's Vietnamese coffee served from 11am, a good-value weekday lunch and the kitchen stays open day and night. Daily 1pm–midnight.

★ **Café de l'Acadèmia** c/de Lledó 1 ☎ 933 198 253; ⓜ Jaume I; map p.46. Great for a date or a lazy lunch, with creative Catalan cooking served in a romantic stone-flagged restaurant or outside in the medieval square, lit by candles

NO SUCH THING AS A FREE LUNCH …

…except, once upon a time, in southern Spain. **Tapas** (from tapar, to cover) originated as free snacks given away as covers for drinks' glasses, perhaps to keep the flies off in the baking sun. It's still a much more southern, Andalucian thing, though the Basques, gallegos and other northerners, all with their own tapas tradition, might disagree. In some parts of Spain, tapas still comes for free with drinks – a dish of olives, a bite of omelette, some fried peppers. But in Barcelona you can expect to pay for every mouthful … unless you count the restaurants which kick off proceedings with an *amuse-gueule* shot glass of soup or designer canapé – free to anyone just about to pay €100 for dinner. The classic old-town tapas bars tend to concentrate on specialities from the Spanish regions, like octopus, peppers and seafood from Galicia; cider, cured meats and cheese from Asturias; or the ubiquitous Basque-style *pintxos*, which are bite-sized concoctions on a slice of bread, held together with a cocktail stick (you're charged by the number of sticks on your plate when you've finished). But contemporary tapas bars in Barcelona think nothing of mixing and matching cuisines, so you could just as easily be munching on a cold soba-noodle salad or a pint-sized lamb kebab.

TOP 5 TRADITIONAL TAPAS

Bar Pinotxo See p.179
Bodega La Plata See opposite
Cal Pep See p.185
Cova Fumada See p.188
Tapería Lolita See p.190

TOP 5 CONTEMPORARY TAPAS

Dos Palillos See p.182
Santa Maria See p.185
Tapas24 See p.191
Sureny See p.193
Tickets See p.190

15

at night. Expect succulent meat grills, fresh fish, rice dishes, and a taste of local favourites like *bacallà* (salt cod), wild mushrooms or grilled veg. Prices are pretty reasonable (mains €11–18) and it's always busy, so dinner reservations are essential. A no-choice *menú del día* is a bargain for the quality (and it's even cheaper eaten at the bar). Mon–Fri 1.30–4pm & 8.45–11.30pm; closed 2 weeks in Aug.
Can Culleretes c/d'en Quintana 5 ☎ 933 173 022, ⊛ culleretes.com; ⊕ Liceu; map p.46. Supposedly Barcelona's oldest restaurant (founded in 1786), serving straight-up Catalan food (*botifarra* sausage and beans, salt cod, spinach and pine nuts, wild boar stew) in cosy, traditional surroundings. Local families come in droves, especially for celebrations or for Sunday lunch, and there are good-value set meals available at both lunch and dinner (around €30, otherwise mains €7–15). Tues–Sat 1.30–4pm & 9–11pm, Sun 1.30–4pm; closed 4 weeks in July/Aug.
Los Caracoles c/dels Escudellers 14 ☎ 933 023 185, ⊛ loscaracoles.es; ⊕ Drassanes; map p.46. A cavernous Barcelona landmark with spit-roast chickens turning on grills outside, dining rooms on various floors adorned with chandeliers and oil paintings, and an open kitchen straight out of Mervyn Peake's *Gormenghast*. The restaurant name means "snails", a house speciality, and the grilled chicken's as good as it looks. However, prices are beginning to look exploitative (€18 for chicken and chips), service can be chaotic, to say the least, and the best that can be said about the whole affair sometimes is that it's been an experience. Daily 1pm–midnight.
Koy Shunka c/d'en Copons 7 ☎ 934 127 939, ⊛ koy shunka.com; ⊕ Jaume I; map p.46. The city's hottest

Japanese chef, Hideki Matsuhisa, has branched out from his *Shunka* original (see p.182) with this sister restaurant nearby that's rather more hip, where peerless sushi and dishes like grilled Wagyu beef and roast black cod await. With pricey rice rolls, mains around €20 and a €75 tasting menu, it's a more rarefied experience all round, but local gourmets thoroughly approve and you'll definitely need to book. Tues–Sun 1–3pm & 8.30–11pm.
Limbo c/de la Mercè 13 ☎ 933 107 699; ⊕ Liceu; map p.46. Designer restaurant that manages to create an intimate feel within a warehouse-style interior of exposed brick and wooden beams. The market-led Mediterrasian menu carries items such as fresh pasta made daily or swordfish tartare with red onion marmalade and wasabi. Most dishes cost between €7 and €18, while the weekday lunch is a really good deal. Mon 8.30pm–midnight, Tues–Sat 1.30–4pm & 8.30pm–midnight (Fri & Sat until 1am).
Matsuri Pl. del Regomir 1 ☎ 932 681 535, ⊛ matsuri -restaurante.com; ⊕ Jaume I; map p.46. A handsome, relaxed place for creative Asian cuisine, with a large menu concentrating on Thai-style noodles, salads and curries, as well as sushi, sashimi and tempura. A daily specials list has some more unusual choices, while a separate sushi bar two doors down provides counter seating for a close-up view of knife-wielding sushi chefs. Around €30 a head. Daily 8pm–midnight.
El Salón c/de L'Hostal d'en Sol 6–8 ☎ 933 152 159, ⊛ www.elsalon.es; ⊕ Jaume I; map p.46. It's easy to fall for the cosy charms of *El Salón*, with its candlelit tables in a Gothic dining room and summer terrace in the nearby

square. The menu changes every few months, with inventive salads giving way to things like a confit of cod with spinach, pine nuts and raisins, or lamb with mustard-and-honey sauce. Most mains are in the range €10–16. Mon–Sat 8.30pm–midnight; closed 2 weeks in Aug.

★ **Shunka** c/dels Sagristans 5 ☎934 124 991; ⓜJaume I; map p.46. Locals figure this to be the best Japanese restaurant in the city – advance reservations are essential, though you might strike lucky if you're prepared to eat early or late. The open kitchen and the bustling staff are half the show, while the food – sushi to udon noodles,

Japanese fried chicken to grilled prawns – is really good. You can eat for around €40, though it's easy to spend more. Tues–Fri 1.30–3.30pm & 8.30–11.30pm, Sat & Sun 2–4pm & 8.30–11.30pm; closed 2 weeks in Aug.

Venus Delicatessen c/d'Avinyó 25 ☎933 011 585; ⓜLiceu/Jaume I; map p.46. Not a deli, despite the name, but a handy place serving Mediterranean bistro cuisine throughout the day and night. It's also good for vegetarians, with dishes like lasagne, couscous, moussaka and salads mostly meat-free and costing around €7–10. Daily noon–midnight.

EL RAVAL

CAFÉS

Café de les Delícies Rambla de Raval 47 ☎934 415 714; ⓜLiceu; map pp.60–61. One of the first off the blocks in this revamped part of the neighbourhood, and still perhaps the best, plonking thrift-shop chairs and tables beneath exposed pipes and girders and coming up with something cute, cosy, mellow and arty. There's breakfast, sandwiches and tapas to share. Mon–Wed 8.30am–11pm, Thurs–Sun 8.30am–2am.

★ **Federal** c/del Parlament 39 ☎931 873 607, ⓦfederalcafe.es; ⓜSant Antoni; map pp.60–61. Sunday brunch is the hottest ticket in town at this effortlessly cool café, squished into a corner townhouse with a great little roof garden on top. Australian owners have imported their own funky vibe, so whether you're looking for a flat white and French toast, a bacon butty and a glass of New Zealand Sauv Blanc or a dandelion soy latte, you can guarantee that there's nowhere else quite like this in Barcelona. Tues–Thurs 8am–10pm, Fri & Sat 8am–1am, Sun 9am–5.30pm.

Granja M. Viader c/d'en Xuclà 4–6 ☎933 183 486, ⓦgranjaviader.cat; ⓜLiceu; map pp.60–61. The oldest traditional *granja* (milk bar) in town is tucked away down a narrow alley just off c/del Carme, with a pavement plaque outside for services to the city. The original owner, Sr. Viader, was the proud inventor of "Cacaolat" (a popular chocolate drink), but for a taste of the old days you could also try *mel i mató* (curd cheese and honey) or *llet Mallorquina* (fresh milk with cinnamon and lemon rind). Mon 5–8.30pm, Tues–Sat 9am–1.30pm & 5–8.30pm; closed 2 weeks in Aug.

★ **El Jardí** c/de l'Hospital 56 ☎933 291 550, ⓦeljardi barcelona.es; ⓜLiceu; map pp.60–61. The "garden bar", hidden in the elegant courtyard of the Gothic Hospital de la Santa Creu is a real away-from-the-bustle find. There's a year-round covered deck offering drinks, snacks, salads and sandwiches during the day, plus a decent lunch menu and a changing list of tapas. Mon–Sat 8am–11pm.

Kasparo Pl. de Vicenç Martorell 4 ☎933 022 072; ⓜCatalunya; map pp.60–61. Sited in the arcaded corner of a quiet square, this tiny café and *terrassa* is popular with parents who come to let their kids play in the adjacent playground. There's muesli, Greek yoghurt and toast and jam for early birds, while later in the day sandwiches, tapas and assorted *platos del día* are on offer – hummus and bread, vegetable quiche, couscous or pasta, for example. Daily 9am–10pm, until midnight in summer; closed Jan.

Mendizábal c/de la Junta de Comerç 2, no phone; ⓜLiceu; map pp.60–61. Don't look for a café because there isn't one. Instead, this cheery stand-up counter across from the Hospital de la Santa Creu dispenses juices, shakes, beer and sandwiches to passing punters. The lucky ones grab a table over the road in the shady little square. Daily 10am–midnight, June–Sept until 1am.

TAPAS BARS

★ **Dos Palillos** c/d'Elisabets 9 ☎933 040 513, ⓦdospalillos.com; ⓜCatalunya; map pp.60–61. Flag-waver for Asian fusion tapas is this hipster hangout, which offers à la carte dim sum in the front galley bar (steamed

---

THE CUP THAT CHEERS

Coffee in Barcelona is invariably espresso – a *café sol* (*café solo*) or simply *un café*. For decaff (*descafeinat*, *descafeinado*), make sure you ask for it *de màquina* ("from the machine") to avoid an instant sachet. A slightly weaker large black coffee is a *café americano*. A *tallat* (*cortado*) is like a *macchiato*, ie a small strong black coffee with a dash of steamed milk; a larger cup with more hot milk is a *café amb llet* (*café con leche*). Chuck brandy, cognac or whisky into a black coffee and it's a *cigaló* (*carajillo*).

Tea comes without milk unless you ask for it, and is often just a teabag in a cup of hot water. If you do ask for milk, chances are it'll be hot and UHT. Better to try an infusion, like mint (*menta*), camomile (*camomila*) and lime (*tila*).

TOP 5 VEGGIE-FRIENDLY RESTAURANTS

La Báscula See p.185
Sesamo See below
Biocenter See below
Venus Delicatessen See opposite
La Verònica See p.184

dumplings to grilled oysters and stir-fried prawns, mostly €5–7) and a back-room, counter-style Asian bar where tasting menus (€50 and €65) wade their way through the highlights. The front bar especially is a playful take on traditional tapas bars (cushions on upturned beer-crates, dusty liqueur bottles and steamer baskets); there are no reservations taken for this, though you do have to book for the Asian bar. Tues & Wed 7.30–11.30pm, Thurs–Sat 1.30–3.30pm & 7.30–11.30pm; closed 2 weeks in Jan & 3 weeks in Aug.

★ **Mam i Teca** c/de la Lluna 4 ☎934 413 335; ⓂSant Antoni; map pp.60–61. An intimate (code for very small) place for superior tapas and fine wines, run by local Slow Food champion Alfons Bach. All the meat is organic, the regional cheeses are well chosen, and market-fresh ingredients go to make up things like daily pasta dishes, a platter of grilled vegetables or a simple serving of lamb cutlets (most dishes €6–12, though some up to €20). Finish with chocolate truffles or home-made ice cream. There are only three or four tables, or you can perch at the bar. Mon, Wed–Fri & Sun 1–4pm & 8.30pm–midnight, Sat 8.30pm–midnight; closed 2 weeks in Aug.

Sesamo c/de Sant Antoni Abat 52 ☎934 416 411; ⓂSant Antoni; map pp.60–61. This classy tapas place (with bar at the front and restaurant tables at the back) offers up a heavily vegetarian-orientated chalkboard menu of innovative dishes. Small and not-so-small dishes roll out of the open kitchen – think Catalan sushi of stuffed courgette rolls, slow-roast tomato tart, coconut curry or a daily risotto and pasta dish, all in the range €7–15. The Catalan wines and cheeses are a high point too. Tues–Sun 7.30pm–2.30am; closed 3 weeks in Aug.

RESTAURANTS

★ **Ànima** c/dels Angels 6 ☎933 424 912; ⓂLiceu; map pp.60–61. Sleek, arty joint attracting a young crowd who come for the seasonally influenced fusion cooking – courgette flowers and mussels tempura is a typical starter dish, or there might be braised oregano pork in autumn – with mains from €10–16. The weekday lunch is the best deal and, if you're lucky, you'll get a table outside. Mon–Sat 1–4pm & 9pm–midnight; Aug open lunch only.

Bar Ra Pl. de la Garduña 3 ☎615 959 872, ⓦratown .com; ⓂLiceu; map pp.60–61. A hip little corner behind the Boqueria market, with a groove-ridden music policy, a

funky feel and a sunny *terrassa*. "It's not a restaurant", they proclaim, but who are they kidding? Breakfast runs from 10am, there's a *menú del dia* served every day (weekends as well) from 1pm, with dinner from 9pm. The menu is eclectic to say the least – veggie lasagne to tuna with wasabi and avocado – but with the market on the doorstep it's all good stuff. Around €25. Daily 9am–1am, closed Sun Nov–March.

★ **Biblioteca** c/de la Junta del Comerç 28 ☎934 126 221, ⓦbibliotecarestaurant.com; ⓂLiceu; map pp.60–61. One of the finest places to sample what Barcelona tends to call "creative cuisine". It's a stylish operation, with an open kitchen turning out fish dishes that might be cooked Japanese- or Basque-style, robust lamb given the local treatment (with parsnip and turnip), or the signature dish of venison pie served with a zippy veg purée of the day (mains €13–19). Clued-up English-speaking staff make it a hassle-free dining experience. Mon–Sat 8pm–midnight; closed 2 weeks in Aug.

Biocenter c/de Pintor Fortuny 25 ☎933 014 583, ⓦrestaurantebiocenter.es; ⓂLiceu; map pp.60–61. One of the longest-running veggie places in town, with a restaurant-bar across the road from the original health-food store. The fixed-price lunch menu (€10, weekends €12.50) starts with soup and a trawl through the salad bar for a first course, followed by a daily changing choice of mains. For dinner, they dim the lights, add candles and sounds and turn out a few more exotic dishes, from red veg curry to ginger tofu (mains around €12). Daily 1–5pm & 8–11.15pm.

Elisabets c/d'Elisabets 2 ☎933 175 826; ⓂCatalunya; map pp.60–61. Catalan home cooking served at cramped tables in a jovial brick-walled dining room. Locals breakfast on a sandwich and a glass of wine, the hearty lunchtime *menú del dia* is hard to beat for price or you can just have tapas, sandwiches and drinks at the bar. Meals Mon–Sat 1–4pm, bar open Mon–Sat 8am–11pm; closed Aug.

★ **Mesón David** c/de les Carretes 63 ☎934 415 934, ⓦmesondavid.com; ⓂParal.lel; map pp.60–61. This down-to-earth Galician bar-restaurant is a firm favourite with neighbourhood families who bring their kids before they can even walk. The weekday *menú* is a steal – maybe lentil broth followed by grilled trout and homemade *flan* while traditional Galician dishes like octopus or the *combinado Gallego* ("ham, salami, ear") go down well with the regulars. Lunch is around €12, otherwise most dishes €7–15, and there's a

TOP 5 CHEAP EATS

Can Maño See p.188
Casa Mari y Rufo See p.186
Elisabets See above
Fast Vínic See p.191
Romesco See p.184

15

CATALAN FOOD AND DISHES

Traditional Catalan food places heavy emphasis on meat, olive oil, garlic, fruit and salad. The cuisine is typified by a willingness to mix flavours, so savoury dishes cooked with nuts or fruit are common, as are salads using both cooked and raw ingredients.

Meat is usually grilled and served with a few fried potatoes or salad, though Catalan sausage served with a pool of haricot beans is a classic menu item. Stewed veal and other casseroles are common, while poultry is sometimes mixed with seafood (chicken and prawns) or fruit (chicken or duck with prunes or pears) for tastes very definitely out of the Spanish mainstream. In season, **game** is also available, especially partridge, hare, rabbit and boar.

As for **fish and seafood**, you'll be offered hake, tuna, squid or cuttlefish, while the local anchovies are superb. Cod is often salted and turns up in *esquiexada*, a summer salad of salt cod, tomatoes, onions and olives. Fish stews are a local speciality, though the mainstays of seafood restaurants are the rice- and noodle-based dishes. **Paella** comes originally from Valencia, but as that region was historically part of Catalunya, the dish has been enthusiastically adopted as Catalunya's own. More certainly Catalan is **fideuà**, thin noodles served with seafood – you stir in the fiery *all i olli* (garlic mayonnaise) provided. **Arròs negre** (black rice, cooked with squid ink) is another local delicacy.

Vegetables rarely amount to more than a few French fries or boiled potatoes, though there are some authentic Catalan vegetable dishes, like spinach tossed with raisins and pine nuts, or *samfaina*, a ratatouille-like stew. Spring is the season for **calçots**, huge spring onions, which are roasted whole and eaten with a spicy *romesco* dipping sauce. Autumn sees the arrival of **wild mushrooms**, mixed with rice, omelettes, salads or scrambled eggs. In winter, a dish of **stewed beans or lentils** is also a popular starter, almost always flavoured with bits of sausage, meat and fat.

For **dessert**, apart from fresh fruit, there's always crème caramel (*flan* in Catalan) – fantastic when home-made – though *crema Catalana* is the local choice, more like a crème brûlée, with a caramelized sugar coating. Or you might be offered *músic*, nuts and dried fruit served with a glass of sweet *moscatel* wine.

---

good-natured bang on the clog-gong for anyone who leaves a tip. Tues–Sun 1–4pm & 8.30pm–1am.

Moti Mahal c/de Sant Pau 103 ☎ 933 293 252, ⓦ moti mahalbcn.com; ⓜ Paral.lel; map pp.60–61. Indian restaurants have sprouted all over the Raval in recent years, and most don't really make the grade, as the spice level is toned down for the local market. But the *Moti Mahal* is considered one of the more authentic places with a typical menu of biryanis, tandoori dishes and curries in various styles and strengths, all around €8 to €12. It's not much to look at, but what proper curry house is? In any case, if it's good enough for Harrison Ford, whose picture is proudly displayed, it's good enough for us. Daily noon–3.30pm & 8pm–midnight, closed Tues lunch.

Pollo Rico c/de Sant Pau 31 ☎ 934 413 184, ⓦ pollo ricosl.com; ⓜ Liceu; map pp.60–61. Barcelona's original "greasy spoon" has been here forever and, while it's not to everyone's taste, if you're in the mood for spit-roast chicken and a glass of rot-gut wine, served in double-quick time, this is the place. The upstairs dining room is a tad more sophisticated (only a tad) – either way, you'll be hard

pushed to spend €15 from a long menu of Spanish and Catalan staples. Daily 10am–midnight; closed Wed.

★ **Romesco** c/de l'Arc de Sant Agustí s/n ☎ 934 189 381; ⓜ Liceu; map pp.60–61. Old Barcelona hands talk lovingly of the *Romesco* – and as long as you accept its limitations (dining under strip-lights, gruff waiters) you can hardly go wrong, as the most expensive thing on the menu is a €9 grilled sirloin and most dishes go for €6 or less. It's basic but good, with big salads, country broths and grilled veg to start, followed by tuna steak, lamb chops or grilled prawns from the market, scattered with parsley and chopped garlic. If you spend more than €15 each you've probably eaten someone else's dinner as well. Mon–Sat 1–11.30pm; closed Aug.

La Verònica Ramba de Raval 2–4 ☎ 933 293 303; ⓜ Liceu/Sant Antoni; map pp.60–61. Funky, retro pizzeria *La Verònica* fits right into the new-look Rambla de Raval. There are loads of crispy pizzas (mostly vegetarian, €10–15) and inventive salads (€8–10), enjoyed by a resolutely young and up-for-a-night-out crowd. Daily noon–1am; closed 2 weeks in Aug.

SANT PERE AND LA RIBERA

CAFÉS

★ **Bar del Convent** Centre Cívic Convent de Sant Agustí, Pl. de l'Acadèmia, C/del Comerç 36, Sant Pere

☎ 932 103 732; ⓜ Jaume I; map p.70. The cloister café-bar in the converted old convent, now cultural centre, is good for drinks at any time and a bargain for lunch and light meals. At night it's more of a bar, with a range of live shows, DJs and concerts. Mon–Thurs 9am–10pm, Fri & Sat 11am–midnight.

★ **La Báscula** c/dels Flassaders 30, La Ribera ☎ 933 199 866; ⓜ Jaume I; map p.70. An old chocolate factory in the backstreets has been given a hippy-chic makeover by a local cooperative and serves up veggie pastas, turnovers, couscous, quiches and salads (dishes around €8.50). Drinks are great too – dozens of teas, coffees, organic wines, juices and shakes – and it's a cool break-from-the-shops spot. Wed–Sat 1pm–midnight, Sun 1–8pm.

Café del Born Pl. Comercial 10, La Ribera ☎ 932 683 272; ⓜ Jaume I; map p.70. No gimmicks, no fusion food and dodgy local art kept to a bare minimum – the recipe for success at this ever-popular neighbourhood café-bar. There's a simple Mediterranean menu on offer, while Sunday brunch is the big weekend draw. Daily 9am–1am (Fri & Sat until 3am).

Pim Pam Burger c/Sabateret 4, La Ribera ☎ 933 152 093, ⓦ pimpamplats.com; ⓜ Jaume I; map p.70. The go-to-choice for a quick bite, *Pim Pam Burger* is the place for burgers, fries, franks and sandwiches (€2.50–6). There are a few stools and tables if you'd rather not eat on the hoof, while *Pim Pam Plats*, just around the corner on c/del Rec is their outlet for budget-beating take-home meals. Daily 1pm–midnight.

TAPAS BARS

El Bitxo c/de Verdaguer i Callis 9, Sant Pere ☎ 932 681 708; ⓜ Urquinaona; map p.70. This is a great find for drinks and tapas, very close to the Palau de la Música Catalana. It's tiny (four small wooden tables and a line of bar stools) but there's a friendly welcome, and the food is good, especially the cured and smoked meats and sausages and regional cheeses (dishes up to €10). Mon 7.30pm–1am, Tues–Thurs 1am–1am, Fri & Sat 1pm–2am, Sun 4.30–11.30pm.

★ **Cal Pep** Pl. de les Olles 8, La Ribera ☎ 933 107 961, ⓦ calpep.com; ⓜ Barceloneta; map p.70. There's no equal in town for fresh-off-the-boat and out-of-the-market tapas. You may have to queue (there are no reservations), and prices are high for what's effectively a bar meal (up to €50 a head) but it's definitely worth it for the likes of impeccably fried shrimp, grilled sea bass, Catalan sausage and beans, and baby squid and chickpeas – the whole show overseen by Pep himself bustling up and down the counter. Mon 7.30–11.30pm, Tues–Fri 1–3.45pm & 7.30–11.30pm, Sat 1.15–3.45pm; closed Easter week & Aug.

Euskal Etxea Pl. de Montcada 1–3, La Ribera ☎ 933 102 185, ⓦ euskaletxea.cat; ⓜ Jaume I; map p.70. The bar at the front of the local Basque community centre is great for *pintxos* – pint-sized tapas, held together by a stick. Just point to what you want (and keep the sticks so that the bill can be

tallied at the end – most things are a couple of euros each). There's a pricier restaurant out back with more good Basque specialities. Bar open daily 10am–12.30am (Fri & Sat until 1am), restaurant 1.30–4pm & 8.30pm–midnight.

★ **Mosquito** c/dels Carders 46, Sant Pere ☎ 932 687 569, ⓦ mosquitotapas.com; ⓜ Jaume I; map p.70. Happy indeed are the locals for whom this is their neighbourhood drink-and-chow joint. The funky Asian tapas bar, festooned with hanging paper lanterns, pours artisan beers and offers an authentic, made-to-order dim sum menu (dishes €3–5), from shrimp dumplings to tofu rolls. Mon 7.30pm–12.30am, Tues–Sun 1pm–12.30am (Fri & Sat until 2.30am).

Santa Maria c/Comerç 17, Sant Pere ☎ 933 151 227; ⓜ Jaume I; map p.70. Paco Guzmán's new-wave tapas bar has a glass-fronted kitchen turning out taste sensations like Catalan sushi, octopus confit, yucca chips and quail with salsa. Around €40 should get you a good range of dishes, finishing on a high note with the famous "Dracula" dessert – a shot glass of strawberry and vanilla cream flavours with pop-rocks that sets off crackles in your mouth. Tues–Fri 8pm–midnight, Sat 1.30–4pm & 8pm–midnight; closed 2 weeks in Aug.

El Xampanyet c/de Montcada 22, La Ribera ☎ 933 197 003; ⓜ Jaume I; map p.70. Traditional blue-tiled bar doing a roaring trade in sparkling cava, cider and tapas (anchovies are the speciality, but there's also marinated tuna, spicy mussels, sun-dried tomatoes, sliced meats and cheese). As is often the way, the drinks are cheap and the tapas turn out to be rather pricey, but there's usually a good buzz about the place. Tues–Sat noon–4pm & 6.30–11pm, Sun noon–4pm; closed Aug.

RESTAURANTS

★ **El Atril** c/dels Carders 23, Sant Pere ☎ 933 101 220, ⓦ atrilbarcelona.com; ⓜ Jaume I; map p.70. Chill out in this fine Aussie-owned bistro-bar, which has a popular *terrassa* in a revamped neighbourhood square. Lunch is always a steal, with tapas served at other times, and dinner from 7pm, from a menu that ranges from *moules frites* to Thai red curry (mains €10–15). The long (until 6pm), lazy Sunday brunch is good, too, while there's a great selection of wines available at the owner's Vino wine store opposite (c/dels Carders 22, opens 5pm, Thurs–Sun 4pm), which you can take as BYO into the restaurant for a small corkage charge. Mon 6pm–midnight, Tues–Sun noon–midnight.

TOP 5 PLACES FOR BRUNCH

Agua See p.189
El Atril See above
Café del Born See above
Federal See p.182
La Soleá See p.190

15

15

★ **Casa Delfín** Pg. del Born 36, La Ribera ☎ 933 195 088; ⓜ Jaume I; map p.70. There are many reasons to like this bubbly, updated taverna, not least its sunny *terrassa* outside the old market. It's a slick operation, inside and out, with a long menu that takes a loving look at traditional Catalan dishes, from sausage and beans to chickpeas and squid, crispy artichokes to roast mountain lamb. It's served tapas-style, so you don't have to come for a full meal (dishes €5–20), but if you've got room don't miss English owner Kate's signature pud, Eton Mess. Daily noon–1am.

Casa Mari y Rufo c/de les Freixures 11, Sant Pere ☎ 933 197 302; ⓜ Jaume I; map p.70. A great place for no-frills market cooking, with a busy family at a smoky range turning out quick-fried sardines, grilled Catalan sausage, stewed oxtail, steak and chips and the like – or ask what's good from the Mercat Santa Caterina fish stalls that day. Expect whitewashed walls, bare light bulbs and chipped tiles, but with lunch for an unbeatable €12 and dinner for around €30, the locals know a good deal when they see one. Mon–Wed 1–4pm, Thurs–Sat 1–4pm & 8–11pm.

Comerç 24 c/del Comerc 24, Sant Pere ☎ 933 192 102, ⓦ carlesabellan.com; ⓜ Jaume I/Arc de Triomf; map p.70. Chef Carles Abellan calls his cutting-edge cuisine "glocal" (ie, global + local) and in the oh-so-cool interior you're presented with tapas-style dishes, mixing flavours and textures (such as foie gras and truffle hamburger, shot glasses of frothy soup and tuna sashimi on pizza) with seeming abandon but to calculated effect. Prices are high (around €80 a head), although you can have a cheaper, less formal meal at Abellan's Eixample tapas bar, *Tapas24* (see p.191), where the food has something of the same panache. Tues–Sat 1.30–3.30pm & 8.30–11pm; closed 2 weeks in Aug.

Cuines Santa Caterina Mercat Santa Caterina, Av. de Francesc Cambó 16, Sant Pere ☎ 932 689 918, ⓦ www .cuinessantacaterina.com; ⓜ Jaume I; map p.70. The handsome neighbourhood market has a ravishing open-plan restaurant, with tables set under soaring wooden rafters. Food in the restaurant touches all bases – pasta to sushi, Catalan rice to Thai curry – with most things costing €9–12, or you can just drink and munch superior tapas at the horseshoe bar. Bar daily 9am–11.30pm (Thurs–Sat until 12.30am); restaurant 1–4pm & 8–11.30pm (Thurs–Sat until 12.30am).

Ikibana Pg. de Picasso 32, La Ribera ☎ 932 956 732, ⓦ ikibana.es; ⓜ Barceloneta; map p.70. Riding the fusion wave is this glam Japanese-Brazilian restaurant with a lounge-bar setting. There's a great weekday lunch deal, in which a mix of zingy rice-and-seaweed-roll combos and exotic tempuras are presented as a series of dainty little dishes, while the full menu also runs to *ceviche* and Kobe beef burgers (dishes €6–13, tasting menu €33). Daily 1.30am–4pm & 8.30pm–midnight, closed Sun lunch.

Kiosko Burger Av. del Marquès de l'Argentera 1, La Ribera ☎ 933 107 413, ⓦ kioskoburger.com; ⓜ Barceloneta; map p.70. Aussie chef Brad Ainsworth has ditched his Asian noodle bar *Wushu*, formerly on this site, in favour of running Barcelona's best gourmet burger outlet. Great-tasting artisan bread rolls and home-made sauces set the tone, while a dozen superb burgers (€5–9) come any way you like, from Catalan (with a roast garlic alioli) to Japanese (teriyaki sauce). Daily 1pm–1am.

Mescladís Pl. de Sant Pere 5, Sant Pere ☎ 932 955 012, ⓦ mescladis.org; ⓜ Arc de Triomf; map p.70. "Tastes of the world" emerge from the kitchen at the Mescladís multi-cultural community project and cookery school, where the menus – using Fair Trade and organic ingredients – feature dishes from couscous to Cameroonian chicken. It's a gregarious, all-sit-down-together place, and full meals cost well under €20. Tues 1–4pm, Wed–Fri 1–4pm & 8.30pm–midnight, Sat 1pm–12.30am.

Salero c/del Rec 60, La Ribera ☎ 933 198 022, ⓦ restaurantesalero.com; ⓜ Barceloneta; map p.70. A crisp, modern space fashioned from a former salt-cod warehouse – if white is your colour, you'll enjoy the experience. The food's Mediterranean-Asian, with things like veggie tempura or a *mee goreng* (fried noodle) of the day, and most dishes costing €12–18. Mon–Sat 1.30–4pm & 8.30pm–midnight, Sun 8.30pm–midnight; closed 2 weeks in Aug.

BARCELONA'S BEST BURGERS

Take one financial crisis, add locals looking for value-for-money dining and the current rage for burger bars becomes more understandable. Of course, being Barcelona, we're talking stylish, gourmet burger places, like the crowd-pleasing **Kiosko Burger** (see above), where artisan-made bread, organic beef, hand-cut fries and perky, home-made sauces keep the punters happy. Others swear by the longstanding **Pim Pam Burger** (see p.185), a hole-in-the-wall place in La Ribera that's well placed for the late-night munchies. A couple of great bars also get honourable burger bravos, namely **Betty Ford's** (see p.198) and **Cerveseria Jazz** (see p.201), while the retro tortilla restaurant, **Flash, Flash** (see p.193), dishes up a mean home-made burger on a plate.

★ **Senyor Parellada** c/de l'Argenteria 37, La Ribera ☎ 933 105 094, ⓦ senyorparellada.com; ⓜ Jaume I; map p.70. An utterly gorgeous renovation of an eighteenth-century building is the mellow backdrop for genuine home-style Catalan cuisine – cuttlefish and cod, stuffed cabbage rolls, duck with figs, a *papillote* of beans with herbs – served from a long menu that doesn't bother dividing starters from mains. Most dishes cost between €8 and €15, while more than a dozen puds await those who struggle through. Daily 1–3.45pm & 8.30–11.30pm.

Set Portes Pg. d'Isabel II 14, La Ribera ☎ 933 192 950, ⓦ 7portes.com; ⓜ Barceloneta; map p.70. A wood-panelled classic with the names of its famous clientele much to the fore – they've all eaten here, from Errol Flynn to Yoko Ono. The decor in the "Seven Doors" has barely changed in almost two hundred years and, while very elegant, it's not exclusive – you should book ahead, though, as the queues can be horrendous. The renowned rice dishes are fairly reasonably priced (€13–20), but for a full meal you're looking at around €50 a head. Daily 1pm–1am.

PORT VELL AND BARCELONETA

CAFÉS

Vioko Pg. de Joan de Borbó 74, Barceloneta ☎ 932 210 652, ⓦ vioko.es; ⓜ Barceloneta; map p.81. Quite simply, the slinkiest, swishiest ice cream and chocolate shop in town – *Vioko's* minimalist white curves serve as the backdrop for artisan *gelati*, gourmet chocs and coffee, hot choc and *xurros*, ready to take away on a stroll along the marina. Daily noon–10pm (June–Aug until midnight).

TAPAS BARS

★ **Cova Fumada** c/del Baluard 56, Barceloneta ☎ 932 214 061; ⓜ Barceloneta; map p.81. Behind brown wooden doors on Barceloneta's market square (there's no sign) is this rough-and-ready tavern with battered marble tables and antique barrels. It might not look like much but the food's great, with ingredients straight from the market (tapas €2–10) – from griddled prawns to fried artichokes. Mon–Wed & Sat 9am–3pm, Thurs & Fri 9am–3pm & 6–8pm; closed Aug.

★ **Jai-Ca** c/de Ginebra 13, Barceloneta ☎ 932 683 265; ⓜ Barceloneta; map p.81. Always a winning choice for seafood tapas, with bundles of razor clams, plump anchovies, stuffed mussels and other platters piled high on the bar. Meanwhile, the fryers in the kitchen work overtime, turning out crisp baby squid, fried shrimp and little green peppers scattered with rock-salt. Take your haul to a tile-topped cane table, or outside onto the tiny street-corner patio. Dishes up to €10. Daily 10am–11pm.

Vaso de Oro c/de Balboa 6, Barceloneta ☎ 933 193 098; ⓜ Barceloneta; map p.81. If you can get in this corridor of a bar you're doing well (Sunday lunch is particularly busy), and there's no menu, but standard bites include *patatas bravas*, fried sausage and tuna salad, with fancier shellfish dishes and meat grills available too (most tapas €4–15). Unusually, they also brew their own beer, which comes in tall schooners, either light or dark. Daily 9am–midnight.

RESTAURANTS

Antiga Casa Solé c/de Sant Carles 4, Barceloneta ☎ 932 215 012, ⓦ cansole.cat; ⓜ Barceloneta; map p.81. Founded in 1903, it was here – it's claimed – that the classic *sarsuela* (Catalan fish stew) was invented. Since then, the quiet, formal *Casa Solé* has been dishing up impeccably cooked, straight-from-the-market fish and seafood, either in stews or casseroles or simply grilled, sautéed or mixed with rice. Baked squid and grilled cod are both house specialities, with mains in the €20–40 range. Tues–Sat 1.30–4pm & 8.30–11pm, Sun 1.30–4pm; closed 2 weeks in Aug.

★ **Can Majo** c/de l'Almirall Aixada 23, Barceloneta ☎ 932 215 455, ⓦ canmajo.es; ⓜ Barceloneta; map p.81. This ticks all the boxes for a quality seaside meal, thanks not least the bonus of a lovely summer *terrassa* by the beach promenade, where you can tuck into wonderful rice dishes, *fideuà* (noodles with seafood), *suquet* (fish stew) or grilled fish. The menu changes daily according to what's off the boat; expect to spend €40–50 a head (and make a reservation if you want an outside table at the weekend). Tues–Sat 1–3.30pm & 8–11.30pm, Sun 1–3.30pm.

IT TAKES TWO

You want a seafood paella or an *arròs negre* (black rice, with squid ink), or maybe a garlicky *fideuà* (noodles with seafood) – of course you do. Problem is, you're on your own and virtually every restaurant that offers these classic Barcelona dishes does so for a minimum of two people (often you don't find out until you examine the menu small print). Solution? Ask the waiter upfront, as sometimes the kitchen will oblige single diners, or look for the dishes on a *menú del dia* (especially on Thursdays, traditionally rice day), when there should be no minimum. Probably best not to grab a stranger off the street to share a paella, however desperate you are.

★ **Can Maño** c/del Baluard 12, Barceloneta ☎ 933 193 082; ⓜ Barceloneta; map p.81. There's rarely a tourist in sight in this old-fashioned diner, packed with noisy locals around formica tables. Basically, your choice is fried or grilled fish, such as sardines, mullet or calamari, supplemented by a few daily seafood specials and basic meat dishes. Expect rough house wine and absolutely no frills, but it's an authentic experience, which is likely to cost you less than €15 a head. Mon–Fri 8–11am, 12.15–4pm & 8–11pm, Sat 8–11am & 12.15–4pm; closed Aug.

Can Ramonet c/de la Maquinista 17, Barceloneta ☎ 933 193 064; ⓦ elnouramonet.com; ⓜ Barceloneta; map p.81. Reputedly the oldest restaurant in the port area, and boasting a shady *terrassa* in front of the neighbourhood market. There's pricey tapas, splendid rice dishes, plus

PORT OLÍMPIC AND POBLE NOU

CAFÉS

El Tío Ché Rambla del Poble Nou 44–46, Poble Nou ☎ 933 091 872, ⓦ eltioche.es; ⓜ Poble Nou, or bus #36 from ⓜ Barceloneta; map p.85. A down-to-earth café in a down-to-earth neighbourhood, run by the same family for four generations. The specialities are orange or lemon *granissat* (crushed ice) and their famous *orxata* (tiger-nut drink), but there are also *torrons* (almond fudge), hot chocolate, coffee, croissants and sandwiches. It's a bit off the beaten track, though you can stroll up easily enough from Bogatell beach (15min) or down the *rambla* from Poble Nou metro (10min). Daily 10am–midnight; reduced hours in winter.

RESTAURANTS

★ **Agua** Pg. Marítim 30, Port Olímpic ☎ 932 251 272, ⓦ grupotragaluz.com; ⓜ Ciutadella-Vila Olímpica; map p.85. Much the nicest boardwalk restaurant on the beachfront strip, perfect for brunch, though if the weather's iffy you can opt for the sleek, split-level dining room. The menu is contemporary Mediterranean – grills, *risotti*, pasta, salads and tapas – and the prices are pretty fair for such a prime spot (most dishes €9–23), so it's usually busy. Daily 1–3.45pm & 8–11.30pm (Fri & Sat until 4.30pm & 12.30am).

Bestial c/Ramon Trias Fargas 2–4, Port Olímpic ☎ 932 240 407, ⓦ grupotragaluz.com; ⓜ Ciutadella-Vila Olímpica; map p.85. Right beside Frank Gehry's fish (under the wooden bridge) you'll find a stylish terrace-garden in front of the beach, great for an alfresco lunch. Inside the feel is sharp and minimalist, while the cooking is Mediterranean, mainly Italian, with dishes given an original twist. Rice, pasta and crisp little wood-fired pizzas are in the €9–14 range, with other dishes up to €25. At weekends there's DJ music and drinks until 2am. Daily 1–4pm & 8–11.30am (Fri & Sat until 12.30am); Nov–Feb closed Sun dinner, Mon, & Tues dinner.

whatever's fresh from the stalls that day, though with dishes running at anything from €10 to €30 the bill soon adds up. Daily noon–midnight (meals from 1pm & 8pm); closed Sun dinner, 2 weeks in Jan, & Aug.

★ **Kaiku** Pg. de Joan de Borbó 74, Barceloneta ☎ 932 219 082; ⓜ Barceloneta; map p.81. You really need to book for this lunch-only place because the secret is out – a prime location on the seafront terrace for fantastic, Basque-influenced seafood meals (dishes €8–17, cheaper lunch menu served Tues–Fri). The ingredients are first-rate, from fish landed from named boats to rice from the famous growing area of Delta de l'Ebre, and tastes are out-of-the-ordinary – think smoked vegetable rice with mushrooms and rocket, or steamed mussels with thyme. Tues–Sun 1–4pm; closed Aug.

15

El Cangrejo Loco Moll de Gregal 29–30, upper level, Port Olímpic ☎ 932 211 748, ⓦ elcangrejoloco.com; ⓜ Ciutadella-Vila Olímpica; map p.85. The terrace at the "Crazy Crab" offers ocean views, and the food is excellent. A mixed fried-fish plate or broad beans with prawns are typically Catalan starters, and the rice dishes are thoroughly recommended. A meal costs from around €40. Daily 1pm–1am.

★ **Els Pescadors** Pl. de Prim 1, Poble Nou ☎ 932 252 018, ⓦ elspescadors.com; ⓜ Poble Nou; map p.85. The best top-class fish restaurant in Barcelona? It's a tough call, but many would choose this hideaway place in a pretty square with gnarled trees in the back alleys of Rambla de Poble Nou. Lunch outside on a sunny day just can't be beaten (reservations advised). The menu offers daily changing fresh fish dishes, and plenty more involving rice, noodles or salt cod (try the latter with *samfaina*, like a Catalan ratatouille). Most dishes cost €10–30 and if you don't go mad with the wine list you'll escape for around €60 a head. Daily 1–4pm & 8–11.30pm; closed Easter week.

Xiringuito Escribà Platja Bogatell, Poble Nou ☎ 932 210 729, ⓦ escriba.es; ⓜ Ciutadella-Vila Olímpica, or bus #36 from Port Vell; map p.85. This glorified beach shack – a *xiringuito* in the parlance – is far enough off the beaten track (a 15min walk along the seafront prom from Port Olímpic) to mark you out as in the know if you make the effort. The paellas, *fideuàs* and daily fish specials are €20 a pop, and there's a ten-percent terrace surcharge, but they still fly out of the kitchen, and what the hell – the food and views are great. Desserts are sensational cakes and pastries from the Escribà family patisserie. Mon–Sat noon–5pm & 8–11pm (Fri & Sat until midnight), Sun noon–5pm; restricted hours in winter, but usually open weekend lunch.

POBLE SEC

TAPAS BARS

⭐ **Quimet i Quimet** c/del Poeta Cabanyes 25 ☎ 934 423 142; ⓜ Paral.lel; map p.98. Poble Sec's cosiest tapas bar is a foodie place of pilgrimage and at busy times everyone has to breathe in to squeeze another punter through the door. The wine bottles are stacked five shelves high (there's a chalkboard menu of wines by the glass), while little plates of classy finger food (mostly €3–10) are served reverently from the minuscule counter – things like roast onions, marinaded mushrooms, stuffed cherry tomatoes, grilled aubergine, anchovy-wrapped olives and a terrific range of regional cheeses. Tues–Sat noon–4pm & 7–11pm, Sun noon–4pm; closed Aug.

Tapería Lolita c/de Tamarit 104 ☎ 934 245 231, ⓦ lolitataperia.com; ⓜ Poble Sec; map p.98. You might have to wait in line to see what all the fuss is about at Joan Martínez's hip bar, which serves cocktails and classic tapas – or "small portions of happiness" – to tuned-in city folk and in-the-know tourists. You can eat and drink for around €25 – don't miss the signature-dish *patatas bravas* or the deep-fried *bombas* and *croquetas*, Barcelona favourites all. Tues–Fri 7pm–2am, Sat 1.30–3.30pm & 7pm–2am; closed Aug.

⭐ **Tickets/41°** Av. Paral.lel 164, no phone, online reservations only on ⓦ ticketsbar.es, ⓦ 41grados.es; ⓜ Poble Sec; map p.98. The hullaballoo shows no sign of abating at *Tickets*, the swanky tapas bar under the star-studded helm of pastry-chef supremo Albert Adrià, his *El Bulli*-famed brother Ferran Adrià and the Iglesias brothers of the renowned *Rías de Galicia* seafood restaurant. It's divided into half-a-dozen quirky seating areas that make a play on fairground and theatrical themes, and the terrifically inventive dishes (€5–20 each, expect to spend €70) mix impeccably sourced ingredients with the flights of fancy expected from the Adrià brothers. With only a hundred covers a night, and online reservations taken up to three months in advance, you can't guarantee a table, though you can also try for a seat at *41°* (or *41 Grados*, ie 41 Degrees), the adjacent and very sleek cocktail and oyster bar where more outré snacks and canapés are served. Tickets Tues–Sat 7–11pm, Sun 1–3pm; 41° Tues–Sat 6pm–2am (snacks until 11pm); closed 2 weeks in Aug.

RESTAURANTS

Bella Napoli c/de Margarit 14 ☎ 934 425 056; ⓜ Poble Sec; map p.98. Authentic Neapolitan pizzeria, right down to the cheery waiters and cheesy pop music. The pizzas – the best in the city – come straight from the depths of a beehive-shaped oven, or there's a big range of pastas, risotti and veal scaloppine, with almost everything priced between €9 and €15. Tues 8.30pm–midnight, Wed–Sun 1.30–4.30pm & 8.30pm–midnight.

La Bodegueta c/de Blai 47 ☎ 934 420 846; ⓜ Poble Sec; map p.98. A true Catalan taverna with food like mother used to make – a relaxed Sunday lunch here brings local families out in force. It's a good-natured, red-check-tablecloth-and-barrels kind of place, specializing in *torrades* (cold cuts on toasted country bread), salads and grills (most dishes €7–16) – the excellent grilled veg platter is a good place to start. Tues–Sun 1–4pm & 8.30pm–midnight; closed Aug.

⭐ **La Soleá** Pl. del Sortidor 14 ☎ 934 410 124; ⓜ Poble Sec; map p.98. This place's *terrassa*, on a down-to-earth square, is a great place for sunny days, while in the cheery if cramped interior there's a backdrop of vibrant colours and young guns behind the counter singing along lustily to *flamenco nuevo* sounds. It's a bistro menu (lunch from 1.30pm, dinner from 8.30pm, dishes €5–10) and all pretty good value – salads and dips to start, followed by proper hamburgers, stir-fries, pasta or a reassuringly old-fashioned Sunday brunch plate of *fideuà* (Catalan noodles). Tues–Sat noon–midnight, Sun noon–5pm.

⭐ **La Tomaquera** c/de Margarit 58, no phone; ⓜ Poble Sec; map p.98. Sit down in this chatter-filled tavern to a dish of olives and two quails' eggs – and any delicacy ends there as the chefs set to hacking steaks and chops from great hunks of meat. It's not for the faint-hearted, but the grilled chicken is sensational and the *entrecôtes* enormous (most mains €8–15). Locals limber up with an appetizer of pan-fried snails with chorizo and tomato. Tues–Sat 1.30–3.45pm & 8.30–10.45pm; closed Aug.

DRETA DE L'EIXAMPLE

CAFÉS

Café del Centre c/de Girona 69 ☎ 934 881 101; ⓜ Girona; map p.104. This quiet coffee stop is only four blocks from the tourist sights on the Passeig de Gràcia but it well off the beaten track as far as most visitors are concerned. It's well worth the walk for a café that's been here since 1873 and that retains its elegant *modernista* decor. Mon–Fri 8am–11pm; closed Aug.

Forn de Sant Jaume Rambla de Catalunya 50 ☎ 932 160 229; ⓜ Passeig de Gràcia; map p.104. Classic uptown *pastisseria* whose glittering windows are piled high with croissants, cakes, pastries and sweets. The small

adjacent café has outdoor *rambla* seats, or you can take away your goodies for later. Mon–Sat 9am–9pm.

TAPAS BARS

La Bodegueta Rambla de Catalunya 100 ☎ 932 154 894; ⓜ Diagonal; map p.104. This long-established basement *bodega* serves cava by the glass, a serious range of other wines and good ham, cheese, anchovies and other tapas (from €3–15) to soak it all up. In summer you can sit outside at tables on the pretty uptown *rambla*. Daily 8am–2am; closed mornings in Aug.

Ciudad Condal Rambla de Catalunya 18 ☎ 933 181

WHAT'S COOKING?

The man behind the reimagining of modern cuisine – the foams, the essences, the vapours, the taste explosions, the deconstructed, laboratory-tested dishes – is Catalan chef **Ferran Adrià**, whose world-famous, triple-Michelin-starred restaurant *El Bulli* (Welbulli.com), on the Costa Brava, set the benchmark for creative contemporary cooking. *El Bulli* closed as a restaurant in 2011 – with plans underway to turn it into a cookery foundation and "centre for creativity" – though Adrià and his brother Albert already have a high-profile presence on the Barcelona dining scene with their new-wave tapas bar, *Tickets*. Meanwhile, the Adrià effect has spawned a generation of regional chefs – many of them alumni of the *El Bulli* kitchens – who have helped put contemporary Spanish cuisine on the map. Talents like Jordi Vilà, Paco Guzmán, Carles Abellan, Ramón Freixa and Fermí Puig are cooking right now in Barcelona, so it's time to brush up on your chemistry and educate your tastebuds.

997; ⓜPasseig de Gràcia; map p.104. The best of the large uptown tapas-hall-style places is a handy city-centre pitstop that caters for all needs. Breakfast sees the bar groan under the weight of a dozen types of crispy baguette sandwich, plus croissants and pastries, while the daily changing tapas selection (€3–10) ranges far and wide, from *patatas bravas* to octopus. It can be standing room only at lunchtime (and not much of that either), so get there early. Daily 7.30am–1.30am.

★ **Tapas24** c/de la Diputació 269 ☎934 880 977, Wcarlesabellan.com; ⓜPasseig de Gràcia; map p.104. Carles Abellan, king of pared-down designer cuisine at his famed restaurant *Comerç 24*, offers a simpler tapas menu at this retro basement bar-diner. There's a reassuringly traditional feel that's echoed in the menu – *patatas bravas*, Andalucian-style fried fish, meatballs, chorizo sausage and fried eggs. But the kitchen updates the classics too, so there's also *calamares romana* (fried squid) dyed black with squid ink or a burger with foie gras. Most tapas cost €4–16. There's always a rush and a bustle at meal times, and you might well have to queue. Mon–Sat 9am–midnight.

RESTAURANTS

Casa Calvet c/de Casp 48 ☎934 124 012, Wcasacalvet .es; ⓜCatalunya/Urquinaona; map p.104. The wonderfully decorated townhouse built by a young Antoni Gaudí for a

Catalan industrialist makes for a truly glam night out. It offers a seasonally changing modern Catalan menu, with desserts that are artworks in themselves, though with mains around the €30 mark, lunch at €40 or tasting menus from €55 to €70, expect it to be a purse-emptying experience. Mon–Sat 1–3.30pm & 8.30–11pm.

El Japonés Ptge. de la Concepció 2 ☎934 872 592, Wgrupotragaluz.com; ⓜDiagonal; map p.104. Designer style – gun-metal grey interior, black-clad staff, sharp service – at moderate prices gives this minimalist Japanese restaurant the edge over its more traditional city rivals. Tick your choices from the long menu of sushi, sashimi, tempura and noodles and hand it to the waiter; average meal cost is around €25 a head. Daily 1.30–4pm & 8.30pm–midnight (Fri & Sat until1am).

Tragaluz Ptge. de la Concepció 5 ☎934 870 621, Wgrupotragaluz.com/tragaluz; ⓜDiagonal; map p.104. This place attracts beautiful people by the score, and the classy Mediterranean-with-knobs-on cooking, served under a glass roof (*tragaluz* means "skylight"), doesn't disappoint. Mains cost €16–30, though cheaper options are available in a separate dining room courtesy of the *Tragarràpid* menu (daily 1–4.30pm), where things like gourmet burgers, salads, *fajitas* and stir-fries cater for those fresh off the *modernista* trail (La Pedrera is just across the way). Daily 1.30–4pm & 8.30pm–midnight (Thurs–Sat until 1am).

ESQUERRA DE L'EIXAMPLE

CAFÉ

★ **Fast Vínic** c/de la Diputació 251 ☎934 873 241, Wfastvinic.com; ⓜPasseig de Gràcia; map p.113. *Fast Vínic* is a designer sandwich bar – but not just any sandwiches and not just any bar. The food emphasis is on top-of-the-range ingredients from sustainable sources (sandwiches mostly €5–10), while at the same time you get to sample from a range of more than twenty Catalan wines, starting at pocket-money prices. It's the more democratic outpost of the hallowed wine-and-foodie temple next door that is *Monvínic* (Wmonvinic.com). Mon–Sat noon–midnight.

TAPAS BARS

Cerveseria Catalana c/de Mallorca 236 ☎932 160 368; ⓜPasseig de Gràcia; map p.113. An uptown beer-and-tapas joint where the counters are piled high with elaborately assembled dishes, supplemented by a blackboard list of daily specials (most tapas €2–10). It gets busy after work and at meal times, and you might have to wait for a table. Daily 9am–1am.

La Taverna del Clínic c/del Rosselló 155 ☎934 104 221, Wlatavernadelclinic.com; ⓜHospital Clinic; map p.113. This sleek *taverna*, so called after the hospital over the road, is a gourmet tapas spot that concentrates on

15

15

TOP 5 MONEY NO OBJECT

Alkimia See below
Cinc Sentits See below
Comerç 24 See p.186
Gaig See below
Els Pescadors See p.189

rigorously sourced regional produce. Snacks at the solid marble bar come in at just a few euros, but the serious food, accompanied by artisan-made olive oil and a high-class wine list, is served at one of the ten tables (book in advance) and runs to more like €10–30 a dish, from artfully arranged grilled market veg with *romesco* sauce to thin slices of seared sushi-quality tuna. Mon–Sat 7.30am–11.30pm.

RESTAURANTS

Cinc Sentits c/d'Aribau 58 ☎ 933 239 490, ⊛ cincsentits .com; Ⓜ Universitat; map p.113. Jordi Artal's "Five Senses" wows diners with his contemporary Catalan cuisine – and the restaurant now has a Michelin star to boot, so you'll need to book. Six- and eight-course "tasting menus" (around €60 and €80, matching wines available) use rigorously sourced ingredients (wild fish, mountain lamb, seasonal vegetables, farmhouse cheeses) in elegant, pared-down dishes that are all about flavour. Tues–Sat 1.30–3pm & 8.30–10pm; closed 2 weeks in Aug.

★ **La Flauta** c/d'Aribau 23 ☎ 933 237 038; Ⓜ Universitat; map p.113. One of the city's best-value lunch menus sees diners queuing for tables early – get there before 2pm to avoid the rush. It's a handsome bar-restaurant of dark wood and deep colours, and while the name is a nod to the house speciality gourmet sandwiches (a *flauta* is a thin baguette), there are also meals served tapas-style, day and night (dishes €4–10), based on local market produce, wild mushrooms to locally landed fish. Mon–Sat 8am–1am; closed 3 weeks in Aug.

★ **Gaig** c/d'Aragó 214 ☎ 934 291 017, ⊛ restaurant gaig.com; Ⓜ Universitat; map p.113. The Gaig family restaurant was first founded in 1869 out in the Horta neighbourhood, but under fourth-generation family member, Carles Gaig, it has a sleek downtown home at the *Hotel Cram*. Its towering reputation (and Michelin star) rests on innovative reinterpretations of traditional Catalan dishes,

so a typical *arròs* (rice) dish might combine foie gras, endive and citrus. But when starters can cost €35, and the *menú degustació* is over €100, you're talking about a true special-occasion place. Mon 9–11pm, Tues–Sat 1–3.30pm & 9–11pm; closed Easter week & 3 weeks in Aug.

Hanoi Pl. de Dr. Letamendi 27 ☎ 934 515 686, Ⓜ Passeig de Gràcia/Universitat; map p.113. Ostensibly a Vietnamese restaurant, though many of the tasty dishes – from little baskets of dim sum to steamed bream with soy and ginger – suggest wider Southeast Asian sources. No matter, the daily weekday lunch is widely recognized as a good deal (otherwise mains €10–13) and the sleek restaurant fills quickly. Mon–Sat 12.30–4pm & 8.30pm–midnight, Sun 12.30–4pm.

★ **Me** c/de Paris 162 ☎ 934 194 933, ⊛ www .catarsiscuisine.com; Ⓜ Diagonal; map p.113. In a stylish neo-colonial setting, *Me* is all the rage for its clever fusion of cuisines from Vietnam and New Orleans by way of Barcelona – all places dear to owner Javier's heart. Expect gumbo and marinated shrimp alongside zingy papaya salad or grilled Saigon rib-eye with lemongrass. Mains are €15–24, though lunch is a simpler, cheaper affair. Tues & Sat 8.45–11.30pm, Wed–Fri 1.45–3.30pm & 8.45–11.30pm.

Out of China c/de Muntaner 100 ☎ 934 515 555, ⊛ outofchinabarcelona.com; Ⓜ Provença; map p.113. Most Chinese restaurants in Barcelona are pretty bland, but not *Out of China*. Black-and-red decor, frilly lanterns and jazz-lounge sounds set the tone for a contemporary Chinese menu that's particularly hot on veggie options, from fried aubergine with market greens to tofu curry. The food doesn't always hit the heights, but lunch is a good deal and even at night prices won't break the bank, with most dishes around €8–10. Mon–Sat 1–4pm & 8pm–midnight, Sun 1–4pm.

★ **El Racó d'en Balta** c/d'Aribau 125 ☎ 934 531 044; Ⓜ Diagonal; map p.113. This funky hangout serves a popular weekday lunch, while at night you can eat for around €30 from a Mediterranean market-led menu, chowing down things like the house burger or veal with béarnaise sauce. Meanwhile, it's drinks and tapas at the cool *Balta Bar* next door, which has been around for a century or so, but is lent a certain style by the hip local punters. Mon 1–3.45pm, Tues–Sat 1–3.45pm & 9–11pm (bar until 2am); closed 1 week in Jan, Easter week & 3 weeks in Aug.

SAGRADA FAMÍLIA AND GLÒRIES

RESTAURANTS

Alkimia c/de la Indústria 79 ☎ 932 076 115, ⊛ alkimia .cat; Ⓜ Sagrada Família; map pp.118–119. Ask Barcelona foodies which is the best new-wave Catalan restaurant in town and once they've all stopped bickering, this is the one they'll probably plump for. "Alchemy" is what's promised by the name, and that's what chef Jordi

Vilà delivers in bitingly minimalist style – think *pa amb tomàquet* (Catalan bread rubbed with tomato and olive oil) liquidized and served in a shot glass. It's a Michelin-starred operation, so reservations are vital – expect a bill north of €100 a head, though the €40 lunch is a comparative bargain. Mon–Fri 1.30–3.30pm & 8.30–11pm; closed Easter week & 3 weeks in Aug.

ROOM SERVICE

The hotels are where it's at for some of the city's fanciest, most creative, Michelin stars-in-their-eyes dining and if you're staying at any of the following you've got some Barcelona's most exciting cooking right on the premises. Currently making waves is **Moo** at the über-fashionable *Hotel Omm* (W hotelomm.es; see p.174), the Barcelona outpost by Girona's celebrated Roca brothers, while Martín Berasategui brings his highly rated Basque style to **Lasarte** in the *Condes de Barcelona* (W condesdebarcelona.com; see p.173) – **Fonda España**, the restaurant at the gloriously decorated *Hotel España* (W hotelespanya.com; see p.170), also forms part of the Berasategui stable. Madrid-based chef Sergi Arola lends his name to the designer tapas place **Arola**, located at the glam waterfront *Arts Barcelona* (W ritzcarlton.com /hotels/Barcelona; see p.172), while holed up in the *Hotel Majestic* (W www.hotelmajestic.es; see p.173) is Fermí Puig's **Drolma**. Other graduates of Ferran Adrià's famed *El Bulli* restaurant are thick on the ground too, whether it's Carles Abellan at **Bravo** in the stunning seafront *W Barcelona* (W w-barcelona.com; see p.172) or Ramón Freixa's **Ávalon** at the *Grand Hotel Central* (W grandhotelcentral.com; see p.171). Finally, for a boutique restaurant-with-rooms experience right in the city, look no further than Jordi Cruz's **Abac** (W www.abacbarcelona .com; see p.176), nestled up in the flash Tibidabo neighbourhood.

15

Gorria c/de la Diputació 421 ☎932 451 164, W restaurantegorria.com; Ⓜ Monumental; map pp.118–119. This elegant family-owned restaurant serves the finest Basque cuisine, like *pochas de Sanguesa* (a sort of white-bean stew), wood-grilled lamb, clams and hake in salsa verde or suckling pig. Prices are on the high side (€50 a head and upwards), but this is regional Spanish cooking of the highest order. Mon 1–3.30pm, Tues–Sat 1–3.30pm &

9–11.30pm; closed Easter week & Aug.

Piazzenza Av. de Gaudí 27–29 ☎934 363 817; Ⓜ Sagrada Família; map pp.118–119. A reliable standby just 5min walk from the Sagrada Família. The tapas, drinks and pizzas are served outdoors in summer, and you can eat for around €20. It's a pretty buzzy place at night, just as popular with locals as with tourists. Daily 1pm–1am; closed 2 weeks in Aug.

GRÀCIA

CAFÉS

Gelateria Caffeteria Italiana Pl. de la Revolució 2 ☎932 102 339; Ⓜ Fontana; map p.126. For real hand-made Italian ice cream, and a stroll around a pretty square in the sun – expect queues at peak times and then more waiting as you struggle to choose from the twenty-odd different flavours. Tues–Sun 3–8pm (Fri & Sat until 11.30pm); closed Jan.

★ **La Nena** c/de Ramon y Cajal 36 ☎932 851 476; Ⓜ Fontana; map p.126. First and foremost, it's the food at "the little girl" that's the main attraction – lovely home-made cakes, plus waffles, quiches, organic ice cream, squeezed juices and the like. But parents love it too, as it's very child-friendly, from the changing mats in the loos to the little seats, games and puzzles. Daily 9am–2pm & 4–10pm; closed Aug.

TAPAS BARS

Bo Pl. de Rius i Taulet 11 ☎933 683 529, W bo restaurant.com; Ⓜ Diagonal; map p.126. Gràcia´s nicest square also has its best selection of café-bars, including this contemporary *tasca* that serves tapas and stuffed sandwiches all day and night. You can easily pick up a decent meal here, from mussels to Caesar salad (most dishes €5–8), but get there early if you want to sit outside. Daily 10am–1am (Fri & Sat until 2am).

★ **Sureny** Pl. de la Revolució 17 ☎932 137 556; Ⓜ Fontana; map p.126. Although strictly speaking a tapas place, this is more of a gourmet experience as you're served at restaurant tables with inventive little dishes from a seasonally changing menu. For around €7 or €8 a time sample clever concoctions like venison tartare with pineapple preserve, a scallop on artichoke cream or monkfish with baby asparagus. Alternatively, a €35 tasting menu gets you seven of the best plus dessert. Tues–Sat 8.30pm–midnight, Sun 1–3.30pm & 8.30pm–midnight; closed Easter week.

RESTAURANTS

★ **Flash, Flash** c/de la Granada del Penedès 25 ☎932 370 990; Ⓜ Diagonal; map p.126. A classic 1970s survivor, *Flash, Flash* does tortillas (€6–9) served any time you like, any way you like, from plain and simple to elaborately stuffed, with sweet ones for dessert. If that doesn't grab you, there's a menu of salads, steaks, burgers and fish. Either way, you'll love the original white leatherette booths and monotone "models-with-cameras" cutouts – very Austin Powers. Restaurant daily 1pm–1.30am, bar open 11am–2am.

★ **Goliard** c/del Progrés ☎932 073 175; Ⓜ Diagonal; map p.126. Smart but casual *Goliard* offers a pared-down dining experience in a contemporary foodie bistro that looks like it should cost three times as much. Dishes are

TOP 5 DATE NIGHTS

Café de l'Acadèmia See p.180
Casa Calvet See p.191
El Salón See p.181
La Singular See below
Senyor Parellada See p.188

of-the-moment – octopus and sweet potato in an almond sauce, tuna sashimi on a chive and tomato salsa – and although the menus is divided into starters and mains (most things €7–15), there are smaller portions available if you want to mix and match. The weekday lunch is a really good deal too. Mon–Fri 1–3.30pm & 9–11.30pm, Sat 9–11.30pm.

Himali c/Milà i Fontanals 60 ☎ 932 851 568; ⓂJoanic; map p.126. There's not much to suggest Barcelona's only Nepalese restaurant will be worth the trip – a few Nepalese flags and pictures adorn an otherwise unassuming neighbourhood eatery. But the food differs from the downtown curry-house offerings, with *momo* (stuffed dumplings), grilled chicken with fragrant walnut curry sauce and slow-cooked mutton and potato typical of the specialities spelt out in English on the menu. Most mains cost around €10, which includes rice and naan bread. Tues–Sun noon–4.30pm & 8pm–midnight.

Nou Candanchu Pl. de Rius i Taulet 9 ☎ 932 377 362; ⓂFontana; map p.126. Good for lunch on a sunny day or a leisurely night out on a budget, when you can sit beneath the clocktower in the ever-entertaining local square. There's a wide menu – tapas and hot sandwiches, but also steak and eggs, steamed clams and mussels, or cod and hake cooked plenty of different ways. It's managed by an affable bunch of young guys, and there's lots of choice for €8–12. Mon, Wed, Thurs & Sun 7am–1am, Fri & Sat 7am–3am.

★ **La Singular** c/de Francesc Giner 50 ☎ 932 375 098; ⓂDiagonal; map p.126. The tiniest of kitchens turns out refined Mediterranean food at moderate prices – say, aubergine and smoked fish salad, or chicken stuffed with dates and ham, with most dishes costing €9–15. There's always something appealing on the menu for veggies too. It's a cornerstone of the neighbourhood, with a friendly – even romantic – atmosphere, but there are only nine tables, so go early or reserve. Mon–Fri 1.30–4pm & 9pm–midnight (Fri until 1am), Sat 9pm–1am; closed 2 weeks in Aug/Sept.

Taverna El Glop c/de Sant Lluís 24 ☎ 932 137 058, Ⓦtavernaelglop.com; ⓂJoanic; map p.126. The rusticity (stone-flagged floors, beams, baskets of garlic) here stops just the right side of parody and the lunch *menú* is one of the city's best deals; otherwise expect to spend €20–25 a head for grills and other tavern specials, prepared on the open kitchen ranges. At the weekend you may have to wait for a table. There are other branches downtown in the Eixample but this is the original and the best. Daily 1–4pm & 8pm–1am.

LES CORTS, PEDRALBES AND SARRIÀ-SANT GERVASI

TAPAS BARS

★ **Bar Tomás** c/Major de Sarrià 49, Sarrià ☎ 932 031 077; FGC Sarrià; map pp.132–133. The best *patatas bravas* in the city? Everyone points you here, to this utterly unassuming, white-formica-table bar in the 'burbs (12min by train from Pl. Catalunya FGC station) for a taste of their unrivalled spicy fried potatoes with garlic mayo and *salsa picante*. They fry between noon and 3pm and 6pm and closing so if it's *bravas* you want, note the hours. Mon, Tues & Thurs–Sun 8am–10pm; closed Aug.

Bar Turó c/del Tenor Viñas 1, Sant Gervasi ☎ 932 006 953; FGC Muntaner; map pp.132–133. A reliable place for tapas, fresh pasta and home-made pizzas (€9–10), right by pretty Turó park. It's a contemporary place, with big windows that overlook a year-round street *terrassa*, and the food is pretty good value for uptown. Mon–Sat 9am–midnight, Sun 9am–4.30pm.

RESTAURANTS

Can Punyetes c/de Marià Cubí 189, Sant Gervasi ☎ 932 009 159, Ⓦcanpunyetes.com; FGC Muntaner; map pp.132–133. Traditional grillhouse-tavern – well, since 1981 anyway – that offers slick city diners a taste of older times. There are simple salads and tapas, and open grills turning out sausage, lamb chops, chicken and pork, accompanied by grilled country bread, white beans and char-grilled potato halves. Prices are very reasonable (almost everything under €10) and locals love it. Daily 1–4pm & 8pm–midnight.

Casa Fernandez c/del Santaló 46, Sant Gervasi ☎ 932 019 308, Ⓦcasafernandez.com; FGC Muntaner; map pp.132–133. The long kitchen hours are a boon for the bar-crawlers in this neck of the woods. It's a contemporary place featuring market cuisine, though they are specialists in – of all things – fried eggs, either served straight with chips or with Catalan sausage, garlic prawns or other variations. Most dishes are in the range €6–15. Daily 1pm–1am.

Bars, clubs and live music

Whatever you're looking for from a night out, you'll find it somewhere in Barcelona – bohemian boozer, underground club, cocktail bar, summer dance palace, techno temple, Irish pub or designer bar, you name it. Some of the finest places for a drink are already covered in the previous chapter, and undoubtedly one of the city's greatest pleasures is to pull up a pavement seat and watch the world go by. However, the bar scene proper operates at a different pace, and with a different set of rules. Specialist bars in Barcelona include *bodegas* (specializing in wine), *cerveserías* (beer), *xampanyerías* (champagne and cava) and *coctelerías* (cocktails). Best known of the city's nightlife haunts are its hip designer bars, while there's a stylish club and music scene that goes from strength to strength fuelled by a potent mix of resident and guest DJs, local bands and visiting superstars.

Generally, the bars and clubs in the old town are a mixture of traditional tourist haunts, party-time Irish bars, local drinking places and fashionista hangouts. In the **Barri Gòtic**, it's the streets around Plaça Reial and Plaça George Orwell that see most of the action, while in **La Ribera**, Passeig del Born is the main focus, though a hip scene is developing up in the neighbouring *barri* of **Sant Pere** too. For a slightly edgier bunch of bars, cross over to **El Raval**, where the coolest places are found in the upper part of the neighbourhood near MACBA (especially along c/de Joaquín Costa). You can still find tradition (and sleaze) further south, closer to the port, in the surviving bars of the old Barri Xinès, while over in the unsung neighbourhood of **Poble Sec** there's an increasing number of mellow bars, music venues and late-night haunts and clubs. **Port Olímpic** is more of a mainstream summer-night playground for locals and tourists alike, with scores of bars, all either themed or otherwise fairly mundane, but with the advantage that you can simply hop from one to another if you don't like your first choice. Up in **Gràcia**, there's a lively bar scene and several off-beat music joints. Meanwhile, the bulk of the big-name warehouse and designer venues are in peripheral areas like **Poble Nou** and **Les Corts**, while also high on the list of any seasoned clubber is the tourist fantasy village of **Poble Espanyol** in Montjuïc.

As for music, major bands include Barcelona on their tours, playing either at sports stadium venues or at the city's bigger clubs. The city's pretty hot on **jazz**, **Latin** and **blues**, while **folk**, **roots** and **world music** aficionados need to scour the club gig lists for home-grown and touring talent alike. All sorts of city venues, museums, galleries and institutions have **live music programmes** too – Caixa Forum is particularly well regarded, while the books-and-music chain **FNAC** (ⓦclubcultura.com) sponsors gigs and events at the concert halls at its stores at Plaça de Catalunya, L'Illa Diagonal and L'Illa Diagonal Mar.

16

ESSENTIALS

What's on Local listings magazines *Guía del Ocio* (ⓦguiadelociobcn.com) and *Time Out Barcelona* (ⓦtimeout.cat) cover current openings, hours and club nights, and most bars, cafés, boutiques and music stores carry flyers and free magazines containing news and reviews. For the Barcelona music scene, check out the websites ⓦatiza.com and ⓦbarcelonarocks.com. For the lowdown on gay and lesbian nightlife in Barcelona, see chapter 18.

Tickets Tickets for major gigs are available from the main ticket agencies (see p.34); in addition, there's a concert ticket desk in the Pl. Catalunya FNAC store (ⓦCatalunya), while the music shops along c/dels Tallers (just off the Ramblas; ⓦCatalunya) also sell gig tickets.

Opening hours Most bars stay open until 2am, or 3am at weekends, while clubs tend not to open much before midnight and stay open until 5am, or even later at weekends – fair enough, as they've often barely got started by 3am. Unlike restaurants, bars and clubs generally stay open throughout August.

Admission charges Some clubs are free before a certain time, usually around midnight. Otherwise, expect to pay €10–20 for club admission, though this usually includes your first drink (if there is free entry, don't be surprised to find that there's a minimum drinks charge of anything up to €10). Tickets for gigs run from €20 to €50, depending on the act though there are cheaper gigs (€5–20) almost every night of the year at a variety of smaller clubs and bars.

MUSIC FESTIVALS

Aside from headline concerts during the Generalitat's summer-long **Festival de Barcelona Grec**, the biggest annual music festivals are the techno, rock and indie showcase that is **Primavera Sound** (May) and the **Sónar** (June) electro bleep-fest. Singer-songwriters are showcased every year at **Barnasants** (Jan–March), while for jazz fans the main event is the **Festival de Jazz** (Nov–Dec), as well as the jazz, blues and Latin-tinged **Festival de Guitarra** (April–May). There's also Gràcia's experimental and electronic music festival, known as **LEM** (Oct). For more on all these music bashes, turn to the "Festivals and holidays" chapter (see p.215).

THE RAMBLAS

BARS

Bosc de les Fades Ptge. de la Banca 5 ☎ 933 172 649, ⓦ museocerabcn.com; Ⓜ Drassanes; map p.38. Tucked away in an alley off the Ramblas, beside the entrance to the wax museum, the "Forest of the Fairies" is festooned with gnarled plaster tree trunks, hanging branches, fountains and stalactites. It's a bit cheesy, which is perhaps why it's a huge hit with the twenty-something crowd who huddle in the grottoes with a cocktail or two. Mon–Thurs & Sun 10am–1am, Fri & Sat 10am–2am.

La Cazalla Ramblas 25, no phone; Ⓜ Drassanes; map p.38. An historic remnant of the old days, the hole-in-the-wall *Cazalla* (under the arch, at the beginning of c/de l'Arc del Teatre) first opened its hatch in 1912. It was closed for some years, but it's now back in business offering stand-up coffees, beers and shots to an assorted clientele of locals, cops, streetwalkers and the occasional stray tourist. Mon–Sat 10am–3am.

BARRI GÒTIC

BARS

★ **L'Ascensor** c/de Bellafila 3 ☎ 933 185 347; Ⓜ Jaume I; map p.46. Sliding antique wooden elevator doors announce the entrance to "The Lift", but it's no theme bar – just an easy-going local hangout, great for a late-night drink. Daily 7pm–3am.

Café Milans c/de Milans 7 ☎ 932 689 932; Ⓜ Drassanes; map p.46. Hidden down a bendy alley, this isn't much more than a hacked-out room in an old Gothic Quarter building, cocktail bar inside, couple of sofas outside, but it works – helped by some wacky art displays, a great soundtrack (Siouxsie to Roxy Music) and one-offs like pop-up vintage clothes sales. Tues–Thurs 6pm–2am, Fri & Sat 6pm–3am.

La Cerveteca c/d'en Gignàs 25 ☎ 933 150 407, ⓦ lacerveteca.com, Ⓜ Jaume I; p.46. The city's biggest and best world beer bar is hardly a beard-and-sandals place, more a cool tasting-bar for ale enthusiasts of all kinds. Mon–Thurs 4–10pm, Fri–Sun 1–11pm.

Glaciar Pl. Reial 3 ☎ 933 021 163; Ⓜ Liceu; map p.46. At this traditional Barcelona meeting point the terrace seating is packed most sunny evenings and at weekends, and the comings and goings in the old town's funkiest square are half the entertainment. Mon–Sat 4pm–2am (Fri & Sat until 3am), Sun 9am–2am.

★ **Milk** c/d'en Gignàs 21 ☎ 932 680 922, ⓦ milk barcelona.com; Ⓜ Jaume I; map p.46. Irish-owned bar and bistro that's carved a real niche as a welcoming neighbourhood hangout. Decor, they say, is that of a "millionaire's drawing room", with its sofas, cushions and antique chandeliers. Get there early for the famously relaxed brunch (Thurs–Sun 10am–4pm), or there's dinner and cocktails every night to a funky soundtrack. Mon–Wed 6pm–1am, Thurs–Sun 10am–3am.

Oviso c/de N'Arai 5, Pl. George Orwell, no phone; Ⓜ Drassanes; map p.46. Holding a mirror onto the neighbourhood, the *Oviso* fits right in with the scruffy urban square outside – a shabby-chic mural-clad café-bar, popular with a hip young crowd. There's a sunny *terrassa*, and the salads and sandwiches are good too, available from breakfast onwards. Daily 10am–2.30am (Fri & Sat 10am until 3am).

Pipa Club Pl. Reial 3 ☎ 933 024 732, ⓦ bpipaclub.com; Ⓜ Liceu; map p.46. Historically a pipe-smoker's private club, this old-fashioned members' bar is a wood-panelled, jazzy, late-night kind of place, with – rare for Barcelona – a pool table. It's on the secretive side – ring the bell for admission and make your way up the stairs – but visitors are welcome. Daily 10pm–3am.

Schilling c/de Ferran 23 ☎ 933 176 787, ⓦ cafeschilling .com; Ⓜ Liceu; map p.46. Something of a haven on this heavily touristed drag, *Schilling* has a certain European "grand-café" style, with its high ceilings, big windows and upmarket feel. It has a loyal gay following, but it's a mixed, chilled place to meet up, grab a *copa* and move on. Mon–Sat 10am–3am, Sun noon–3am.

★ **Zim** c/de Dagueria 20, no phone; Ⓜ Jaume I; map p.46. Katherine (of the adjacent *Formatgeria La Seu* cheese shop) and co-owner Francesc offer up this tiny, hole-in-the-wall tasting bar for selected wines from boutique Spanish producers. For a soothing glass or two accompanied by farmhouse cheese, wonderful cured meats from the Pyrenees and artisan-made bread, you really can't beat it – and closing time is often somewhat flexible if you're in the mood for more wine. Mon–Sat 6–11pm; closed Aug.

CLUBS AND LIVE MUSIC

Fantástico Ptge. dels Escudellers 3 ☎ 933 175 411, ⓦ fantasticoclub.com; Ⓜ Drassanes; map p.46. A cheery music bar for the pop, indie, new-folk and shoegazer crowd, bopping to the The Killers, The Pigeon Detectives, Get Cape and the like. Admission usually free. Wed–Sat 11pm–3am.

★ **Harlem Jazz Club** c/de la Comtessa de Sobradiel 8 ☎ 933 100 755, ⓦ harlemjazzclub.es; Ⓜ Jaume I; map p.46. For many years, *the* hot place for jazz, where every

16

TOP 5 HISTORIC BARS

Almirall See p.198
La Confitería See p.198
Dry Martini See p.202
Marsella See p.198
Velódromo See p.202

HERE FOR THE BEER?

Until recently, **beer** (*cervesa* in Catalan, *cerveza* in Spanish) in Barcelona meant lager, and only lager, but a growing interest in artisan beers, craft brews and foreign imports means a wider choice in many bars these days. For the best selection of Catalan and Spanish craft beers you need to make a special trip out by metro to **2D2D Spuma** (c/de la Maniqua 8, Sant Andreu ☎661 230 209, ⊛2d2dspuma.com; Ⓜ Congrés; Mon–Thurs 6pm–midnight, Fri & Sat 6pm–2am), a beer-bar and associated shop for over two hundred microbrews of all kinds, from unpasteurized wheat beers to organic ales. It's in a residential neighbourhood several metro stops north of Glòries, but if this seems like taking things too seriously, then beer-bar **La Cerveteca** (see p.197) in the Barri Gòtic is a far easier find, while there are artisan beers made on the premises in Gràcia at **La Cervesera Artesana** (see p.204), Barcelona's original brew-pub. A few pioneering city bars also serve a decent handcrafted beer – stand-outs are the Asian tapas joint **Mosquito** in Sant Pere (see p.185) and Poble Sec's beer-and-music bar **Cervesería Jazz** (see p.201).

style gets an airing, from African and gypsy to flamenco and fusion. There are two shows a night; it's best to get advance tickets for the second spot. Entry €5–10, depending on the night and the act. Gigs daily at 10pm & 1am (weekends 11pm & 2am); closed Aug.

Jamboree Pl. Reial 17 ☎933 191 789, ⊛masimas .com; Ⓜ Liceu; map p.46. They don't get the big jazz names here that they used to, but the nightly gigs (from €10) still pull in the crowds, while the wild Monday night WTF jazz, funk and hip-hop jam session (from 9pm; €5) is a city fixture. Stay on for the club, which kicks in after midnight (entry €10) and you get funky sounds until the small hours. Gigs daily at 9pm & 11pm, club daily midnight–5am.

Karma Pl. Reial 10 ☎933 025 680, ⊛karmadisco.com; Ⓜ Liceu; map p.46. A stalwart of the scene, this old-school studenty basement place can get claustrophobic at times.

Sounds are indie, Britpop and US college, while a lively crowd gathers at the square-side bar and *terrassa* which is open from 6pm. Club admission around €10. Tues–Sun midnight–5am.

La Macarena c/de Nou de Sant Francesc 5; no phone, ⊛macarenaclub.com; Ⓜ Drassanes; map p.46. Once a place where flamenco tunes were offered up to La Macarena, the Virgin of Seville – now a heaving temple to all things electro. Entry free until around 1am, then from €5. Daily midnight–4.30am (Fri & Sat until 5am).

★**Sidecar** Pl. Reial 7 ☎933 021 586, ⊛sidecar factoryclub.com; Ⓜ Liceu; map p.46. The hippest concert space in the old town – pronounced "See-day-car" – has nightly gigs and DJs that champion rock, indie, roots, electronica and fusion acts. Entry €7–10, though some gigs up to €20. Tues–Sun 8pm–5am, gigs usually at 10.30pm, DJs at 12.30am.

EL RAVAL

BARS

★**Almirall** c/de Joaquín Costa 33 ☎933 189 917; Ⓜ Universitat; map pp.60–61. Dating from 1860, Barcelona's oldest bar is a *modernista* design classic – check out the doors, counter and stupendous glittering bar. Not too young, not too loud, and always good for a late-night drink. Daily 6pm–2am (Fri & Sat until 3am).

Betty Ford's c/de Joaquín Costa 56 ☎933 041 368; Ⓜ Universitat; map pp.60–61. With a vibe somewhere between a student lounge and a beach bar, *Betty's* is a bouncy place full of bouncy young things, sipping colourful cocktails and cold Australian beer. Deal with the late-night ~~nchies~~ by getting to grips with their famed burger ~~...ly~~ 6pm–1am (Fri & Sat until 2am).

~~...do~~ Sant Pau 128 ☎934 430 458; Ⓜ Paral. ~~...~~ one-time bakery and confectioner's ~~...~~ood bar, faded tile floor, murals, anti- ~~...~~mirrored cabinets – is now a popular bar ~~...~~ It's a handy stop-off on the way to a night ~~...~~ Mon–Sat 8pm–3am, Sun 7pm–2am.

London Bar c/Nou de la Rambla 34 ☎933 185 261; Ⓜ Liceu; map pp.60–61. Opened in 1910, the well-known *London Bar* attracts a mostly tourist clientele these days, but it's still worth looking in as time has not dulled the exuberant *modernista* decor (nor the authentic old-town sleaze just up the street). Tues–Sat 7pm–4am; closed 2 weeks in Aug.

Marmalade c/de la Riera Alta 4–6 ☎934 423 966, ⊛marmaladebarcelona.com; Ⓜ Sant Antoni; map pp.60–61. A hugely glam facelift for the old Muebles Navarro furniture store has gone for big, church-like spaces and a back-lit Art Deco bar that resembles a high altar. Cocktails, bistro meals and gourmet burgers pull in a relaxed dine-and-lounge crowd, and there's a popular weekend brunch too. If you like the style, give the more informal Barri Gòtic sister bar, *Milk* (see p.197) a whirl as well. Mon–Fri 7pm–3am, Sat & Sun 10am–3am.

★**Marsella** c/de Sant Pau 65 ☎934 427 263; Ⓜ Liceu; map pp.60–61. Authentic, atmospheric 1930s bar – named after the French port of Marseilles – where absinthe is the

16

drink of choice. It featured in Woody Allen's *Vicky Cristina Barcelona*, so expect a spirited mix of film fans, oddball locals and young dudes, all looking for a slice of the old Barri Xinès. Mon–Sat 10pm–3am; closed 2 weeks in Aug.

Muy Buenas c/del Carme 63 ☎ 934 425 053; Ⓜ Liceu; map pp.60–61. Arguably the Raval's nicest traditional watering-hole, with a restored *modernista* interior and eager-to-please staff. A long marble trough does duty as the bar, and the beer's pulled from antique beer taps. Tues–Sat 9am–3am.

★ **Resolis** c/de la Riera Baixa 22 ☎ 934 412 948; Ⓜ Sant Antoni; map pp.60–61. The team behind *Ànima* restaurant rescued this decayed, century-old bar and turned it into a cool hangout with decent tapas. They didn't do much – a lick of paint, polish the panelling, patch up the brickwork – but now punters spill out of the door onto "secondhand clothes street" and a good time is had by all. Mon–Wed 1pm–1am, Thurs–Sat 1pm–2.30am.

Zelig c/del Carme 116 ☎ 934 415 622, Ⓦ zelig-barcelona .com; Ⓜ Sant Antoni; map pp.60–61. The photo-frieze on granite walls and a fully stocked cocktail bar make it very much of its *barri* but *Zelig* stands out from the crowd – two Dutch owners offer a chatty welcome, a tendency towards 1980s sounds and a slight whiff of camp. Mon 8.30am–7pm, Tues–Fri 8.30pm–3am, Sat & Sun 7pm–3am.

CLUBS AND LIVE MUSIC

La Concha c/de Guardia 14 ☎ 933 024 118; Ⓜ Drassanes; map pp.60–61. The Arab–flamenco fusion throws up a great atmosphere, worth braving the slightly dodgy area

TOP 5 MUSIC BARS
Belchica See p.202
Casa Paco See p.200
Cervesería Jazz See p.201
Soló Bar See p.201
Vinilo See p.204

for. It's a kitsch, gay-friendly joint, dedicated to the "incandescent presence" of Sara Montiel, Queen of Song and Cinema, with uninhibited dancing by tourists and locals alike. Admission free. Daily 5pm–3am.

★ **Jazz Sí Club** c/de Requesens 2 ☎ 933 290 020, Ⓦ tallerdemusics.com; Ⓜ Sant Antoni; map pp.60–61. This is a great place for inexpensive (€5–8) gigs in a tiny sweat-box of a club associated with the Taller de Musics (Music School). Every night from around 8.30 or 9pm there's something different, from exuberant rock, blues, jazz and jam sessions to the popular weekly Cuban (Thurs) and flamenco (Fri) nights. There are usually a couple of sessions a night, with an interval in between. Your first drink is included in the price, and the bar is as cheap as chips. Daily 8–11.30pm.

★ **Moog** c/de l'Arc del Teatre 3 ☎ 933 017 282, Ⓦ masimas.com/moog; Ⓜ Drassanes; map pp.60–61. One of the most influential clubs around for electronic sounds, playing techno, electro, drum 'n' bass and trance to a cool but up-for-it crowd. The bigger-name international DJs tend to play Wednesday nights. Admission €10. Daily midnight–5am.

16

SANT PERE AND LA RIBERA

BARS

Black Horse c/d'Allada Vermell 16, Sant Pere ☎ 932 683 338; Ⓦ pubblackhorse.com; Ⓜ Jaume I; map p.70. Barcelona has embraced the "English" pub and "Irish" bar with a vengeance, and every *barri* has a place where the stag and hen groups can feel right at home.

On the whole, there's little to choose between them, though by common consent, the *Black Horse* is the best, with an off-the-beaten-track feel, despite being just a few minutes from the Picasso museum. Mon–Thurs 6pm–2am, Fri 6pm–3am, Sat 1pm–3am, Sun 1pm–2am.

THE BEAT FROM THE STREET

The Barcelona sound – *mestiza* – is a cross-cultural musical fusion whose heartland is the immigrant melting-pot of the Raval. The local postcode – **08001** – lends a name to the sound's hippest flagbearers, while also typically "Raval" is the collective called **Cheb Balowski**, an Algerian-Catalan fusion band. The biggest star on the scene is the Paris-born, Barcelona-resident **Manu Chao**, whose infectious, multi-million-selling album *Clandestino* (1998) kick-started the whole genre. He's widely known abroad, and influenced many Barcelona bands, including the world music festival favourites **Ojos de Brujo** (Eyes of the Wizard), who present a fusion reinvention of flamenco and Catalan rumba. Other hot sounds come from the Latin American dub and reggae band **GoLem System**, and the fusion-freestyle merchants **LA Kinky Beat**. There's more information on the useful *mestiza* portal Ⓦ radiochango.com, while you can hear all the above – and more – on three great samplers, *Barcelona Raval Sessions*, *Barcelona Raval Sessions 2* and *Barcelona Zona Bastarda*. For new-wave Catalan rumba, get hold of the *Rambla Rumble Rumba* compilation.

★ **Casa Paco** c/d'Allada Vermell 10, Sant Pere ☎ 935 073 719; Ⓜ Jaume I; map p.70. Sant Pere's signature bar is this cool music joint that's a hit on the weekend DJ scene – the tagline "not a disco, just a bar with good music" says it all. There's a great *terrassa* under the trees, and if you can't get a table here try one of several other alfresco bars down the traffic-free boulevard. Meanwhile, the associated *Pizza Paco* across the way (also with its own terrace) means you don't have to go anywhere else for dinner. Daily 9am–2am (Fri & Sat until 3am), Oct–March 6pm–2am (Fri & Sat until 3am).

Espai Barroc c/de Montcada 20, La Ribera ☎ 933 100 673; Ⓜ Jaume I; map p.70. Every evening the doors are thrown open at the Palau Dalmases for drinks and cocktails in a remodelled medieval mansion known as the *Espai Barroc*, or "Baroque Space". The rather grand and pricey candlelit bar (minimum charge €7) certainly looks the part – it's your opportunity to dress to the nines – and if you come on Thursday evening you'll catch singers belting out arias as you sip fine wines under the chandeliers (recital at 11pm, €20, first drink included). Tues–Sat 8pm–2am, Sun 6–10pm.

★ **La Fianna** c/dels Banys Vells 19, La Ribera ☎ 933 151 810, Ⓦ lafianna.com; Ⓜ Jaume I; map p.70. Flickering candelabras, parchment lampshades, rough plaster walls and deep colours set the Gothic mood in this stylish lounge-bar that's "putting the beat in the Born". Relax on the chill-out beds and velvet sofas, or book ahead to eat – the fusion-food restaurant is open from 8.30pm. Mon–Wed & Sun 6pm–1.30am, Thurs–Sat 6pm–2.30am.

Mudanzas c/de la Vidrería 15, La Ribera ☎ 933 191 137; Ⓜ Barceloneta; map p.70. Locals like the relaxed feel (especially if you can hide yourself away in the cosy upper room) at *Mudanzas*, while those in the know come for the wide selection of rums, whiskies and vodkas from around the world. Daily 10am–2.30am, Aug opens at 6pm.

★ **El Nus** c/dels Mirallers 5, La Ribera ☎ 933 195 355; Ⓜ Jaume I; map p.70. *El Nus* still has the feel of the shop it once was, down to the antique cash register, though it's now a kind of jazz bar-cum-gallery – a quiet, faintly old-fashioned, late-night place. Daily 7.30pm–2.30am, closed Wed.

La Vinya del Senyor Pl. de Santa Maria 5, La Ribera ☎ 933 103 379; Ⓜ Jaume I; map p.70. A great wine bar with front-row seats onto the lovely church of Santa Maria del Mar. The wine list is really good – with a score available by the glass – and there are oysters, smoked salmon and other classy tapas available. Tues–Thurs noon–1am, Fri & Sat noon–2am, Sun noon–midnight.

PORT VELL AND BARCELONETA

BARS

★ **Can Paixano** c/de la Reina Cristina 7, Port Vell ☎ 933 100 839, Ⓦ canpaixano.com; Ⓜ Barceloneta; map p.81. A must on everyone's itinerary is this back-street joint where the drink of choice – all right, the only drink – is cava (Catalan champagne). Don't go thinking sophistication – it might come in traditional champagne saucers (the sort of thing Dean Martin used to stack in a pyramid and then pour wine over), but this is a counter-only joint where there's fizz, tapas and tapas-in-sandwiches and that's your lot. And who could want more? Mon–Sat 9am–10.30pm; closed 1 week in Feb & 2 weeks in Aug.

Le Kasbah Pl. de Pau Vila, behind Palau de Mar, Port Vell ☎ 932 216 225, Ⓦ ottozutz.com; Ⓜ Barceloneta; map p.81. The *terrassa* is the big summer draw here, when nothing but a reviving cocktail and a breath of fresh air will do, though the funky, sort-of-Oriental interior has a chilled-out charm. Post-beach happy hours see the bar open earlier on some summer nights too. Tues–Sat 11pm–3am.

Luz de Gas Moll de Diposit, in front of Palau de Mar, Port Vell ☎ 934 842 326, Ⓦ luzdegas.com; Ⓜ Barceloneta; map p.81. Sip a chilled drink on the polished deck of the moored boat, and soak up some great marina and harbour views. Queues form on hot days, when every parasol-shaded seat is taken, but it's especially nice at dusk as the city lights begin to twinkle. March–Oct daily noon–3am.

PORT OLÍMPIC AND POBLE NOU

CLUBS AND LIVE MUSIC

CDLC Pg. Marítim 32, Port Olímpic ☎ 932 240 470, Ⓦ cdlcbarcelona.com, Ⓜ Ciutadella-Vila Olímpica; map p.85. With a clientele of A-list celeb, footy player and WAG, well-heeled tourist and local rich kid, this beautiful-person lounge-club hangout is for those who want to dine, dance and kick back in like-minded company. Restaurant open daily from noon, club midnight–3am.

Club Catwalk c/de Ramon Trias Fargas 2–4, Port Olímpic ☎ 932 216 161, Ⓦ clubcatwalk.net; Ⓜ Ciutadella-Vila Olímpica; map p.85. The sleek, chic portside club of choice for the beautiful of Barcelona, playing house, funk, soul and R&B to well-heeled locals and visitors. It's under the landmark *Hotel Arts Barcelona*. Admission €20. Thurs–Sun midnight–5am.

Sala Razzmatazz c/de Pamplona 88, Poble Nou ☎ 933 208 200, Ⓦ salarazzmatazz.com; Ⓜ Bogatell; map p.85. *Razzmatazz* hosts the biggest in-town rock gigs (the concert hall capacity is 3000), while at weekends the former warehouse turns into "five clubs in one", spinning indie, rock, pop, techno, electro, retro and more in variously named music bars like "The Loft", "Pop Bar" or "Lolita". Admission (€15) gets you entrance to all the bars. Fri & Sat 1–6am.

16

MONTJUÏC

BARS

La Caseta del Migdia Mirador del Migdia ⓦlacaseta .org; cable car (Telefèric de Montjuïc) or bus #193 to Castell de Montjuïc, then follow signs to "Mirador" (15min walk); map p.91. It's cooler in every sense up on the heights of Montjuïc, as a welcome summer breeze whistles through the trees and chill-out sounds cosset intrepid visitors to the panoramic, open-air bar of *La Caseta*, around the back of the castle. Hours variable, but usually weekends noon–sunset, plus summer weekend DJ nights.

CLUBS AND LIVE MUSIC

La Terrrazza Poble Espanyol, Av. Francesc Ferrer i Guàrdia ☎ 932 724 980, ⓦlaterrrazza.com; ⓜEspanya; map p.91. Open-air summer club that's *the* place to be in Barcelona. Nonstop dance, house and techno, though don't get there until at least 3am, and be prepared for the style police. May–Oct Thurs–Sat midnight–6am.

POBLE SEC

BARS

⭐ **Bar Seco** Pg. de Montjuïc 74 ☎ 933 296 374; ⓜ Paral.lel; map p.98. The "Dry Bar" is a local hit, with its mellow vibe, freshly squeezed juices, Free Trade drinks and artisan beers. Stand-out dish from the Slow Food-inspired, veggie-friendly menu is *patatas salvajes* ("wild potatoes") – fried organic skin-on spuds with a fiery *alioli*. Big picture windows look out onto the corner plot, and there's *terrassa* seating over the road. Mon 9am–8pm, Tues–Thurs 9am–1am (Nov–April Tues & Wed closes at 8pm), Fri 9am–2am, Sat 10am–2am, Sun 10am–1am.

Celler Cal Marino c/de Margarit 54 ☎ 933 294 592; ⓜ Poble Sec; map p.98. The wines in the barrels are to take away at knockdown prices, and you can drink a *copa* for under two euros, but there's also a more sophisticated wine selection available in this cavernous, stone-walled tavern. Add cheap tapas and a jolly neighbourhood crowd, and there's no reason not to stop by. Tues–Fri 11.30am–3pm & 7–11pm, Sat & Sun 11.30am–3pm.

Cervesería Jazz c/de Margarit 43 ☎ 934 433 259; ⓜ Poble Sec; map p.98. Grab a stool at the carved bar and shoot the breeze over a Catalan craft beer. It's an amiable joint with great music, jazz to reggae, and locals swear that the burgers are the best in town. Tues–Sat 7pm–2.30am.

La Tieta c/de Blai 1 ☎ 646 077 936; ⓜ Paral.lel; map p.98. Small but perfectly formed, "The Aunt" is a cool drinks and tapas place, with selected wines served by the glass, an open window onto the street and just enough room inside for a dozen or so good friends. Tues–Sun 11am–11pm.

⭐ **Xix Bar** c/de Rocafort 19 ☎ 934 234 314, ⓦxixbar .com; ⓜ Poble Sec; map p.98. "Chicks" is an old *granja* (milk bar) – which explains the milk pail and big cow photos – turned candlelit, but completely unstuffy, cocktail bar. Gin's the big drink here (they claim over 100 varieties), and they mix stonking gin cocktails and even have their own specialist gin shop on site, with tasting courses and other activities. Mon–Sat 5pm–2.30am (Fri & Sat until 3am).

CLUBS AND LIVE MUSIC

⭐ **Maumau** c/d'en Fontrodona 33 ☎ 934 418 015, ⓦmaumaunderground.com; ⓜ Paral.lel; map p.98. If you're really in the know, then *Maumau* is one of your first weekend ports of call – a great underground lounge-club, cultural centre and chill-out space with comfy sofas, nightly film and video projections, exhibitions and a roster of guest DJs playing deep, soulful grooves. Strictly speaking it's a private club, but they tend to let foreign visitors in for free – if you do join, the "Carnet Maumau" (Maumau Card, currently €12) gives you all sorts of discounts and deals at hot venues right across the city. Thurs–Sat 11pm–2.30am.

Sala Apolo c/Nou de la Rambla 113 ☎ 934 414 001, ⓦsala-apolo.com; ⓜ Paral.lel; map p.98. Old-time ballroom turned hip concert venue with gigs on two stages (local acts to big names) and an eclectic series of club nights with names to reckon with (Nasty Mondays, Crappy Tuesdays etc). Sounds range far and wide, from punk or Catalan rumba to the weekend's long-running techno/electro Nitsa Club (ⓦ www.nitsa.com). Gigs €10–35, clubs nights €10–15. Daily midnight–5am.

Soló Bar c/de Margarit 18 ☎ 933 297 618; ⓜ Poble Sec; map p.98. Bare-bones boho music bar with free live gigs most nights around 9pm, from Latin American beats to alt-rock. Mon, Tues & Thurs–Sun 7.30pm–2.30am.

Tinta Roja c/de la Creu dels Molers 17 ☎ 934 433 243, ⓦtintaroja.net; ⓜ Poble Sec; map p.98. More of an experience than most bars, this highly theatrical tango bar features a succession of over-the-top crimson rooms leading to a stage at the back. There's cabaret and live music (tango, rumba, Cuban, flamenco, African) – often free – a couple of nights a week, though special shows are €5–10. Wed, Thurs & Sun 8pm–1.30am, Fri & Sat 8pm–3am; closed 2 weeks in Aug.

16

TOP 5 LEFT-FIELD MUSIC VENUES

Elèctric Bar See p.204
Heliogàbal See p.204
Jazz Sí Club See p.199
Sala Apolo See opposite
Tinta Roja See opposite

DRETA DE L'EIXAMPLE

BARS

★ **La Pedrera de Nit** La Pedrera, Pg. de Gràcia 92 ☎ 902 101 212, ⊛ www.telentrada.com; Ⓜ Diagonal; map p.104. The city's most exciting pop-up bar has a regular summer season on the extraordinary Gaudí roof terrace at La Pedrera (see p.109). It's a unique location for drinks and views, with sounds ranging from jazz trios to chamber ensembles. Tickets cost €25; advance booking essential, either at the Pedrera ticket office or from TelEntrada. June, July & Aug only, Fri & Sat 8.30–11pm.

CLUBS AND LIVE MUSIC

City Hall Rambla de Catalunya 2–4 ☎ 932 380 722, ⊛ grupo-ottozutz.com; Ⓜ Catalunya; map p.104. Very popular mainstream dance joint – the handy location helps – which hosts some of the most varied club nights around, from 80s revival to electro. Admission €12, though usually free before 2am. Daily midnight–6am.

ESQUERRA DE L'EIXAMPLE

BARS

Belchica c/du Villaroel 60 ☎ 934 511 355, ⊛ belchica .es; Ⓜ Urgell; map p.113. Barcelona's first Belgian beer bar guarantees a range of decent brews (including hard-to-find Trappist ales). It's also a muso's joint, playing electronica, new jazz, lounge, reggae and other left-field sounds, and there are live acts once or twice a week. Mon–Fri 6pm–3am, Sat 7pm–3am.

Danzarama Gran Via de les Corts Catalanes 604 ☎ 933 019 743, ⊛ danzarama.com; Ⓜ Universitat; map p.113. Stalwart of the uptown gastro-club scene, with a flashy fusion restaurant (open day and night), summer *terrassa* and cool bar and lounge, great for starting the night before some serious dancing elsewhere. Daily 7am–2am (Fri & Sat until 3am).

★ **Dry Martini** c/d'Aribau 166 ☎ 932 175 072, ⊛ drymartinibcn.com; Ⓜ Provença; map p.113. White-jacketed bartenders, dark wood and brass fittings, a self-satisfied air – it could only be the city's legendary uptown cocktail bar. To be fair, though, no one mixes drinks better and the regulars aren't the one-dimensional business types you might expect. There's also a mysterious hideaway back-room restaurant, *Speakeasy*, where you can play at being Al Capone. Mon–Fri 1pm–2.30am (open 6.30pm in Aug), Sat & Sun 6.30pm–3am.

★ **Velódromo** c/de Muntaner 213 ☎ 934 306 022; Ⓜ Hospital Clinic; map p.113. A gleaming facelift for one of uptown Barcelona's most iconic addresses has put the glam back into this Art Deco gem. With a lofty, *Parisien* feel,

a swooping staircase and a gleaming bar, it's ideal for swish drinks and cocktails, though with fancy breakfasts, brunch and a tapas-and-bistro menu by renowned chef Carles Abellan it's also made for early starts and later dinners. Daily 6am–2.30am.

CLUBS AND LIVE MUSIC

Antilla BCN Latin Club c/d'Aragó 141–143 ☎ 934 514 564, ⊛ antillasalsa.com; Ⓜ Hospital Clinic/Urgell; map p.113. Latin and Caribbean tunes galore – rumba, son, salsa, merengue, mambo, you name it – for out-and-out good-time dancing. There are live bands, killer cocktails and dance classes most nights. Wed 11pm–4am, Thurs 11pm–5am, Fri & Sat 11pm–6am, Sun 7pm–1am.

Luz de Gas c/de Muntaner 246 ☎ 932 097 711, ⊛ luzdegas.com; Ⓜ Diagonal; map p.113. Former ballroom venue popular with a slightly older crowd, with live music (rock, blues, soul, jazz and covers) every night around midnight. Foreign acts appear regularly, too, mainly jazz-blues types but also old soul acts and up-and-coming rockers. Admission up to €20. Daily 11.30pm–5am, also occasional gigs from 9.30pm.

Quilombo c/d'Aribau 149 ☎ 934 395 406, Ⓜ Diagonal; map p.113. Unpretentious music bar – just a bare box of a room really – that's rolled with the years since 1971, featuring live guitarists, Latin American bands and a clientele that joins in enthusiastically, maracas in hand. Mon–Thurs & Sun 9pm–3am, Fri & Sat 7.30pm–3.30am.

GRÀCIA

BARS

La Baignoire c/de Verdi 6, no phone; Ⓜ Fontana; map p.126. A small corner of sophistication on an otherwise rowdy street – Ella Fitzgerald warbling away in the background, a dozen good wines by the glass and cheesy nibbles. Mon–Sat 7pm–1am (Fri & Sat until 2am), Sun 4pm–1am.

Café del Sol Pl. del Sol 16 ☎ 934 155 663; Ⓜ Fontana; map p.126. The grandaddy of the Pl. del Sol scene sees

action day and night. On summer evenings, when the square is packed, there's not an outdoor table to be had, but even in winter this is a popular drinking den – the pubby interior has a back room and gallery, often rammed to the rafters. Daily 1pm–2.30am.

★ **Canigó** Pl. de la Revolució 10, no phone; Ⓜ Fontana; map p.126. Family-run neighbourhood bar now entering its third generation. It's not much to look at,

16

TOP 5 WINE BARS

Can Paixano See p.200
La Baignoire See p.202
La Tieta See p.201
La Vinya del Senyor See p.200
Zim See p.197

but the drinks are cheap and it's a real Gràcia institution, packed out at weekends with a young, hip and largely local crowd. Tues–Sun 8pm–2am.

La Cervesera Artesana c/de Sant Agustí 14 ☎ 932 379 594, ⓦ lacervesera.net; ⓜ Diagonal; map p.126. A score of identikit Irish pubs in town serve Guinness and other imported beers, but for real-ale, Catalan style – including an own-brew stout – the city's original microbrewery is well worth a visit. Mon–Thurs & Sun 6pm–2am, Fri & Sat 6pm–3am.

Châtalet c/de Torrijos 54 ☎ 932 849 590; ⓜ Fontana/Joanic; map p.126. Handy for a drink and a sandwich before or after the movies (both Verdi cinemas are on the doorstep), but Châtalet also has a pretty cool indie vibe, with old movies playing on the TV and a bubbly clientele who like their music. Daily 6pm–2am (Fri & Sat until 3am).

★ **Vinilo** c/Matilde 2 ☎ 626 464 759; ⓜ Diagonal; map p.126. Wear a beret, surgically attached to your iPad, drool over *Bladerunner*, Jeff Buckley and Band of Horses? This hipster music joint is just for you – a dive bar with the lighting set at a perpetual dusk, where time easily slips away. Daily 7pm–2am (Fri & Sat until 3am).

Virreina Pl. de la Virreina 1 ☎ 932 379 880, ⓦ virreina bar.com; ⓜ Fontana; map p.126. Another real Gràcia favourite, on one of the neighbourhood's prettiest squares, with a very popular summer *terrassa*. It's one of those places where you drop by for a quick drink and find yourself staying for hours. Daily 10am–1am (Fri & Sat until 2am).

CLUBS AND LIVE MUSIC

★ **Centre Artesà Tradicionàrius (CAT)** Trav. de Sant Antoni 6–8 ☎ 932 184 485 ⓦ tradicionarius.cat; ⓜ Fontana; map p.126. The best place in town for folk, traditional and world music by Catalan, Spanish and visiting performers, including some occasional big names. Admission is usually €5–15 and you can expect anything from Basque bagpipes to Brazilian singers. There are also music and instrument workshops, while CAT sponsors all sorts of outreach concerts and festivals, including an annual international folk and traditional dance festival between January and April. Concerts usually at 9 or 10pm.

Elèctric Bar Trav. de Gràcia 233 ⓦ myspace.com /electricbarcelona; ⓜ Joanic; map p.126. The bar of choice for Gràcia's counterculture crowd, who come for the wildly varied live programming, with something on every night, from poetry slams to electro-folk gigs. It's free if you just want to drink in the grungy bar – performances in the space out back start at 10pm (weekends at 11pm), with admission usually €3–5. Daily 7pm–2am (Fri & Sat until 3am).

★ **Heliogàbal** c/Ramon y Cajal 80 ⓦ heliogabal.com; ⓜ Joanic; map p.126. Not much more than a boiler room given a lick of paint, but filled with a cool, twenty-something crowd here for the live poetry and music – expect something different every night (Catalan versifying, jazz jam sessions and earnest singer-songwriters), starting at 10pm. Admission is usually €3–10, depending on the act, and drinks aren't expensive. Tues–Sun 9pm–2am (Fri & Sat until 3am).

Otto Zutz c/de Lincoln 15 ☎ 932 380 722, ⓦ grupo -ottozutz.com; FGC Gràcia; map p.126. It first opened as a club in 1985 and has since lost some of its glam cachet, but this three-storey former textile factory still has a shed-load of pretensions. The sounds are basically hip-hop, R&B and house, and with the right clothes and face, you're in (you may or may not have to pay, depending on how impressive you are, the day of the week, the mood of the door staff etc). Admission €15. Wed–Sat midnight–6am.

LES CORTS, PEDRALBES AND SARRIÀ-SANT GERVASI

BARS

Gimlet c/de Santaló 46, Sant Gervasi ☎ 932 015 306; FGC Muntaner; map pp.132–133. This favoured cocktail joint is especially popular in summertime, when the street-side tables offer a great vantage point for watching the party unfold. There are also two or three other late-opening bars on the same stretch. Daily 7.30pm–3am.

CLUBS AND LIVE MUSIC

★ **Bikini** Av. Diagonal 547, Les Corts ☎ 933 220 800, ⓦ bikinibcn.com; ⓜ Les Corts/Maria Cristina; map pp.132–133. This traditional landmark of Barcelona nightlife (behind L'Illa shopping centre) offers a regular diet of great indie, rock, roots and world gigs, followed by club

sounds from house to Brazilian, according to the night. Admission €15–25, though some big-name gigs cost up to €40. Wed–Sun midnight–5am; closed Aug.

Elephant Club Pg. dels Til.lers 1, Pedralbes ☎ 933 340 258, ⓦ elephantbcn.com; ⓜ Palau Reial; map pp.132–133. A gorgeous designer stage-set for gorgeous designer people. There's dancing, but mostly there's preening in a series of ornamental, Oriental-style gardens that spill out from a fancy uptown mansion. Admission €15. Thurs 11.30pm–4am, Fri & Sat 11.30pm–5am.

Sala BeCool Pl. Joan Llongueras 5, Sant Gervasi ☎ 933 620 413, ⓦ salabecool.com; ⓜ Hospital Clinic/FGC Muntaner; map pp.132–133. Thumping uptown club venue for local and national rock, indie and electro/techno bands and DJs. Gigs currently run Thurs to Sat nights, followed by DJ sessions, with admission for either running from €10 to €20, depending on who's appearing. They also sponsor free Friday-night acoustic nights at the next-door Irish bar *Dublin*. Thurs–Sat: gigs at 10pm; club midnight or 1am until 4am.

Universal c/de Marià Cubí 182, Sant Gervasi ☎ 934 146 362, ⓦ universalbcn.com; FGC Muntaner; map pp.132–133. A classic designer music bar and dance club that's been at the cutting edge of Barcelona style since 1985 – and there are still queues. Sounds are less of-the-moment (house to back-to-the-80s) and be warned: drinks are fairly pricey and they operate a strict door policy, so if your face doesn't fit you might not get in. Admission charged weekends, from €10. Mon–Thurs 11pm–3.30am, Fri & Sat 11pm–5am.

TOP 5 GOOD-TIME DANCE CLUBS

Antilla BCN Latin Club See p.202
La Macarena See p.198
Moog See p.199
Sala Razzmatazz See p.200
La Terrrazza See p.201

TIBIDABO

BARS

Mirablau Pl. del Dr Andrea, Av. Tibidabo ☎ 934 340 035, ⓦ mirablaubcn.com; FGC Av. del Tibidabo then Tramvia Blau, or taxi; map p.139. This chic bar by the tram and funicular terminus has unbelievable city views. By day it's a great place for drinks, while at night it's more of an upmarket tapas and music joint. Daily 11am–5am.

16

CONCERT HALL, PALAU DE LA MÚSICA CATALANA

Arts and culture

As you would expect from a city of its size, Barcelona has a busy arts and culture calendar – there will always be something worth catching, whether it's a contemporary dance performance, cabaret show or night at the opera. Classical and contemporary music, in particular, gets an airing in some stunning auditoriums, and while local theatre is less accessible for non-Catalan or -Spanish speakers, many cinemas at least show films in their original language. Local performers have always steered away from the classics and gone for the innovative, so the city boasts a long tradition of street and performance art, right down to the human statues plying their trade on the Ramblas. Barcelona excels in the visual arts, too – from traditional exhibitions of paintings to contemporary photography or installation works – and dozens of arts centres and galleries put on varied shows throughout the year.

ESSENTIALS

Tickets and information A useful first stop for tickets and information is the Palau de la Virreina, Ramblas 99 (daily 10am–8.30pm; ☎ 933 161 000; Ⓜ Liceu). ServiCaixa (☎ 902 332 211, Ⓦ servicaixa.com) and TelEntrada (☎ 902 101 212, Ⓦ telentrada.com) are the main advance booking agencies for music, theatre, cinema and exhibition tickets.

What's on The city council's Institute of Culture website, Ⓦ bcn.cat/cultura, is invaluable – it covers every aspect of art and culture in the city, with links to daily updated arts stories and a comprehensive calendar of events. Otherwise, the best listings magazines are the weekly *Guía del Ocio* (Ⓦ guiadelociobcn.com) and *Time Out Barcelona* (Ⓦ timeout.cat), online or from any newspaper stand. There's also a free monthly "Cultural Agenda" guide in English available from tourist offices and the Palau de la Virreina.

17

CLASSICAL, CONTEMPORARY AND OPERA

Most of Barcelona's **classical** music concerts take place in the *modernista* Palau de la Música Catalana or at the purpose-built, contemporary L'Auditori, while **opera** is performed at its traditional home, the Gran Teatre del Liceu on the Ramblas. Many of the city's churches, including the cathedral and Santa María del Mar, also host concerts and recitals, while other interesting venues holding concerts include the historic Saló del Tinell in the Ajuntament, Palau Robert, FNAC Triangle at Plaça de Catalunya, Caixa Forum, the Fundació Joan Miró and CCCB (these last two particularly for **contemporary** music). Notable **festivals** include the summer-long Festival de Barcelona Grec, Nous Sons ("New Sounds"), the annual contemporary music festival (March–April), the Festival de Música Antiga (May), the Festa de la Música (June 21), and the Festival Opera Butxaca (Pocket Opera Festival; Nov), while there are free concerts in Barcelona's parks each July, the so-called Clàssics als Parcs.

VENUES

★ **Ateneu Barcelonès** c/de la Canuda 6, Barri Gòtic ☎ 933 426 121, Ⓦ ateneubcn.org; concert information ☎ 933 191 789, Ⓦ masimas.com; Ⓜ Catalunya; map p.46. Jazz-flamenco promoters Mas i Mas sponsor an excellent chamber music programme at the 150-year-old Ateneu cultural association, under the banner "30 minutes of music". Performances are on Fri, Sat and Sun at 6pm, 7pm & 8pm (entry €8) while the Ateneu also hosts plenty of other activities and concerts.

L'Auditori c/de Lepant 150, Glòries ☎ 932 479 300, Ⓦ auditori.org; Ⓜ Marina/Glòries; map pp.118–119. The city's main contemporary concert hall is home to the Orquestra Simfònica de Barcelona i Nacional de Catalunya (OBC), whose weekend concert season runs Sept–May. L'Auditori also puts on other orchestral and chamber works, jazz and world gigs and music for children and families, while it's the main venue for the annual Early Music and Contemporary Music festivals. Under-26s with ID get fifty-percent discount on all tickets, 1hr before performances. Box office Mon–Sat noon–9pm, Sun 1hr before performance.

Casa Elizalde c/de València 302, Dreta de l'Eixample ☎ 934 880 590, Ⓦ casaelizalde.com; Ⓜ Passeig de Gràcia; map p.104. Small-scale classical concerts and recitals, plus more offbeat contemporary performances, are held at this cultural centre, usually with free entry.

Gran Teatre del Liceu Ramblas 51–59 ☎ 934 859 900; box office c/de Sant Pau 1 ☎ 934 859 913, Ⓦ liceu barcelona.com; Ⓜ Liceu; map p.38. One of Europe's finest opera houses hosts a wide-ranging programme of opera and dance productions, plus other concerts and recitals including the extremely popular *sessions golfes* (late-night concerts). The season runs Sept–June. Make bookings well in advance by phone or online – sales for the next season go on general sale in mid-July. Box office Mon–Fri 1.30–8pm, Sat & Sun 1hr before performance.

★ **Palau de la Música Catalana** c/del Palau de la Música 4-6, off c/Sant Pere Més Alt, Sant Pere ☎ 932 957 200 or ☎ 902 442 882, Ⓦ palaumusica.org; Ⓜ Urquinaona; map p.70. The extravagantly decorated Catalan concert hall is home to the Orfeó Català choral group and venue for concerts by the Orquestra Ciutat de Barcelona among others, though there's a broad remit here – over a season you can catch anything, from *sardanes* to pop concerts. Concert season Sept–June. Box office Mon–Sat 10am–9pm, Sun 2hr before performance.

DANCE

Barcelona is very much a contemporary dance city, with its own dedicated dance venue, Mercat de les Flors, as well as regular performances by regional, national and international artists and companies at theatre venues (see p.210) like the TNC, Teatre Lliure and Institut del Teatre – the latter, the city's theatre and dance school, has its own youth dance company, IT Dansa. The Dies de Dansa (Days of Dance) **festival** in July offers up brief (10–20min) contemporary dance performances of all kinds in courtyards at places like MACBA, CCCB, Caixa Forum and the Picasso and Miró museums. Although its home is indisputably Andalucia, flamenco also has deep roots in and around Barcelona, courtesy of its *andaluz* immigrants – unless you're looking for a showy night out, the pricey, tourist-oriented *tablaos* (flamenco and dinner shows) are best passed up in favour of the smaller clubs and restaurants that put on performances. If you're here at the end of April, don't

17

THE SARDANA – DANCING WITH CATALANS

If you're intrigued by what looks like a mass dance flash mob outside the cathedral, La Seu, chances are you've stumbled upon a performance of the Catalan national dance – the **sardana**. Its origins are obscure, though similar folk dances in the Mediterranean date back hundreds if not thousands of years. It was established in its present form during the mid-nineteenth-century Renaixença (Renaissance), when Catalan arts and culture flourished, and was so identified with expressions of national identity that public dancing of *sardanes* was banned under the Franco regime. Sometimes mocked elsewhere in Spain, Catalans claim it to be truly democratic – a circle-dance open to all, danced in ordinary clothes (though some wear espadrilles) with no restriction in age or number. The dancers join hands, heads held high, arms raised, and though it looks deceptively simple and sedate it follows a precise pattern of steps, with shifts in pace and rhythm signalled by the accompanying *cobla* (band) of brass and wind instruments. This features typically Catalan instruments like the *flabiol* (a type of flute), and both tenor and soprano oboes, providing the characteristic high-pitched music. A strict etiquette applies to prevent the circle being broken in the wrong place, or a breakdown in the steps, and some of the more serious adherents may not welcome an intrusion into their circle by well-meaning first-timers. But usually visitors are encouraged to join the dance, especially at festival times, when the *sardana* breaks out spontaneously in the city's squares and parks.

There are regular *sardana* dances held outside La Seu, in Plaça de la Seu (M Jaume I), every Sunday at noon, plus every Saturday at 6pm from Easter until the end of November. The **Federació Sardanista de Catalunya** (W fed.sardanista.cat) also publishes a calendar of dances and events on its website.

---

miss the wild flamenco shows and parties of the Feria de Abril de Catalunya, a ten-day **festival** held down at the Fòrum site, and there are also two other flamenco festivals each year, De Cajón in winter (Jan–March) and the old town's Festival de Flamenco in May.

DANCE VENUE
Mercat de les Flors c/de Lleida 59, Montjuïc ☎ 934 261 875, W mercatflors.cat; M Poble Sec; map p.91. The city's old flower market serves as the "national centre for movement arts", with dance the central focus of its varied programme – from Asian performance art to European contemporary dance.

FLAMENCO CLUBS
El Tablao de Carmen Poble Espanyol, Montjuïc ☎ 933 256 895, W tablaodecarmen.com; M Espanya; map p.91. The long-standing *tablao* in the Poble Espanyol at least looks the real deal, sited in a replica Andalucian street and featuring a variety of flamenco styles from both

seasoned performers and new talent. From €35 for the show and a drink, rising to €70 for the show plus dinner. Advance reservations essential. Tues–Sun, shows at 7.30pm & 10pm.

★ **Tarantos** Pl. Reial 17, Barri Gòtic ☎ 933 191 789, W masimas.com; M Liceu; map p.46. Some purists are sniffy about the experience, but for a cheap flamenco taster you can't beat *Tarantos* – a couple of rows of seats and a small bar in front of a stage where young singers, dancers and guitarists perform nightly. It's the sister club to jazz/dance club *Jamboree*, at the same address. Entry €7. Performances at 8.30pm, 9.30pm & 10.30pm, plus extra nightly session in July & Aug.

FILM

At most of the larger cinemas and multiplexes films are usually shown dubbed into Spanish or Catalan. However, several cinemas do show mostly **original-language** (*versión original* or V.O.) foreign films; the best are listed below. Tickets cost around €8, and most cinemas have one night (usually Mon or Wed) when entry is **discounted**, usually to around €6. Many cinemas also feature **late-night** screenings (*madrugadas*) on Fri and Sat nights, which begin at 12.30 or 1am. The city hosts

several small film **festivals** throughout the year, including an international festival of independent short films, plus festivals devoted specifically to animation, women's, gay and lesbian, Asian, and African film. The Generalitat's FilmoTeca is often the venue for festival screenings. The sci-fi, horror and fantasy fest that is the Festival Internacional de Cinema de Fantastic (W sitgesfilmfestival.com) is held down the coast in nearby Sitges in October.

TOP 5 CULTURE ON A BUDGET
L'Antic Teatre See p.210
Ateneu Barcelonès See p.207
Casa Elizalde See p.207
FilmoTeca See opposite
Tarantos See above

CINEMAS

★ **Cinema Maldà** c/del Pi 5, Barri Gòtic ☎ 933 019 350, ⓦ cinemamalda.net, Ⓜ Liceu; map p.46. Hidden away in a little shopping centre just up from Plaça del Pi, the Maldà is a great place for independent movies and festival winners, all in V.O.

Filmoteca Av. de Sarrià 33, Esquerra de l'Eixample ☎ 934 107 590, ⓦ gencat.cat/cultura/icic/filmoteca; Ⓜ Hospital Clinic; map p.113. Run by the Catalan government, the Filmoteca shows three or four different films (often foreign-language, and usually in V.O.) every day – the programme changes every couple of weeks, and themed seasons, classic films, retrospectives and obscure world cinema releases are its stock-in-trade. Tickets are just €3 per film, or there's an €40 pass allowing entry to twenty films. A new cinema building is being constructed in the Raval for the FilmoTeca, but for the time being it will still be based at Av. de Sarrià.

Méliès Cinemes c/de Villaroel 102, Esquerra de l'Eixample ☎ 934 510 051, ⓦ cinesmelies.net; Ⓜ Urgell; map p.113. A repertory cinema specializing in V.O. showings (classics, indie and art-house), with three to five different films daily in its two salas. Discount night is Mon.

Verdi/Verdi Park Verdi c/de Verdi 32, Gràcia; Verdi Park, c/de Torrijos 49, Gràcia; ☎ 932 387 990, ⓦ cines-verdi.com; Ⓜ Fontana; map p.126. Gràcia's popular sister cinemas are in adjacent streets, showing independent, art-house and V.O. movies from around the world on nine screens. Late-night films at Verdi on Fri & Sat; discount night Mon.

Yelmo-Icaria c/de Salvador Espriu 61, Centre de la Vila, Port Olímpic ☎ 932 217 585, ⓦ yelmocines.es; Ⓜ Ciutadella-Vila Olímpica; map p.85. Fifteen screens showing mainstream Hollywood V.O. movies at a shopping centre multiplex, a few minutes' walk from the Port Olímpic. Late-night screenings Fri & Sat; discount night Mon.

OPEN-AIR CINEMA

Sala Montjuïc Castell de Montjuïc ☎ 933 023 553, ⓦ salamontjuic.org, ⓦ servicaixa.com; cable car (Telefèric de Montjuïc) or cinema bus (normal tickets and passes valid) from Pl. d'Espanya (Ⓜ Espanya), departures from 8.30pm, returns when film finishes; map p.91. Every July there's a giant-screen open-air cinema established on the grass under the walls at Montjuïc castle (Mon, Wed & Fri night; tickets €5, deck-chair rental €3) – you're encouraged to bring a picnic. Screenings are in the original language, with Spanish subtitles, and range from current art-house hits to film club stalwarts like *Some Like it Hot*. The films usually start at 10.15pm, with live music first from 9pm, but with space limited to 2500 it's best to get there at opening time (8.30pm) or buy in advance through ServiCaixa.

THEATRE AND CABARET

The **Teatre Nacional de Catalunya** (Catalan National Theatre) was specifically conceived as a venue to promote Catalan productions, and features a repertory programme of translated classics (such as Shakespeare in Catalan), original works and productions by guest companies from Europe. The other big local theatrical project is the **Ciutat del Teatre** (Theatre City) on Montjuïc, which incorporates the fringe-style Mercat de les Flors, the progressive Teatre Lliure and the Institut del Teatre theatre and dance school. The centre for commercial theatre is on and off the Ramblas and along Avinguda Paral.lel and the nearby streets. For **children's theatre**, see Chapter 22. Some theatres draw on the city's

---

ON LOCATION

You can fall in love with Barcelona all over again with a stack of DVDs and a giant bucket of popcorn. Major movie event of recent years for the city was Woody Allen's extended homage to its photogenic landmarks in **Vicky Cristina Barcelona** (2008), a frothy love triangle – partly financed by the city administration, who definitely got their money's worth – that bounced from the Barri Gòtic to the Sagrada Família. However, film buffs point back to 1975 and Michelangelo Antonioni's **The Passenger** as the first major film to showcase the city's attractions, as Jack Nicholson negotiates Gaudí rooftops and cable cars in a cryptic case of stolen identity. Madrid's inimitable Pedro Almodóvar gave his own seedy, oddball take on Barcelona in **All About My Mother** (1999) – an Oscar winner for Best Foreign Language Film – while in Tom Tykwer's **Perfume** (2006), the city's atmospheric old town stood in for eighteenth-century Paris in the adaptation of Patrick Süskind's cult novel. However, the two most arresting Barcelona movies to date show not a single colourful landmark or famous sight, being set entirely within the confines of a Rambla de Catalunya mansion block. All you glean of the city from Jaume Balagueró and Paco Plaza's zombie-virus-shockers **Rec** (2007) and **Rec 2** (2009) is never to join the Barcelona fire brigade, and never to take a hand-held camera (*rec* = record) into a locked-down apartment building…

17

CATALAN THEATRE COMPANIES

Els Comediants (W comediants.com) – a travelling collective of actors, musicians and artists, established in 1971, who use any open space as a stage to celebrate "the festive spirit of human existence".

La Cubana (W lacubana.es) is a highly original company that started life as a street theatre group, though it has since moved into television and theatre proper. It still hits the streets occasionally, taking on the role of market traders in the Boqueria or cleaning cars in the street in full evening dress.

Dagoll Dagom (W dagolldagom.com) specializes in hugely theatrical, over-the-top musicals.

La Fura del Baus (Vermin of the Sewer; W lafura.com) are performance artists who aim to shock and lend a new meaning to audience participation. They've subsequently taken on opera, cabaret, film and installations, lending each a wild, challenging perspective.

Els Joglars (W elsjoglars.com) present political theatre, and are particularly critical of the Church and government, who come in for regular satirical attacks.

Teatre Nu (Naked Theatre; W teatrenu.com) was founded in 1991 by young Catalan actors who wanted to bring theatre back to its essence and "provoke social, moral and ideological dialectic between the audience and public".

Tricicle (W tricicle.com) – a very successful three-man mime, circus and theatre group – has branched off into film and television, but always places its humour "somewhere between reality and the absurd".

strong **cabaret** tradition – particularly burlesque, music-hall entertainment – which is far more accessible to non-Catalan or Spanish speakers than straight theatre. **Tickets** are available from theatre box offices, or the usual agency outlets, while for last-minute tickets visit the counter at the Palau de la Virreina (Ramblas 99; Mon–Sat 10am–8.30pm), which offers same-day half-price tickets from three hours before the start of the show. The summer **Festival de Barcelona Grec** always has a strong theatre and dance programme; many performances are at the open-air Teatre Grec on Montjuïc (see p.96).

THEATRES

Institut del Teatre Pl. de Margarida Xirgu, Montjuïc ☎ 932 273 900, W institutdelteatre.org; M Poble Sec; map p.91. The school for dramatic arts and dance has a regular programme of events scheduled at its two theatres, where you can catch performances by the current crop of students.

Teatre Lliure Pl. de Margarida Xirgu, Montjuïc ☎ 932 892 770, W teatrelliure.cat; M Poble Sec; map p.91. The "Free Theatre" performs the work of contemporary Catalan and Spanish playwrights, as well as reworkings of the classics, from Shakespeare to David Mamet (some productions have English surtitles). It also hosts visiting dance companies, concerts and recitals. The original theatre, a smaller auditorium in Gràcia, also has a full programme.

Teatre Nacional de Catalunya (TNC) Pl. de les Arts 1, Glòries ☎ 933 065 700, W tnc.cat; M Glòries; map pp.118–119. Intended to foster Catalan works, the national theatre – built as a modern emulation of an ancient Greek temple – features major productions by Catalan, Spanish and European companies, as well as smaller-scale plays, experimental works and dance productions.

Teatre Poliorama Ramblas 115, El Raval ☎ 933 177 599, W teatrepoliorama.com; M Catalunya; map p.38. Specializes in modern drama (Catalan and translation) and

musicals, often utilizing the talents of offbeat companies like Tricicle and Dagoll Dagom (see box above).

Teatre Romea c/de l'Hospital 51, El Raval ☎ 933 181 431, W teatreromea.com; M Liceu; map pp.60–61. Has an emphasis on contemporary Catalan and Spanish playwrights and pan-European productions, and gives space to new theatre groups and radical directors.

CABARET AND OTHER VENUES

L'Antic Teatre c/de Verdaguer i Callis 12, Sant Pere ☎ 933 152 354, W lanticteatre.com; M Urquinaona; map p.70. A small, independent theatre with a wildly original programme of events, many free, from video shows and art exhibitions to offbeat cabaret performances, modern dance and left-field music. In the end though, the best bit may just be the bar (open daily 4–11pm) and summer garden *terrassa*.

★ **Café Teatre Llantiol** c/de la Riereta 7, El Raval ☎ 933 299 009, W llantiol.com; M Sant Antoni; map pp.60–61. Idiosyncratic cabaret café-theatre whose varied shows feature a mix of mime, song, clowning, magic and dance, and sometimes there's English-language stand-up comedy by local and visiting acts. Shows (€10–15) normally begin at 9pm & 11pm (6pm & 9pm on Sun), with an additional late-night Saturday special. Closed Mon.

El Molino c/Vila i Vilà 99, Av. Paral.lel, Poble Sec ☎ 932 055 111, ⓦ elmolinobcn.com; Ⓜ Paral.lel; map p.98. One of Barcelona's most famous old cabaret theatres reopened in 2010 after many years in mothballs, and the self-styled "Little Moulin Rouge" has a classy new look for its traditional burlesque and music stage shows. There are big-production lunch and dinner shows – signature show is "Made in Parallel", an all-singing, all-dancing tribute to the city of Barcelona – with performances daily from Wed to Sun (lunch show from €45, evening show and drink from €40, show plus dinner

TOP 5 BIG NIGHTS OUT 17

L'Auditori See p.207
El Molino See above
Gran Teatre del Liceu See p.207
Palau de la Música Catalana See p.207
Teatre Nacional de Catalunya See opposite

from €80), plus Mon tango and Tues flamenco nights (varied prices).

VISUAL ARTS

Barcelona has dozens of **private art galleries** and exhibition halls in addition to the temporary displays on show in its art centres, museums and galleries. Major venues with regularly changing art exhibitions include Caixa Forum, CCCB, MACBA and Fundació Antoni Tàpies for contemporary art; Espai 13 at Fundació Joan Miró for young experimental artists; MNAC and La Pedrera for blockbuster international art shows; FAD for industrial and graphic art, design, craft and architecture; and Arts Santa Mònica for contemporary Catalan art and photography. A few more specialist places are listed below. **Commercial galleries** cluster together in the Barri Gòtic on c/de la Palla and c/de Petritxol near the church of Santa María del Pi; in La Ribera on c/de Montcada and Passeig del Born; in El Raval on c/dels Àngels and c/del Doctor Dou near the MACBA; and in the Eixample on Passeig de Gràcia, c/del Consell de Cent and Rambla Catalunya. Note that most commercial galleries are closed on Sun, Mon and in August. The weekly *Guía del Ocio* and the Associació de Galeries d'Art Contemporani (ⓦ artbarcelona.es) have gallery listings and exhibition news. In spring **photography** fans should look out for the Primavera Fotogràfica, when photography exhibitions are held at various venues around the city.

ART AND CULTURAL CENTRES

La Capella c/de l'Hospital 56, El Raval ☎ 934 427 171, ⓦ bcn.cat/lacapella; Ⓜ Liceu; map pp.60–61. This space in the medieval Hospital de la Santa Creu promotes contemporary art of all kinds, though is often a platform for work by young Barcelona artists.

Fundació Foto Colectania c/de Julian Romea 6, Gràcia ☎ 932 171 626, ⓦ colectania.es; Ⓜ Fontana; map p.126. A private foundation that puts on exhibitions culled from the work of more than sixty Spanish and Portuguese photographers, with works from the 1950s onwards.

Gap Gallery c/de Sant Honorat 11, Barri Gòtic ☎ 931 862 865, ⓦ gapgallery.com; Ⓜ Jaume I; map p.46. Part of the not-for-profit "Gràcia Arts Project" (ⓦ graciaarts project.com), which has a long-term plan to open an arts centre in Gràcia, this old-town gallery meanwhile hosts a widely varied programme of arts shows, installations and music and multimedia events.

Palau Robert Pg. de Gràcia 107, Dreta de l'Eixample ☎ 932 388 091, ⓦ gencat.cat/palaurobert; Ⓜ Diagonal; map p.104. The Catalan government's information office and gallery space sponsors a wide range of shows, all with a Catalan connection.

Palau de la Virreina Ramblas 99, Barri Gòtic ☎ 933 161 000, ⓦ bcn.cat/virreinacentredelaimatge; Ⓜ Liceu; map p.38. Changing shows at the city council's cultural HQ concentrate on contemporary culture, social studies and photography.

Sala d'Art Jove de la Generalitat c/Calabria 147, Esquerra de l'Eixample ☎ 934 838 361; Ⓜ Rocafort; map p.113. The Generalitat's youth art space is for artists under 30 – expect anything from formal portraiture to one-off installations. Closed Aug.

COMMERCIAL GALLERIES

Galleria Joan Prats Rambla de Catalunya 54, Dreta de l'Eixample ☎ 932 160 290, ⓦ galeriajoanprats.com; Ⓜ Passeig de Gràcia; map p.104. One of the city's best-regarded galleries for the works of contemporary Catalan artists and photographers.

H2O c/de Verdi 152, Gràcia ☎ 934 151 801, ⓦ h2o.es; Ⓜ Fontana/Lesseps; map p.128. Independent gallery working in the fields of architecture, design, photography and contemporary art.

Kowasa c/de Mallorca 235, Esquerra de l'Eixample ☎ 934 876 137, ⓦ kowasa.com; Ⓜ Diagonal; map p.113. Traditional and contemporary photography and photographic art, featuring Spanish and international photographers; it's above the photography bookshop of the same name.

Sala Parés c/de Petritxol 5–8, Barri Gòtic ☎ 933 187 020, ⓦ salapares.com; Ⓜ Liceu; map p.46. Possibly the most famous gallery in the city, established in the mid-nineteenth century, Sala Parés hosted Picasso's first show. It still deals exclusively in nineteenth- and twentieth-century Catalan art, putting on around twenty exhibitions a year, including a biannual "Famous Paintings" exhibition of works by some of the best-known Spanish and Catalan names.

ARENA

Gay and lesbian Barcelona

There's a vibrant gay and lesbian scene in Barcelona (or "Gaycelona", as some would have it), backed up by an established organizational infrastructure and a generally supportive city council. Information about the scene – known in Spanish as el ambiente, "the atmosphere" – is pretty easy to come by, while locals and tourists alike are well aware of the lure of Sitges, mainland Spain's biggest gay resort, just forty minutes south by train. Bars, clubs, restaurants and hotels aimed specifically at a gay and lesbian clientele are scattered across Barcelona, though there's a particular concentration in the so-called Gaixample, the "Gay Eixample", an area of a few square blocks just northwest of the university in the Esquerra de l'Eixample. But you'll also be well received at plenty of other nominally straight dance bars and clubs in a city that's generally welcoming to its gay and lesbian visitors.

ESSENTIALS

Accommodation Finding sympathetic accommodation in the city isn't a problem, as there's any number of chic, boutique properties with a gay-friendly vibe. Barcelona also has one out-and-out gay hotel, the very cool, "heterofriendly" *Hotel Axel* (see p.174), which is right in the middle of the Gaixample district. Or contact Outlet4Spain (☎ 938 102 711, ⓦ outlet4spain.com), an accommodation agency that specializes in gay-friendly hotels, villas, apartments and flat-shares in Barcelona and Sitges.

Information For up-to-date information and other advice on the gay scene, you can call any of the organizations listed under "Useful contacts" below, or try the lesbian and gay city telephone hotline on ☎ 900 601 601 (toll free; daily 6–10pm only).

What's on Aside from the weekly bar and club listings in *Guía del Ocio* (ⓦ guiadelociobcn.es, in Spanish) and *Time Out Barcelona* (ⓦ timeout.cat, in Catalan), there's also a good free magazine called *Nois* (ⓦ revistanois.com, in Spanish), which carries an up-to-date review of the scene in Barcelona and Catalunya. Single best English-language website is the excellent 60by80 (ⓦ 60by80.com), which has its finger on the pulse of all things hot, from shopping to partying.

18

USEFUL CONTACTS

Antinous c/de Josep Anselm Clavé 6, Barri Gòtic ☎ 933 019 070, ⓦ antinouslibros.com; ⓜ Drassanes. Gay and lesbian bookshop with useful contacts and information board, and a café at the back. Mon–Fri 10am–2pm & 5–8pm, Sat noon–2pm & 5–8pm.

Ca la Dona c/de Casp 38, Dreta de l'Eixample ☎ 934 127 161, ⓦ caladona.org; ⓜ Urquinaona. A women's centre with library and bar, used for meetings by various feminist and lesbian organizations; information available to callers.

Casal Lambda c/de Verdaguer i Callís 10, Sant Pere ☎ 933 195 550, ⓦ lambda.cat; ⓜ Urquinaona. A gay and lesbian centre with a wide range of social, cultural and educational events.

Cómplices c/de Cervantes 2, Barri Gòtic ☎ 934 127 283, ⓦ libreriacomplices.com; ⓜ Liceu. Exclusively gay and lesbian bookshop; also magazines and DVDs. Mon–Fri 10.30am–8pm, Sat noon–8pm.

Coordinadora Gai-Lesbiana de Catalunya (CGL) c/de Violant d'Hongria 156, Sants ☎ 932 980 029, ⓦ cogailes.org; ⓜ Plaça del Centre. The CGL issues the "Rainbow Card", which, for €10 per month, gives discounts, free admission and other advantages at a wide variety of businesses and venues across the city.

Front d'Alliberament Gai de Catalunya (FAGC) c/de Verdi 88, Gràcia ☎ 932 172 669, ⓦ fagc.org; ⓜ Fontana. Association for gay men, with a library, meetings and events.

CAFÉS AND BARS

Aire c/de Valencia 236, Esquerra de l'Eixample ☎ 934 515 812, ⓦ arenadisco.com; ⓜ Passeig de Gràcia; map p.113. The hottest, most stylish lesbian bar in town is a relaxed place for a drink and a dance to pop, house and retro sounds. Gay men are welcome too. Thurs–Sat 11pm–3am, July & Aug also Tues & Wed.

Átame c/del Consell de Cent 257, Esquerra de l'Eixample ☎ 934 549 273; ⓜ Universitat; map p.113. Contemporary music bar with a change of pace, from early evening drinks and gentility to late-night hot sounds. Daily 6pm–2am.

Bim Bam Bum Zeltas c/de Casanova 75, Esquerra de l'Eixample ☎ 934 541 902, ⓦ bimbambum.es;

ⓜ Universitat; map p.113. Pumped-up house-music bar for the pre-club crowd. Wed–Sun 10.30pm–3am.

Dietrich c/del Consell de Cent 255, Esquerra de l'Eixample ☎ 934 517 707; ⓜ Universitat; map p.113. Cornerstone of the Gaixample scene is this well-known music bar and "teatro-café" – *tranquilo* during the week, but ever more hedonistic as the weekend wears on, with drag shows, acrobats and dancers punctuating the DJ sets. Daily 10pm–2.30am (Fri & Sat until 3am).

People Lounge c/de Villarroel 71, Esquerra de l'Eixample ☎ 935 327 743, ⓦ peoplebcn.com; ⓜ Urgell; map p.113. Stylish cafe-bar where you shouldn't feel out

PARTY TIME

The biggest event of the year – in the country's biggest gay-friendly resort – is **Carnival** in Sitges (see p.146), while the main city bash is Barcelona's annual LGBT **Pride** festival (ⓦ pridebarcelona.org), which has events running over ten days each June, from street parades and stiletto races to Tibidabo fun-fair parties. Barcelona is also often the venue of choice for other international gatherings – in the past, the city has hosted the **Eurogames** (the European Gay and Lesbian Sports Championships), while the gay and lesbian **Circuit** festival (ⓦ circuitfestival.net) is a Barcelona stalwart. For movie buffs there's the annual **Barcelona International Gay and Lesbian Film Festival** (ⓦ www.cinemalambda.com), usually in July, while the appearance of the sun also sees the city's **Mar Bella** beach come into its own as Barcelona's own gay summer beach zone.

TOP 5 GAY-FRIENDLY BARS

Betty Ford See p.198
La Concha See p.199
Schilling See p.197
Universal See p.205
Velòdromo See p.202

---

18 CLUBS

Arena Madre c/de Balmes 32, Esquerra de l'Eixample; Classic c/de la Diputació 233; VIP Grand Via de les Corts Catalanes 593; Dandy Grand Via de les Corts Catalanes 593; ☎ 934 878 342, ⓦ arenadisco.com; Ⓜ Passeig de Gràcia; map p.113. The *Madre* "mother" club sits at the helm of the Arena empire, all within a city block (pay for one, get in to all) – frenetic house at *Arena Madre*, high disco antics at *Arena Classic*, more of the same plus dance, R&B, pop and rock at the more mixed *Arena VIP* and vintage chart hits at *Arena Dandy*. Fri & Sat 12.30–6am, Madre daily till 5.30am.

Matinée Ronda de Sant Pere 19–21, Dreta de l'Eixample, no phone, ⓦ matineegroup.com; Ⓜ Urquinaona; map

p.104. The Matinée group ring the changes at their club HQ according to the night, starting on Friday with DMix (for everyone), and moving on with DBoy (Saturday) and La Madame (Sunday), all offering a nonstop fusion of beats. Fri, Sat & Sun midnight–6am.

Metro c/de Sepúlveda 158, Esquerra de l'Eixample ☎ 933 235 227, ⓦ metrodiscobcn.com; Ⓜ Universitat; map p.113. A gay institution in Barcelona, with cabaret nights and other events midweek, and extremely crowded club nights at weekends, playing current dance, techno and retro disco. Daily midnight–5am (Fri & Sat until 6am).

of place if you're over 40. Mon–Sat 8pm–3am, Sun 7pm–3am.

Punto BCN c/de Muntaner 63–65, Esquerra de l'Eixample ☎ 934 536 123, ⓦ arenadisco.com; Ⓜ Universitat; map p.113. A Gaixample classic that attracts a lively crowd for drinks, chat and music. Wednesday happy hour is a blast, while Friday night is party night. Daily 6pm–2.30am.

FESTES DE LA MERCÈ

Festivals and holidays

Almost any month you choose to visit Barcelona you'll coincide with a saint's day, festival or holiday, and it's hard to beat the experience of arriving to discover the streets decked out with flags and streamers, bands playing and the entire population out celebrating. Traditionally, each neighbourhood celebrates with its own festa, though the major ones – like Gràcia's Festa Major and the Mercè – have become city institutions, complete with music, dancing, traditional parades and firework displays. The religious calendar has its annual highlights too, with Carnival, Easter and Christmas as popular times for parades, events and festivities across the city. Meanwhile, biggest and best of the annual arts and music events are the summer Festival de Barcelona Grec, the ever-expanding Sónar extravaganza of electronic music and multimedia art and the rock and indie fest that is Primavera Sound.

There's a **month-by-month calendar** below of the best annual festivals, holidays, trade fairs and events, though it's not an exhaustive list. For more information about what's going on at any given time, call into the cultural information office at the **Palau de la Virreina**, Ramblas 99, or check out the Ajuntament's useful **website** (ⓦbcn.cat/cultura).

Incidentally, not all **public holidays** coincide with a festival, but many do (see p.33). In addition, saints' day festivals – indeed all Catalan celebrations – can vary in date, often being observed over the weekend closest to the dates given.

JANUARY

Cap d'Any New Year's Eve. Street and club parties, and mass gatherings in Pl. de Catalunya and other main squares. You're supposed to eat twelve grapes in the last twelve seconds of the year for twelve months of good luck. The next day, Jan 1, is a public holiday.

Cavalcada dels Reis Afternoon of Jan 5. This is when the Three Kings (who distribute Christmas gifts to Spanish children) arrive by sea at the port and ride into town, throwing sweets as they go. The parade begins at about 5pm on Jan 5; the next day is a public holiday.

Festa dels Tres Tombs Jan 17. The first big festival of the year is the costumed horseback parade through the Sant Antoni neighbourhood, with local saint's day festivities to follow. *Tomb* is the Catalan word for a circuit, or tour, so the riders make three processional turns of the neighbourhood.

Barnasants Dates vary, Jan–April ⓦbarnasants.com. A singer-songwriter festival (Catalan/Spanish, plus Brazilian and Latin American artists), with more than a hundred gigs held over three months in city clubs and concert venues.

De Cajón! Jan–March ⓦtheproject.cat. Big-name flamenco stars perform a series of one-off concerts in major city concert halls.

FEBRUARY

Festes de Santa Eulàlia Feb 12 ⓦbcn.cat/santa eulalia. The depths of winter are interrupted by festivities in honour of Eulàlia, the young Barcelona girl who suffered a beastly martyrdom by the Romans. She's a revered patron of the city, and her saint's day falls on Feb 12, around which are held a weeks worth of celebrations with a focus on children and families – parades of giants, *sardanes*, dances, concerts, *castellers* (see box below) and fireworks. Lots of historic buildings and museums are also open for free on the day.

Carnaval/Carnestoltes Week before Lent, sometimes in March. Costumed parades, dances, concerts, open-air barbecues and other traditional carnival events take place in every city neighbourhood. The big city parade is down Av. Paral.lel, where you're encouraged to don a mask and join in. However, it's Sitges, on the coast, which has the most outrageous celebrations.

MARCH/APRIL

Festes de Sant Medir de Gràcia First week in March. A horse-and-carriage parade around Gràcia, which then heads to the Sant Medir hermitage in the Collserola hills. Later, the procession returns to Gràcia, where thousands of sweets are thrown to children along the route, and there's plenty of traditional dancing and feasting.

Setmana Santa Easter, Holy Week. Religious celebrations and services at churches throughout the city. Special services are on Thurs and Fri in Holy Week at 7–8pm, Sat at 10pm; there's a procession from the church of Sant Agustí on c/de l'Hospital (El Raval) to La Seu, starting at around 4pm on Good Friday; and Palm Sunday

CASTLES IN THE SKY

Guaranteed to draw crowds at every festival are the teams of **castellers** – castle-makers – who pile person upon person, feet on shoulders, to see who can construct the highest, most aesthetically pleasing tower. It's an art that goes back over two hundred years, combining individual strength with mutual cooperation – perhaps this is why it was discouraged as an activity under Franco. Nowadays, it's very popular once again, with societies known as *colles* in most Catalan towns who come together to perform at annual festivals and events. There's a real skill to assembling the *castell*, with operations directed by the *cap de colla* (society head) – the strongest members form the crowd at the base, known as the *pinya*, with the whole edifice topped by an agile child, the *anxaneta*, who lifts their palm above their head to "crown" the castle. Ten human storeys is the record. For more see ⓦcastellersdebarcelona.cat.

CLOCKWISE FROM TOP FLAMING LIPS, PRIMAVERA SOUND (P.218); FESTES DE LA MERCÈ (P.219); ACROBATS, FESTIVAL GREC (P.218) >

sees the blessing of the palms at La Seu. Public holidays on Good Friday and Easter Monday.

Dia de Sant Jordi St George's Day, April 23. St George's Day, dedicated to Catalunya's dragon-slaying patron saint, is a day of national identity – the Catalan flag appears everywhere and red roses (the colour of the dragon's blood) are the bloom of choice, with the two coming together at the Palau de la Generalitat, the home of the Catalan government. The saint's day has been entwined over the years with two other occasions, so that it's also a kind of local Valentine's Day (traditionally, men give their sweethearts a rose…) and International Book Day (…and receive a book in return). You'll be hard pushed to escape stumping up for either as you run the gauntlet of stalls down the Ramblas.

Feria de Abril de Catalunya Last week in April ⓦ fecac.com. The region's biggest Andalucian festival, with ten days of food, drink and flamenco. All the action goes down at the big marquees erected at the Parc del Fòrum plaza (Diagonal Mar).

Festival de Guitarra April & May ⓦ theproject.cat. A spring-season perennial, the annual guitar festival showcases all sorts of musical styles – jazz and Latin, blues and fusion – with some big names playing every year. Gigs are at concert halls across the city.

Saló Internacional del Còmic Dates vary, April or May ⓦ ficomic.com. The International Comic Fair takes place over three days, with stalls, drawing workshops and children's activities at one of the city's exhibition halls.

19 MAY

Dia del Treball May 1. May Day/Labour Day is a public holiday, with union parades along main city thoroughfares.

Dia de San Ponç May 11. A traditional saint's day, celebrated by a market running along c/de l'Hospital in the Raval, with fresh herbs, flowers, aromatic oils and sweets.

Festival de Música Antiga Usually first two weeks ⓦ auditori.org. The Early Music Festival attracts medieval and Baroque groups from around the world, with concerts based at L'Auditori concert hall and free fringe shows outdoors in old-town squares.

Barcelona Poesia Second or third week ⓦ bcn.cat /barcelonapoesia. Week-long poetry festival with readings and recitals in venues across the city. It incorporates the Jocs Floral (Floral Games), a medieval Catalan poetry competition, while Spanish and foreign poets converge for the International Poetry Festival at the Palau de la Música Catalana.

Dia Internacional dels Museus May 18. On International Museum Day, there's free entrance to all city-run museums – local press have details of participating museums, opening hours and special events.

Corpus Christi Late May/early June. See box, p.50.

Primavera Sound Usually last week ⓦ primavera sound.com. The city's hottest music festival heralds a massive three-day bash down at the Parc del Fòrum (Diagonal Mar), attracting superstar names in the rock, indie and electronica world. It's extended into the city and Poble Espanyol too, with club gigs and free street gigs now part of the scene.

Festival de Flamenco de Ciutat Vella Usually last week ⓦ flamencociutatvella.com, ⓦ tallersdemusics. com. Annual old-town flamenco bash, organized by the Taller de Músics (music workshop) and centred on the CCCB. Five days of guitar recitals, singing and dancing, plus DJ sessions and chill-out zone, and lectures and conferences on all matters flamenco.

JUNE

Sónar Usually 2nd or 3rd week ⓦ sonar.es. The International Festival of Advanced Music and Multimedia Art is Europe's biggest and most cutting-edge electronic music, multimedia and urban art festival, attracting up to 100,000 visitors for three days of brilliant noise and spectacle. Sónar by day centres on events at MACBA and the CCCB; by night the action shifts to out-of-town L'Hospitalet, with all-night buses running from the city to the Sónar bars and clubs. Separate day, night and general tickets available – buy well in advance.

Festa de la Música June 21. Every year on this day scores of free concerts are held in squares, parks, civic centres and museums in every neighbourhood across the city – from buskers to orchestras, folk to techno. There are concerts in the two or three preceding days too, so you're bound to catch something you like.

Verbena/Dia de Sant Joan June 23–24. The "eve" and "day" of St John herald probably the wildest celebrations in the city, with a "night of fire" of bonfires and fireworks across Barcelona. It marks a hedonistic welcome to summer, with parties in full swing in every neighbourhood and pyrotechnics on Montjuïc and Tibidabo. *Coca de Sant Joan*, a sweet flatbread, and cava are the traditional accompaniments to the merriment. The traditional place to end the night is on the beach, watching the sun come up – thankful that the dawning day (June 24) is a public holiday.

Festival de Barcelona Grec June–Aug ⓦ barcelona festival.com. Since the 1970s, the summer's foremost arts and music festival has centred its performances on Montjuïc's open-air Greek theatre (see p.96) – a dramatic location for cutting-edge Shakespearean productions or events by Catalan avant-garde performance artists, while music ranges from the likes of Philip Glass to African rap. There are also concerts, plays and dance productions at the CCCB and city theatres – in total, around fifty different events held over a six-week period.

JULY

Dies de Dansa 1st week ⓦ marato.com. Part of the summer Grec festival, this five-day contemporary dance extravaganza sees free daytime performances in buildings, parks, streets, squares, museums and galleries across the city, plus evening events and video projections at the CCCB.

Montjuïc de Nit 1st week ⓦ bcn.cat/cultura/montjuicnit. Once a year, Montjuïc's galleries throw open their doors for the night, while parks, spaces and buildings across the whole hillside throb with free gigs, dance, theatre, films, street art and family events, running until the small hours.

AUGUST

Festa Major de Gràcia Mid-Aug ⓦ festamajordegracia .cat. What was once a local village festival is now an annual city highlight, with banging music, boisterous dancing, wackily decorated floats and streets transformed into magical scenes, plus the usual noisy fireworks, parades of giants and devils and human castle-building in main squares. The festivities last a week – don't miss them if you're in town.

Festa Major de Sants Last week of Aug. Another week's worth of traditional festivities in an untouristed neighbourhood, in the streets behind Barcelona Sants station.

San Miguel Mas i Mas Festival ⓦ masimas.com. The quietest summer month gets a shot in the arm with a music festival by promoters Mas i Mas that crosses genres, hip-hop to classical jazz, at a variety of venues across the city.

19

SEPTEMBER

Diada Nacional Sept 11. Catalan national day, commemorating the eighteenth-century defeat at the hands of the Bourbons. It's a public holiday in Barcelona, and special events include the city's more radical Catalan nationalists throwing bricks through burger-bar windows, fighting with the police and showing their patriotism by spraying graffiti on every available space.

Festes de la Mercè Sept 24 ⓦ bcn.cat/merce. The biggest annual festival, held around Sept 24 (a public holiday), is dedicated to Our Lady of Mercy, co-patroness of the city, whose image is paraded from the church of la Mercè near the port. It's an excuse for a week of merrymaking,

including costumed giants, breathtaking firework displays and competing teams of *castellers* – not to mention outdoor concerts, bicycle races, children's events and even free admission to city museums and galleries on the saint's day. During the week, the concurrent alternative music festival, known as BAM (ⓦ bcn.cat/bam), puts on free rock, world and fusion gigs at emblematic old-town locations and at Parc del Fòrum.

Festa Major de Sant Miquel Last week. Traditional festivities on the waterfront as Barceloneta celebrates its saint's day with fireworks, parades, *castellers*, music and dancing.

OCTOBER/NOVEMBER

LEM Throughout Oct ⓦ gracia-territori.com. Experimental and electronic music and art festival organized by the Gràcia Territori Sonor collective, with free or cheap concerts, events and happenings held in Gràcia's bars, cafés and galleries.

Festival de Tardor Ribermúsica Third week ⓦ riber musica.org. Wide-ranging four-day music festival held in the Born, with free concerts in historic and picturesque locations.

Festival Internacional de Jazz Last week in Oct and through Nov ⓦ barcelonajazzfestival.com. The biggest annual jazz festival in town has been going for more than four decades and attracts superstar solo artists and bands to the clubs and concert halls, as well as putting on smaller-scale street concerts.

Festival Opera Butxaca Last week in Oct and through Nov ⓦ festivaloperabutxaca.org. The "Pocket Opera

CELEBRATING CATALAN-STYLE

Central to any Catalan festival is the parade of **gegants**, the overblown five-metre-high giants with a costumed frame (to allow them to be carried) and papier-mâché or fibreglass heads. Barcelona has its own official city gegants of King Jaume and his queen (there's more at ⓦ gegantsbcn.cat), while each neighbourhood cherishes its own traditional figures, from elegant noblewomen to turban-clad sultans – the Barri Gòtic's church of Santa Maria del Pi has some of the most renowned. Come festival time they congregate in the city's squares, dancing cumbersomely to the sound of flutes and drums, and accompanied by smaller, more nimble figures known as **capgrossos** (bigheads) and by outsized lions and dragons. Also typically Catalan is the **correfoc** (fire-running), where brigades of drummers, fire-breathing dragons and demons with firework-flaring tridents cavort in the streets. It's as devilishly dangerous as it sounds, with intrepid onlookers attempting to stop the dragons passing, as firecrackers explode all around – approach with caution.

SOME THINGS YOU MIGHT HAVE MISSED ...

If you look beyond the big-name acts and the major annual celebrations, there's a whole world of off-the-radar festive fun in Barcelona, with some events just putting a toe in the water and others growing more elaborate with each year. February's **Minifestival** (Ⓦ minifestival.net), for example, provides a neat suburban counterpoint to the bigger city music fests, highlighting international indie acts that you've definitely never heard of. In May, **Loop** (Ⓦ loop-barcelona .com), the international fair and festival for video art, attracts hundreds of artists from dozens of countries. September sees the ever-improving **Festival Àsia** (Ⓦ casaasia.es/festival), with dance, theatre, music, DJs, children's activities, performance art and workshops showcasing the culture of Asia and the Pacific Region. By October, digi-heads and Second Lifers are ready for **Artfutura** (Ⓦ artfutura.org), the digital culture and creativity festival, while alternative Christmas shopping is best done at **Drap-Art** (Ⓦ drapart.org), the Festival of Creative Recycling, which puts on its annual bash and market at the CCCB.

19

Festival" showcases new Catalan and European operas, with performances in the smaller theatres and spaces at the Liceu, TNC, L'Auditori and other venues.

Tots Sants All Saints' Day, Nov 1. When the Spanish remember their dead with cemetery visits and special meals, it's traditional to eat roast chestnuts (*castanyes*), sold by street vendors, sweet potatoes and *panellets* (almond-based sweets). It's also a public holiday.

DECEMBER

Fira de Santa Llúcia Dec 1–22. For more than two hundred years the Christmas season has seen a special market and crafts fair outside the cathedral. Browse for gifts or watch the locals snapping up Christmas trees, Nativity figures and traditional decorations.

Nadal/Sant Esteve Dec 25–26 Ⓦ bcn.cat/nadal. Christmas Day and St Stephen's Day are both public holidays, which Catalans tend to spend at home – the traditional gift-giving is on Twelfth Night (Jan 6). Each year, there's a Christmas Nativity scene erected in Pl. de Sant Jaume, Barri Gòtic, which stays there for the whole of Dec and the first week in Jan.

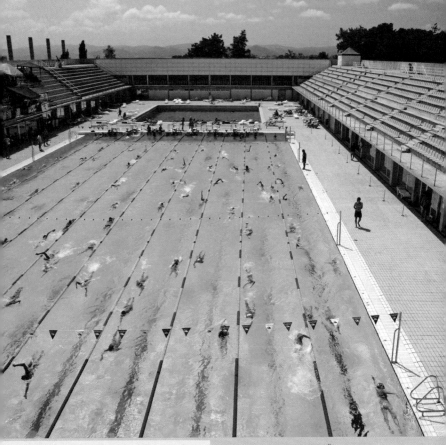

PISCINA MUNICIPAL DE MONTJUÏC

Sports and outdoor activities

Barcelona is well placed for access to the sea and mountains, which is one of the reasons it was picked for the 1992 Olympics – the event that really put the modern city on the map. A spin-off from the games was an increased provision of top-quality sports and leisure facilities throughout Catalunya, which have attracted an increasing number of major games events – half a million spectators watched the European Athletics Championships when they were held here in 2010, the IAAF World Junior Championships hit the city in 2012, and the World Swimming Championships arrive in 2013. However, while there are scores of sports centres and swimming pools in Barcelona, there aren't actually that many that will appeal to tourists or casual visitors. Most people are content to relax on the city beaches or take off for a hike or jog in the surrounding hills of the Parc del Collserola.

ESSENTIALS

Information Servei d'informació Esportiva (☎010, ⓦbcn.cat, look under "Esports"), the city council's sports information service, is the main source of information about municipal sports facilities. It also has a drop-in office (Direcció d'Esports) on Montjuïc at Av. de l'Estadi 30–40 (ⓜEspanya), at the side of the Picornell swimming pool.

Tickets Tickets for all major sporting events can be bought from the agencies, ServiCaixa (☎902 332 211, ⓦservi caixa.com), TelEntrada (☎902 101 212, ⓦtelentrada.com) or Ticketmaster (☎902 150 025, ⓦticketmaster.es).

BASKETBALL

Second only to football in popularity in Catalunya, basketball has been played in Barcelona since the 1920s. Games are usually played September to June at weekends, with most interest in the city's two main teams. **Club Joventat de Badalona**, founded in 1930, were European champions in 1994, while **FC Barcelona** finished runners-up five times before finally becoming European champions in 2003, a title they regained in 2010. It's easiest to go and watch FC Barcelona, as Badalona is out in the sticks. The team plays at the Palau Blaugrana, adjacent to the Camp Nou.

Tickets Tickets to games are fairly inexpensive (€13–65, depending on the seat and game), and you can either buy tickets online (ⓦfcbarcelona.com) or go to the stadium (the day before the game) – see "Football" opposite for main stadium contact details.

CYCLING

Cycling is being heavily promoted by the city authorities as a means of transport. There's a successful **bike-sharing scheme** (known as Bicing) while around 160km of cycle paths traverse the city, with plans to double the network in the future. Not all locals have embraced the bike, and some cycle paths are still ignored by cars or are clogged with pedestrians, indignantly reluctant to give way to two-wheelers. But, on the whole, cycling around Barcelona is not the completely hairy experience it was. The nicest place to get off the road is the **Parc del Collserola**, where there are bike trails for varying abilities through the woods and hills. **Montjuïc** is another popular place for mountain-biking – there's a weekend rental outfit up behind the castle. Bikes are allowed on the metro, on FGC trains and on the Montjuïc and Vallvidrera funiculars.

Bike tours The best way to see the city by bike – certainly as a first-time visitor – is to take a bike tour (see p.26); bikes and equipment will be provided.

Bike rental You can rent a bike from one of the outlets listed in "City tours" (see p.25).

Maps You might want to pick up the map detailing current cycle paths. It's available from the tourist office, or on the city council's website ⓦbcn.cat/bicicleta.

Races and festivals The city hosts a variety of annual cycling events, including the main regional race, the Volta a Catalunya (ⓦvoltacatalunya.cat) every March. June sees the Ajuntament's annual Festa de la Bici (Bicycle Fiesta), while September is another big month, with races during the Mercè festival and a day during the city's "Mobility Week" dedicated to cycling. In October, there's the Escalada a Montjuïc, an annual international hill-climb race on Montjuïc

BYE-BYE BULLS

Bullfights are an integral part of many southern Spanish festivals, and while Catalunya too has had a long, if less renowned bullfighting tradition, the more progressive city of Barcelona has always stood somewhat apart. The one surviving bullring, the **Plaza de Toros Monumental**, Gran Via de les Corts Catalanes 749 (ⓜMonumental) – site, incidentally, of the Beatles' only ever concert in Barcelona, in 1965 – kept going for many years with the dwindling support of local aficionados and tourists from the Costa Brava, but the writing had been on the wall since Barcelona roundly declared itself an anti-bullfight city in 2004. In July 2010 the Catalan parliament followed suit, with an historic vote to ban bullfighting in Catalunya, the second autonomous community to do so (after the Canary Islands). The 2011 bullfight season was the last in Barcelona, with the future of the Monumental bullring still undecided – though whatever happens to it, the impressive, circular Moorish-style facade is likely to be retained as an historic part of the city patrimony.

USEFUL CONTACTS

Amics de la Bici c/Demóstenes 19, Sants ☎ 933 394 060, ⓦ amicsdelabici.org; ⓜ Plaça de Sants. The "Friends of the Bike" organize a full range of events and activities, from rides to bike-mechanic courses.

Esport Ciclista Barcelona ⓦ ecbarcelona.net. Founded in 1929, the cycle sports club organizes the Escalada a Montjuïc – details available on their website.

TOP 5 GREATEST EVER BARCELONA PLAYERS

Carles Rexach (1965–81)
Johan Cruyff (1973–78)
Ronaldinho (2003–08)
Samuel Eto'o (2004–09)
Lionel Messi (2004–)

FOOTBALL

To be honest, there's only one sport in Barcelona and that's football, as played by local heroes **FC** (Futbol Club) **Barcelona**. The team is worshipped at the Camp Nou stadium in the north of the city and, even if you don't coincide with a game, the stadium's football museum and tour alone is worth the trip (see p.131). The other local team – though not to be compared – is **RCD** (Reial Club Deportiu) **Espanyol**, whose games are played at their 40,000-seater stadium at Cornellà, west of the city centre. The season runs from late August until May, with games usually played on Sundays (though sometimes on other days). You'll have little problem getting a ticket to see an Espanyol game – you can usually just turn up on the day – and, perhaps surprisingly, it's also fairly straightforward to get tickets for FC Barcelona. The Camp Nou seats 98,000, which means it's only really full for big games against rivals like Real Madrid, or for major European ties.

TEAM CONTACTS

FC Barcelona Camp Nou, Av. Arístides Maillol, Les Corts ☎ 934 963 600, ⓦ fcbarcelona.com; ⓜ Collblanc/Maria Cristina; map pp.132–133. Tickets go on general sale (online or at the stadium) a week or more before each match, or try ServiCaixa or Ticketmaster. Season-ticket holders who aren't attending the match put their seats up for sale through the club, right up until kick-off

time, so it's not advised to buy tickets from touts at the ground. For a typical league game you're likely to pay from €50 (and be seated *very* high up), though prices run as high as €140.

RCD Espanyol Av. Baix Llobregat 100, Cornellà de Llobregat ☎ 932 927 700, ⓦ rcdespanyol.com; ⓜ Cornellà Centre, then 20min walk. Most tickets cost €40–90; you can buy online and pick your tickets up on the day.

HORSERIDING

Escola Municipal d'Hípica La Foixarda Av. Montanyans 1, Montjuïc ☎ 934 261 066, ⓦ hipicalafoixarda.com; ⓜ Espanya, then bus #50; map p.91. The municipal riding school on Montjuïc offers lessons and

courses for adults (beginners especially welcome), children and disabled people, or you can just have a taster with an hour-long riding session from around €15. Office open Mon–Fri 5.30–8pm, Sat & Sun 9am–1.30pm & 5–9pm.

ICE-SKATING

There are a couple of ice rinks in the city, including one at FC Barcelona's Camp Nou stadium, and a seasonal rink at the Parc del Fòrum at Diagonal Mar. At the Roger de Flor rink there's a café-bar from where you can watch the action. It's a good idea to check hours and restrictions before you go, as weekends and holidays especially can see the rinks inundated with children. Note that gloves are compulsory for all skaters and helmets for under 12s, and both can be rented at the rinks.

ICE RINKS

Pavelló Pista Gel Camp Nou, c/d'Arístides Maillol 12, Les Corts ☎ 934 963 630, ⓦ fcbarcelona.com; ⓜ Collblanc/Maria Cristina; map pp.132–133. Morning and afternoon skating sessions daily throughout the year, times vary; closed Aug. Admission €12, including skate rental. Also a skating school, for classes of all ages and levels.

Skating Pista de Gel c/de Roger de Flor 168, Dreta de l'Eixample ☎ 932 452 800, ⓦ skatingclub.cat; ⓜ Tetuan; map pp.118–119. Morning and afternoon skating sessions daily throughout the year, times vary. Admission €14, including skate rental.

ROLLERBLADING, SKATING AND SKATEBOARDING

The Passeig Marítim and Port Olímpic area (ⓜ Ciutadella-Vila Olímpica) see heavy **skate and blade** traffic, while other popular runs include Arc de Triomf (ⓜ Arc de Triomf), Parc Joan Miró (ⓜ Tarragona) and Barceloneta, next to the Palau del Mar (ⓜ Barceloneta). The Fòrum site down at Diagonal Mar (ⓜ El Marseme Forum) has acres of wide open space. You're supposed to keep off all marked cycle paths. Meanwhile, *the* place for **skateboarders** is the piazza outside MACBA, the contemporary art gallery in the Raval.

20

RUNNING AND JOGGING

The **Passeig Marítim** (ⓦ Ciutadella-Vila Olímpica) is the best place for a seafront run – there's a five-kilometre promenade from Barceloneta all the way to the River Besòs, with a fitness circuit on the way at Mar Bella beach. To get off the beaten track, you'll need to head for the heights of Montjuïc or the Parc del Collserola.

Races and festivals There's a half-marathon (Mitja Marató de Barcelona) held in the city every February or March, while the full Barcelona Marathon (Marató Barcelona; application forms and details on ⓦ barcelonamarato.es) takes place in March. There are more road races during the September Mercè festival, while La Cursa (ⓦ cursaelcorteingles.com; April), the annual twelve-kilometre run organized by El Corte Inglés department store, attracts over 50,000 fun-runners onto the streets. It's one of the longest-established city runs, held since 1979, and the 1994 event, attracting 110,000 runners, stills hold the Guinness world record for number of participants.

SPORTS CENTRES

Every city neighbourhood has a sports centre, most with swimming pools but also offering a variety of other sports, games and activities. Schedules and prices vary, so it's best to contact the centres directly for any sport you might be interested in. Most have a general daily admission fee (€15–20) if all you want is a swim and use of the gym. A couple of the more useful centres are listed below, but for a full rundown call ❼ 010 or consult the sports section database on ⓦ bcn.cat.

Poliesportiu Marítim Pg. Marítim 33, Vila Olímpica ❼ 932 240 440, ⓦ claror.cat; ⓦ Ciutadella-Vila Olímpica; map p.85. Large complex by the Port Olímpic with a pool, gym and sauna, plus a wide range of organized activities, games and treatments, from aerobics, dance and yoga to indoor biking, beach tennis and hydrotherapy. Mon–Fri 7am–midnight, Sat 8am–9pm, Sun 8am–4pm.

Poliesportiu Municipal Frontó Colom Ramblas 18, Barri Gòtic ❼ 933 023 295, ⓦ frontocolom.com; ⓦ Drassanes; map p.38. Centrally situated sports centre with pool and gym, where you can see traditional Spanish *frontón* (handball) or Basque *jai alai*, reputedly the fastest sport in the world. Mon–Fri 7.30am–10.30pm, Sat 9am–8pm, Sun 9am–2.30pm.

SWIMMING

The city **beaches** are fine for a stroll across the sand and an ice cream, but the water's none too welcoming and you'd do best to save your swimming for the region's coastal beaches (Sitges is the best) or one of Barcelona's many municipal **pools**. There are scores of them, but we've picked out three of the best below. You may be required to show your passport before being allowed in, and you'll need to wear a swimming cap. If you're hardy enough, the annual Christmas Swimming Cup involves diving into the port on December 25 and racing other like-minded fools.

SWIMMING POOLS

Club Natació Atlètic Barceloneta Pl. del Mar, Barceloneta ❼ 932 210 010, ⓦ cnab.org; ⓦ Ciutadella-Vila Olímpica; map p.79. One indoor pool, two outdoor, plus bar, restaurant and gym facilities. Mon–Fri 6.30am–11pm, Sat 7am–11pm, Sun 8am–5pm (until 8pm mid-May to Sept). Daily admission for non-members is €11, under-10s €7.

Piscina Municipal de Montjuïc Av. Miramar 31, Montjuïc ❼ 934 430 046; Funicular de Montjuïc; map p.91. The city's most beautiful outdoor pool, low on facilities but high on Montjuïc – it was built for the Olympic diving competitions. Mid-June to early Sept: daily 11am–6.30pm. Admission €5, under-14s €3.50.

Piscines Picornell Av. de l'Estadi 30–38, Montjuïc ❼ 934 234 041, ⓦ picornell.cat; ⓦ Espanya, then bus #50; map p.91. Remodelled and expanded for the Olympics, the fifty-metre indoor pool is open all year, while the outdoor pool is open to the public from June to Sept. Nudist sessions all year on Sat night, plus Sun pm Oct–May.

FOLLOW THAT CAR

Catalunya's motor racing circuit, the **Circuit de Catalunya** (ⓦ circuitcat.com), hosts the annual Formula 1 Spanish Grand Prix in April/May, as well as a whole series of other Spanish and Catalan bike and motor races throughout the year, from truck-racing to endurance rallies. The track is out near Granollers, north of the city (trains from Sants/Pg. de Gràcia, a twenty-minute walk from Montmeló station, but during the Grand Prix there are also shuttle-bus services and direct buses from Barcelona. For Formula 1, you need to sort out tickets well in advance (they go on sale the previous August; check the website), while sports travel companies can offer special race packages.

20

Indoor pool and other facilities Mon–Fri 7am–midnight, Sat 7am–9pm, Sun 7.30am–4pm (until 8pm July–Sept); outdoor pool usually 9am–9pm. Outdoor €5.50 (under-14s €4), indoor €10 (under-14s €7), includes gym and sauna.

TENNIS

Municipal tennis courts, including Vall d'Hebron, are listed on the city council website ⓦ bcn.cat or the English-language ⓦ barcelona-tennis.com, while for private clubs consult the website of the Federació Catalana de Tennis (ⓦ fctennis.cat). One of these, the Reial Club de Tennis Barcelona-1899 (ⓦ rctb1899.es), hosts the **Barcelona Open** every April.

TENNIS COURTS

Centre Municipal de Tenis Pg. Vall d'Hebron 178–196, Vall d'Hebron ☎ 934 276 500; Ⓜ Montbau. The main municipal tennis centre at Vall d'Hebron, in the northeastern suburbs, is the best place to play. Unlike many clubs in the city, you can rent courts by the hour without being a member. There are asphalt and clay courts, costing around €20–25 an hour, plus a pool, gym and café. Rackets are available for rent. Public hours Mon–Fri 8am–11pm, Sat & Sun 8am–9pm.

WATERSPORTS

Base Nàutica Municipal Av. Litoral, Platja Mar Bella ☎ 932 210 432, ⓦ basenautica.org; Ⓜ Ciutadella-Vila Olímpica, then bus #41; map p.85. You can rent catamarans and windsurfers, and there's a popular bar here as well. Prices vary considerably, but you can expect to pay from around €40 for a couple of hours' windsurfer rental or €200 for a two-day elementary sailing course. Open all year: hours vary, though April–Sept daily 10am–7pm.

Centre Municipal de Vela Moll de Gregal, Port Olímpic ☎ 932 257 940, ⓦ velabarcelona.com; Ⓜ Ciutadella-Vila Olímpica; map p.85. Port Olímpic's sailing club has courses and instruction in catamaran and Laser sailing, kayaking and windsurfing, from two hours to two days. Prices are much the same as at Base Nàutica Municipal. Mon–Fri 9am–9pm, Sat & Sun 9am–8pm.

20

CASA GISPERT

Shopping

While for sheer size and scope Barcelona cannot compete with Paris or other fashion capitals, it is one of the world's most stylish cities – architecture, fashion and decoration are thoroughly permeated by Catalan *disseny* (design). All of this makes for great shopping, whether you're looking for unique clothing by a hot local designer or something stylish for the home. Traditional arts and crafts have a place here too, from basketware to ceramics, and many artists and craftworkers have workshops that are open to the public. Antiques and curios abound, while souvenirs range from the gloriously tacky to the outrageously wacky – a walk down the Ramblas and through the Barri Gòtic alone throws up anything from Picasso T-shirts to Peruvian bangles, not to mention Barcelona football scarves, handmade soap, carnival masks, designer chocolates and vintage dresses.

21

The best **general shopping area** for clothes, souvenirs, arts and crafts is the Barri Gòtic, particularly between the upper part of the Ramblas and Avinguda Portal de l'Àngel. Established designer and **high-street fashion** is at home in the Eixample, along Passeig de Gràcia, Rambla de Catalunya and c/de Pelai, as well as along Avinguda Diagonal in Les Corts. Hot **new designers and boutiques** – including shoe, street- and skatewear specialists – can be found in La Ribera, around Passeig del Born (c/dels Flassaders, c/del Rec, c/de Calders, c/de l'Espartería, c/de la Vidrería, c/del Bonaire), but also down c/d'Avinyó in the Barri Gòtic, between c/del Carme and MACBA in El Raval, and along c/de Verdi in Gràcia. For **secondhand and vintage clothing**, stores line the whole of c/de la Riera Baixa (El Raval), with others nearby on c/del Carme and c/de l'Hospital, and on Saturdays there's a street market here. More bargains are in the **remainder stores, wholesalers and discount outlets** found along c/de Girona in the Eixample, between the Gran Via and Ronda Sant Pere.

For **antiques** – books, furniture, paintings and artefacts – you need to trawl c/de la Palla, c/dels Banys Nous and surrounding streets in the Barri Gòtic, best combined with the antique market on Thursdays in front of the cathedral. **Delis and specialist food shops** tend to be concentrated around the Passeig del Born in La Ribera. Independent **music and CD stores** are found on and around c/dels Tallers (El Raval), just off the top of the Ramblas. And don't forget the city's **museums and galleries**, where you'll find reasonably priced items ranging from postcards to wall-hangings.

ESSENTIALS

Opening hours Shop opening hours are typically Mon–Sat 10am–1.30/2pm & 4.30–7.30/8pm, though all the bigger shops stay open over lunchtime, while smaller shops close on Saturday afternoons and/or may vary their hours in other ways. Major department stores and shopping malls open Mon–Sat 10am–10pm, though the cafés, restaurants and leisure outlets in malls are usually open on Sunday too. Barcelona's daily food markets, all in covered halls, are generally open from Mon–Sat 8am–3pm & 5–8pm (local variations apply),

though the most famous, La Boqueria on the Ramblas, opens throughout the day.

Sales The annual sales (*rebaixes*, *rebajas*) follow the main fashion seasons – mid-January until the end of February, and throughout July and August.

Tax refunds Non-EU residents can get an IVA (ie VAT) refund on each purchase over the value of €90; if there's a "Tax-Free Shopping" sticker displayed at the store (🆆 spain refund.com), ask for the voucher and claim the refund at the airport before leaving.

ANTIQUES

★ **L'Arca de l'Avia** c/dels Banys Nous 20, Barri Gòtic ☎ 933 021 598, 🆆 larcadelavia.com; 🅜 Liceu; map p.46. Catalan brides used to fill up their nuptial trunk (*arca*) with embroidered bed linen and lace, and this shop is a treasure-trove of vintage and antique textiles. Period (eighteenth to early-twentieth century) costumes can be hired or purchased as well – one of Kate Winslet's *Titanic* costumes came from here. Mon–Fri 10am–2pm & 5–8pm, Sat 10am–2pm; closed Aug.

Bulevard dels Antiquarius Pg. de Gràcia 55–57, Dreta de l'Eixample ☎ 932 154 499, 🆆 bulevarddels antiquaris.com; 🅜 Passeig de Gràcia; map p.104. An arcade with over seventy shops full of antiques of all kinds,

from toys and dolls to Spanish ceramics and African art. Mon–Sat 10am–8.30pm; closed Sat in Aug.

Mercantic c/Rius i Taulet 120, Sant Cugat del Vallès ☎ 936 744 950, 🆆 mercantic.com; FGC Sant Cugat. This permanent antiques and collectables market is out in the suburbs but makes a great trip for casual browsers and serious collectors alike. You'll find everything from furniture to farm machinery, old radios to vintage jewellery, postcards to erotic drawings, plus an outdoor flea market (Sun until 3pm), weekly lot auctions (Sat) and trade markets (1st Sun of each month). Tues–Sat 9.30am–8pm, Sun 9.30am–3pm; closed Aug.

ARTS, CRAFTS AND GIFTS

Artesania Catalunya c/dels Banys Nous 11, Barri Gòtic ☎ 934 674 660, 🆆 artesania-catalunya.com; 🅜 Liceu; map p.46. It's always worth a look in the "Emprentes de Catalunya" showroom of the local government's arts and

crafts promotion board. Exhibitions change, but most of the work is contemporary in style, from basketwork to glassware, though traditional methods are still very much encouraged. Mon–Sat 10am–8pm, Sun 10am–2pm.

21

CRAFT WORKSHOPS

Crafts have always been central to Barcelona's industry, with a history dating back to the Middle Ages. Many of the street names in the Born (ⓂJaume I/Barceloneta), particularly, refer to the crafts once practised there; eg c/de la Argenteria, silversmith's street, c/dels Mirallers, the street where they used to make mirrors, c/de la Vidriería, glassmakers' street, or c/dels Sombrerers, where hats (*sombreros*) were made. Over the last couple of decades, neighbourhoods like the Born, El Raval and Poble Nou have once again become craft centres as empty buildings and warehouses have been opened up as workshops. Some artists work behind closed doors, while others have a space at the front where they sell their limited series or unique pieces.

A good way to see the Ciutat Vella (old town) workshops is to coincide with the **Tallers Oberts**, or open workshops (ⓦtallersoberts.net), usually held over the last two weekends of May, when there are studio visits, exhibitions, children's workshops, guided tours and lots of other events. Or contact Barcelona tour agency My Favourite Things (ⓦmyft.net), who can organize a workshop tour on request, introducing you directly to selected artists.

Cereria Subirà Bxda. de la Llibreteria 7, Barri Gòtic ☎933 152 606; ⓂJaume I; map p.46. Barcelona's oldest shop (it's been here 1760) has a beautiful interior, and sells unique hand-crafted candles. Mon–Fri 9am–1.30pm & 4–7.30pm, Sat 9am–1.30pm.

★ **Espai Drap Art** c/d'en Groc 1, Barri Gòtic ☎932 684 889, ⓦdrapart.org; ⓂJaume I; map p.46. The Drap-Art creative recycling organization has a shop and exhibition space for artists to show their wildly inventive wares, from trash-bangles to tin bags. Tues–Fri 11am–2pm & 5–8pm, Sat 6–9pm.

★ **Fantastik** c/de Joaquín Costa 62, El Raval ☎933 013 068, ⓦfantastik.es; ⓂUniversitat; map pp.60–61. Beguiling gifts, crafts and covetable objects from four continents. You'll never know how you lived without them, whether it's Chinese robots, African baskets, Russian domino sets or Vietnamese kitchen scales. Mon–Thurs 11am–2pm & 4–9pm, Fri & Sat 11am–9pm.

Papirum Bxda. de la Llibreteria 2, Barri Gòtic ☎933 105 242, ⓦpapirum-bcn.com; ⓂJaume I; map p.46. For all your writing needs – hand-painted paper, draughtsman's pens, leather-bound notebooks, calligraphy sets and more. Mon–Fri 10am–8.30pm, Sat 10am–2pm & 5–8.30pm.

Taller Textil Teranyina c/del Notariat 10, El Raval ☎933 179 436, ⓦteresarosa.com; ⓂCatalunya; map pp.60–61. Teresa Rosa Aguayo opened her Raval textile workshop in 1987, and continues to weave striking contemporary carpets, rugs and wall-hangings, and make textile jewellery and other objects. You can call in any time to see the design work being carried out, or sign up for one of the courses. Mon–Fri 11am–3pm & 5–8pm.

BOOKS

GENERAL

Casa del Llibre Pg. de Gràcia 62, Dreta de l'Eixample ☎932 723 840, ⓦcasadellibro.com; ⓂPasseig de Gràcia; map p.104. Barcelona's biggest book emporium, strong on literature, humanities and travel, with plenty of English-language titles and Catalan literature in translation. Mon–Sat 9.30am–9.30pm.

★ **La Central del Raval** c/d'Elisabets 6, El Raval ☎902 884 990, ⓦlacentral.com; ⓂCatalunya; map pp.60–61. Occupying a unique space in the former Misericordia chapel, La Central is a fantastically stocked arts and humanities treasure-trove, with books piled high in every nook and cranny. There's a big English-language section (and other European languages too), while other La Central outlets are found in MACBA (contemporary art museum) and MUHBA (Barcelona History Museum). Mon–Fri 9.30am–9pm, Sat 10am–9pm.

Come In c/de Balmes 129, Esquerra de l'Eixample ☎934 531 204, ⓦlibreriainglesa.com; ⓂDiagonal; map p.113. Stocks only English-language books and literature, and is also a good place for language-learning and teaching aids. Mon–Fri 9.30am–8.30pm, Sat 9.30am–2pm & 4.30–8pm.

Laie c/de Pau Claris 85, Dreta de l'Eixample ☎933 181 739, ⓦlaie.es; ⓂPasseig de Gràcia; map p.104. This has been one of Barcelona's favourite bookshops for years, though probably just as much for its café-restaurant, which is a good place to unwind. Other speciality Laie arts outlets are found in galleries like Caixa Forum, CCCB, La Pedrera, Museu Picasso and the Liceu. Mon–Fri 10am–9pm, Sat 10.30am–9pm.

ART, DESIGN AND PHOTOGRAPHY

Kowasa c/de Mallorca 235, Esquerra de l'Eixample ☎932 158 058, ⓦkowasa.com; ⓂDiagonal; map p.113. The city's best bookshop for photography and photographic art. Mon–Fri 10am–8.30pm, Sat 11am–2pm & 5–8.30pm.

Museu Nacional d'Art de Catalunya Palau Nacional, Montjuïc ☎936 220 376, ⓦmnac.cat; ⓂEspanya; map p.91. Doubled in size since the museum refurbishment, the MNAC bookshop has the city's widest selection of books on

Catalan art, architecture, design and style. Tues–Sat 10.15am–6.45pm, Sun 10.15am–2.30pm.

★ **Ras** c/del Doctor Dou 10, El Raval ☎ 934 127 199, ⓦ rasbcn.com; ⓜ Catalunya; map pp.60–61. Specializes in books and magazines on graphic design, architecture, photography and contemporary art. It's a cutting-edge gallery space, too, so the exhibitions here are always worth a look. Tues–Sat noon–8pm.

COMICS AND GRAPHIC BOOKS

Norma Comics Pg. de Sant Joan 9, Dreta de l'Eixample ☎ 932 448 423, ⓦ normacomics.com; ⓜ Arc de Triomf; map p.118. Spain's best comic and graphic-novel shop, for everything from manga to the Caped Crusader, plus DVDs and all kinds of related gear and gizmos. Mon–Sat 10.30am–8.30pm.

SECONDHAND

★ **Hibernian Books** c/de Montseny 17, Gràcia ☎ 932 174 796, ⓦ hibernian-books.com; ⓜ Fontana; map p.126. Barcelona's best secondhand English bookshop has around 40,000 titles in stock, and there are always plenty of giveaway bargains available. There are new titles available as well and you can part-exchange. Mon 4–8.30pm, Tues–Sat 10.30am–8.30pm.

TRAVEL, GUIDES AND MAPS

★ **Altaïr** Gran Via de les Corts Catalanes 616, Esquerra de l'Eixample ☎ 933 427 171, ⓦ altair.es; ⓜ Universitat; map p.113. Europe's biggest travel superstore has a massive selection of travel books, guides, maps and world music, plus a programme of travel-related talks and exhibitions. Mon–Sat 10am–8.30pm.

Llibreria Quera c/de Petritxol 2, Barri Gòtic ☎ 933 180 743, ⓦ llibreriaquera.com; ⓜ Liceu; map p.46. The most knowledgeable place in town for Catalan and Pyrenean maps and trekking guides, plus anything else to do with the great outdoors. Tues 10am–8pm, Wed–Sat 10am–1.30pm & 4.30–8pm; closed Sat in Aug.

CLOTHES, SHOES AND ACCESSORIES

DESIGNER FASHION

Antonio Miró c/del Consell de Cent 349, Dreta de l'Eixample ☎ 934 870 670, ⓦ antoniomiro.es; ⓜ Passeig de Gràcia; map p.104. The showcase for Barcelona's most innovative designer, Antonio Miró – especially good for classy suits, though now also branding accessories and household design items. Mon–Sat 10.30am–8.30pm.

Armand Basi Pg. de Gràcia 49, Dreta de l'Eixample ☎ 932 151 421, ⓦ armandbasi.com; ⓜ Passeig de Gràcia; map p.104. Colourful men's and women's jackets, jeans, dresses and casual wear from the hot Spanish designer. There's also a full range of accessories – watches to fragrances – though the must-have items are the designer table- and kitchenware created with superchef Ferran Adrià. Also outlets also at La Roca Village and El Corte Inglés. Mon–Sat 10.30am–8.30pm.

Camisería Pons c/Gran de Gràcia 49, Gràcia ☎ 932 177 292, ⓦ camiseriapons.com; FGC Gràcia; map p.126. Originally a *modernista* shirt shop, this beautiful space has been transformed into a showcase for contemporary Spanish fashion designers. Mon–Sat 10am–2pm & 5–8.30pm.

Custo Barcelona Pl. de les Olles 7, La Ribera ☎ 932 687 893; ⓜ Barceloneta; map p.70; Pl. del Pi 2, Barri Gòtic ☎ 933 042 753; ⓜ Liceu; map.46; ⓦ custo-barcelona .com. Selling hugely colourful designer tops and sweaters for men and women, this is where the stars get their T-shirts. There are lots of Custo stores all over the city, but La Ribera's adds a bright splash to the medieval alleys, while last season's gear gets another whirl at the Pl.del Pi discount outlet in the Barri Gòtic. Mon–Sat 10am–9pm, Sun noon–8pm.

Jean-Pierre Bua Av. Diagonal 469, Esquerra de l'Eixample ☎ 934 397 100, ⓦ jeanpierrebua.com; ⓜ Hospital Clínic; map p.113. The city's high temple for fashion victims: a postmodern shrine for Yamamoto, Gaultier, Miyake, McQueen, McCartney, Westwood and other international stars. Mon–Sat 10am–2pm & 4.30–8.30pm.

★ **Naifa** c/del Doctor Dou 11, El Raval ☎ 933 024 005; ⓜ Liceu; map pp.60–61. Original, colourful and informal men's and women's collections by Argentinian designer Paula Guillaumin. Mon–Sat 11.30am–3pm & 4.30–9pm.

★ **Natalie Capell** Atelier de Moda c/dels Banys Vells 4, entrance at c/de la Carassa 2, La Ribera ☎ 933 199 219, ⓦ nataliecapell.com; ⓜ Jaume I; map p.70. Where "each dress carries a story", the boutique stocks her own very elegant designs, in 1920s- and 1930s-style, every one sewn and colour-dyed by hand. Tues–Sat noon–8.30pm.

Purificación García Pg. de Gràcia 21, Dreta de l'Eixample ☎ 934 877 292, ⓦ purificaciongarcia.es; ⓜ Passeig de Gràcia; map p.104. A hot designer with an eye for fabrics – García's first job was in a textile factory. She's also designed clothes for films, theatre and TV, and her costumes were seen at the opening ceremony of the Barcelona Olympics. The eponymous shop's a beauty, with the more casual items and accessories not particularly stratospherically priced. Mon–Sat 10am–8.30pm.

HIGH-STREET FASHION

Mango Pg. de Gràcia 8–10, Dreta de l'Eixample ☎ 934 121 599; Pg. de Gràcia 65, Dreta de l'Eixample

21

☎ 932 157 530; ⊛ mango.com; Ⓜ Passeig de Gràcia; map p.104. Now available worldwide, Barcelona is where Mango began and prices here are generally a bit cheaper than in North America or other European countries. These two are the flagship stores, but there are branches all over the city. Mon–Sat 10.15am–9.30pm.

Zara Pg. de Gràcia 16, Dreta de l'Eixample ☎ 933 187 675, ⊛ zara.com; Ⓜ Passeig de Gràcia; map p.104. Trendy but cheap seasonal fashion for men, women and children from the Spanish chain. The Pg. de Gràcia branch is the flagship store, but you'll find outlets right across the city. Mon–Sat 10am–8.30pm.

JEWELLERY, TEXTILES AND ACCESSORIES

★ **Almacenes del Pilar** c/de la Boqueria 43, Barri Gòtic ☎ 933 177 984, ⊛ almacenesdelpilar.com; Ⓜ Liceu; map p.46. A world of frills, lace, cloth and materials used in the making of Spain's traditional regional costumes. You can pick up a decorated fan for just a few euros, though quality items go for a whole lot more. Mon–Sat 10am–2pm & 4.30–8pm; closed Aug.

Iriarte Iriarte c/de l'Esquirol 1, La Ribera ☎ 933 198 175, ⊛ iriarteiriarte.com; Ⓜ Jaume I; map p.70. Atelier-showroom for sumptuous handmade leather bags and belts. The alley (off c/dels Cotoners) has several other interesting craft workshops and galleries to browse. Tues–Fri 10am–2pm & 4–8.30pm, Sat noon–8.30pm.

Joaquín Berao Rambla de Catalunya 74, Dreta de l'Eixample ☎ 932 150 091, ⊛ joaquinberao.com; Ⓜ Passeig de Gràcia; map p.104. Avant-garde jewellery by a Madrid designer in a beautifully presented shop. Mon–Sat 10am–8.30pm.

Obach Sombrería c/del Call 2, Barri Gòtic ☎ 933 184 094; Ⓜ Liceu; map p.46. For traditional titfers of all kinds, hats and caps to berets and stetsons. Mon–Sat 10am–1.30pm & 4–8pm.

SECONDHAND, VINTAGE AND DISCOUNT OUTLETS

Espácio de Creadores c/Comtal 22, Barri Gòtic ☎ 934 127 958; Ⓜ Urquinaona; map p.46. Looking for glad-rags and super-stylish clothes on a budget? This is a fashionista bargain-hunter's dream, selling top-name haute couture from Spanish designers at thirty- to sixty-percent discounts. Mon–Sat 10am–9pm.

Holala! Plaza Pl. de Castella 2, El Raval ☎ 933 020 593, ⊛ holala-ibiza.com; Ⓜ Universitat; map pp.60–61. Vintage heaven in a warehouse setting (up past CCCB) for denim, flying jackets, Hawaiian shirts, baseball gear and much, much more. Mon–Sat 11am–9pm.

★ **Lailo** c/de la Riera Baixa 20, El Raval ☎ 934 413 749; Ⓜ Liceu; map pp.60–61. Secondhand and vintage clothes shop with a massively wide-ranging stock, plus fancy dress costumes, tuxes and gowns available for hire. If you're serious about the vintage scene, this is your first stop – and if you don't find what you want, just move on down the street to the neighbouring stores and outlets. Mon–Sat 11am–2pm & 5–8.30pm.

Mango Outlet c/de Girona 37, Dreta de l'Eixample ☎ 934 122 935, ⊛ mangooutlet.com; Ⓜ Girona; map p.104. Last season's Mango gear at unbeatable prices, with items starting at just a few euros. The shop is in the city's "garment district" and there are other outlet stores in the same neighbourhood. Mon–Sat 10.15am–9pm.

El Mercadillo c/de la Portaferrissa 17, Barri Gòtic ☎ 933 183 872; Ⓜ Liceu; map p.46. The camel at the entrance marks this hippy-dippy indoor street market of shops and stalls selling T-shirts, skatewear, vintage gear and jewellery. Mon–Sat 10am–8.30pm.

La Roca Village La Roca del Vallès ☎ 938 423 900, ⊛ larocavillage.com. The out-of-town outlet mall is one for serious designer discount-hounds, with a hundred stores selling designer gear at up to sixty percent off normal prices. It's half an hour from the city centre and you can get there directly by bus – there are full transport details on the website. Mon–Sat 10am–9pm.

SHOES

Camper c/de Pelai 13–37, El Triangle, Dreta de l'Eixample ☎ 933 024 124, ⊛ camper.com; Ⓜ Catalunya; map p.38. Spain's favourite shoe store opened its first shop in Barcelona in 1981. Providing hip, well-made, casual city footwear at a good price has been the cornerstone of its success – there's a store seemingly on every corner and in every mall, including this one, right at the top of the Ramblas. Mon–Sat 10am–9pm.

Czar Pg. del Born 20, La Ribera ☎ 933 107 222; Ⓜ Jaume I; map p.70. A galaxy of running shoes, pumps, sneakers, bowling shoes and baseball boots – if your Starsky and Hutch Adidas SL76s have worn out, you can pick up another pair here. Mon 4–9pm, Tues–Sat noon–9pm.

★ **La Manual Alpargatera** c/d'Avinyó 7, Barri Gòtic ☎ 933 010 172, ⊛ lamanualalpargatera.com; Ⓜ Liceu; map p.46. In this traditional workshop they make and sell *alpargatas* (espadrilles) to order, as well as producing other items using straw, rope- and basketwork. Mon–Fri 9.30am–1.30pm & 4.30–8pm, Sat 10am–1.30pm & 4.30–8pm.

TOP 5 ONLY-IN-BARCELONA SOUVENIRS

Almacen Marabi See p.235
La Campana See p.232
Els Encants See p.234
Espai Drap Art See p.228
Papabubble See p.234

21

★ **U-Casas** c/de l'Espaseria 4, La Ribera ☎ 933 100 046, ⓦ casasclub.com; ⓜ Jaume I; map p.70. Casas has four lines of shoe stores across Spain, with the U-Casas brand at the young and funky end of the market. Never mind the shoes, the stores themselves (right across town) are pretty spectacular, especially at the branch in the Born where an enormous shoe-shaped bench-cum-sofa takes centre-stage. Mon–Thurs 10.30am–8.30pm, Fri & Sat 10.30am–9pm.

DEPARTMENT STORES AND SHOPPING MALLS

Arenas de Barcelona Gran Via de les Corts Catalanes 373–385, Esquerra de l'Eixample ☎ 932 890 244, ⓦ arenasdebarcelona.com; ⓜ Espanya; map p.113. The city's newest designer mall is a glam refit of a former bullring, and while it's bigger on leisure facilities than shops and boutiques, you won't want to miss the view from the circular rooftop promenade. Mon–Sat 10am–10pm.

El Corte Inglés Pl. de Catalunya 14, Dreta de l'Eixample ☎ 933 063 800; ⓜ Catalunya; map p.38; Av. del Portal de l'Àngel 19–21, Barri Gòtic ☎ 933 063 800, ⓦ elcorte ingles.es; ⓜ Catalunya; map p.46. The city's largest department store – visit the flagship Pl. de Catalunya branch for nine floors of clothes, accessories, cosmetics, household goods, toys and top-floor café. For music, books, computers and sports gear, head for the Portal de l'Àngel branch. Mon–Sat 10am–10pm.

Diagonal Mar Av. Diagonal 3, Diagonal Mar ☎ 902 530 300, ⓦ diagonalmarcentre.es; ⓜ Maresme Forum or T4 tram; map p.86. The largest mall in Catalunya anchors the Diagonal Mar zone, and features the usual high-street suspects (El Corte Inglés, H&M, Zara, Mango, Sephora and FNAC) plus designer clothes and accessories, cafés, restaurants and cinema. Mon–Sat 10am–10pm.

Glòries Av. Diagonal 208 at Pl. de les Glòries Catalanes, Glòries ☎ 934 860 404, ⓦ www.lesglories.com; ⓜ Glòries; map p.118. Huge 230-store mall with all the national high-street fashion names (H&M, Zara, Bershka, Mango) as well as a big Carrefour supermarket, children's wear, toys and games, ice-cream parlours, a dozen bars, cafés and restaurants and a seven-screen cinema complex. Mon–Sat 10am–10pm.

L'Illa Av. Diagonal 545–559, Les Corts ☎ 934 440 000, ⓦ lilla.com; ⓜ Maria Cristina; map pp.132–133. The landmark uptown shopping mall is stuffed full of designer fashion (including the local Custo), plus Camper (shoes), FNAC (music, film and books), Sfera (cosmetics), Decathlon (sports), El Corte Inglés (department store), Caprabo (supermarket), gourmet food hall and much more. Mon–Sat 10am–9.30pm.

El Triangle Pl. de Catalunya 4, Dreta de l'Eixample ☎ 933 180 108, ⓦ eltriangle.es; ⓜ Catalunya; map p.38. Shopping centre at the top of the Ramblas, dominated by the flagship FNAC store, which specializes in books (good English-language selection), music, film and computer stuff. Also a Camper (for shoes), Habitat (homeware) and Sephora (cosmetics), plus lots of boutiques, and a café on the ground floor next to the extensive newspaper and magazine section. Mon–Sat 10am–10pm.

DESIGN, DECORATIVE ART AND HOUSEHOLD GOODS

Cubiña c/de Mallorca 291, Dreta de l'Eixample ☎ 934 765 721, ⓦ cubinya.es; ⓜ Verdaguer; map p.104. The building itself is stupendous – Domènech i Montaner's *modernista* Casa Thomas – while the inside holds the very latest in household design, from slinky CD racks to €5000 dining tables. Mon–Sat 10am–2pm & 4.30–8.30pm.

Ganivetería Roca Pl. del Pi 3, Barri Gòtic ☎ 933 021 241; ⓜ Liceu; map p.46. Handsome old shop dating from 1911, selling a big range of knives, cutlery, corkscrews and other household goods, including a fine array of gentlemen's shaving gear. Mon–Fri 10am–1.30pm & 4.30–8pm, Sat 10am–2pm & 5–8pm.

Germanes García c/dels Banys Nous 15, Barri Gòtic ☎ 933 186 646; ⓜ Liceu; map p.46. Who knew you could make quite so much stuff out of basket-, raffia- and wicker-work? The enormous warehouse-showroom has everything from cradles to tables, plant-holders to wardrobes. Mon 4.30–7.30pm, Tues–Sat 9.30am–1.30pm & 4.30–7.30pm.

★ **Gotham** c/de Cervantes 7, Barri Gòtic ☎ 934 124 647, ⓦ gotham-bcn.com; ⓜ Jaume I; map p.46. The place to come for retro (1950s to 1980s) furniture, lighting, homeware and accessories, plus original designs. Mon–Fri 11am–2pm & 5–8pm, Sat 11am–2pm; closed Sat in Aug.

Indio c/del Carme 24, El Raval ☎ 933 175 442; ⓜ Catalunya; map pp.60–61. When locals of a certain age want linen, pillows, blankets, sheets and tablecloths, this is where they come – and the beautiful *modernista* facade, long cutting counters, and wood panels and marble floor survive from its nineteenth-century glory days. Mon–Sat 10am–1.30pm & 4–7.30pm.

★ **Vinçon** Pg. de Gràcia 96, Dreta de l'Eixample ☎ 932 156 050, ⓦ vincon.com; ⓜ Passeig de Gràcia; map p.104. The grandaddy of household style, pioneered by Fernando Amat. It's a fantastic building, never mind what's on sale, with various separate street entrances and separate sections for bedroom (Tinc Çon; c/de Rosselló 246) and kitchen (Kitchen Çon; c/de Pau Claris 179) stuff, plus temporary art and design exhibitions in La Sala Vinçon. Mon–Sat 10am–8.30pm.

Vitra Pl. Comercial 5, La Ribera ☎ 932 687 219, ⓦ www .vitra.com; ⓜ Jaume I; map p.70. Home and workplace furniture specialist with stunning chairs and furniture by the likes of Frank O. Gehry, Philippe Starck, Charles and Ray Eames and Ron Arad. Mon–Thurs 9am–2pm & 5–7pm, Fri 9am–2pm.

21

FOOD AND DRINK

There's a full list of city **markets** at ⓦ bcn.cat/mercatsmunicipals. The ones picked out below are all covered more fully in the Guide. The main local **supermarket** chain is Caprabo (ⓦ caprabo.es), which has a useful branch in the Mercat de la Barceloneta, though most other branches are located in residential neighbourhoods, away from the tourist sights. The most convenient downtown supermarket is that in the basement of El Corte Inglés (Pl. de Catalunya), and there's also the fairly basic Carrefour Express at Ramblas 113.

DAILY FOOD MARKETS

Mercat de la Barceloneta Pl. de la Font, Barceloneta; Ⓜ Barceloneta; map p.81. See p.83.

Mercat de la Concepció c/de Valencia, Dreta de l'Eixample; Ⓜ Passeig de Gràcia; map p.104. See p.108.

Mercat de Galvany c/de Santaló 65, Sant Gervasi; Ⓜ Maria Cristina; map pp.132–133. See p.131.

Mercat de la Llibertat Pl. de la Llibertat, Gràcia; Ⓜ Fontana; map p.126. See p.126.

Mercat del Ninot c/de Mallorca 133, Esquerra de l'Eixample; Ⓜ Hospital Clínic; map p.113. See p.114.

Mercat Sant Antoni Ronda de Sant Antoni, El Raval; Ⓜ Sant Antoni; map pp.60–61. See p.65.

Mercat Sant Josep/La Boqueria Ramblas; Ⓜ Liceu; map p.38. See p.40.

Mercat Santa Caterina Av. Francesc Cambó, Sant Pere; Ⓜ Jaume I; map p.70. See p.68.

SPECIALIST FOOD STORES

★ **La Botifarreria de Santa Maria** c/de Santa Maria 4, La Ribera ☎ 933 199 123, ⓦ labotifarreria.com; Ⓜ Jaume I; map p.70. If you ever doubted the power of the humble Catalan pork sausage, drop by this designer temple-deli where otherwise beautifully behaved locals jostle at the counter for the day's home-made *botifarra*, plus rigorously sourced hams, cheeses, pâtés and salamis. True disciples can even buy the T-shirt. Mon–Fri 8.30am–2.30pm & 5–8.30pm, Sat 8.30am–3pm.

Bubó c/Caputxes 10, La Ribera ☎ 932 687 224, ⓦ bubo .ws; Ⓜ Jaume I; map p.70. There are chocolates and then there are Bubó chocolates – jewel-like creations and playful desserts by pastry maestro Carles Mampel. This very classy shop (with tastings and drinks de rigueur) is complemented by their minimalist new-wave tapas place, *Bubobar*, a couple of doors down at no. 6. Daily 10am–1pm (Fri & Sat until 1am).

La Campana c/de la Princesa 36, La Ribera ☎ 933 197 296; Ⓜ Jaume I; map p.70. This gorgeous shop from 1890 stocks handmade pralines and truffles, but it's best known for its beautifully packaged squares and slabs of *turrón*, traditional Catalan nougat. Daily 10am–9pm.

★ **Casa Gispert** c/dels Sombrerers 23, La Ribera ☎ 933 197 535, ⓦ casagispert.com; Ⓜ Jaume I; map p.70. Roasters of nuts, coffee and spices for over 150 years, Casa Gispert have a truly delectable store of wooden boxes,

baskets, stacked shelves and tantalizing smells. There are organic nuts and dried fruit, teas and gourmet deli items available too. Tues–Fri 9.30am–2pm & 4–7.30pm (also Mon, same times, Oct–Dec), Sat 10am–2pm & 5–8pm.

★ **A Casa Portuguesa** c/de Verdi 58, Gràcia; also at c/de l'Or 8, Gràcia; ☎ 933 683 528, ⓦ acasaportuguesa .com; Ⓜ Fontana; map p.126. This sleek café and deli on Gràcia's buzziest street is a showcase for the food, wine and culture of Portugal. Call in for a break while trawling the designer and streetwear stores of Carrer de Verdi – they make Portuguese specialities daily (including the famous *pasteis de Belém*, little custard tarts), and have a full programme of wine tastings, food festivals and other events. Tues–Fri 5–11pm, Sat & Sun 11am–11pm.

Colmado Quílez Rambla de Catalunya 63, Dreta de l'Eixample ☎ 932 152 356, ⓦ lafuente.es; Ⓜ Passeig de Gràcia; map p.104. This classic Catalan grocery has windows and shelves piled high with tins, preserves, bottles, jars and packets, plus a groaning *xarcuteria* counter, all overseen by sober gents in collar and tie and blue smocks. Mon–Fri 9.30am–2pm & 4.30–8.30pm, Sat 9.30am–2pm, plus Sat afternoons Sept–Dec.

★ **Formatgeria La Seu** c/de la Daguería 16, Barri Gòtic ☎ 934 126 548, ⓦ formatgerialaseu.com; Ⓜ Jaume I; map p.46. Sells the best farmhouse cheeses from independent producers all over Spain. Chatty Scottish owner Katherine is usually on hand to advise, and you can try before you buy with a €2.50 tasting plate – ask about the *formatgelat*, a cheese-ice cream fusion that's unique to the shop. Tues–Thurs 10am–2pm & 5–8pm, Fri & Sat 10am–3.30pm & 5–8pm; closed Aug.

Forn Baluard c/del Baluard 38–40, Barceloneta ☎ 932 211 208, ⓦ baluardbarceloneta.com; Ⓜ Barceloneta; map p.81. There are scores of bakeries in Barcelona and every neighbourhood has its favourite, but when push comes to shove, foodies pick the *Baluard*, right next to Barceloneta market, where their passion for artisan bread, cakes and pastries knows no bounds. Mon–Sat 8am–9pm.

Jamonísimo c/de Provença 85, Esquerra de l'Eixample ☎ 934 390 847, ⓦ jamonisimo.com; Ⓜ Hospital Clínic; map p.113. When Ferran Adrià, Heston Blumenthal and other kitchen maestros are in town, this is where they come to taste and buy the world's finest, artisan-made cured hams from happy, acorn-fed pigs. Mon–Fri 9.30am–2.30pm & 5–9pm, Sat 9.30am–2.30pm.

21

Olive Pl. de les Olles 2, La Ribera ☎933 105 883; ⓜBarceloneta; map p.70. The best place to investigate the properties of the humble olive – if you thought that organic, single-estate, cold-pressed, extra-virgin olive oil was as good as it gets, this Mediterranean deli goes a step further with its olive-oil preserves, soaps and face-creams, not to mention Portuguese sea-salt and Provençal herbs. Mon–Sat 10.30am–9pm.

Papabubble c/Ample 28, Barri Gòtic ☎932 688 625, ⓦpapabubble.com; ⓜDrassanes; map p.46. Groovy young things rolling out home-made candy to a chill-out soundtrack. Come and watch them at work, sample a sweetie, and take home a gorgeously wrapped gift. Mon–Fri 10am–2pm & 4–8.30pm, Sat 10am–8.30pm; closed Aug.

WINE

Vila Viniteca c/dels Agullers 7 & 9, La Ribera ☎937 777 017, ⓦvilaviniteca.es; ⓜBarceloneta; map p.70. A very knowledgeable specialist in Catalan and Spanish wines. Pick your vintage and then nip over the road for the gourmet deli part of the operation. Mon–Sat 8.30am–8.30pm (closes Sat at 2.30pm in July & Aug).

MARKETS

Antiques Av. de la Catedral, Barri Gòtic; ⓜJaume I; harbourside, Port Vell; ⓜBarceloneta. The weekly antiques market outside the cathedral is quite a spectacle but attracts high prices. Better for bargains is the weekend market on the Port Vell harbourside. Cathedral market every Thurs from 9am, closed Aug; harbourside market Sat & Sun from 11am.

Art Pl. Sant Josep Oriol, Barri Gòtic; ⓜLiceu. The square is filled with stalls and easels every weekend from 11am, with local artists banging out still lifes, harbour views etc.

Christmas Av. de la Catedral and surrounding streets, Barri Gòtic; ⓜJaume I. Traditional decorations, gifts, Christmas trees and more at the annual Fira de Santa Llúcia. Daily Dec 1–22 10am–9pm.

Coins, books and postcards Mercat Sant Antoni, Ronda de Sant Antoni, El Raval; ⓜSant Antoni. The rare coin and secondhand/antiquarian book stalls around Sant Antoni market are also good for posters, trading cards and comic collectables. Sun 9am–2pm.

Coins and stamps Pl. Reial, Barri Gòtic; ⓜLiceu. Specialist coin and stamp dealers and collectors do regular weekend battle under the arcades of Barcelona's most emblematic old-town square. Sun 10am–2pm.

Farmers' market Pl. del Pi, Barri Gòtic; ⓜLiceu. Specializes in honey, cheese, cakes and other produce. Also takes place during the Festa de la Mercè (Sept), and the Festa de Sant Ponç in c/de l'Hospital (May 11). Last Sat and Sun of the month.

Flea market Els Encants, c/Dos de Maig, northwest side of Pl. de les Glòries Catalanes, Glòries; ⓜGlòries/Encants. The most entertaining place to trawl through old clothes, jewellery, antiques, junk and furniture is the city's oldest flea market (see p.123). It's still open for now, but is eventually due a move because of the remodelling of the Glòries district. Every Mon, Wed, Fri & Sat 9am–3pm, plus Dec 1 to Jan 5 Sun 9am–3pm.

Flowers and birds Ramblas, between Pl. de Catalunya and Mercat de la Boqueria; ⓜLiceu; Mercat de la Concepció, c/de Valencia, Dreta de l'Eixample, ⓜPasseig de Gràcia. The Ramblas flower stalls always put on a pretty show, but locals are more likely to do serious flower and plant shopping at the Mercat de la Concepció.

MUSEUMS, GALLERIES AND ATTRACTIONS

L'Aquàrium Moll d'Espanya, Port Vell ⓦaquariumbcn.com; ⓜDrassanes or Barceloneta; map p.81. A fish-related extravaganza, from the mundane (T-shirts, stationery, posters, games, toiletries) to cult must-haves (Mariscal-designed bathroom transfers). Daily: July & Aug 9.30am–11pm; Sept–June 9.30am–9pm, until 9.30pm at weekends.

CosmoCaixa c/Teodor Roviralta 47–51, Tibidabo ⓦcosmocaixa.com; FGC Avinguda del Tibidabo; map p.139. The shop in the science museum is the place to buy space jigsaws, planet mobiles, model lunar-rovers, dinosaur kits, star charts and natural history books. Tues–Sun 10am–8pm.

Museu d'Art Contemporani de Barcelona Pl. dels Àngels, El Raval ⓦmacba.cat; ⓜUniversitat; map pp.60–61. Designer aprons, espresso cups, T-shirts, posters, gifts and toys, plus art and design books. Mon & Wed–Fri 11am–7.30pm (mid-June mid-Sept till 8pm), Sat 10am–8pm, Sun & hols 10am–3pm.

Museu Barbier-Mueller c/de Montcada 14, La Ribera ⓦbarbier-mueller.ch; ⓜJaume I; map p.70. The pre-Columbian art museum shop has a wide range of ethnic artefacts, from wall-hangings and jewellery to terracotta pots and figurines. Definitely the place to pick up your Panama hat. Tues–Fri 11am–7pm, Sat & Sun 11am–8pm, hols 11am–3pm.

MUSIC

Casa Beethoven Ramblas 97 ☎933 014 826, ⓦcasabeethoven.com; ⓜLiceu; map p.38. Wonderful old shop selling sheet music, CDs and music reference books – classical, but also rock, jazz and flamenco. Mon–Fri 9am–2pm & 4–8pm, Sat 9am–2pm & 5–8pm; closed Aug.

MADE IN BARCELONA

The world owes Barcelona, big time. For a start, in the fashion world there are the global brands **Mango** (women's clothes), **Camper** (shoes) and **Custo** (designer T-shirts), each of which started out in the city. Suitably togged up, you don't just drink a beer here, it's an **Estrella Damm** (tagline, the "beer of Barcelona"), a brew that sponsors everything from the Primavera Sound rock festival to Americas Cup yacht racing – in a neat bit of local synergy, they got Custo to knock up a typically colourful limited-edition design bottle to celebrate their 130th birthday in 2006. And then there are **Chupa Chups** (from the Spanish *chupar*, to lick), the lolly on a stick invented by one Enric Bernat in 1958 – Salvador Dalí, no less, designed the company logo. Kojak in the 1970s TV series wouldn't be seen without one; and Chupa Chups even made it aboard the *Mir* space station. Meanwhile, radical poet, publisher and inventor Alejandro Finisterre (admittedly, born in Galicia) was convalescing outside Barcelona after a bomb injury suffered during the Civil War, when he first came up with the idea for the game of **table football** (*bar football, foosball*). He took out a patent in Barcelona in 1937 and, though there are competing claims, is often regarded as the man subsequently responsible for endless hours wasted in bars worldwide.

Discos Castelló c/dels Tallers 3, El Raval ⓣ933 182 041; c/dels Tallers 7, El Raval ⓣ933 025 946, ⓦcastellodiscos.com; ⓜCatalunya; map pp.60–61. You can track down pretty much anything you want from the c/dels Tallers music stores, including classical recordings at no. 3 and pop, rock, *mestiza*, electronica, hardcore and Spanish and Catalan sounds at no. 7. If these are no good other nearby specialists should do the job. Mon–Sat 10am–8pm

★ **Etnomusic** c/del Bonsuccés 6, El Raval ⓣ933 011 884, ⓦetnomusic.com; ⓜCatalunya; map pp.60–61. World-music specialist, especially good for *mestiza*, reggae, Latin and all types of South American music. Mon–Sat 11am–2pm & 5–8pm.

★ **Wah Wah Discos** c/de la Riera Baixa 14, El Raval ⓣ934 423 703, ⓦwah-wahsupersonic.com; ⓜLiceu; map pp.60–61. Vinyl heaven for record collectors – rock, indie, garage, 70s punk, electronica, blues, folk, prog, jazz, soul and rarities of all kinds. Mon–Sat 11am–2pm & 5–8.30pm.

SPORTS

Botiga del Barça FC Barcelona, Camp Nou, Les Corts ⓣ934 923 111, ⓦshop.fcbarcelona.com; ⓜMaría Cristina; map pp.132–133. For official merchandise the stadium megastore has it all – including that all-important lettering service for the back of the shirt that elevates you to the squad. Mon–Sat 10am–8.30pm, Sun 10am–2.30pm, match days until kick-off.

Decathlon c/de la Canuda 20, at Pl. Vila de Madrid, Barri Gòtic ⓣ933 426 161, ⓦdecathlon.es; ⓜCatalunya; map p.46. They've got clothes and equipment for 63 sports in the old-town megastore, so you're bound to find what you want. Also bike rental and repair. Mon–Sat 9.30am–9.30pm.

TOYS, MAGIC, COSTUME AND PARTY WEAR

★ **Almacen Marabi** c/dels Flassaders 30, La Ribera, no phone ⓦalmacenmarabi.blogspot.com; ⓜJaume I; map p.70. Mariela Marabi, originally from Argentina, makes handmade felt finger dolls, mobiles, puppets and animals of extraordinary invention. She's often at work at the back, while her eye-popping workshop also has limited-edition pieces by other selected artists and designers. Tues–Sat noon–2.30pm & 5–8.30pm.

Drap c/del Pi 14, Barri Gòtic ⓣ933 181 417, ⓦminiaturasdrap.com; ⓜLiceu; map p.46. *Everything* is in miniature in this extraordinary dolls' house outfitters – asking for a set of bedroom furniture hardly stretches the talents of a place that can fit out a minuscule dentist's surgery or a complete art gallery. Mon–Fri 9.30am–1.30pm & 4.30–8.30pm, Sat 10am–1.30pm & 5–8.30pm.

★ **El Ingenio** c/d'en Rauric 6–8, Barri Gòtic ⓣ933 177 138, ⓦel-ingenio.com; ⓜLiceu; map p.46. Juggling, magic and street-performer shop with a *modernista* storefront. It's also the place to come for carnival costumes and masks, made in the workshop on the premises. Mon–Fri 10am–1.30pm & 4.15–8pm, Sat 10am–2pm & 5–8.30pm.

El Rey de la Màgia c/de la Princesa 11, Sant Pere ⓣ933 193 920, ⓦelreydelamagia.com; ⓜJaume I; map p.70. Spain's oldest magic shop contains all the tricks of the trade, from rubber chickens to Dracula capes. They also have an associated magic school and theatre, with events and performances posted on the website. Mon–Fri 11am–2pm & 5–8pm, Sat 11am–2pm.

PARC ZOOLÒGIC

Children's Barcelona

Taking your children to Barcelona doesn't pose insurmountable travel problems. On the whole, once you're happily ensconced, and have cracked the transport system, you'll find that your children will be given a warm welcome almost everywhere you go. There's plenty to do, whether it's a day at the beach or a daredevil cable-car ride, while if you coincide with one of Barcelona's festivals, you'll be able to join in with the local celebrations, from sweet-tossing and puppet shows to fireworks and human castles. "Children's attractions" rounds up the best of the options for keeping everybody happy; for sporting suggestions and outdoor activities, see Chapter 20. Finally, for plenty more ideas, check out the English-language resource and support site ⓦkidsinbarcelona.com, which is packed with information on everything from safe play areas to babysitting services.

PUBLIC TRANSPORT

The metro and FGC With very young children, the main problem is using public transport, especially the metro, which seems almost expressly designed to thwart access for pushchairs and buggies. Most stations are accessed by stairs or escalators, and there are steps and stairs within the system itself, making it difficult for single travellers with young children to get around easily. Even with two adults, you often face a stiff climb out of stations with the pushchair. However, the stations on lines 1 and 2 – including Universitat, Catalunya, Passeig de Gràcia and Sagrada Família – are accessible by lift from street level, and many FGC stations have lifts to the platforms, too, including Espanya (for Montserrat trains) and Avinguda del Tibidabo (for Tibidabo).

Buses All city buses have been adapted for wheelchair access and so have room to handle a buggy.

Tickets Children under 4 travel free on public transport, while there are reduced prices for tickets on the sightseeing Bus Turístic and the cable cars.

PRODUCTS, CLOTHES AND SERVICES

Products Disposable nappies (diapers), baby food, formula milk and other standard items are widely available in pharmacies and supermarkets, though not necessarily with the same range or brands that you will be used to at home. Organic baby food, for example, is often hard to come by – it's best to look in health-food stores rather than supermarkets – and most Spanish non-organic baby foods contain small amounts of sugar or salt. If you require anything specific for your baby or child, either bring it with you or check with the manufacturer about equivalent brands.

Clothing For relatively cheap, well-made babies' and children's clothing, Prénatal (⟨⟩ prenatal.es) has an excellent range, and there are branches all over the city. Chicco (branches at Ronda de Sant Pere 13 and in Diagonal Mar shopping centre; ⟨⟩ www.chicco.es) is the place for baby and toddler clothes and gear. Or go to Galeries Malda (c/de la Portaferrissa 22, Barri Gòtic) or El Corte Inglés (see p.231) for more children's and babies' clothes and designer labels.

Services Most establishments are baby-friendly in the sense that you'll be made very welcome if you turn up with a child in tow. Many museum cloakrooms, for example, will be happy to look after your pushchair as you carry your child around the building, while restaurants will make a fuss of your little one. However, specific facilities are not as widespread as they are in the UK or US. Baby-changing areas are relatively rare, except in department stores and shopping centres, and even where they do exist they are not always up to scratch. By far the best is at El Corte Inglés, though most major shopping centres now have pull-down changing tables in their public toilets.

RESTAURANTS, ACCOMMODATION AND BABYSITTING

Restaurants Local restaurants tend not to offer children's menus (though they will try to accommodate specific requests), highchairs are rarely provided, and restaurants open relatively late for lunch and dinner. Despite best intentions, you might find yourself eating in one of the international franchise restaurants, which tend to be geared more towards families and open throughout the day.

Accommodation Suitable accommodation is easy to find, and most hotels and pensions will be welcoming. However, bear in mind that much of the city's budget accommodation is located in buildings without lifts; while, if you're travelling out of season, it's worth noting that some older-style pensions don't have heating systems – and it can get cold. If you want a cot provided, or baby-listening and -sitting services, you'll have to pay the price of staying in one of the larger hotels – and, even then, never assume that these facilities are provided, so always check in advance. Renting an apartment is often a good idea, even for just a weekend or short stay, as you'll get a kitchen and a bit more space for the kids to play in.

Babysitting You'll pay from around €10–15 per hour for babysitting if arranged through your hotel; or contact Tender Loving Canguros (from €8 per hour, plus fee; enquiries Mon–Sat 9am–9pm; ☎ 647 605 989, ⟨⟩ tlcanguros.com), whose nannies and babysitters all speak English.

CHILDREN'S ATTRACTIONS

If you've spent too much time already in the showpiece museums, galleries and churches, any of the suggestions below should head off a children's revolt. Most have been covered in the text, so you can get more information by turning to the relevant page. **Admission charges** are almost always reduced for children, though the cut-off age varies from attraction to attraction.

CINEMA, SHOWS AND THEATRE

Cinema Children's film sessions are held at the FilmoTeca (see p.209), Sun 5pm, admission €2.

Font Màgica The sound-and-light show in front of the Palau Nacional on Montjuïc (p.90) is always a hit, though it starts quite late.

IMAX Port Vell Giant-screen and 3D documentaries and adventure shows about nature, space and the human body. See p.82.

Magic shows The magic shop, El Rey de la Màgia (see p.235), has weekend magic shows (Sat 6pm, Sun noon & 6.30pm; €12), with an hour of magic plus a visit to the shop's magic museum.

Statues and street theatre The Ramblas is one big outdoor show for children, with human statues a speciality, not to mention buskers, pavement artists, magicians and food, bird and flower markets.

Theatre There are often children's puppet shows, music, mime and clowns at the Fundació Joan Miró (see p.98), usually at weekends and holidays. Jove Teatre Regina (c/de Sèneca 22, Gràcia ⓣ932 181 512, ⓦjtregina.com; ⓜDiagonal; map p.126) also puts on music and comedy productions for children (Sat & Sun 6pm; adult admission €10, includes children).

MUSEUMS, GALLERIES AND ATTRACTIONS

L'Aquàrium Adults might find the Aquarium a bit of a disappointment, but there's no denying its popularity with children. Under-4s get in free, and there are discounts for 4- to 12-year-olds. See p.80.

Museums Most of the major museums and galleries run children's activity programmes, especially in school holidays. The "Niños" section in the weekly *Guía del Ocio* magazine lists the possibilities, from art and craft workshops at the Fundació Joan Miró and MACBA to chocolate-making at the Museu de la Xocolata. Museums with a special interest for children include Museu Blau (Natural Sciences Museum; see p.87), CosmoCaixa (Science Museum; see p.139), Museu del Futbol (FC Barcelona Museum; see p.131), Museu d'Història de Barcelona (Barcelona History Museum; see p.49), Museu de Cera (Wax Museum; see p.42), and Museu Marítim (Maritime Museum; see p.78).

Parc Zoològic All the usual suspects, plus children's zoo and dolphin shows; free for under-3s, discounts for under-12s. See p.76.

Poble Espanyol Open-air "museum" of Spanish buildings, craft demonstrations, gift shops, bars and restaurants. Family ticket available. See p.91.

PARKS AND GARDENS

Gardens Top choice is the Parc del Laberint in Horta (see p.129), where the hillside gardens, maze and playground provide a great day out. For a city-centre surprise, seek out the Jardins de la Torre de les Aigües (c/Roger de Llúria 56, Dreta de l'Eixample; see p.107), which from the end of June to the end of Aug, transform from an urban garden into a beach, complete with sand and paddling pool.

Parks In the city, the Parc de la Ciutadella has the best range of attractions, with a boating lake and a zoo. Older children will love the bizarre gardens and buildings of Gaudí's Parc Güell, while the Parc del Collserola is a good target for a walk in the hills and a picnic. At Parc del Castell de l'Oreneta (daily 10am–dusk), behind Pedralbes monastery, there are miniature train rides and pony rides on Sun and public holidays (not Aug); it's at the end of c/de Montevideo (take bus #66 from Pl. Catalunya or #64 from Pl. Universitat to the end of the line and walk up Av. d'Espasa; map pp.132–133).

Playgrounds Most city kids use the squares as playgrounds, under parental supervision. In Gràcia, Pl. de la Virreina and Pl. de Rius i Taulet are handsome traffic-free spaces with good bars with attached *terrassas*. Wherever your children play, however, you need to keep an eagle eye out for dog dirt. In the old town, the nicest dog- and traffic-free playground is in Pl. de Vicenç Martorell, in El Raval, where there are some fenced-off swings in front of a great café, *Kasparo* (see p.182). Parc del Fòrum, at Diagonal Mar, also has a good children's playground and lots of other child-oriented attractions.

RIDES AND VIEWS

Bike tours Join a group bike tour for a safe way to see the sights on two wheels. See p.26.

Cable cars The two best rides in the city are the cross-harbour cable car from Barceloneta to Montjuïc (see p.89), and the Telefèric de Montjuïc (see p.89), which then takes you up to the castle at the top of Montjuïc. Neither is for the faint-hearted child or sickly infant.

Las Golondrinas Sightseeing boat rides around the port and local coast. See p.26.

Mirador de Colón See the city from the top of the Columbus statue at the bottom of the Ramblas. See p.78.

Torre de Collserola Stunning views from the telecommunications tower near Tibidabo. Under-3s go free. See p.140.

THEME PARKS

Catalunya en Miniatura Torrelles de Llobregat, 17km southwest of Barcelona (A2 highway, exit 5) ⓣ936 890 960, ⓦcatalunyaenminiatura.com. A theme park with 170 Catalan monuments in miniature, plus mini-train rides, children's shows and playground. Daily 10am–6pm, later opening April–Sept; closed Mon Nov–Feb. Admission €11, under-12s €8, under-4s free.

Illa Fantasia Vilassar de Dalt, 25km north of Barcelona, just short of Mataró (exit 92 on the main highway) ⓣ937 514 553, ⓦillafantasia.com. Supposedly the largest water park in Europe, with slides, splash pools, swimming pools, water games and picnic areas. Buy a combined ticket (*billete combinado*) at Barcelona Sants station and you can travel free on the train to Premià de Mar, and then take the free connecting bus to the park. Admission €21, children under 1.4m high €15, children under 1m high free. Mid-May to mid-Sept daily 10am–7pm.

Port Aventura 1hr south of Barcelona, near Salou and La Pineda (exit 35 on A7) ☎ 977 779 090, ⓦ portaventura.es. Universal Studios' massive theme park is based on five different cultures – Mexico, the Wild West, Polynesia, China and the Mediterranean – and also features the Costa Caribe water adventure park. There are four on-site hotels, a beach club, shops, restaurants and shows, as well as fairground rides (including the biggest roller-coaster in Europe). Two-day (€69, under-10s €56) and two-park (€79, under-10s €64) combination tickets offer the best value. Renfe trains from Passeig de Gràcia/Barcelona Sants run directly to Port Aventura's own station (1hr 15min; ⓦ renfe.com), or the park is just 15min from Reus airport. Daily April–Oct 10am–7/8pm (July & Aug until midnight); Nov–Dec Sat & Sun only 10am–7/8pm.

Tibidabo Dubbed "La Muntanya Magica", the rides and shows in the mountain-top amusement park (see p.140) are unbeatable as far as location goes, though tame compared with those at Port Aventura.

22

DETAIL FROM THE MIRADOR DE COLÓN

Contexts

Barcelona snapshot

It only takes a few minutes in Barcelona to realize that wherever you might be, you're emphatically not in Spain. Or, rather you are – just not in the clichéd Spain of paella, sangria, bullfights and flamenco. Instead, Barcelona is a dynamic modern city that considers itself almost a place apart, with a deeply felt Catalan identity rooted in a rich, and at times, glorious past. The language is an easy identifier, with Catalan street and business signs taking precedence over Castilian Spanish by law. Or just take note of the burgeoning number of .cat domain names to know that the least Spanish city in Spain always does things its own way.

City and state

Barcelona is one of the biggest cities on the Mediterranean coast, with a population of 1.6 million (metropolitan population 4.8 million). It's the capital of the province of Catalunya (population 7.1 million), whose official title is the **Comunitat Autonoma de Catalunya**. It's also one of seventeen "autonomous communities" recognized by the new Spanish constitution of 1978, with Catalunya defined as a "nationality" (rather than, crucially, a "nation") by the original 1979 Statute of Autonomy and its 2006 successor.

The Catalan government – the **Generalitat** – based in Barcelona, enjoys a high profile, employing eighty thousand people in various departments or ministries controlling social services, urban planning, culture, regional transport, industry, trade, tourism, fisheries and agriculture. However, as long as the budget is based on **tax** collected by central government and then returned proportionately, the scope for real independence is limited, as the Generalitat has no tangible resources of its own and is forced to **share jurisdiction** on strategic matters such as health, education and justice with the Spanish state. In addition, although an autonomous part of Spain, Catalunya is not officially recognized at international level.

However, over the years steps have been taken to create at least the illusion of independence. Catalan (as opposed to Spanish) tourism, trade and industry are increasingly promoted abroad, while two of the most visible symbols of the Spanish state, the Guardia Civil and the Policía Nacional, are gradually being scaled down, with urban **policing** and rural and highway duties being taken over by the Mossos d'Esquadra, Catalunya's autonomous police force. Culturally, emphasis has been on the promotion of the **Catalan language** – currently one of the fastest-growing languages in the world. All Catalunya's children are taught in Catalan, while the entire machinery of regional government and business is conducted in Catalan, and there are ongoing discussions about making Catalan an official EU language.

Parliament and administration

The **Parlament de Catalunya** (Parliament of Catalunya) comprises a single chamber of 135 members, with elections held every four years. It sits in the old Ciutadella arsenal building in Parc de la Ciutadella, in parliamentary sessions that run from September to December and February to June, though extraordinary sessions can be called outside these months. As well as legislating for Catalunya within the strictures of the Statute of Autonomy, parliament also appoints the senators who represent the Generalitat in the Spanish Senate and has the right to initiate legislation in the Spanish Congress.

Catalunya is divided into four **provinces** – Barcelona, Girona, Lleida and Tarragona – and further subdivided into counties and municipalities. Barcelona itself is divided into ten **administrative districts**, including the Ciutat Vella, Eixample, Gràcia, Sants-Montjuïc and Sarrià-Sant Gervasi. The city is run by a mayor and 41 city councillors who are elected by each municipal area. The seat of the city council, the **Ajuntament**, is in Plaça de Sant Jaume, opposite the Generalitat building.

Catalan politics

From 1980 (the first elections after autonomy) until 2003, and again since 2010, **Catalunya** has consistently elected right-wing governments – initially led by the conservative Convergència i Unió (CiU) president of the Generalitat, **Jordi Pujol i Soley**, and currently by their pro-nationalist leader, **Artur Mas i Gavarró**. The Catalan predilection for the Right may come as a surprise in view of the past, but Catalunya is nothing if not pragmatic, and such administrations are often seen as better able to protect Catalan business interests – especially in times of economic crisis.

The main opposition is usually provided by the **Partit Socialista de Catalunya** (PSC), sister party of the national PSOE, and the centre-right, unionist **Partido Popular de Catalunya** (PPC), while other Catalan parties, such as the left-wing, pro-independence **Esquerra Republicana de Catalana** (ERC) and the **Catalunya Verds** (ICV; Greens), usually attract minority support. Pro-independence coalitions are slowly gaining traction in parliamentary elections, though another point of view is presented by the **Ciutadans** (Citizens) party, a left-leaning, non-nationalistic grouping that takes exception to the official exclusive promotion of all things Catalan (especially language). It won three seats in both the 2006 and 2010 parliamentary elections, offering a less partisan, social democratic view of how Catalunya might develop.

City politics

After Franco, the first democratic municipal elections were held in 1979 (which the PSC socialists won), and between 1982 and 1997, the Ajuntament was led by an incredibly popular and charismatic socialist mayor, **Pasqual Maragall i Mira**, who took much of the credit for the hosting of the 1992 Olympic Games and consequent reshaping of the city. Maragall and his PSC successors, Joan Clos and Jordi Hereu i Boher, were re-elected over the years with relative ease, but ultimately the PSC paid the price of incumbents right across Europe as the economic meltdown continued to bite. The big headline after the 2011 municipal elections was the end of 32 years of socialist rule in Barcelona, with the right-wing nationalist coalition **Convergència i Unió** (CiU) repeating its Catalan parliamentary success. New mayor Xavier Trias is a fairly unknown quantity in a city that – by way of contrast to conservative Catalunya – has historically been a socialist stronghold.

The economy

The recession, and the flat-lining Spanish economy, informs all current political debate, and Catalunya has no immunity from national and international problems. Since 2010, the CiU in the Catalan parliament has promoted regional austerity plans and huge budget cuts to social services – and claims its economic approach has been effectively endorsed by popular vote following its success in the 2011 municipal elections. However, as elsewhere in Europe, there have been vociferous public protests against the cuts. The so-called Spanish "15-M" movement (which started with demonstrations in Madrid on May 15, 2011) has seen massive social-media-organized demos and occupations in Plaça de Catalunya, Ciutadella park and Plaça de Sant Jaume – there has already been tension and violence in the

CHANGING THE FACE OF BARCELONA

The 1992 **Olympics** are still regarded as a turning point in the city's recent history. They were an important boost, involving radical restoration of the old-town and port areas and prompting massive new developments – at a pace that the city has endeavoured to maintain ever since. In recent years, among countless other ambitious projects, this has meant the complete renovation of the **Port Vell** neighbourhood, a cleanup of **El Raval**, the development of **Diagonal Mar and the Fòrum** convention and leisure site, and the ongoing regeneration of **Poble Nou** as part of the so-called **Project 22@**. This last project alone has already attracted more than a thousand companies and created over 30,000 jobs, with new social-housing schemes to follow.

Other **current development schemes** include the complete remodelling of the Glòries district, the further expansion of the city's airport and metro system, the completion of high-velocity train (AVE) links with other Spanish cities and France, and the building of a new transport interchange at Sant Andreu-Sagrera. Over the next decade, massive new city **business and residential areas** are also being planned near the port and by the river Besòs – all evidence that Barcelona's development is far from finished.

city as blockades and camps have been forcibly cleared by the local police in the interests of "safety".

So far, so normal, though as always in Spain, there are two stories going on, since the budget deficits in autonomous communities like Catalunya are not as severe as in Spain as a whole. And while further cuts are almost inevitable (as are further violent protests), there's a general feeling among the political classes that the region is well placed to bounce back. After all, along with the Basque Country and Madrid, Catalunya has long been one of the most prosperous areas in the country. The number of firms in Barcelona accounts for fifteen percent of all the companies in Spain, while around a fifth of all new companies starting business in Spain do so in Catalunya. Barcelona is Europe's most popular convention site and the continent's number-one port for cruise ships, while the airport is in Europe's top ten for passenger numbers. Catalunya boasts the highest GDP of all Spain's autonomous communities, attracts almost a quarter of Spain's total inward investment and has Europe's largest savings bank, La Caixa.

Tourism is an important factor, accounting for sixteen percent of Catalunya's GDP, with over twelve million visitors a year now coming to the region. Other major employers are telecommunications, metal products and the chemical and pharmaceutical industries, though it's as a self-proclaimed "**city of knowledge**" that Barcelona is now positioning itself, attracting an increasing amount of information and communications technology business, as well as big-budget biotechnology and aerospace companies. MareNostrum, Spain's most powerful supercomputer, for example, is located in Barcelona, not Madrid, while the Catalan city also hosts the annual Mobile World Congress (3GSM), the world's biggest wireless communications trade fair.

Immigration

While immigrants from elsewhere in Spain have long settled in Barcelona (indeed, were encouraged to do so by Franco to dilute Catalan nationalism), those bearing the brunt of **racism** are the newcomers from North Africa, the Indian subcontinent and South America. While the large Pakistani community in El Raval is generally respected for the life and business it's injected into the neighbourhood, popular local wisdom has come to equate North Africans with petty crime, and Romanies are treated largely as pariahs. It's dangerous nonsense, with at least some of its roots in a Catalan nationalism that prides itself on a certain cultural superiority, but such bigoted views aren't simply confined to the Right – while the regional Peoples' Party (PP) bangs on about immigration ad nauseam, senior figures on the Left, too, have warned of the "dangers" of allowing too many "foreigners" into Catalunya.

NO NUDES PLEASE, WE'RE CATALAN

Barcelona is one of Europe's most popular city-break destinations, but tourism has brought its own problems, as Barcelona has acquired a not-always-welcome reputation as a beach resort and party town. The roaming stag parties and antisocial late-night behaviour by visitors causes much hand-wringing at City Hall (and much street-hosing early each morning), while certain old-town areas are now virtual tourist-only zones for much of the year. After Spanish newspapers published pictures in 2009 of tourists having sex with prostitutes on the Ramblas, locals talked sadly of the city being sullied, and it was no surprise when in 2011 – following regular local media complaints – the city council banned resort-style behaviour on Barcelona's streets. You can take your shirt off, or walk around in swimwear on the beach or on the beach promenade (complete nudity is allowed on just one beach), but strolling up and down the Ramblas as if you're on the Costa del Sol will no longer be tolerated by the local police.

The facts, of course, tell a different story. Just eleven percent of the Catalan population at large has its origin outside Spain, though as most of these people live or work in the capital it's easy to construct a prejudice from their higher profile in the city. In contrast, almost a third of the Catalan population comes from other parts of Spain, while the fastest-growing immigrant population is actually that of other Europeans, free to settle in Catalunya with the relaxation of EU residency rules. All told, 160 different nationalities are represented in Barcelona, with foreign residents amounting to almost fifteen percent of the population (broadly similar to other major European cities).

Social life and community

Barcelona faces some familiar urban social problems. Almost two-thirds of Catalunya's seven million inhabitants now live in the city and its metropolitan region, with many complaining that the high-profile regeneration projects do little for their needs. That said, both the Olympic and Project 22@ schemes have incorporated social housing, leisure facilities and green spaces, while the **public transport** system in particular is something of a European model of excellence.

Nonetheless, there are tensions in an increasingly crowded, developed city. Noise in residential areas is a perennial problem, and the Ajuntament has been getting tough in enforcing **noise restrictions** and closing down transgressing bars and clubs. The city council has also been getting more serious about dealing with squatters, known as **okupas**, whose banner- and graffiti-clad buildings have long been a familiar sight, especially in and around Gràcia. In the past, Barcelona has been tolerant of the *okupas*, but concern from some residents about drugs and noise has persuaded the city council to close down many squats in recent years. In the same vein, the police have come down hard on **botellóns** – the mass, impromptu outdoor drinking parties that sprout up in Barcelona and other Spanish cities from time to time.

Green Barcelona

From the huge photovoltaic plant at the Fòrum site to the city buses powered by compressed natural gas, Barcelona likes to see itself as a future "sustainable" city. Its hosting of the 2004 **Universal Forum of Cultures** expo might have been politically controversial, but at its heart was a vision of **sustainable development** that the city authorities embraced with vigour. Subsequent urban-renewal projects have all incorporated innovative "green" methodology, while the city has pioneered many successful green schemes, from neighbourhood recycling of rubbish and rain-water to the Bicing **bike-sharing** project and charge-points for electric vehicles. It's well worth a visit to the **Fábrica del Sol** eco-centre in Barceloneta (see p.83), which throws light on all the city's efforts in sustainable living.

A history of Barcelona and Catalunya

Catalan cultural identity can be traced back as far as the ninth century. From the quilt of independent counties of the eastern Pyrenees, a powerful dynastic entity, dominated by Barcelona, and commonly known as the Crown of Aragón, developed over the next six hundred years. Its merger with Castile-León in the late 1400s led to eventual inclusion in the new Spanish empire of the sixteenth century – and marked the decline of Catalan independence and its eventual subjugation to Madrid. It has rarely been a willing subject, which goes some way to explaining how ingrained are the Catalan notions of social and cultural divorce from the rest of the country.

Early civilizations

During the **Upper Paleolithic** period (35,000–10,000 BC), cave-dwelling hunter-gatherers lived in parts of the Pyrenees, and **dolmens**, or stone burial chambers, from around 5000 BC still survive. No habitations from this period have been discovered but it can be conjectured that huts of some sort were erected, and farming had certainly begun. By the start of the **Bronze Age** (around 2000 BC), the Pyrenean people had begun to move into fortified villages in the coastal lowlands.

The first of a succession of **invasions** of the region began sometime after 1000 BC, when the Celtic "urnfield people" crossed the Pyrenees into the region, settling in the river valleys. These people lived side by side with indigenous Iberians, and the two groups are commonly, if erroneously, referred to as **Celtiberians**.

Foundation of Barcelona

On the coast, the **Greeks** had established trading posts at Roses and Empúries by around 550 BC. Two centuries later, though, the coast (and the rest of the peninsula) had been conquered by the North African **Carthaginians**, who founded **Barcino** (later Barcelona) in around 230 BC, probably on the heights of Montjuïc. The Carthaginians' famous commander, Hannibal, went on to cross the Pyrenees in 214 BC and attempted to invade Italy. But the result of the Second Punic War (218–201 BC) – much of which was fought in Catalunya – was to expel the Carthaginians from the Iberian peninsula in favour of the **Romans**, who made their new base at the former Carthaginian stronghold of Tarraco (Tarragona).

Roman Catalunya

The Roman colonization of the Iberian peninsula was far more intense than anything previously experienced and met with great resistance from the Celtic and Iberian tribes.

c.230 BC	218–201 BC	304 AD	c.350
Carthaginians found the settlement of "Barcino", probably on the heights of Montjuïc.	Romans expel Carthaginians from Iberian peninsula in Second Punic War. Roman Barcino is established around today's Barri Gòtic.	Santa Eulàlia – the city's patron saint – is martyred by Romans for refusing to renounce Christianity.	Roman city walls built as threat of invasion grows.

BARCINO – TARRAGONA'S LITTLE SISTER

Barcelona does its best to champion its Roman remains, and the sketchy ruins of **Barcino** – or Colonia Julia Augusta Faventia Pia, as it was dubbed in 15 BC by the emperor Augustus – can be traced today in a walk around the Barri Gòtic, centred on the cathedral area (see box, p.49). However, Roman Barcino was always second-best to the provincial capital of Tarragona, known as **Tarraco**, whose extremely fine monuments can still be seen in and around that city. Imperial Tarraco (see p.156) boasted two forums, a theatre and a circus, plus temples and necropolises, not to mention an infrastructure of roads, bridges and aqueducts – much of which was used well into modern times.

It was almost two centuries before the conquest was complete, by which time Spain had become the most important centre of the Roman Empire after Italy. In the first two centuries AD, the Spanish mines and the granaries of Andalucia brought unprecedented wealth, and **Roman Spain** enjoyed a period of stable prosperity in which the region of Catalunya played an influential part. In Tarraco, Barcino and the other Roman towns, the inhabitants were granted full Roman citizenship; the former Greek settlements on the Costa Brava had accepted Roman rule without difficulty and consequently experienced little interference in their day-to-day life.

Towards the third century AD, the Roman political framework began to show signs of decadence and corruption, becoming increasingly vulnerable to **barbarian invasions** from northern Europe. The Franks and the Suevi swept across the Pyrenees, sacking Tarraco in 262 and destroying Barcelona. Within two centuries Roman rule had ended, forced on the defensive by new waves of Suevi, Alans and Vandals and finally superseded by the **Visigoths** from Gaul, former allies of Rome.

Visigothic Spain

The **Visigoths** established their first Spanish capital at Barcelona in 415 (before eventually basing themselves further south at Toledo), and built a kingdom encompassing most of modern Spain and the southwest of modern France. Their triumph, however, was relatively short-lived. Ruling initially as a caste apart from the local people, with a distinct status and laws, the Visigoths lived largely as a warrior elite, and were further separated from the local people by their adherence to Arian Christianity, which was considered heretical by the Catholic Church. Under their domination, the economy and the quality of life in the former Roman towns declined, while within their ranks a series of plots and rivalries pitted members of the ruling elite against each other.

Moorish conquest

Divisions within the Visigothic kingdom coincided with the Islamic expansion in North Africa, which reached the shores of the Atlantic in the late seventh century. In 711 Tariq ibn Ziyad, governor of Tangier, led a force of several thousand troops across the Straits of Gibraltar and routed the Visigothic nobility. With no one to resist, the stage for the **Moorish conquest of Spain** was set. Within ten years, the Muslim Moors

415	711	801
Visigoths sweep across Spain and establish temporary capital in Barcino.	Moorish conquest of Spain. Barcelona eventually forced to surrender (719).	Barcelona retaken by Louis the Pious, son of Charlemagne. Frankish counties of Catalunya become a buffer zone, known as the Spanish Marches.

had advanced a long way north, destroying Tarragona and forcing Barcelona to surrender – although the more inaccessible parts of the Pyrenees retained their independence. In most places, a limited autonomy was granted to the local population in exchange for payment of tribute. There was no forced conversion to Islam, and Jews and Christians lived securely as second-class citizens. In areas of the peninsula that remained under direct Muslim power during the ninth century, a new ethnic group emerged: the **Mozarabs**, Christians who lived under Muslim rule, and adopted Arabic language, dress and social customs.

The Spanish Marches

Moorish raiding parties reached beyond the Pyrenees as far north as Poitiers, where in 732 Charles Martel, the de facto ruler of Merovingian France, dealt them a minor defeat, which convinced them to withdraw. Martel's son Pepin and his famous grandson **Charlemagne** (768–814) both pushed back the invaders further, with Charlemagne's empire including the southern slopes of the Pyrenees and much of Catalunya. After being ambushed and defeated by the Basques at Roncesvalles in 778, Charlemagne switched his attention to the Mediterranean side of the Pyrenees, attempting to defend his empire against the Muslims. He took Girona in 785 and his son Louis directed the successful siege of Barcelona in 801. With the capture of Barcelona, the Frankish counties of Catalunya became a sort of buffer zone, known as the **Spanish Marches**. Separate territories were established, each ruled by a count and theoretically owing allegiance to the Frankish king or emperor.

The birth of Catalunya

As the Frankish empire of Charlemagne disintegrated in the decades following his death, the counties of the Marches enjoyed greater independence, which was formalized in 878 by Guifré el Pelós – or **Wilfred the Hairy**. Wilfred was count of Urgell and the Cerdagne and, after adding Barcelona to his holdings, named himself its first count, founding a dynastic line that was to rule until the 1400s. In the wake of the Muslim withdrawal from the area, **Christian outposts** had been established throughout Catalunya, and Wilfred continued the process, founding Benedictine monasteries at Ripoll (about 880) and Sant Joan de les Abadesses (888), where his daughter was the first abbess.

Wilfred was followed by a succession of rulers who attempted to consolidate his gains. Early counts, like **Ramon Berenguer I** (1035–76), concentrated on establishing their superiority over the other local counts, which was bitterly resisted. **Ramon Berenguer III** (1144–66) added considerable territory to his realms with his marriage in 1113 to a Provençal heiress, and made alliances and commercial treaties with Muslim and Christian powers around the western Mediterranean.

The most important stage in Catalunya's development, however, came in 1137 with the marriage of **Ramon Berenguer IV** to Petronella, the two-year-old daughter of King Ramiro II of Aragón. This led to the **dynastic union of Catalunya and Aragón**. Although this remained a loose and tenuous federation – the regions retained their own parliaments and customs – it provided the platform for rapid expansion over the next

878	985	1137	1213–1276
Guifré el Pelós (Wilfred the Hairy) declared first Count of Barcelona, founding a dynastic line that rules until 1410.	Moorish sacking of city. Sant Pau del Camp – city's oldest surviving church – built after this date.	Dynastic union of Catalunya and Aragón established.	Reign of Jaume I, "the Conqueror", expansion of empire and beginning of Catalan golden age.

three centuries. Ramon also managed to force most of the other counts to recognize his superior status, and subsequently issued the **Usatges de Barcelona**, a code of laws and customs defining feudal duties, rights and authorities – sneakily putting Ramon I's name on them to make them appear older than they were. He also captured Muslim Tortosa and Lleida in 1148–49, which mark the limits of the modern region of Catalunya, but now the region began to look east for its future, across the Mediterranean.

The Kingdom of Catalunya and Aragón

Ramon Berenguer IV was no more than a count, but his son **Alfons I** (who succeeded to the throne in 1162) also inherited the title of King of Aragón (where he was Alfonso II) and became the first count-king of what historians later came to call the **Crown of Aragón**. To his territories he added Roussillon and much of southern France, becoming known as "Emperor of the Pyrenees".

Alfons's son, Pere (Peter) the Catholic, gained glory as one of the military leaders in the decisive defeat of Muslim forces at the **Battle of Las Navas de Tolosa** in 1212. But through his ties of lordship to the French counts of Toulouse, Pere found himself on the wrong side in the Albigensian wars (the Catholic Church's crusade against the Cathar heresy), and he was killed by Catholic forces a year later. These were uncertain times in Catalunya, but a golden age was about to dawn.

Jaume I

Pere was succeeded by his five-year-old son, **Jaume I** (1213–76), whose extraordinary reign started unpromisingly when he was initially entrusted to the care of the Knights Templar while his crown was disputed by rival counts. Shrugging off the tutelage of his Templar masters at the age of 13, Jaume personally took to the field to tame his rebellious nobility, before embarking on a series of campaigns of conquest, which brought him Muslim Mallorca in 1229, Menorca in 1231 and Ibiza in 1235. Next he turned south and conquered the city of Valencia in 1238, establishing a new kingdom of which he was also ruler. Recognizing that **Mediterranean expansion** was where Catalunya's future lay, Jaume signed the **Treaty of Corbeil** in 1258, renouncing his rights in France (except for Montpellier, the Cerdagne and Roussillon), in return for the French King Louis's renunciation of claims in Catalunya.

Catalan expansion

On Jaume's death, his kingdom was divided between his sons, one of whom, **Pere II** ("the Great"), took Catalunya, Aragón and Valencia. Connected through marriage to the Sicilian crown, Pere used the 1282 "Sicilian Vespers" rising against Charles of Anjou to press his claim to the island. In August that year, Pere was crowned at Palermo, and Sicily became the base for Catalan exploits throughout the Mediterranean. Athens and Neopatras were taken between 1302 and 1311 by Catalan mercenaries, the **almogávares**, and famous sea-leaders-cum-pirates such as Roger de Flor and Roger de Llúria fought in the name of the Catalan-Aragonese crown. Malta (1283), Corsica (1323), Sardinia (1324) and Naples (1423) all fell under the influence of successive count-kings.

1282–1387	1348	1391	1410
Barcelona at centre of a Mediterranean empire. Successive rulers construct most of Barcelona's best-known Gothic buildings.	Black Death strikes, killing half of Barcelona's population.	Pogrom against the city's Jewish population.	Death of Martí el Humà (Martin the Humane), last of Catalan count-kings. Beginning of the end of Catalan influence in the Mediterranean.

CATALAN ROOTS

Conflicting loyalties in the territories of the Spanish Marches (see p.247) in the ninth century sparked the construction of many local fortifications to protect and control the population, which led to the term *catlá* ("lord of the castle") being used to refer to the people of the area – the root of today's "**Catalan**" (Castilian has an analogous root). Also, and as happened across much of the former Roman Empire, spoken Latin had taken on geographical particularities, and the "Romance" languages, including Catalan, had begun to develop. A document from 839 recording the consecration of the cathedral at La Seu d'Urgell in the Pyrenees is seen as the first Catalan-language historical document.

Barcelona's medieval mercantile class were quick to see the possibilities of Mediterranean commerce. Maritime customs were codified in the so-called *Llibre del Consolat de Mar*, trade relations were established with North Africa and the Middle East, and Catalan became used as a trading language throughout the Mediterranean.

Catalunya in the golden age

The **Corts**, Catalunya's first parliament – and one of the earliest such bodies in Europe – was established during Jaume I's reign, while in 1249, the first governors of Barcelona were elected, nominating councillors to help them who became known as the Consell de Cent. In 1289 there was the first recorded meeting of a body that became known as the **Generalitat**, a sort of committee of the Corts. Within it were represented each of the three traditional estates – commons, nobility and clergy – and the Generalitat gradually became responsible for administering public order, justice and defence of the realm.

By the mid-fourteenth century Catalunya was at its economic peak. Barcelona had impressive new buildings to match its status as a regional superpower – the cathedral, the church of Santa María del Mar, the Generalitat building, the Ajuntament (with its Consell de Cent meeting room) and the Drassanes shipyards all testify to Barcelona's wealth in this period. Catalan became established as a **literary language**, and Catalan works are recognized as the precursor of much of the great medieval European literature: Ramon Llull's romance *Blanquerna* was written a century before Chaucer's *Canterbury Tales*. **Architecture** progressed from Romanesque to Gothic styles, with churches displaying features that have become known as Catalan-Gothic – such as spacious naves, hexagonal belfries and a lack of flying buttresses.

The rise of Castile

The last of Wilfred the Hairy's dynasty of Catalan count-kings, Martin the Humane (Martí el Humà), died in 1410 without an heir. After nearly five hundred years of continuity, there were six claimants to the throne, and in 1412 nine specially appointed counsellors elevated Ferdinand (Ferran) de Antequera, son of a Catalan princess, to the vacant throne.

Ferdinand ruled for only four years, but his reign and that of his son, Alfons, and grandson, John (Joan) II, spelled the end for Catalunya's influence in the Mediterranean. The Castilian rulers were soon in dispute with the Consell de Cent, and non-Catalans started to be appointed to key positions in the Church, state offices

1469	1479	1493	1516
Marriage of Ferdinand of Aragón and Isabel of Castile.	Ferdinand succeeds to Catalan-Aragese crown. Inquisition introduced to Barcelona, leading to forced flight of the Jews.	Christopher Columbus received in Barcelona after triumphant return from New World.	Spanish crown passes to Habsburgs and Madrid is established as capital of Spanish empire.

THE INQUISITION IN CATALUNYA

The Catholic monarchs, Ferdinand and Isabel, shared in the religious bigotry of their contemporaries, although Isabel, under the influence of her personal confessor, Tomás de Torquemada, was the more reactionary of the two. In Catalunya, the **Inquisition** was established in 1487, and aimed to purify the Catholic faith by rooting out heresy. It was directed mainly at the secret **Jews**, most of whom had been converted by force (after the pogrom of 1391) to Christianity. It was suspected that their descendants, known as **New Christians**, continued to practise their old faith in secret, and in 1492, an edict forced some seventy thousand Jews to flee the country. The Jewish population in Barcelona was completely eradicated in this way, while communities elsewhere – principally in Girona, Tarragona and Lleida – were massively reduced, and those who remained were forced to convert to Christianity.

and the armed forces. In 1469 John's son, Prince Ferdinand (Ferran), who was born in Aragón, married Isabel of Castile, a union that would eventually finish off Catalan independence. Both came into their inheritances quickly, Isabel taking Castile in 1474 and the Catalan-Aragónese crown coming to Ferdinand in 1479.

Ferdinand and Isabel

Under **Ferdinand and Isabel**, the two largest kingdoms in Spain were united under a ruling pair known as "**Los Reyes Católicos**" ("Els Reis Catòlics" in Catalan) – the Catholic monarchs. Their energies were devoted to the reconquest and unification of Spain: they finally took back Granada from the Moors in 1492, and initiated a wave of Christian fervour at whose heart was the **Inquisition** (see box above).

Also in 1492, the final shift in Catalunya's outlook occurred with the triumphal return of **Christopher Columbus** from the New World, to be received in Barcelona by Ferdinand and Isabel. Castile, like Portugal, looked away from the Mediterranean to the Americas for trade and conquest, and the exploration and exploitation of the New World was spearheaded by the Andalucian city of Seville. Meanwhile, Ferdinand gave the Supreme Council of Aragón control over Catalan affairs in 1494. The Aragonese nobility, who had always resented the success of the Catalan maritime adventures, now saw the chance to complete their control of Catalunya by taking over its ecclesiastical institutions – with Catalan monks being thrown out of the great monasteries of Poblet and Montserrat.

Habsburg rule

Charles I, a **Habsburg**, came to the throne in 1516 as a beneficiary of the marriage alliances made by the Catholic monarchs. Five years later he was elected emperor of the **Holy Roman Empire** (as Charles V), inheriting not only Castile, Aragón and Catalunya, but also Flanders, the Netherlands, Artois, the Franche-Comté and all the American colonies. With such responsibilities, it became inevitable that attention would be diverted from Spain, whose chief function became to sustain the Holy Roman Empire with gold and silver from the Americas. It was in this era that Madrid was established as capital city of the Spanish empire, and the long rivalry began between Madrid and Barcelona.

1640–1652	1714	1755
Uprising known as "War of the Reapers" declares Catalunya an independent republic. Barcelona besieged and surrenders to Spanish army.	After War of Spanish Succession, Spanish throne passes to Bourbons. Barcelona finally subdued on September 11 (now Catalan National Day); Ciutadella fortress built.	Barceloneta district laid out – gridded layout is early example of urban planning.

Throughout the **sixteenth century**, Catalunya continued to suffer under the Inquisition, and – deprived of trading opportunities in the Americas – became an impoverished region. Habsburg wars wasted the lives of Catalan soldiers, banditry increased, and the poverty of the mass of the population was a source of perpetual tension.

With Spain and France at war in 1635, the Catalans took advantage of the situation and revolted, declaring themselves an **independent republic** under the protection of the French King Louis XIII. This, the **War of the Reapers** – after the marching song *Els Segadors* ("The Reapers"), later the Catalan national anthem – ended in 1652 with the surrender of Barcelona to the Spanish army. The **Treaty of the Pyrenees** in 1659 finally split the historical lands of Catalunya as the Spanish lost control of Roussillon and part of the Cerdagne to France.

Bourbon repression

In 1700, when the Habsburg king Charles II died heirless, France's Louis XIV saw an opportunity to fulfil his longtime ambition of putting a Bourbon on the Spanish throne. He secured the succession of his grandson, Philippe d'Anjou, under condition that the latter renounced his rights to the throne of France. This deal put a Bourbon on the throne of Spain, but led to war with the other claimant, Archduke Charles of Austria: the resulting **War of the Spanish Succession** lasted thirteen years from 1701, with Catalunya (along with England) lining up on the Austrian side in an attempt to regain its ancient rights.

However, the **Treaty of Utrecht** in 1714 gave the throne to the **Bourbon** (*Borbón* in Castilian, *Borbó* in Catalan) Philippe, now Philip V of Spain, and initiated a fresh period of repression from which the Catalans took a century to recover. Barcelona lay under siege for over a year, and with its eventual capitulation a fortress was built at Ciutadella to subdue the city's inhabitants – the final defeat, on September 11, is still commemorated every year as a Catalan holiday, **La Diada**. The university at Barcelona was closed, the Catalan language was banned, the Consell de Cent and Generalitat were abolished – in short, Catalunya was finished as even a partially autonomous region.

Napoleonic and Peninsular Wars

When neighbouring France became aggressively expansionist following the Revolution of 1789, Spain was a natural target, first for the Revolutionary armies and later for the machinations of Napoleon. In 1805, during the **Napoleonic Wars**, the French fleet (along with the Spanish who had been forced into an alliance) was defeated at Trafalgar. Shortly after, Charles IV was forced to abdicate, and Napoleon installed his brother Joseph on the throne three years later. Attempting to broaden his appeal among Spain's subjects, the French emperor proclaimed a separate government of Catalunya – independent of Joseph's rule – with Catalan as its official language. The region's response was an indication of how far Catalunya had become integrated into Spain during the Bourbon period – despite their history the Catalans supported the Bourbon cause solidly during the ensuing **Peninsular War** (1808–14), ignoring Napoleon's blandishments. Girona was defended heroically from the French in a seven-month

1778	1814	1848	1850
Steady increase in trade with America; Barcelona's economy improves.	After Peninsular War, French finally driven out, with Barcelona the last city to fall.	Rapid expansion and industrialization.	Plaça Reial – emblematic old-town square – is laid out.

siege, while Napoleon did his cause no good at all by attacking and sacking the holy shrine and monastery at Montserrat. Fierce local resistance was eventually backed by the muscle of a British army, and the French were at last driven out.

The slow Catalan revival

Despite the political emasculation of Catalunya, there had been signs of **economic revival** during the eighteenth century, not least as (from 1778) Catalunya was allowed to trade with the Americas for the first time; in this way, the shipping industry received a boost and Catalunya was able to export its textiles to a wider market. After the Napoleonic Wars, Catalunya experienced **industrialization** on a scale like nowhere else in Spain. In the mid-nineteenth century, the country's first **railway** was built from Barcelona to Mataró, later to be extended south to Tarragona and north to Girona and the French border. **Manufacturing** industries encouraged a shift in population from the land to the towns; Catalan olive oil production helped supply the whole country; and previously local industries flourished on a wider scale – for example, cava (champagne-like wine) production was introduced in the late nineteenth century, supported closely by the age-old cork industry of the Catalan forests. From 1890, hydroelectric power was harnessed from the Pyrenees, and by the end of the century Barcelona was the fastest-growing city in Spain – one of only six with more than 100,000 inhabitants.

Cultural renaissance

Equally important was the first stirring of what became known as the **Renaixença** (Renaissance), in the mid-nineteenth century. Despite being banned in official use and public life, the Catalan **language** had never died out. Books began to appear again in Catalan, and the language was revived among the bourgeoisie and intellectuals as a means of making subtle nationalist and political points. Catalan **poetry** became popular, and the late medieval **Jocs Florals** (Floral Games), a sort of literary competition, were revived in 1859 in Barcelona: one winner was the great Catalan poet, Jacint Verdaguer (1845–1902). Catalan **drama** developed (although even in the late nineteenth century there were still restrictions on performing wholly Catalan plays), led mainly by the dramatist Pitarra.

Prosperity led to the rapid **expansion of Barcelona**, particularly the mid-nineteenth-century addition to the city of the planned Eixample district. Encouraged by wealthy patrons and merchants, architects such as Josep Puig i Cadafalch, Lluís Domènech i Montaner and Antoni Gaudí i Cornet were in the vanguard of the **modernista** movement which changed the face of the city. Culture and business came together with the **Universal Exhibition** of 1888, based around the *modernista* buildings of the Parc de la Ciutadella, and later the **International Exhibition** on Montjuïc in 1929.

The seeds of civil war

In 1814, the repressive Ferdinand VII had been restored to the Spanish throne, and, despite the Catalan contribution to the defeat of the French, he stamped out the least hint of liberalism in the region, abolishing virtually all Catalunya's remaining privileges.

1859	1882	1888	1893
Old city walls demolished and Eixample district built to accommodate growing population.	Work begins on Sagrada Família; Antoni Gaudí takes charge two years later.	Universal Exhibition held at Parc de la Ciutadella. *Modernista* architects start to make their mark.	First stirrings of anarchist unrest. Liceu opera house bombed.

On his death, the crown was claimed both by his daughter Isabel II (with liberal support) and by his brother Charles (backed by the Church and the conservatives). The ensuing **First Carlist War** (1833–39) ended in victory for Isabel, who came of age in 1843. Her reign was a long record of scandal, political crisis and constitutional compromise, until liberal army generals under the leadership of General Prim eventually effected a coup in 1868, forcing Isabel to abdicate. However, the experimental **First Republic** (1873–75) failed, and following the **Second Carlist War** the throne went to Isabel's son, Alfonso XII.

Against this unstable background, local dissatisfaction increased and the years preceding World War I saw a growth in working-class **political movements**. Barcelona's textile workers organized a branch affiliated to the Communist First International, founded by Karl Marx, and the region's wine growers also banded together to seek greater security. Tension was further heightened by the **loss of Cuba** in 1898, which only added to local economic problems, with the return of soldiers seeking employment in the cities where there was none.

Conflict in Barcelona

A call-up for army reserves to fight in Morocco in 1909 provoked a general strike and, at the end of July, a solid week of rioting in Barcelona, and then throughout Catalunya, in which over one hundred people died. Working-class Catalans objected violently to the suggestion that they should go to fight abroad for a state that did little for them at home, and Barcelona's streets saw the widespread burning of churches and other religious institutions – symbols of the power of the state that dominated their lives. Battle lines were drawn in the very name given to the disturbances – what was a glorious "July revolution" to the rioters came later to be known by the nervous bourgeoisie as the so-called **Tragic Week** (Setmana Trágica). Mass arrests, executions and repression followed, as the rioters were put down, but future seeds were sown as Catalan workers realized the need to be better organized. A direct result was the establishment of the Confederación Nacional del Trabajo – the **CNT** – in 1911, which included many previously unconnected Catalan working-class organizations.

World War I and the start of dictatorship

During **World War I** Spain was neutral, though inwardly turbulent since soaring inflation and the cessation of exports following the German blockade of the North Atlantic hit the country hard. As rumblings grew among the workers and political organizations, the army moved decisively, crushing a general strike of 1917. However, the situation did not improve. Violent strikes and assassinations plagued Barcelona, while the CNT and the union of the socialists, the CGT, both saw huge increases in their membership. In 1923, **General Primo de Rivera**, the captain-general of Catalunya, overthrew the national government in a military coup that had the full backing of the Catalan middle class, establishing a dictatorship that enjoyed initial economic success. The general resigned in 1930, dying a few months later, but the hopes of some for the restoration of the monarchy's political powers were short-lived. The success of the anti-monarchist parties in the municipal elections of 1931 led to the abdication of the king and the foundation of the **Second Republic**.

1901	1909	1922	1926	1929
Pablo Picasso's first public exhibition held at *Els Quatre Gats* tavern.	Setmana Trágica (Tragic Week) of rioting. Many churches destroyed.	Parc Güell opens to the public.	Antoni Gaudí run over by a tram; Barcelona stops en masse for his funeral.	International Exhibition held at Montjuïc.

The Second Republic

In 1931, Catalunya, under Francesc Macià, leader of the Republican Left, declared itself to be an **independent republic**, and the Republican flag was raised over the Ajuntament in Barcelona. Madrid refused to accept the declaration, though a statute of limited autonomy was granted in 1932. Despite initial optimism, the government was soon failing to satisfy raised local expectations. **Anarchism** in particular was gaining strength among the frustrated middle classes as well as among workers and peasantry. The **Communist Party** and the left-wing **socialists**, driven into alliance by their mutual distrust of the "moderate" socialists in government, were also forming a growing bloc. On the Right, the **Falangists** (founded in 1923 by José Antonio Primo de Rivera, son of the dictator) made uneasy bedfellows with conservative traditionalists and dissident elements in the army upset by modernizing reforms.

In this atmosphere of growing confusion, the left-wing **Popular Front** alliance, including the Catalan Republican Left, won the general election of January 1936 by a narrow margin, and an all-Republican government was formed. In Catalunya, **Lluís Companys** became president of the Generalitat. But with the economy crippled by strikes, the government singularly failed to exert its authority over anyone. Finally, on July 17, 1936, the military garrison in Morocco rebelled under **General Francisco Franco**'s leadership, to be followed by uprisings at military garrisons throughout the country. Much of the south and west quickly fell into the hands of the Nationalists, but Madrid and the industrialized northeast remained loyal to the Republican government. In Barcelona, although the military garrison supported Franco, it was soon subdued by local Civil Guards and the workers, while local leaders set up militias in preparation for the coming fight.

In October 1936, Franco was declared military commander and head of state; fascist Germany and Italy recognized his regime as the legitimate government of Spain in November. The Civil War was on.

Civil War

The **Spanish Civil War** (1936–39) was one of the most bitter and bloody the world has seen. Violent reprisals were visited on their enemies by both sides – the Republicans shooting priests and local landowners wholesale, and burning churches and cathedrals; the Nationalists carrying out mass slaughter of the population of almost every town they took. It was also to be the first modern war – Franco's German allies demonstrated their ability to inflict terror on civilian populations with their bombing raids on Gernika and Durango, while radio became an important propaganda weapon, with Nationalists offering starving Republicans the "white bread of Franco".

Despite sporadic help from Russia and the 35,000 volunteers of the **International Brigades**, the Republic could never compete with the professional armies and the massive assistance from fascist Italy and Nazi Germany that the Nationalists enjoyed. Eventually, the non-intervention of other European governments was effectively to hand victory to the Nationalists. The Republican government fled Madrid first for Valencia, and then moved on to base itself at Barcelona in 1937. The **Battle of the Ebro** around Tortosa saw massive casualties on both sides; Nationalist troops advanced on Valencia in 1938, and from the west were also approaching Catalunya from their bases in Navarre. When Bilbao was taken by the Nationalists, the Republicans' fight on the

1936–1939	1939–1975	1975
Spanish Civil War. Barcelona at heart of Republican cause, with George Orwell and other volunteers arriving to fight. City eventually falls to Nationalists in January 1939.	Spain under Franco. Generalitat president Lluís Companys executed, Catalan language banned and Catalan identity threatened by Madrid.	Death of General Franco, who is succeeded as head of state by King Juan Carlos.

Aragón front was lost. The final Republican hope – that war in Europe over Czechoslovakia would draw the Allies into a war against fascism – evaporated in September 1938 with the British Prime Minister Chamberlain's capitulation to Hitler at Munich. Franco was able to call on new arms and other supplies from Germany for a final offensive against Catalunya.

The **fall of Barcelona** came on January 25, 1939 – the Republican parliament held its last meeting at Figueres a few days later. Republican soldiers, cut off in the valleys of the Pyrenees, made their way across the high passes into France, joined by women and children fearful of a fascist victory. Among the refugees and escapees was **Lluís Companys**, president of the Generalitat, who was later captured in France by the Germans, returned to Spain and, under orders from Franco, was shot at the castle prison on Montjuïc in 1940.

Catalunya in Franco's Spain

Although the Civil War left more than half a million dead, destroyed a quarter of a million homes and sent a third of a million people (including 100,000 Catalans) into exile, Franco was in no mood for reconciliation. With his government recognized by Allied powers, including Britain and France, he set up **war tribunals** that ordered executions and created concentration camps in which upwards of two million people were held until "order" had been established by authoritarian means.

The **Catalan language** was banned again, in schools, churches, the press and in public life; only one party was permitted, and censorship was rigorously enforced. The economy was in ruins, and Franco did everything possible to further the cause of Madrid against Catalunya, starving the region of investment and new industry. After **World War II** (during which the country was too weak to be anything but neutral), Spain was economically and politically isolated.

What saved Franco was the acceptance of **American aid**, offered on the condition that Franco provide land for US air bases. Prosperity increased after this, fuelled in the 1960s and 1970s by a growing tourist industry, but Catalunya (along with the Basque Country, another thorn in Franco's side) remained economically backward. Absentee landlords took much of the local revenue, a situation exacerbated by Franco's policy of encouraging emigration to Catalunya from other parts of Spain (and granting the immigrants land) in an attempt to dilute regional differences.

Despite the **cultural and political repression**, the distinct Catalan identity was never really obliterated: the Catalan Church retained a feisty independence, while Barcelona emerged as the most important publishing centre in Spain. Clandestine language and history classes were conducted, and artists and writers continued to produce work in defiance of the authorities. Nationalism in Catalunya, however, did not take the same course as the Basque **separatist movement**, which engendered the terrorist organization ETA (Euzkadi ta Azkatasuna; "Basque Homeland and Freedom"). There was little violence against the state in Catalunya and no serious counterpart to ETA. The Catalan approach was subtler: an audience at the Palau de la Música sang the unofficial Catalan anthem when Franco visited in 1960; a massive petition against language restrictions was raised in 1963; and a sit-in by Catalan intellectuals at Montserrat was organized in protest against repression in the Basque Country.

1977	1978–1980	1992
First democratic Spanish elections for forty years.	Generalitat re-established and Statute of Autonomy approved. Socialist mayor and municipal government elected (1979); Conservative nationalist government elected (1980).	Olympics held in Barcelona. Massive rebuilding projects transform Montjuïc and the waterfront.

Franco's death and the new democracy

When Franco died in 1975, **King Juan Carlos** was officially designated to succeed as head of state – approved of by the powerful army and groomed for the succession by Franco himself. The king's initial moves were cautious in the extreme, though to his credit, Juan Carlos recognized that some real break with the past was inevitable, and, accepting the resignation of his prime minister, set in motion the process of **democratization**. His newly appointed prime minister, Adolfo Suárez, steered through a Political Reform Act, which allowed for a two-chamber parliament and a referendum in favour of democracy; he also legitimized the Socialist Party (the PSOE) and the Communists, and called elections for the following year, the first since 1936.

In the elections of 1977, the **Pacte Democratico per Catalunya** – an alliance of pro-Catalan parties – gained ten seats in the lower house of the Spanish parliament, which was otherwise dominated by Suárez's own centre-right UCD party but also had a strong Socialist presence. In a spirit of consensus, it was announced that Catalunya was to be granted a degree of autonomy, and a million people turned out on the streets of Barcelona to witness the re-establishment of the Generalitat and to welcome home its president-in-exile, **Josep Tarradellas**.

A new Spanish constitution of 1978 allowed for a sort of devolution within a unitary state, and the **Statute of Autonomy** for Catalunya was approved on December 18, 1979, with the first regional elections taking place in March 1980. The conservative **Jordi Pujol i Soley** and his coalition party **Convergència i Unió** (CiU) gained regional power – and proceeded to dominate the Catalan parliament for the next quarter of a century. In a way, the pro-conservative vote made it easy for the central government to deal with Catalunya, since the demands for autonomy here did not have the extreme political dimension they had in the Basque Country.

The 1980s and 1990s

The **elections of 1982** saw Felipe González's PSOE elected with a massive swing to the Left in a country that had been firmly in the hands of the Right for 43 years. The **1986 general election** gave González a renewed mandate, during which time Spain entered the **European Community**, decided by referendum to stay in NATO and boasted one of the fastest-growing economies in Western Europe. Narrow victories in two more elections kept the Socialists in power, but after the 1993 results were counted it was clear that they had failed to win an overall majority and were forced to rely on the support of the Catalan nationalist coalition, CiU, to retain power. This state of affairs well suited Jordi Pujol, who was now in a position to pursue some of the Catalan nationalists' more long-cherished aims, in particular the right to retain part of the region's own income-tax revenue.

Following allegations of sleaze and the disclosure of the existence of a secret "dirty war" against the Basque terrorists, the calling of a **general election in 1996** came as no surprise and neither did the overall result. In power for almost fourteen years, the PSOE finally succumbed to the greater appeal of the conservative Partido Popular (PP), under **José Maria Aznar** – the first conservative government in Spain since the return of democracy. However, the PP came in well short of an outright majority, and Aznar was

1995	2004	2006	2008
MACBA (contemporary art museum) opens, signalling regeneration of El Raval district.	Diagonal Mar hosts Universal Forum of Cultures, heralding transformation of Poble Nou district.	New statute of autonomy agreed with Spain.	Montjuïc castle symbolically handed over from state to city, to become a peace museum.

THE STATE THEY'RE IN

While it's never had the same high profile or the violence associated with Basque separatism, Catalan independence is a hot topic. It's not supported by either of the main national parties, the PSOE or the PP, but recent Spanish minority governments have had the issue forced upon them, notably following the overwhelming approval by the Catalan parliament in September 2005 of the **Estatut** – the proposed reform of the 1979 Catalan Statute of Autonomy. This opened up all sorts of national fault-lines, with the bill going well beyond Spanish constitutional limits, defining Catalunya as a "nation" within Spain and claiming full tax-raising powers and a parallel judicial system. Not surprisingly, the proposed reform caused political mayhem: to the PP and conservatives (and much of the Madrid-based media), granting more regional autonomy puts the Spanish nation at risk; to the Socialists, declaring Catalunya a "nation" is a welcome step towards a strong federal state; while for the separatists, it's nothing less than a call to independence.

A watered-down version of the statue was **approved by referendum** in 2006, increasing Catalunya's tax-raising powers and redefining in general (though not legal) terms the region as a "nation". But it satisfied few, and the statute was subsequently contested in the courts by other autonomous Spanish regions and by the PP, before being substantially altered again by the **Constitutional Court of Spain** in 2010 – which reiterated that Spain remained the only "nation" recognized by the constitution. Regional outrage led to a surge of **unofficial, non-binding referendums** held throughout Catalunya (including in Barcelona, in April 2011), indicating around twenty-percent support for full independence, something that would, ultimately, require approval by both the Spanish parliament and a full national referendum.

left with the same problem as González before him – relying on the Catalan nationalists and other smaller regionalist parties to maintain his party in power.

Contemporary politics

In the **general election of 2000**, the PP won a resounding victory in the national parliament, while Catalunya was left under CiU control. For the first time, the PP was no longer dependent on other parties to pass legislation and was high on confidence, though within two years Aznar's government had begun to lose its way. In particular, Aznar's fervent support of US and British **military action in Iraq** in 2003 led to huge discontent, with polls showing that ninety percent of Spaniards opposed the conflict.

However, in the local elections of 2003, Aznar and the PP defied the polls, holding off the PSOE in many major cities (Barcelona excepted). With the PSOE beset by corruption scandals and affected by the strong separatist showing in regional elections, it seemed that the best the PSOE could hope for was to deny the PP an absolute majority in the **2004 general election**. That was before the dramatic events of March 11, 2004, when terrorists killed two hundred people in coordinated **train bombings in Madrid**. Spain went to the polls in shock a few days later, and voted in the PSOE against all expectations.

The Socialists took power in a minority administration led by PSOE prime minister **José Luis Rodríguez Zapatero**, forced to rely on parliamentary support from Catalan separatists and other regional parties. Over the term, Zapatero played his cards well,

2010	2011
Catalan parliament bans bullfighting; Catalunya becomes first region in mainland Spain to do so.	FC Barcelona are European football champions for fourth time; Socialists lose city mayoral and municipal vote; centre-right Catalan nationalists win Barcelona vote for first time since return to democracy.

pointing to measures such as the withdrawal of troops from Iraq, an increase in the minimum wage and maternity leave and even the legalization of gay marriage as evidence of a new direction for Spain.

After a decade of spectacular growth, he fought the **2008 general election** largely on his handling of the economy, and he and the PSOE were re-elected to office, though with just short of an absolute majority.

But as the **international banking crisis** began to hit home, and with the government's **austerity measures** increasingly unpopular, Zapatero called time on his leadership in April 2011, announcing that he wouldn't stand for a third term. With high Spanish unemployment and a disintegrating economy, the election due in spring 2012 promises to be difficult – to say the least – for the incumbent Socialists, though (following two successive general election defeats) the PP's leader, Mariano Rajoy, is just as unpopular among many mainstream voters. Every analyst of every political colour agrees that Spain requires long-term structural reform – but it's not at all clear who will clean up the current mess.

Books

The selection of books reviewed below provides useful background on the city's history, people and institutions. Despite a long pedigree, Catalan literature is hard to find in translation, though novels set in Barcelona by (mostly foreign) authors provide a feel of the city past and present. In Barcelona, most of the major bookshops (see p.228) carry English-language guides and titles about the city; or look in the museum bookshops (particularly in MNAC, MACBA, Caixa Forum, Museu Picasso and Fundació Joan Miró) for books on art, design and architecture. The online literary magazine ⓦbarcelonareview.com has plenty in the archive on Spanish and Catalan writers, art, culture and life, and there's also the very useful Lletra (ⓦlletra.net), an excellent online resource (in English) for Catalan literature.

HISTORY

BARCELONA

★ **Jimmy Burns** *Barça: A People's Passion*. On one level, it's simply an informative history of the city's famous football team, alma mater of Cruyff, Lineker, Maradona, Ronaldinho et al. However, like the club itself, the book is so much more than that, as Burns examines Catalan pride and nationalism through the prism of sport.

Felipe Fernandez-Armesto *Barcelona: A Thousand Years of the City's Past*. An expertly written appraisal of what the author sees as the formative years of the city's history, from the tenth to the early twentieth century.

★ **Robert Hughes** *Barcelona*. The renowned art critic casts his accomplished eye over two thousand years of Barcelona's history and culture, with special emphasis on the nineteenth and early twentieth centuries – explaining, in his own words, "the zeitgeist of the place and the connective tissue between the cultural icons".

★ **Matthew Stewart** *Monturiol's Dream*. Witty and engaging account of the life and work of Narcís Monturiol, the nineteenth-century Catalan utopian visionary, revolutionary and inventor of the world's first true submarine. Stewart places Monturiol firmly at the centre of Barcelona's contemporary social and political turmoil – printing seditious magazines, manning the barricades in the 1850s, fleeing into exile and returning to pursue his pioneering invention.

Colm Tóibín *Homage to Barcelona*. Echoing Orwell, the Irish writer pays his own homage to the city, tracing Barcelona's history through its artists, architects, personalities, organizations and rulers.

SPAIN

John Hooper *The New Spaniards*. Excellent portrait of post-Franco Spain and the new generation – the second revised edition of 2006 brings the twenty-first-century country into focus.

Hugh Thomas *Rivers of Gold: The Rise of the Spanish Empire*. Thomas's scholarly but eminently accessible history provides a fascinating snapshot of Spain's most glorious period – the meteoric imperial rise in the late fifteenth and early sixteenth centuries, when characters such as Ferdinand and Isabel, and Columbus and Magellan, shaped the country's outlook for the next three hundred years.

★ **Giles Tremlett** *Ghosts of Spain*. The *Guardian's* Madrid correspondent takes a warts-and-all look at contemporary Spain, and finds the dark days of the Civil War never very far from the surface, even now. It's a terrific read – if you buy just one book for general background on how modern Spain works and what its people think, this should be it.

THE CIVIL WAR

Gerald Brenan *The Spanish Labyrinth*. First published in 1943, Brenan's record of the background to the Civil War is tinged by personal experience, yet still impressively rounded.

★ **George Orwell** *Homage to Catalonia*. Stirring account of the Civil War fight on the Aragón front and Orwell's participation in the early exhilaration of revolution in Barcelona. A forthright, honest and entertaining tale, covering Orwell's injury and subsequent flight from the factional infighting in Republican Spain.

Paul Preston *A Concise History of the Spanish Civil War; Franco; The Spanish Holocaust*. From the leading historian of twentieth-century Spain, *Civil War* is an easily accessible introduction to the subject, while *Franco* offers a penetrating, monumental biography of Franco and his regime. His latest, *The Spanish Holocaust*, is a controversial account of the murders and massacres that took place in

Spain during and after the Civil War – violence that still engenders dark passions on both sides of the argument in contemporary Spain.

Hugh Thomas *The Spanish Civil War*. Exhaustive political study of the period that is still the best single telling of the convoluted story of the Civil War.

ART AND ARCHITECTURE

★ **Gijs van Hensbergen** *Gaudí: The Biography*. A worthy biography of "arguably the world's most famous architect". Van Hensbergen puts substantial flesh on the man while placing his work firmly in context, as Spain lost its empire and Catalunya slowly flexed its nationalist muscles.

John Richardson *A Life of Picasso*. The definitive multi-volume biography – Volume 1, covering the period 1881–1906, is an extremely readable account of the artist's early years, covering the whole of his time in Barcelona.
Philippe Thiébaut *Gaudí: Builder of Visions*. Read van Hensbergen for the life, but pick up this pocket-sized volume

CATALAN LITERATURE AND WRITERS

Catalan was established as a literary language as early as the thirteenth century, and a **golden age** of medieval Catalan literature followed, lasting until the mid-sixteenth century, with another cultural and literary flowering in the nineteenth century known as the **Renaixença** (Renaissance). However, this long pedigree has suffered two major interruptions: first, the rise of Castile and later Bourbon rule, which saw the Catalan language eclipsed and then suppressed; and a similar suppression under Franco, when there was a ban on Catalan books and publications. In the post-Civil War period, there was some relaxation of the ban, but it's only been since the return of democracy to Spain that Catalan literature has once again flourished.

Catalan and Spanish speakers and readers are best served by the literature, since there's little still in translation. The vernacular works of mystic and philosopher **Ramon Llull** (1233–1316) mark the onset of a true Catalan literature – his *Blanquerna* was one of the first books to be written in any Romance language, while the later chivalric epic *Tirant lo Blanc* (*The White Tyrant*) by **Joanot Martorell** (1413–68) represents a high point of the golden age. None of the works of the leading lights of the nineteenth-century *Renaixença* is readily available in translation, and it's to *Solitud* (*Solitude*) by **Victor Català** (1869–1966) that you have to look for the most important pre-Civil War Catalan novel. This tragic tale of a woman's life and sexual passions in a Catalan mountain village was first published in 1905, pseudonymously by Caterina Albert i Paradís, who lived most of her life in rural northern Catalunya.

During and after the Civil War, many authors found themselves under forcible or self-imposed exile, including perhaps Spain's most important modern novelist, **Juan Goytisolo** (born 1931), a bitter enemy of the Franco regime (which banned his books). Goytisolo has spent most of his life abroad – in Paris and Marrakesh – with his great trilogy (*Marks of Identity*, *Count Julian* and *Juan the Landless*) confronting the whole ambivalent idea of Spain and Spanishness. Other notable exiles included **Pere Calders i Rossinyol** (1912–94), best known for his short stories, and **Mercè Rodoreda i Gurgui** (1909–83), whose *Plaça del Diamant* (*The Time of Doves*), *El Carrer de les Camèlies* (*Camellia Street*) and *La Meva Cristina i Altres Contes* (*My Cristina and Other Tales*) are relatively easily found in translation. For something lighter, there are the works of **Maria Antònia Oliver i Cabrer** (born 1946), novelist, children's author and short-story writer born in Mallorca, whose early novels were influenced by her birthplace, but whose *Estudi en Lila* (*Study in Lilac*) and *Antipodes* introduce fictional Barcelona private eye Lonia Guiu. More detectives – this time, oddball twins Eduard and Pep – comb the city in the work of contemporary Catalan novelist **Teresa Solana** (born 1962).

Not all Catalan writers write in Catalan, but rather in Spanish, including perhaps the best-known of all – **Manuel Vasquez Montalban** (1939–2003), crime writer *par excellence*, and novelist, poet, journalist, political commentator and committed Communist to boot. His Pepe Carvalho books do nothing less than expose the shortcomings of the new Spanish democracy in fast-changing Barcelona. Montalban's contemporary **Juan Marse** (born 1933) uses the post-Civil War dictatorship as the background for many of his Barcelona-set novels, and it's the same period that spawned the Barcelona blockbuster *The Shadow of the Wind* by **Carlos Ruiz Záfon** (born 1964), and its prequel *The Angel's Game*. For other new Catalan writers, such as **Albert Sánchez Piñol** (born 1965), nationality seems incidental at best – his well-regarded first novel, *Cold Skin*, is a creepy psychological sci-fi tale of solitude on an Antarctic island, while literary adventure story *Pandora in the Congo* starts in the dark heart of the African jungle.

for its excellent photographic coverage – not just Gaudí buildings and interiors, but sketches, historical photographs

and architectural insights that add up to a useful gateway to his work in the city and surroundings.

FOOD AND WINE

★ **Colman Andrews** *Catalan Cuisine*. The best available – possibly the *only* available – English-language book dealing with Spain's most adventurous regional cuisine. Full of historical and anecdotal detail, it's a pleasure to read, let alone cook from (no pictures, though).

Penelope Casas *The Foods and Wines of Spain*. Casas roams across every region of Spain in this classic Spanish

cookery book, including the best dishes that Catalunya has to offer. Her *Paella* and *Tapas: The Little Dishes of Spain* cover the rest of the bases.

Jan Read *Wines of Spain*. All you need to know to sort out your Penedès from your Priorat – an explanation of regions and producers, plus tasting notes and tips for wine tourists.

NOVELS SET IN BARCELONA

John Bryson *To the Death, Amic*. Barcelona, under siege during the Civil War, is the backdrop for a coming-of-age novel recounting the adventures of 10-year-old twins Enric and Josep.

Miguel Cervantes *Don Quixote*. Barcelona is the only city to which Cervantes gives its real name in his picaresque classic – in the Barcelona chapters, Don Quixote and Sancho Panza see the ocean for the first time, and Quixote fights a duel on Barceloneta beach against the Knight of the White Moon.

Ildefonso Falcones *Cathedral of the Sea*. Falcones, a lawyer living in Barcelona, sets his first novel in the expansionist years of the fourteenth century, where work is under way on the building of the city's most magnificent church, Santa María del Mar. It's a highly realistic, excitingly plotted tale that lifts the skirts of medieval Barcelona to show an authentic picture of a city on the make. It was a Spanish award-winner on publication and has become something of a publishing sensation, in the manner of *The Shadow of the Wind*.

Juan Marse *Lizard Tails* and *Shanghai Nights*. Marse spent his formative years in a Barcelona scarred by the Civil War, and ruptured childhood and family hardship are themes that emerge in much of his work. Only a couple of titles have thus far been translated into English: *Lizard Tails* is an evocation of post-Civil War childhood, while *Shanghai*

Nights – again, Barcelona and war to the fore – is billed as "a tale of the human spirit".

★ **Eduardo Mendoza** *City of Marvels*, *The Truth About the Savolta Case* and *The Year of the Flood*. Mendoza's first and best novel, *City of Marvels*, is set in the expanding Barcelona of 1880–1920, full of rich underworld characters and riddled with anarchic and comic turns. The milieu is reused with flair in *The Truth About the Savolta Case*, while *The Year of the Flood* adds a light touch to an unusual amorous entanglement in 1950s Barcelona.

Raul Nuñez *The Lonely Hearts Club*. A parade of grotesque and hard-bitten characters haunt the city in this oddball but likeable romantic comedy.

Colm Tóibín *The South*. Barcelona provides the background for Tóibín's first novel about an Irish woman looking for a new life.

★ **Carlos Ruiz Záfon** *The Shadow of the Wind*. Top holiday read is the international bestseller by the Barcelona-born, one-time LA screenwriter Záfon. It's a Gothic literary thriller set in the aftermath of the Civil War, full of atmospheric Barcelona locations, and it generated rave reviews, not to mention selling over ten million copies worldwide. Záfon followed up with a similarly intricate, similarly successful plot-within-plot prequel called *The Angel's Game*.

THRILLERS AND CRIME NOVELS

Bernado Atxaga *The Lone Man*. The noted Basque writer set his well-received psychological thriller during the 1982 World Cup, when two ETA gunmen hole up in a Barcelona hotel.

★ **Manuel Vasquez Montalban** *Murder in the Central Committee*, *Southern Seas*, *The Angst-Ridden Executive*, *An Olympic Death*, *Offside*, *The Man of My Life* and *Tatoo*. Montalban's greatest creation, the fast-living gourmand-detective Pepe Carvalho, ex-Communist and CIA agent, first appeared in print in 1972, investigating foul deeds in the city in a series of wry and racy Chandleresque thrillers. *Murder in the Central Committee* is a good place to start, as Carvalho confronts his Communist past. *Southern Seas* won the Planeta, Spain's biggest literary prize, while the city's businesses, institutions and events come under typical scrutiny in *The Angst-Ridden Executive*, *An Olympic Death*

and *Offside*. Twenty-first-century Catalan politics and business come under the spotlight in the last Carvalho novel, *The Man of My Life*, while the early *Tatoo*, published for the first time in English in 2008, plunges you right back into "sex, death and food in 1970s Barcelona".

Teresa Solana *A Not So Perfect Crime; A Shortcut to Paradise*. In her first two Barcelona noir novels, Solana introduces bumbling detective twins Eduard and Pep – they don't look alike and they don't solve cases, but they do skewer contemporary high society, whether in politics (*A Not So Perfect Crime*) or literary circles (*A Shortcut to Paradise*).

Barbara Ellen Wilson *Gaudí Afternoon*. Pacy feminist thriller making good use of Gaudí's architecture as a backdrop for deception and skulduggery.

Language

In Barcelona, Catalan (Català) has more or less taken over from Castilian (Castellano) Spanish as the language on street signs, maps, official buildings and notices, and so on. On paper, it looks like a cross between French and Spanish and is generally easy to read if you know those two. Spoken Catalan is harder to come to grips with, as the language itself is not phonetic, and accents vary from region to region.

Few visitors realize how important Catalan is to those who speak it: never commit the error of calling it a dialect. However, despite the preponderance of the Catalan language, you'll get by perfectly well in Spanish, as long as you can learn to understand Catalan in timetables, on menus, and the like. You'll find some basic pronunciation rules below, for both Spanish and Catalan, and a selection of words and phrases in both languages. Spanish is certainly easier to pronounce, but don't be afraid to try Catalan, especially in the more out-of-the-way places – you'll generally get a good reception if you at least try communicating in the local language.

Numerous **Spanish phrasebooks** are available, not least the *Spanish Rough Guide Phrasebook*, laid out dictionary-style for instant access, and featuring 24 typical travel scenarios which can also be downloaded for free as audio files. In Barcelona, *Parla Català* (Pia) is the only readily available English–Catalan phrasebook, though there are more extensive Catalan–English dictionaries and teach-yourself Catalan guides available online.

PRONUNCIATION

CASTILIAN (SPANISH)

Unless there's an accent, words ending in "D", "L", "R" or "Z" are **stressed** on the last syllable, all others on the second last. All **vowels** are pure and short; combinations have predictable results.

A somewhere between the "A" sound of "back" and that of "father".

E as in "get".

I as in "police".

O as in "hot".

U as in "rule".

C is lisped before "E" and "I", hard otherwise: "cerca" is pronounced "thairka".

G works the same way, a guttural "H" sound (like the "ch" in "loch") before "E" or "I", a hard "G" elsewhere – "gigante" becomes "higante".

H is always silent.

J the same sound as a guttural "G": "jamón" is pronounced "hamon".

LL sounds like an English "Y": "tortilla" is pronounced "torteeya".

N is as in English unless it has a tilde (accent) over it, when it becomes "NY": "mañana" sounds like "man-yaana".

QU is pronounced like an English "K".

R is rolled, "RR" doubly so.

V sounds more like "B", "vino" becoming "beano".

X has an "S" sound before consonants, normal "X" before vowels.

Z is the same as a soft "C", so "cerveza" becomes "thairbaitha".

CATALAN

With Catalan, don't be tempted to use the few rules of Spanish pronunciation you may know – in particular the soft Spanish "Z" and "C" don't apply, so unlike in the rest of Spain the city is not "Barthelona" but "Barcelona", as in English.

A as in "hat" if stressed, as in "alone" when unstressed.

E varies, but usually as in "get".

I as in "police".

IG sounds like the "tch" in the English scratch; "lleig" (ugly) is pronounced "yeah-tch".

O a round full sound, when stressed, otherwise like a soft "U" sound.

U somewhere between the "U" of "put" and "rule".

Ç sounds like an English "S"; "plaça" is pronounced "plassa".

C followed by an "E" or "I" is soft; otherwise hard.

G followed by "E" or "I" is like the "zh" in "Zhivago"; otherwise hard.

H is always silent.

J as in the French "Jean".

TALKING THE TALK

Catalan (Català) is a Romance language, stemming directly from Latin, and closely resembling the language of Occitan, spoken in southern France. Catalan is spoken by over ten million people in total, in Barcelona and Catalunya, part of Aragón, much of Valencia, the Balearic islands, Andorra and parts of the French Pyrenees – and its use is thus much more widespread than Danish, Finnish and Norwegian. Other Spaniards tend to belittle it by saying that to get a Catalan word you just cut a Castilian one in half but, in fact, the grammar is more complicated and it has eight vowel sounds compared with Castilian's five. During Franco's time in power, Catalan was banned from the radio, TV, daily press and schools, which is why many older people cannot read or write it (even if they speak it all the time) – the region's best-selling Catalan-language newspaper sells far fewer copies than the most popular Castilian-language daily paper. Virtually every Catalan is bilingual, but most regard Catalan as their mother tongue and it's estimated that it is the dominant language in over half of Catalunya's households – a figure that's likely to grow given the amazing revival of the language in recent times.

L.L is best pronounced (for foreigners) as a single "L" sound; but for Catalan speakers it has two distinct "L" sounds.

LL sounds like an English "Y" or "LY", like the "yuh" sound in "million".

N as in English, though before "F" or "V" it sometimes sounds like an "M".

NY corresponds to the Castilian "Ñ".

QU before "E" or "I" sounds like "K", unless the "U" has an umlaut (Ü), in which case, and before "A" or "O", as in "quit".

R is rolled, but only at the start of a word; at the end, it's often silent.

T is pronounced as in English, though sometimes it sounds like a "D"; as in "viatge" or "dotze".

V at the start of a word sounds like "B"; in all other positions it's a soft "F" sound.

W is pronounced like a "B/V".

X is like "SH" or "CH" in most words, though in some, like "exit", it sounds like an "X".

Z is like the English "Z" in "zoo".

USEFUL WORDS AND PHRASES

Words and phrases below are given in the following order: **English** - Spanish - *Catalan*.

BASICS

Yes, No, OK	Sí, No, Vale	*Sí, No, Val*
Please, Thank you	Por favor, Gracias	*Si us plau, Gràcies*
Where? When?	Dónde? Cuando?	*On? Quan?*
What? How much?	Qué? Cuánto?	*Què? Quant?*
Here, There	Aquí, Allí/Allá	*Aquí, Allí/Allá*
This, That	Esto, Eso	*Això, Allò*
Now, Later	Ahora, Más tarde	*Ara, Mès tard*
Open, Closed	Abierto/a, Cerrado/a	*Obert, Tancat*
With, Without	Con, Sin	*Amb, Sense*
Good, Bad	Bueno/a, Malo/a	*Bo(na), Dolent(a)*
Big, Small	Gran(de), Pequeño/a	*Gran, Petit(a)*
Cheap, Expensive	Barato, Caro	*Barat(a), Car(a)*
Hot, Cold	Caliente, Frío	*Calent(a), Fred(a)*
More, Less	Más, Menos	*Mes, Menys*
I want	Quiero	*Vull (pronounced "vwee")*
I'd like	Quisiera	*Voldria*
Do you know?	¿Sabe?	*Vostès saben?*
I don't know	No sé	*No sé*
There is (is there?)	(¿)Hay(?)	*Hi ha(?)*
What's that?	¿Qué es eso?	*Què és això?*
Give me (one like that)	Deme (uno así) (a bit brusque)	*Doneu-me*
Do you have?	¿Tiene?	*Té ?*
The time	La hora	*L'hora*

Today, Tomorrow	Hoy, Mañana	*Avui, Demà*
Yesterday	Ayer	*Ahir*
Day before yesterday	Ante ayer	*Abans-d'ahir*
Next week	La semana que viene	*La setmana que ve*
Next month	El mes que viene	*El mes que ve*

GREETINGS AND RESPONSES

Hello, Goodbye	Hola, Adiós	*Hola, Adéu*
Good morning	Buenos días	*Bon dia*
Good afternoon/night	Buenas tardes/noches	*Bona tarde/nit*
See you later	Hasta luego	*Fins després*
Sorry	Lo siento/Disculpéme	*Ho sento*
Excuse me	Con permiso/Perdón	*Perdoni*
How are you?	¿Cómo está (usted)?	*Com va?*
I (don't) understand	(No) Entiendo	*(No) Ho entenc*
Not at all/You're welcome	De nada	*De res*
Do you speak English?	¿Habla (usted) inglés?	*Parleu anglès?*
I (don't) speak Spanish/Catalan	(No) Hablo español	*(No) Parlo Català*
My name is …	Me llamo …	*Em dic …*
What's your name?	¿Como se llama usted?	*Com es diu?*
I am English/	Soy inglés(a)	*Sóc anglès(a)*
… Scottish/	… escocés(a)	*… escocès(a)*
… Australian/	… australiano(a)	*… australian(a)*
… Canadian/	… canadiense(a)	*… canadenc(a)*
… American/	… americano(a)	*… americà (a)*
… Irish	… irlandes(a)	*… irlandès (a)*

FINDING ACCOMMODATION

Do you have a room?	¿Tiene una habitación?	*Té alguna habitació?*
… with two beds/double bed	… con dos camas/cama matrimonial	*… amb dos llits/llit per dues persones*
… with shower/bath	… con ducha/baño	*… amb dutxa/bany*
It's for one person (two people)	Es para una persona (dos personas)	*Per a una persona (dues persones)*
For one night (one week)	Para una noche (una semana)	*Per una nit (una setmana)*
It's fine, how much is it?	¿Está bien, cuánto es?	*Esta bé, quant és?*
It's too expensive	Es demasiado caro	*És massa car*
Don't you have anything cheaper?	¿No tiene algo más barato?	*En té de mé sbon preu?*

DIRECTIONS AND TRANSPORT

How do I get to …?	¿Por donde se va a …?	*Per anar a …?*
Left, right, straight on	Izquierda, derecha, todo recto	*A la dreta, a l'esquerra, tot recte*
Where is …?	¿Dónde está …?	*On és …?*
… the bus station	… la estación de autobuses	*… l'estació de autobuses*
… the train station	… la estación de ferrocarril	*… l'estació*
… the nearest bank	… el banco más cercano	*… el banc més a prop*
… the post office	… el correos/la oficina de correos	*… l'oficina de correus*
… the toilet	… el baño/aseo/servicio	*… la toaleta*
It's not very far	No es muy lejos	*No és gaire lluny*
Where does the bus to … leave from?	¿De dónde sale el autobús para …?	*De on surt el autobús a …?*
Is this the train for Barcelona?	¿Es este el tren para Barcelona?	*Aquest tren va a Barcelona?*
I'd like a (return) ticket to …	Quisiera un billete (de ida y vuelta) para …	*Voldria un bitlet (d'anar i tornar) a …*
What time does it leave (arrive in)?	¿A qué hora sale (llega a)?	*A quina hora surt (arriba a)?*

NUMBERS

1	un/uno/una	*un(a)*
2	dos	*dos (dues)*
3	tres	*tres*
4	cuatro	*quatre*
5	cinco	*cinc*
6	seis	*sis*
7	siete	*set*
8	ocho	*vuit*
9	nueve	*nou*
10	diez	*deu*
11	once	*onze*
12	doce	*dotze*
13	trece	*tretze*
14	catorce	*catorze*
15	quince	*quinze*
16	dieciseis	*setze*
17	diecisiete	*disset*
18	dieciocho	*divuit*
19	diecinueve	*dinou*
20	veinte	*vint*
21	veintiuno	*vint-i-un*
30	treinta	*trenta*
40	cuarenta	*quaranta*
50	cincuenta	*cinquanta*
60	sesenta	*seixanta*
70	setenta	*setanta*
80	ochenta	*vuitanta*
90	noventa	*novanta*
100	cien(to)	*cent*
101	ciento uno	*cent un*
102	ciento dos	*cent dos (dues)*
200	doscientos	*dos-cents (dues-centes)*
500	quinientos	*cinc-cents*
1000	mil	*mil*
2000	dos mil	*dos mil*

DAYS AND MONTHS

Monday	lunes	*dilluns*
Tuesday	martes	*dimarts*
Wednesday	miércoles	*dimecres*
Thursday	jueves	*dijous*
Friday	viernes	*divendres*
Saturday	sábado	*dissabte*
Sunday	domingo	*diumenge*
January	enero	*gener*
February	febrero	*febrer*
March	marzo	*març*
April	abril	*abril*
May	mayo	*maig*
June	junio	*juny*
July	julio	*juliol*
August	agosto	*agost*
September	septiembre	*setembre*

October	octubre	*octobre*
November	noviembre	*novembre*
December	diciembre	*desembre*

FOOD AND DRINK

Words and phrases below are given in the following order: **English** - Spanish - *Catalan*.

SOME BASIC WORDS

To have breakfast	Desayunar	*Esmorzar*
To have lunch	Comer	*Dinar*
To have dinner	Cenar	*Sopar*
The bill	La cuenta	*El compte*
I'm a vegetarian	Soy vegetariano/a	*Sóc vegetarià/vegetariana*
Knife	Cuchillo	*Ganivet*
Fork	Tenedor	*Forquilla*
Spoon	Cuchara	*Cullera*
Table	Mesa	*Taula*
Bottle	Botella	*Ampolla*
Glass	Vaso	*Got*
Menu	Carta	*Carta*
Soup	Sopa	*Sopa*
Salad	Ensalada	*Amanida*
Hors d'oeuvres	Entremeses	*Entremesos*
Omelette	Tortilla	*Truita*
Sandwich	Bocadillo	*Entrepà*
Toast	Tostadas	*Torrades*
Tapas	Tapes	*Tapes*
Butter	Mantequilla	*Mantega*
Eggs	Huevos	*Ous*
Bread	Pan	*Pa*
Olives	Aceitunas	*Olives*
Oil	Aceite	*Oli*
Vinegar	Vinagre	*Vinagre*
Salt	Sal	*Sal*
Pepper	Pimienta	*Pebre*
Sugar	Azucar	*Sucre*

GENERAL MENU TERMS

Assorted	Surtido/variado	*Assortit*
Baked	Al horno	*Al forn*
Char-grilled	A la brasa	*A la brasa*
Fresh	Fresco	*Fresc*
Fried	Frito	*Fregit*
Fried in batter	A la romana	*A la romana*
Garlic mayonnaise	Alioli	*All i oli*
Grilled	A la plancha	*A la plantxa*
Pickled	En escabeche	*En escabetx*
Roast	Asado	*Rostit*
Sauce	Salsa	*Salsa*
Sautéed	Salteado	*Saltat*
Scrambled	Revuelto	*Remenat*
Seasonal	Del tiempo	*Del temps*
Smoked	Ahumado	*Fumat*
Spit-roasted	Al ast	*A l'ast*

Steamed	Al vapor	*Al vapor*
Stewed	Guisado	*Guisat*
Stuffed	Relleno	*Farcit*

FISH AND SEAFOOD/PESCADO Y MARISCOS/PEIX I MARISC

Anchovies	Anchoas/Boquerones	*Anxoves/Seitons*
Baby squid	Chipirones	*Calamarsets*
Bream	Dorada	*Orada*
Clams	Almejas	*Cloïses*
Crab	Cangrejo	*Cranc*
Cuttlefish	Sepia	*Sipia*
Eels	Anguilas	*Anguiles*
Hake	Merluza	*Lluç*
Langoustines	Langostinos	*Llagostins*
Lobster	Langosta	*Llagosta*
Monkfish	Rape	*Rap*
Mussels	Mejillones	*Musclos*
Octopus	Pulpo	*Pop*
Oysters	Ostras	*Ostres*
Perch	Mero	*Mero*
Prawns	Gambas	*Gambes*
Razor clams	Navajas	*Navalles*
Red mullet	Salmonete	*Moll*
Salmon	Salmón	*Salmó*
Salt cod	Bacalao	*Bacallà*
Sardines	Sardinas	*Sardines*
Scallops	Vieiras	*Vieires*
Sea bass	Lubina	*Llobarro*
Sole	Lenguado	*Llenguado*
Squid	Calamares	*Calamars*
Swordfish	Pez espada	*Peix espasa*
Trout	Trucha	*Truita (de riu)*
Tuna	Atún	*Tonyina*
Whitebait	Chanquete	*Xanguet*

MEAT AND POULTRY/CARNE Y AVES/CARN I AVIRAM

Beef	Buey	*Bou*
Boar	Jabalí	*Senglar*
Charcuterie	Embutidos	*Embotits*
Chicken	Pollo	*Pollastre*
Chorizo sausage	Chorizo	*Xoriço*
Cured ham	Jamón serrano	*Pernil serrà*
Cured pork sausage	Longaniza	*Llonganissa*
Cutlets/Chops	Chuletas	*Costelles*
Duck	Pato	*Ànec*
Ham	Jamón York	*Pernil dolç*
Hare	Liebre	*Llebre*
Kid/goat	Cabrito	*Cabrit*
Kidneys	Riñones	*Ronyons*
Lamb	Cordero	*Xai/Be*
Liver	Hígado	*Fetge*
Loin of pork	Lomo	*Llom*
Meatballs	Albóndigas	*Mandonguilles*
Partridge	Perdiz	*Perdiu*

Pigs' trotters	Pies de cerdo	*Peus de porc*
Pork	Cerdo	*Porc*
Rabbit	Conejo	*Conill*
Sausages	Salchichas	*Salsitxes*
Snails	Caracoles	*Cargols*
Steak	Bistec	*Bistec*
Tongue	Lengua	*Llengua*
Veal	Ternera	*Vedella*

VEGETABLES AND PULSES/VERDURAS Y LEGUMBRES/VERDURES I LLEGUMS

Artichokes	Alcachofas	*Carxofes*
Asparagus	Esparragos	*Esparrecs*
Aubergine	Berenjena	*Albergínia*
Avocado	Aguacate	*Alvocat*
Broad/lima beans	Habas	*Faves*
Cabbage	Col	*Col*
Carrots	Zanahorias	*Pastanagues*
Cauliflower	Coliflor	*Col-i-flor*
Chickpeas	Garbanzos	*Cigrons*
Courgette	Calabacín	*Carbassó*
Cucumber	Pepino	*Concombre*
Garlic	Ajo	*All*
Haricot beans	Judías blancas	*Mongetes*
Herbs	Hierbas	*Herbes*
Leeks	Puerros	*Porros*
Lentils	Lentejas	*Llenties*
Mushrooms	Champiñones	*Xampinyons*
Onion	Cebolla	*Ceba*
Peas	Guisantes	*Pèsols*
Peppers	Pimientos	*Pebrots*
Potatoes	Patatas	*Patates*
Spinach	Espinacas	*Espinacs*
Tomatoes	Tomates	*Tomàquets*
Turnips	Nabos	*Naps*
Wild mushrooms	Setas	*Bolets*

FRUIT/FRUTA/FRUITA

Apple	Manzana	*Poma*
Apricot	Albaricoque	*Albercoc*
Banana	Plátano	*Plàtan*
Cherries	Cerezas	*Cireres*
Figs	Higos	*Figues*
Grapes	Uvas	*Raïm*
Melon	Melón	*Meló*
Orange	Naranja	*Taronja*
Peach	Melocotón	*Pressec*
Pear	Pera	*Pera*
Pineapple	Piña	*Pinya*
Strawberries	Fresas	*Maduixes*

DESSERTS/POSTRES/POSTRES

Cake	Pastel	*Pastís*
Cheese	Queso	*Formatge*
Crème caramel	Flan	*Flam*

Fruit salad	Macedonia	*Macedonia*
Ice cream	Helado	*Gelat*
Rice pudding	Arroz con leche	*Arròs amb llet*
Tart	Tarta	*Tarta*
Yoghurt	Yogur	*Yogur*

CATALAN SPECIALITIES

Amanida Catalana Salad served with sliced meats (sometimes cheese)

Ànec amb peres Duck with pears

Arròs a banda Rice with seafood, the rice served separately

Arròs a la Cubana Rice with fried egg and home-made tomato sauce

Arròs a la marinera Paella: rice with seafood and saffron

Arròs negre "Black rice", cooked – risotto-style – in squid ink

Bacallà a la llauna Salt cod baked with garlic, tomato and paprika

Bacallà amb mongetes Salt cod with stewed haricot beans

Botifarra (amb mongetes) Grilled Catalan pork sausage (with stewed haricot beans)

Bunyols Fritters, which can be sweet (like little doughnuts, with sugar) or savoury (salt cod or wild mushroom)

Calçots Large char-grilled spring onions, eaten with romesco sauce (available Feb–March)

Canelons Cannelloni

Conill all i oli Rabbit with garlic mayonnaise

Conill amb cargols Rabbit with snails

Crema Catalana Crème caramel, with caramelized sugar topping

Entremesos Hors d'oeuvres of mixed meat and cheese

Escalivada Grilled aubergine, pepper and onion

Escudella i carn d'olla A winter dish of stewed mixed meat and vegetables, served broth first, meat and veg second

Espinacs a la Catalana Spinach cooked with raisins and pine nuts

Esqueixada Salad of salt cod with peppers, tomatoes, onions and olives – a summer dish

Estofat de vedella Veal stew

Faves a la Catalana Stewed broad beans, with bacon and botifarra – a regional classic

Fideuà Short, thin noodles (the width of vermicelli) served with seafood, accompanied by all i olli

Fideus a la cassola Short, thin noodles baked with meat

Fricandó (amb bolets) Braised veal (with wild mushrooms)

Fuet Catalan salami

Llagosta amb pollastre Lobster with chicken in a rich sauce

Llenties guisades Stewed lentils

Mel i mató Curd cheese and honey – a typical dessert

Oca amb naps Goose with turnips

Pa amb tomàquet Bread (often grilled), rubbed with tomato, garlic and olive oil

Panellets Marzipan cakes – served for All Saints' Day

Perdiu a la vinagreta Partridge in vinegar gravy

Perdiu amb col Partridge with cabbage dumplings

Pollastre al cava Chicken with cava (champagne) sauce

Pollastre amb gambes Chicken with prawns

Postres de músic Cake of dried fruit and nuts

Rap amb all cremat Monkfish with creamed garlic sauce

Salsa romesco Spicy sauce (with chillis, ground almonds, hazelnuts, garlic, tomato and wine), often served with grilled fish

Samfaina Ratatouille-like stew (onions, peppers, aubergine, tomato), served with salt cod or chicken

Sarsuela Fish and shellfish stew

Sípia amb mandonguilles Cuttlefish with meatballs

Sopa d'all Garlic soup, often with egg and bread

Suquet de peix Fish and potato casserole

Xató Mixed salad of olives, salt cod, preserved tuna, anchovies and onions

DRINKS

Beer	Cerveza	*Cervesa*
Wine	Vino	*Vi*
Champagne	Champan	*Xampan/Cava*
Sherry	Jerez	*Xerès*
Coffee	Café	*Cafè*
Espresso	Café solo	*Cafè sol*
Large black coffee	Café Americano	*Cafè Americà*
Large white coffee	Café con leche	*Cafè amb llet*
Small white coffee	Café cortado	*Cafè tallat*
Decaff	Descafeinado	*Descafeinat*
Tea	Té	*Te*
Drinking chocolate	Chocolate	*Xocolata*
Juice	Zumo	*Suc*

Crushed ice drink	Granizado	*Granissat*
Milk	Leche	*Llet*
Tiger nut drink	Horchata	*Orxata*
Water	Agua	*Aigua*
Mineral water	Agua mineral	*Aigua mineral*
... **(sparkling)**	... (con gas)	... *(amb gas)*
... **(still)**	... (sin gas)	... *(sense gas)*

A GLOSSARY OF CATALAN WORDS

Ajuntament Town hall (city council)
Avinguda Avenue
Barcino Roman name for Barcelona
Barri Suburb or quarter
Bodega Cellar, wine bar or warehouse
Caixa Savings bank
Call Jewish quarter
Camí Path
Capella Chapel
Carrer Street
Casa House
Castell Castle
Cava Catalan "champagne"
Comarca County
Correus Post office
Església Church
Estació Station
Estany Lake
Festa Festival
Font Waterfall
Forn Bakery
Generalitat Catalan government
Gòtic Gothic (eg Barri Gòtic, Gothic Quarter)
Granja Milk bar/café

Guiri Foreigner
Llotja Stock exchange building
Mercat Market
Modernisme Catalan Art Nouveau
Monestir Monastery or convent
Museu Museum
Palau Aristocratic mansion/palace
Passatge Passage
Passeig Promenade/boulevard; also the evening stroll thereon
Pastisseria Cake/pastry shop
Pati Inner courtyard
Plaça Square
Platja Beach
Pont Bridge
Porta Gateway
Rambla Boulevard
Renaixença Renaissance
Ríu River
Sant/a Saint
Sardana Catalunya's national folk dance
Serra Mountain range
Seu Cathedral
Terrassa Outdoor terrace

Small print and index

A ROUGH GUIDE TO ROUGH GUIDES

Published in 1982, the first Rough Guide – to Greece – was a student scheme that became a publishing phenomenon. Mark Ellingham, a recent graduate in English from Bristol University, had been travelling in Greece the previous summer and couldn't find the right guidebook. With a small group of friends he wrote his own guide, combining a highly contemporary, journalistic style with a thoroughly practical approach to travellers' needs.

The immediate success of the book spawned a series that rapidly covered dozens of destinations. And, in addition to impecunious backpackers, Rough Guides soon acquired a much broader readership that relished the guides' wit and inquisitiveness as much as their enthusiastic, critical approach and value-for-money ethos.

These days, Rough Guides include recommendations from budget to luxury and cover more than 200 destinations around the globe, as well as producing an ever-growing range of eBooks and apps.

Visit **roughguides.com** to see our latest publications.

Rough Guide credits

Editor: Edward Aves
Layout: Nikhil Agarwal
Cartography: Rajesh Chhibber
Picture editor: Rhiannon Furbear
Proofreader: Jennifer Speake
Managing editor: Keith Drew
Assistant editor: Jalpreen Kaur Chhatwal
Production: Rebecca Short
Cover design: Nicole Newman, Rhiannon Furbear
Photographers: Chris Christoforou, Roger d'Olivere Mapp
Editorial assistant: Lorna North

Senior pre-press designer: Dan May
Design director: Scott Stickland
Travel publisher: Joanna Kirby
Digital travel publisher: Peter Buckley
Reference director: Andrew Lockett
Operations coordinator: Becky Doyle
Operations assistant: Johanna Wurm
Publishing director (Travel): Clare Currie
Commercial manager: Gino Magnotta
Managing director: John Duhigg

Publishing information

This ninth edition published January 2012 by
Rough Guides Ltd,
80 Strand, London WC2R 0RL
11, Community Centre, Panchsheel Park,
New Delhi 110017, India
Distributed by the Penguin Group
Penguin Books Ltd,
80 Strand, London WC2R 0RL
Penguin Group (USA)
375 Hudson Street, NY 10014, USA
Penguin Group (Australia)
250 Camberwell Road, Camberwell,
Victoria 3124, Australia
Penguin Group (NZ)
67 Apollo Drive, Mairangi Bay, Auckland 1310,
New Zealand
Rough Guides is represented in Canada by Tourmaline
Editions Inc. 662 King Street West, Suite 304, Toronto,
Ontario M5V 1M7
Printed in Singapore
© Jules Brown 2012

Maps © Rough Guides
No part of this book may be reproduced in any form
without permission from the publisher except for the
quotation of brief passages in reviews.
296pp includes index
A catalogue record for this book is available from the
British Library
ISBN: 978-1-40538-697-5
The publishers and authors have done their best to
ensure the accuracy and currency of all the information in
The Rough Guide to Barcelona, however, they can accept
no responsibility for any loss, injury, or inconvenience
sustained by any traveller as a result of information or
advice contained in the guide.
1 3 5 7 9 8 6 4 2

Help us update

We've gone to a lot of effort to ensure that the ninth
edition of **The Rough Guide to Barcelona** is accurate
and up-to-date. However, things change – places get
"discovered", opening hours are notoriously fickle,
restaurants and rooms raise prices or lower standards. If
you feel we've got it wrong or left something out, we'd like
to know, and if you can remember the address, the price,
the hours, the phone number, so much the better.

Please send your comments with the subject line
"**Rough Guide Barcelona Update**" to ✉ mail@uk
.roughguides.com. We'll credit all contributions and send a
copy of the next edition (or any other Rough Guide if you
prefer) for the very best emails.
Find more travel information, connect with fellow
travellers and book your trip on ⓦ roughguides.com

ABOUT THE AUTHOR

Jules Brown first visited Barcelona in 1985. Apart from this book, he has also written and researched several more Rough Guides, as well as various titles for other publishers and numerous newspaper and magazine articles.

Readers' letters

Thanks to all the readers who have taken the time to write in with comments and suggestions (and apologies if we've inadvertently omitted or misspelt anyone's name):

Anne Baker; Gavin Bell; Roger Dean; Terence Foster; Sarah Frankland; Anthony Herniman; Chris Hinton; Rob Jackson; Stephen Jenkins.

Photo credits

All photos © Rough Guides except the following:
(Key: t-top; b-bottom; c-centre; l-left; r-right)

p.1 Axiom Photographic Agency, Stefano Buonamici
p.2 Pictures Colour Library, Rafael Campillo
p.4 Superstock, Travel Library Limited
p.7 Neri Hotel & Restaurant (tr)
p.8 Dos Palillos
p.9 Axiom Photographic Agency, Luis Castaneda/Tips
p.10 Superstock, Robert Harding
p.11 Corbis, Gregorio/Alterphotos/EXPA/NewSport (b)
p.12 Museu del Modernisme Català (b)
p.13 Museu Blau (tl); Getty Images, Sylvain Sonnet (bl); Palau Moxó, Barcelona (br)
p.14 Alamy, John Kellerman (t); Corbis, Tom Grill (bl)
p.15 Getty Images, Xavier Arnau Serrat (c)
p.18 Alamy, wronaphoto.com
p.36 AWL Images, Travel Pix Collection
p.77 Corbis, Sylvain Sonnet

p.95 AWL Images, Carlos Sanchez Pereyra (tl)
p.116 Superstock, Guido Krawczyk
p.121 Getty Images, Sylvain Sonnet
p.142 Superstock, age fotostock
p.151 Getty Images, John Miller/Robert Harding (t)
p.206 Superstock, photononstop
p.215 Pictures Colour Library, Rafael Campillo
p.217 Corbis, Gianluca Battista/Demotix (t); Alberto Estevez/epa (bl); Pictures Colour Library, Rafael Campillo (br)
p.240 Superstock, Fotosearch

Front cover La Pedrera, 4Corners/Massimo Borchi
Back cover Camp Nou, Rough Guides/Roger d'Olivere Mapp (t); Giant cat sculpture, Rambla de Raval, Rough Guides/Chris Christoforou (br); Casa Batlló, Rough Guides/Roger d'Olivere Mapp (bl)

Index

Maps are marked in grey

Maps

Index

Listings key

- ● Accommodation
- ● Café/tapas bar/restaurant
- ● Bar/club/live music venue
- ● Shop

City plan

The **city plan** on the pages that follow is divided as shown:

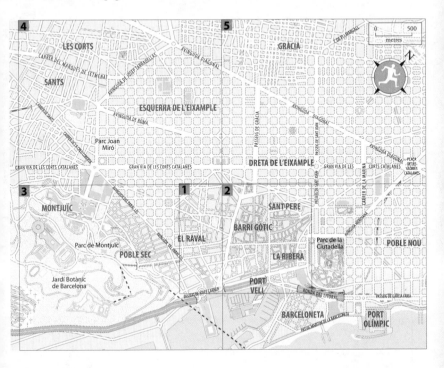

Map symbols

- ⚘ Viewpoint
- ⊙ Statue
- ⓘ Information office
- 🅿 Parking
- 🏊 Swimming pool
- Ⓣ Tram stop
- 🌴 Gardens

- ✉ Post office
- ✚ Hospital
- ✡ Synagogue
- ✈ Airport
- Ⓜ Metro station
- Ⓖ FGC station

- Building
- Church / cathedral / chapel
- Market
- Park/garden
- Forest
- Beach
- Cemetery

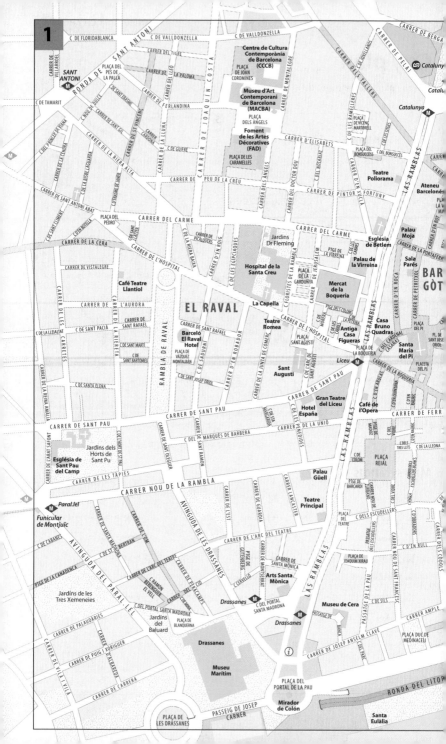

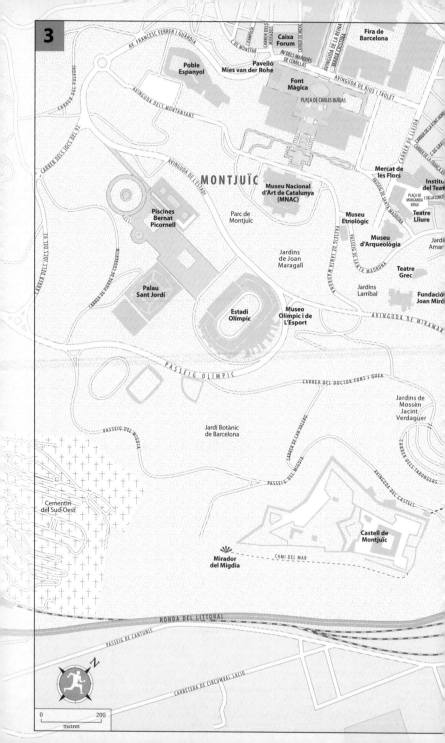

3

AV. FRANCESC FERRER I GUÀRDIA

Poble Espanyol

Pavelló Mies van der Rohe

Caixa Forum

Fira de Barcelona

AV DELS MARQUÉS DE COMILLAS

AVINGUDA DE LA REINA MARIA CRISTINA

Font Màgica

AVINGUDA DE RIUS I TAULET

PLAÇA DE CARLES BUÏGAS

C DE MONTFAR

CARRER DELS MORABOS

CARRER DE MER

AV DE COMPOSIT

AVINGUDA DELS MONTANYANS

CARRER DEL POLVOR

CARRER DELS JOCS DEL 92

AVINGUDA DE L'ESTADI

MONTJUÏC

Museu Nacional d'Art de Catalunya (MNAC)

CARRER DE LLEIDA

CARRER DE LA FONT FLORIDA

CARRER DE LA FRANCA X

Mercat de les Flors

Institut del Teat

PASSEIG DE SANTA MADRONA

PLAÇA DE MARGARIDA XIRGU

C DE LA CONCE

Piscines Bernat Picornell

Parc de Montjuïc

Museu Etnològic

Teatre Lliure

CARRER DELS JOCS DEL 92

Jardins de Joan Maragall

Museu d'Arqueologia

Jardi Amar

CARRER DE PIERRE DE COUBERTIN

Palau Sant Jordi

Teatre Grec

Jardins Larribal

Fundació Joan Miró

Estadi Olímpic

Museo Olímpic i de L'Esport

AVINGUDA DE MIRAMAR

PASSEIG OLÍMPIC

CARRER DEL DOCTOR FONT I QUER

Jardins de Mossèn Jacint Verdaguer

PASSEIG DEL MIGDIA

Jardí Botànic de Barcelona

CARRER DE CARABELEU

CARRER DELS TARONGERS

Cementiri del Sud-Oest

PASSEIG DEL MIGDIA

AVINGUDA DEL CASTELL

Castell de Montjuïc

Mirador del Migdia

CAMÍ DEL MAR

RONDA DEL LITTORAL

PASSEIG DE CANYUNIS

CARRETERA DE CIRCUMVAL LACIO

N

0   200
metres

5

C DE LA PROVIDENCIA

C DELS MADRAZO

Fontana Ⓜ

CARRER D'ASTÚRIES

PL. DEL DIAMANT

C DEL OR

✝ **Sant Joan**

RAMBLA DEL PRAT

PL. DE LA VIRREINA

Casa Rubinet

C DE MARIA CUBÍ

Ⓢ *Gràcia*

GRÀCIA

Verdi Cinema

Verdi Park Cinema

C DE MONTSENY

Mercat de la Llibertat

CARRER DE MONTSENY

CARRER DE LA PERLA

C DE SANT LLUÍS

C DE JOAN BLANQUES

C DE STA EUGENIA

C ROS DE OLANO

TRAVESSERA DE GRÀCIA

Mercat Abaceria Central

C DE LA GRANADA DEL PENEDÈS

CARRER DE PUIGMARTÍ

PLAÇA DE RIUS I TAULET

CARRER DE SIRACUSA

C DE BALMES

C DE LUÍS ANTÚNEZ

CARRER DE LA TRAVESSIA

CARRER DE TORDERA

VIA AUGUSTA

GRAN DE GRÀCIA

CARRER DE TORRES

C DE BANYOLES

C DE IGUALADA

C DEL COMTE DE SALVATIERRA

Casa Fuster

CARRER DE LA LLIBERTAT

C DE MONISTROL

CARRER DE SÈNECA

CARRER DE BONAVISTA

CARRER DE LA LLIBERTAT

C DE SANTA EULÀLIA

C DE CAMPRODON

PASSEIG DE GRÀCIA

PASSEIG DE SANT JOAN

Casa Serra

CARRER DE CÒRSEGA

CARRER DE CÒRSEGA

CARRER DE BAILÈN

PL DE JOAN CARLES I

Provença Ⓢ

Palau Robert ⓘ Ⓜ *Diagonal*

Ⓜ *Diagonal*

CARRER DEL ROSSELLÓ

CARRER DEL ROSSELLÓ

Ⓜ *Diagonal*

Casa Àsia

Ⓜ *Verdaguer*

PTGE DE LA CONCEPCIÓ

Vinçon

Casa de la Punxes

La Pedrera

CARRER DE PROVENÇA

CARRER DE PROVENÇA

Ⓜ *Verdaguer*

AVINGUDA DIAGONAL

Kowasa Gallery

Fundació Joan Brossa

Casa Thomas

CARRER DE MALLORCA

CARRER DE MALLORCA

Palau Montaner

CARRER DE VALÈNCIA

Museu Egipci

CARRER DE VALÈNCIA

Fundació Antoni Tàpies

Ⓜ *Passeig de Gràcia*

La Concepció ✝

Mercat de la Concepció

CARRER D'ARAGÓ

Galeria Joan Prats

Casa Amatller

Casa Batlló

Ⓜ *Girona*

CARRER DEL CONSELL DE CENT

Museu del Perfum Casa Lleó Morera

Museu del Modernisme Català

PTGE DE PERMANYER

Jardins de les Torres de les Aigües

Ⓜ *Girona*

CARRER DE LA DIPUTACIÓ

CARRER DE LA DIPUTACIÓ

Fundació Francisco Godia

DRETA DE L'EIXAMPLE

Plaça Tetuan

Ⓜ

Universitat de Barcelona

Ⓜ *Passeig de Gràcia*

PLAÇA TETUAN

GRAN VIA DE LES CORTS CATALANES

RONDA DE LA UNIVERSITAT

CARRER DE CASP

Ⓜ *Catalunya*

RONDA DE SANT PERE

PLAÇA DE CATALUNYA

Casa Calvet

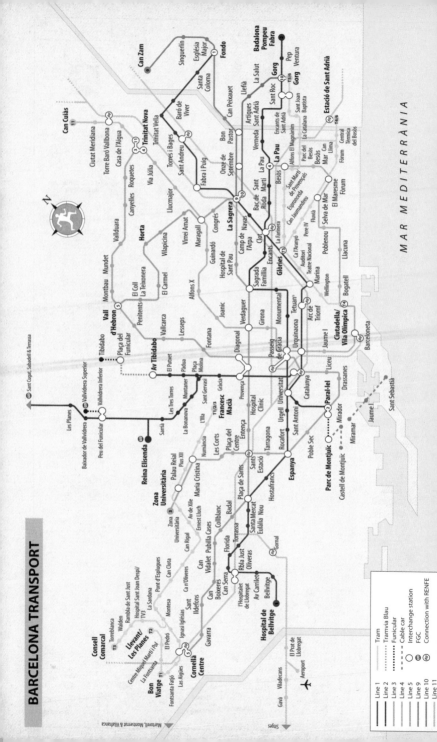

BARCELONA TRANSPORT